Centerville Library
Washington-Centerville Public Library
Center
D0667991

SMOKE

HOW A
SMALL-TOWN GIRL
ACCIDENTALLY
WOUND UP SMUGGLING
7,000 POUNDS OF
MARIJUANA WITH THE
POT PRINCESS
OF BEVERLY HILLS

DEY ST.
AN IMPRINT OF WILLIAM MORROW PUBLISHERS

SMOKE

MEILI CADY

DEY ST.

This is a work of nonfiction. The events and experiences detailed herein are all true and have been faithfully rendered as I have remembered them, to the best of my ability. Some names, identities, and circumstances have been changed in order to protect the integrity and/or anonymity of the various individuals involved. Though conversations come from my keen recollection of them, they are not written to represent word-for-word documentation; rather, I've retold them in a way that evokes the real feeling and meaning of what was said, in keeping with the true essence of the mood and spirit of the event. In some cases, events have been compressed to maintain narrative flow.

SMOKE. Copyright © 2015 by Meili Cady. All rights reserved. Printed in the United States of America. No part of this book may be used or reproduced in any manner whatsoever without written permission except in the case of brief quotations embodied in critical articles and reviews. For information address HarperCollins Publishers, 195 Broadway, New York, NY 10007.

HarperCollins books may be purchased for educational, business, or sales promotional use. For information please e-mail the Special Markets Department at SPsales@harpercollins.com.

FIRST EDITION

Designed by Shannon Plunkett

Library of Congress Cataloging-in-Publication Data has been applied for.

ISBN 978-0-06-228190-6

15 16 17 18 19   OV/RRD   10 9 8 7 6 5 4 3 2

FOR MOM AND DAD
AND FOR FIELD

CONTENTS

PART ONE
GATEWAY

1

ONE TOKE OVER THE LINE

The last time I went to a federal building in Ohio, I was escorted in handcuffs by an army of DEA agents carrying submachine guns and enough evidence to send me to prison for forty years. Now I'm escorted by my attorney to meet with the prosecutor to explain how the hell I ended up on a private jet with a quarter ton of weed packed into thirteen suitcases.

The conference room is stale and windowless, much like the interrogation room I was in for four hours while officers grilled me about my friendship with Lisette Lee, the alleged heiress to the Samsung electronics fortune. She was my best friend for four years in Los Angeles, the first close friend I made in town. We were ride or die "partners in crime." We brought new meaning to the phrase. Growing up, I had a tight-knit group of best friends in Washington, and we shared a lot of friendship bracelets, but none like I shared with Lisette. We both took that ride in the DEAs SUV, where we sat side by side in matching handcuffs.

I take a seat next to Mike Proctor, my attorney, on one side of a long conference table. Two DEA agents and a prosecutor sit across from us. I'm wearing the same black blazer and figure-hugging pencil skirt I wore when we were arrested, but today the ensemble hangs on me. Staring down a decades-long prison sentence can do a lot to curb a girl's appetite. I set aside my black quilted Chanel tote, a gift from Lisette in better times, and remind myself to breathe. Mike gives me a reassuring nod. We've spent the past four weeks preparing for this moment.

The prosecutor, Tim Pritchard, reminds me of a male mannequin with an athletic build and a poker face. This is the first time I've met him, but I met Agent Heufelder, a stern no-nonsense DEA agent, when he put handcuffs behind my back before a trip to DEA headquarters last month. The second agent is here as a formality. I met him on the other end of a submachine gun at our last arrival at the private airport in Columbus.

Tim Pritchard and the DEA agents have pens and pads of paper in front of them, ready to take notes during the interview, and a stack of police documents for reference. Tim explains the terms of the proffer session and asks me if I understand and agree to speak under these terms. After I agree, I feel the energy on the other side of the conference table shift. Tim and Agent Heufelder seem wound up and ready to begin firing questions at me. Mike and I both know that the first thing they will ask, and the thing they will continue to ask until they get a straight answer, is whether I knew it was weed in the suitcases. No one will believe that I didn't know. Mike is a brilliant attorney and a good man, and he's helped me prepare for how to handle this moment.

As Tim opens a manila folder in front of him, I take a dry swallow of air. I know what I have to do. "If it's okay, I'd like to say something before we begin," I say. Tim looks up from his folder, then closes it. Both DEA agents stare intently at me.

"Go ahead," Tim says, narrowing his focus on me as he folds his hands over the conference table.

With everyone's full attention, I begin slowly. "I'm here today because I was involved in an operation that moved thousands of pounds of marijuana from Los Angeles to Ohio using private planes." I pause for a moment, stifled by the sound of my own voice. The words seem so surreal coming from my mouth. I still can't believe that what I'm saying is true.

"I want you to know that I knew what I was doing. I knew it was marijuana in the suitcases, and I did it anyway. The stupid decisions I've made have disappointed not only myself, but my family and all my loved ones as well. What's done is done, and I can't take any of it back. I can't go back in time and make better decisions. The only thing I can do is try to start making good ones now and help you with your investigation as much as I can. That's what I'm here to do." When I finish, I look around the table at Tim Pritchard and the DEA agents. Each one of their postures has changed. The heat that was building in the room has begun to diffuse. They appear to be relieved.

"Well," Agent Heufelder says as he exchanges a glance with the prosecutor, "I'd say that's a good way to start the meeting." He picks up a pen and leans forward with his elbows on the table. "All right, Meili," he says. "We're ready to listen to you. Why don't you begin by telling us why you moved to Los Angeles?"

2

FRESH OFF THE BUS

Five years earlier. I was nineteen when I left my small hometown of Bremerton, Washington, to become a movie star in Los Angeles.

Ever since I could remember, a career in film seemed like a perfectly reasonable pursuit. I'd never found anything, short of the Backstreet Boys, that excited me in the way that acting did, and almost nothing else that made me feel particularly special. I was a strange, chubby child during my early years of elementary school, with a misguided sense of fashion and a misinformed belief that shampooing one's hair too often could be destructive. My wardrobe was a combination of colorful L.L.Bean vacation clothes and GAP denim hand-me-downs from my male cousins. I had my ears pierced at a young age, and I had an obsession with dangling earrings. I would beg my mother to let me wear hers to school. I most adored her Christmas earrings. In my opinion, they were the most beautiful of all her jewelry, with their intricate balls of glitter, vibrant jewel tones, and even one pair that had blinking red and green lights. I never viewed myself as being pretty, but I felt a little pretty when I wore her holiday earrings, with no regard for the ridicule that they might inspire from my classmates. My mother would look at me with hesitation and concern when she'd find me wearing them after January and well into the summer, but she never had the heart to tell me not to.

I'd grown accustomed to being bullied at school, mostly about my weight. I was only marginally overweight, but, combined with all my other oddities, it was enough to fill any afternoon recess with cruel jokes at my expense. I compensated for my apparent social repulsiveness by acting goofy and playful, and it won me friends, though it came at the cost of daily badgering. I think we were all just trying to fit in.

Throughout every awkward and often painful phase of my childhood, my involvement in local theater was my escape, my happy place. I planned to one day escape forever to L.A. and the artful world of cinema, where I was sure I'd find acceptance.

My great-aunt on my mother's side, who died years before I was born, was a silent film star known as Wanda Hawley. That was her stage name; her real name was Selma Pittack. She was a contract actress with Paramount Studios and rose to fame as the ingénue in a string of Cecil B. DeMille films. Wanda became the envy of many women of the time when she starred as the love interest to screen legend Rudolph Valentino in a film called *The Young Rajah*. I read online that at the peak of her career, she was receiving just as much fan mail as, if not more than, Gloria Swanson.

According to family lore, Wanda was disowned by some of the family after it was discovered that she had been dancing naked on a table with some other actress at a party. When I heard the story from my parents, I was awed by how confident and free-spirited she must have been to do such a thing. Unfortunately, my great-aunt's career never thrived beyond the advent of sound in movies, and the small amount of money she had left from her days as a screen star was gone by the time she died. She was buried in the famous Hollywood Forever Cemetery on Santa Monica Boulevard, right across the street from her former home at Paramount Studios. Just outside of her concrete resting place, the Paramount Water Tower is in plain view, looming in the skyline.

In my bedroom growing up, I had two framed photos on my wall that had once belonged to Wanda. One was an old headshot that she'd signed on the back "with love" to her brother. The other was a photo of her being interviewed by a journalist for *Harper's Magazine*. I kept both pictures in their original frames as keepsakes from Wanda's better days. I looked up to her. She had gumption. She was one of the first big stars in the history of the industry, one of the first people who really made it. Though it didn't last, she had her moment in the sun. I could only imagine how invigorating it must have been, to be a working actress in Hollywood. I longed to experience that, and I swore that someday I would.

By the time I entered junior high, I had slimmed down and grown into a full C cup. I joined a neighborhood gym and started going to Weight Watchers meetings with my mother. I lost almost fifteen pounds and was stunned to find myself getting positive attention from boys, for the first time in my life. Fresh from summer vacation, I came back to school tan and toned in a way that I'd never been. I was armed with makeup and a hair straightener, and my parents were kind to supply me with a new wardrobe of well-fitting clothes.

In high school I was active in the Rotary Interact Club and the Honor Society. I was voted Rotary Student of the month, student body president, homecoming princess, and "Most Likely to be Famous" by the time I graduated. I'd managed to save five thousand dollars working at a coffee stand on the lot of a gas station near my house and spent the money on a backpacking trip through Europe the summer after graduation. I came back ready to make good on a promise I'd made to myself years before.

APRIL 2005

Dressed for the road, I stood in our living room. The walls to our Northwest house were covered by long windows, and from almost anyplace upstairs one could see a landscape of grass, garden, and dense forest that surrounded our property. My father made a fire in the woodstove that kept us warm all morning as we prepared for the drive south to Los Angeles. He'd tried many times to teach me how to build a fire, but I never really learned; maybe now I'd never need to know. I wondered if I would ever miss Bremerton and its morning frost. It's beautiful here, but often so cold—I was looking forward to the sunshine of Southern California. Spring had barely arrived, but I could see from the living room window that the apple tree in our backyard had already started to bloom. I wouldn't be around for Mom's apple pies this year. Over our acre of trimmed lawn, I took in the view of the Hood Canal and the Olympic Mountains one last time before turning to go outside.

With the help of my parents, I loaded the greater part of my worldly possessions into my used Volkswagen Jetta. My mother stood in her nursing scrubs and worn clogs on our gravel driveway. She works at a clinic in town. My dad is a real estate agent and makes his own schedule. He insisted on driving down to Los Angeles with me, and I wouldn't have had it any other way. He secured the last of my boxes into the trunk. "Well, looks like we're all set, sweetie," he said. "I'll grab the cooler. Mom packed us up some snacks. And I smoked the last of that salmon from Neah Bay. I thought we could have a little on the drive. I'll tell you, it's pretty good! Might make you want to rethink your move! I can always turn the car around." He grinned at me. My parents always knew that I would move to Los Angeles someday, but it didn't stop them from trying to lure me away from the plan with homemade goods and the best smoked salmon this side of the Olympic Mountains.

My mom put her arm around me. "I hope you can forgive me for working today," she said. "I just thought that because you're leaving before I am, that it would be okay."

"Mom, no," I said. "Why would you take the day off? It's perfectly fine." She nodded and leaned her head against mine, squeezing my arm as she pulled me in closer to her. She brushed a long strand of rust-brown hair from my face and looked at me with wet eyes. Her hands were soft and smelled like Oil of Olay. I kissed her on the cheek. My father arrived back with the cooler and looked at his watch.

"Okay. We have to hit the road if we want to beat traffic," he said.

After a few minutes of increasingly tight hugs and "be safes," my mother stayed anchored on our porch. I climbed into the passenger seat of my now fully packed car and rolled down the window as Dad started the engine. My eyes were locked on my mother's. I had so many memories of seeing her standing at that same spot, on the porch at the doorway to our home. My older brother, Nick, and I used to come back from school and she would be there and open the door for us before we could reach it. Now, it had been over a year since Nick left to study physics at Stanford, and I, the youngest, was about to be the last to leave.

Mom waved as my Jetta pulled down our driveway, bound for Hollywood. I watched her get smaller in the rearview mirror. She blew kisses and wiped away tears that poured down over a tight smile. She continued to wave to us with her free hand. The image ripped at my heart. I knew it would.

My father and I drove as close to the ocean as we could. The Jetta had a sunroof, and we cruised down the West Coast with our hands stretched toward the sun, catching salt air and blowing it into the car. The sound track to the movie *Chicago* blared through the speakers, and the only noise that could be heard above it was the off-key caw of our voices as we sang along at full volume. We turned a twenty-two-hour drive into a three-day road trip, with my father enthusiastically stopping us at every conceivable tourist attraction along the way. We followed the Pacific Coast Highway through Malibu and, when we saw palm trees and giant movie billboards on the Sunset Strip, we'd finally arrived at my new home in Hollywood.

The movies I saw glowing on those billboards were filmed here. The actors who starred in them lived here. I knew I could be one of them soon. There were curbside taco trucks with neon signs that flashed bright long after the bars were closed. Drunks stumbled out of nightclubs like zombies, ready to commit carbocide (i.e., death to one's diet by extreme intake of carbs) after other more salacious ambitions for the evening had been abandoned. This town had a pulse. Good, bad, or perverse, it was alive.

I SETTLED INTO THE SPARE bedroom of a small duplex near Sony Studios in Culver City, close to the ocean, though just out of reach of the salt air. My roommate was an elderly Mexican woman named Esther, the mother of a family friend in Washington. She spoke very little English, and my three years of Spanish in high school didn't help much to bridge the gap; but Esther seemed nice, and the rent was cheap.

I was finally in Hollywood, where everything started for Aunt Wanda, and now where I was beginning my own career.

I enrolled at an acting studio in the San Fernando Valley. I'd found out about the class from one of Dad's coworkers back home, who claimed to have been an agent at William Morris once upon a time. The class was in a room on the upstairs level of an aging strip mall on Ventura Boulevard, next to a Mexican restaurant. The studio space held forty theater seats that had been recovered from old movie houses, facing a spot-lit stage area.

The instructor was a flamboyant, blond sixty-something woman named Bonnie Chase who talked about "the good old days of Hollywood" and a former love affair with Jack Nicholson. The walls inside her studio were plastered with actor headshots; some of the photos were new, in color, and some were old and stained in black and white. I recognized a few of the faces from movies and television. There was a picture of Bonnie with Anthony Hopkins taped to the door, amid a collage of personal photos of Bonnie with other celebrities whom she said had studied with her over the years.

MY FATHER AND I HAD flown down to visit Los Angeles a month before my move. That was when we first came to the studio and met Bonnie Chase, following up on his coworker's referral. Dad wanted to meet the woman who was about to be my acting coach, and of course I was eager to get a look at the class.

Bonnie had told us to come in on the Thursday that we'd be in town during our visit. Thursdays at the studio were showcase nights, when Bonnie invited "industry professionals," such as directors and agents, to come watch her actors put up scenes, similar to a variety theater performance. When we came to watch the showcase that night, Bonnie had introduced my dad to her students as a "producer." He laughed it off, though we both thought it was odd.

The talent at the showcase was intimidating, a far cry from my high school drama department, and these actors had steel in their eyes. They were fighting in every scene to be the best, and some of them were pretty damned good. The competition in this town was fierce.

After the showcase, Bonnie invited us to a birthday party the next night for someone named Daniel, who was apparently a friend to many people at the studio. Daniel wasn't an actor, but he was peripheral to the film industry as the former assistant to a well-known director. Dad and I accepted the offer, thrilled to be invited to my first party in L.A. The birthday celebration was to be held at a hotel bar in Hollywood; being nineteen, I was worried that I wouldn't be allowed in, but an actor from Bonnie's studio said that security was usually pretty loose and I'd have a good chance of getting by without showing an ID.

At our hotel room before the event, I unpacked a black-and-gold sequined dress from Forever 21. Dad had bought it for me the week before our trip, just in case we went out while we were here. He'd wanted me to have something new to wear. I wore bright yellow stilettos from Ross I'd been saving to wear for a special occasion. They were the tallest shoes I'd ever owned, but I thought they were sexy and worth a little discomfort. Bonnie had told me to look my best: there might be directors or people in casting at Daniel's party, and it could be a good opportunity for networking.

I was nervous as we walked into the crowded hotel bar, tugging at my dress to make sure it was lying flat. My feet were already throbbing from the stilettos. Just as the actor at the showcase had predicted, no one asked to see my ID. The party was loud and overwhelming, and I stayed close to my father as we scanned the room for Bonnie. We found her in a group of actors from the showcase.

"You made it!" she shrieked as she threw her arms around me and gave me a half kiss on my cheek. "Meili. Let me get a look at you, my darling." She took my hands in hers and stepped back to take in my appearance, nodding approval.

"You look like a star. I'm so thrilled that you're joining the studio. We're going to have a lot of fun." Her eyes shined as she smiled at me. She turned to my father.

"Don't worry," she said. "She's in good hands. Now. Honey, have you met Daniel?" Bonnie led us to Daniel, standing nearby holding a beer and wearing a black button-down shirt with jeans.

"Hi, kiddo. Welcome to Hollywood," he said as he shook my hand.

He was Mexican with a stocky build and curly gelled hair. Daniel had an easy disposition, and something about him made me feel comfortable right away. Most of the people I'd met here so far seemed vaguely uninterested in me, like they were looking for someone behind me and hoping to give no more than a cordial hello. Daniel seemed genuinely content to talk with me, even when he was the center of attention at his own birthday party.

My father and I didn't stay long at the party. While I enjoyed speaking with Daniel and Bonnie for a few minutes at the beginning, I felt awkward, like an outsider. My feet were aching and blistered from my shoes within an hour, and I began to feel silly wearing them. The actors from the studio were polite but stayed at a distance. After wandering through the hordes of strangers and eyeballing men in suits who looked important, I was tired and ready to leave.

I saw Daniel again on my way out with my father. We wished him a happy birthday and he told me to take his phone number in case I needed a friend when I moved into town next month.

A FEW WEEKS AFTER MY move to Los Angeles, I got my first visitor from home. Cate had been my best friend for as long as I could remember. She was beautiful, obsessed with fashion, wild, and politically savvy. Back in the day, our mischief was watching R-rated movies and tying up our parents' phone lines until four in the morning. Now she was visiting me in L.A. to shop and look for movie stars.

I pulled into arrivals at the Los Angeles International Airport. Cate was waving at me from the curb and looking ready for L.A. with oversized sunglasses and too much luggage. Her shiny brown hair looked longer than it was when we said our farewells at my parents' house before I left.

We greeted each other in a tight hug. "Get it together, girl," she said. "You're going to ruin your makeup."

"It's just . . . really good to see you," I said as I quickly wiped my eye and lifted a floral-patterned suitcase into the trunk of my Jetta. I hadn't realized how much I missed Cate. Close friendships were much harder to come by here than I'd expected. Los Angeles can be a lonely city.

We drove to Beverly Hills and found parking at Barneys New York. The potpourri of expensive perfume hit us as we passed through the cosmetics department, and white balloons and loud music filled the room—we'd stumbled into some kind of fancy summer shopping event. Thin women with long hair and perfect breasts sauntered through the space like models, smiling at consumers and handing out glasses of champagne from a silver tray. I wondered if that was real champagne. It couldn't be. I hadn't seen a single person be asked to show ID.

"All right! This is what I'm talkin' about. I'm going to go do some damage in the shoe department," Cate said. It occurred to me that she was more at home here than I was at this point. "You coming?" she asked. "It's all you," I said. "Have fun."

Cate was a workaholic as a waitress in Washington, and she had always seemed to afford her taste for designer labels. I was on a tight budget with no job and a modest allowance from home, so I had no business in the shoe department at Barneys. Cate left me standing wide-eyed near a makeup counter.

I was startled when I realized that someone was speaking to me, convinced that I was invisible here. They were probably going to ask me to stand somewhere else—I was standing too close to the display and this would understandably interfere with their marketing strategy. I was clearly a departure from their desired demographic.

"Would you like one?" It was one of the fembots with the fake champagne. She handed me a glass from the silver tray before I could tell her that I don't care much for cider. I took a sip. *Oh boy. This is definitely not cider.* I looked around me to make sure that I wasn't in trouble, but no one seemed to notice or care. I took another long sip. I was nineteen years old and drinking real champagne at Barneys in Beverly Hills. *This is awesome.*

Any sense of time or normalcy escaped me as I sat down in a makeup chair. A beautician layered my face with product. Apparently, I was due for a makeover. I was polishing off my second glass of champagne when Cate reappeared with two massive bags of shoes. "I just met Frasier!"

"What?" I asked. "How? What do you mean? You met Kelsey Grammer?" I slid off the chair, not wanting to miss out on any excitement.

"I don't know what his name is, but it's definitely Frasier. Him and his wife. I helped her pick out shoes. I told her that I'm a fashion student and that she should choose the shoes that make her feel the most beautiful, because that is what the designer had in mind when he designed them." Cate glowed with pride.

"Are they still here?" I asked, checking my new look in the mirror. "What was he like? I love *Frasier!*"

I bought a twenty-dollar eye shadow to be polite to the beautician, then hurried off to the shoe department with Cate. "I just want to see him," I told her, scanning the room. "There he is," she whispered to me. The actor stood at the opposite end of the room with his blond wife. She looked like one of the fembots. I'd had only a moment to be starstruck when I saw their eyes land on us and he called out (in the same imperial tone as his TV alter ego), "There she is!" He pointed a finger straight at Cate. The couple made a beeline to us, and before I could process this absurdity, we were face-to-face with the celebrity.

He smiled at us. "We just wanted to thank you again," he told Cate. "I'm so glad that we were able to find you. We were afraid that you might have left. What you said back there—it was beautiful." They introduced themselves and asked us where we were from. When we told him that we were from "around Seattle," I waited for him to say something about *Frasier* because the show was set in Seattle, but of course he never did. He told us to enjoy our day and left with his wife.

As they walked away, I turned to Cate. "Want some champagne?" We exchanged smiles and hurried back to the cosmetics department.

The next day, Cate tagged along to acting class with me. Bonnie had insisted that I study there five days a week, and I religiously followed her instructions, even if it cost half my monthly allowance to do so. Cate sat at the back of the studio and read fashion magazines to keep her occupied for the six hours that I'd be there. Though she was anxious to leave and hit up L.A.'s hottest vintage shops, she was curious about what I'd been doing.

There were about twenty students in every class. We signed in at the entrance and paid twenty-five dollars to be there. Each class began with an introduction by Bonnie, and then we moved into emotional warm-ups and improvisations to loosen us up before we began scene work. Bonnie gave us an exercise that involved repeating letters of the alphabet and channeling emotional meaning into them. In turn, five actors took the lit-up stage area and repeated, "A, b, c, 1, 2, 3." The idea was to repeat this sequence aloud and explore a gamut of emotions through it. I took the stage with four other actors and we all began. "A, b, c, 1, 2, 3. A, b, c, 1, 2, 3. A, b, c, 1, 2, 3!" Bonnie urged us along, hovering over each of us individually, intent on excavating some emotion as she passed.

After I'd repeated the phrase twice, I found Bonnie in front of me, like a drill sergeant addressing a soldier. "I want to hear your heart BREAKING, Meili! You need to go there. You need to LET GO! Pull that stick out from under your ass! What happened?! Oh, it broke your heart, DIDN'T IT?!" Tears welled up in my eyes on command, and I screamed passionately at the top of my lungs, "A, B, C, 1, 2, 3!" Bonnie was delighted. She threw her hands up in success. "YES! Now, Meili, I want to see something else. I want LUST. Give me your LUST. Stick your tits out! I WANT TO HEAR YOUR OVARIES CLANGING TOGETHER!" Feeling the eyes of the class, I struggled to follow her instruction.

Confused and somewhat disoriented, I yelled, "A, B, C—" My concentration was instantly broken by the growing sound of giggling at the back of the room, as Bonnie whipped around to face the interruption. From the stage, I could see brown hair shaking suspiciously behind a summer issue of *Vogue*. Cate stood up, shaking with uncontrollable laughter, and excused herself from the studio without a word. The class watched in stunned silence as she left; a final explosion of amusement was audible after the door shut behind her.

To my amazement, Cate was allowed to return the next evening to observe the Thursday night showcase. After five weeks of class, Bonnie had deemed me ready to perform in my first "industry showcase." I was excited that she thought I was making progress, but anxious. Every girl who came into the studio had to do the same scene for her first showcase, and it involved an orgasm. Or rather, faking an orgasm. I'd experienced neither in real life.

I'd only ever slept with one guy back in Washington, and I could say with certainty that an orgasm was not what I experienced. Now I had to play Meg Ryan's part in the scene from *When Harry Met Sally*, when she faked a climax in the middle of dinner at a restaurant—in front of about fifty people, including my best friend since first grade and graying industry professionals Bonnie was going to seat in the front row. These "professionals" were usually older men, and I'd seen them shift around in their seats and smile as they watched Bonnie's young actresses shake and moan their way through the famous scene. Now it was my turn for this rite of passage, and I felt sick to my stomach. At least Daniel, one of my only friends here, said he would be there for moral support.

The last sun of the day was casting shadows over Ventura Boulevard as Cate and I walked the stairs up to class. Actors stood outside the open door to the studio, smoking cigarettes and running lines for their scenes. Loud music played from speakers inside near the stage, setting the atmosphere for the evening. The male actors wore button-down shirts and slacks, some with ties and jackets if it was right for the material they'd be performing; for actresses, Bonnie insisted that we showed a lot of skin on showcase night, regardless of what was appropriate for the scenes. "You want to get cast? Show 'em what you got!" she said. So the girls came to the studio gussied up like prize pigs headed to the county fair. I was now a part of the livestock show. Dreading the risk of potential wardrobe malfunctions in a skirt—though certain that any such malfunctions would be quickly forgiven—I decided to wear jean shorts and a tank top. Bonnie brushed past me holding a script, deep in conversation with another actor. She noticed my bare legs and gave a subtle nod of approval as she passed. Though I felt exposed, I was content to know that I was pleasing my mentor.

Daniel spotted me and walked up to offer advice before I entered the packed studio. "Be as loud as you can, and if she tells you to climb on top of the table, just try not to fall off. And definitely don't fall into the audience. Or do. At least you'll stand out."

"What do you mean 'climb on the table'?" I asked.

"Well, sometimes Bonnie likes to have the girls jump up on the table and do the orgasm from there. Like a music video girl on the hood of a car, circa 1985."

"Wait a second . . ." I began. Daniel stopped me. "Meili, your sexuality is going to be a powerful tool in this town. Don't be afraid to use it. Besides, if you don't do a good enough job, Bonnie will bring another actress onstage and put her on the table to do it better than you, and it will be embarrassing. Good luck, kiddo."

I couldn't believe how pretty some of these actresses were. I bet that they could fake an orgasm. Even more, I bet that they'd had real orgasms. If I could have one, maybe I wouldn't be so uptight all the time. This would be good practice for me. Yes.

Bonnie took center stage to open the showcase by introducing the "industry professionals" in the front row to the studio, including Daniel, whom she introduced as a director, though he had never been employed as a director, and as far as I knew he had no intention of becoming one. She looked down at the scene list on a clipboard and shouted, "Okay! *Harry Met Sally* is up! Meili!"

I nervously teetered on three-inch heels as I stepped into the hot studio lights with my male scene partner. The audience quieted as we settled into the chairs. I cleared my throat a little too loud. *Er, not sexy.* Apparently I had to use my sexuality, and repulsing anyone within earshot the moment that I step into the lights was not a good step in that direction.

I tried to stop my hands from shaking, but it seemed impossible. *Just don't fall into the audience.* I barely knew my scene partner's name, but he'd been in class far longer than I had and was intimidatingly handsome sitting across the table from me in a tight T-shirt. I wondered if he could give me an orgasm. *Maybe we should have rehearsed this in private.*

Bonnie positioned herself directly in front of us, just out of the spotlights.

"All right!" she said. "Let's see it."

We made it through the short dinner dialogue at the table. I reprised Meg Ryan's role and said, "It's just that all men are sure it never happened to them, and most women at one time or another have done it. So, you do the math." The male actor said Billy Crystal's line, "You don't think that I can tell the difference?"

I felt everyone in the studio watching me from the edges of their decrepit theater seats, waiting for me to start. My scene partner stared at me with a blank expression. A long moment passed. I closed my eyes, pursed my lips together, and took in slow, deep breaths. I let out a quiet sigh as I lifted my hands, still shaking, to run them through my hair. "Ooh. Yes. Oh, yeah . . ." Bonnie said nothing. I moaned as I touched my neck, bringing my fingers to my mouth and running them back and forth along my lips. My fingers smelled like the Subway sandwich I ate for dinner. *I'm always still hungry after I eat Subway. What do they put in that stuff?* No sound was heard from the audience. *Good? Bad? Almost over?*

I moaned louder, breathed faster, and attempted to reach my fake crescendo. "Oh God! Oh! Yes! Oh! Oh!" My hands had almost stopped shaking. I was in the clear. I rolled my head back and felt my way down from my neck until I was touching myself within an inch of my cleavage, moaning out, louder, louder. My scene partner gasped at me, in character. I could see Bonnie from the corner of my eye, moving closer to us. It seemed like she was about to cut the scene and declare the time of death. Finally.

"Meili! YES! That's PERFECT!"

I breathed out and took my hands down. Relief. I began to get up and free myself from this farce. But Bonnie wasn't done.

"Now!" Bonnie went on. "I want to see you UP! Into the lights, where you belong! I want to see you moving! Get on top of the table!"

No. Please, no. For a moment, I wondered how forgiving Bonnie would be if I just got up and ran out of the studio. A dramatic exit! Or perhaps I could pretend that I simply misheard Bonnie, stand in the lights to take a bow, then pass out headshots to the front row before sitting back into the audience with Cate.

Every showcase night at the studio comprised two shows: the actors in their scenes, and Bonnie. Her theatrical directing was a main attraction, second only to the fishnet stockings and plunging necklines that she encouraged all the young actresses to wear.

Still trying to stay in the moment, I leaned my upper body weight onto the rickety table. My handsome scene partner was still sitting at it, staring at me. I felt like a sea lion attempting to hurl itself onto a raft. The table began to creak. I was certain I'd crush it like a taco shell at any moment, but by the grace of God it didn't collapse as I climbed on top. Bonnie seemed pleased. "Yes!" she said. "Now, Meili, I want to hear your ovaries clanging together!" I sat on my knees on top of the table and moaned as loud as I could, breathing heavily, tossing my hair back. "Ooh!" I decided that it was time to just give Bonnie what she wanted, so I could crawl off the stage and hide in a seat. I swiveled my hips around in an awkward motion, as if I were struggling to move a Hula-Hoop. There was no way that this was a realistic demonstration of what an orgasm looked like, but Bonnie seemed to love it. I shrieked as loudly as I could, "OH!," and threw my hands up in an exaggerated hallelujah. Bonnie clapped like a seal and faced the audience. "Aha! Now, THAT'S a print!"

I saw Daniel outside the studio after the showcase. He walked up to me with an amused grin. "Jesus. You did good, kid. I mean, I think I've seen better fake orgasms, but that was pure entertainment."

"Thanks," I said. "I'm just glad it's over."

Cate congratulated me on my bizarre induction into the class. "I won't pretend to understand how this whole acting business works. That shit was crazy. But! It's your thing and I'm happy if you're happy." She left to warm up the car as I said good night to everyone at the studio. Daniel offered to walk me to the parking lot. He walked slowly, like he had something to say. "Ya know, you need to make some girlfriends here. I should introduce you to my friend Lisette. She's the Samsung heiress."

"The Samsung heiress? As in Samsung electronics?" I asked.

Daniel pulled out his phone and showed me a picture of a beautiful young Asian woman. She had dark, long hair and big, almost catlike eyes that stared out from the image as if to challenge anyone who dared to look at it. Though she looked anything but friendly, there was something intriguing about her. She exuded a kind of rare, regal confidence. Still, she appeared entirely unapproachable. I saw nothing in her of the fun-loving friends I'd known back home.

"She's . . . really pretty," I said. I decided not to share any of my negative impressions of her with him. I thought it was odd that Daniel thought that I would have anything in common with this person.

She was the Samsung heiress, and I was an actress from a small town who drove a used Jetta and hunted for sales in the produce section at Ralphs. I told him that I didn't think we'd be a good match, and that a meeting probably wasn't a good idea. Daniel put his phone away as we started to walk again.

He shrugged and said, "Ya know, think about it. I think you two could get along."

CATE WENT BACK TO WASHINGTON, and I again felt the absence of any close friendships in my new city. I existed in a haze of isolation and Del Taco binges. I signed with a small talent agency, which led to a hair commercial and a few student films. I booked the lead role in an independent comedy movie, but after filming, arguments among the producers stopped it from getting a theatrical release and the film was shelved indefinitely, right along with my deferred paycheck. I quickly learned that the term "deferred payment" meant no payment, ever. It was exciting to be getting some work as an actress, but it was harder to get than I'd expected. Much harder. Most things didn't seem to pay anything, and my agency wasn't sending me out on many auditions; unless you had a scroll of credits and an established agent, it was difficult to get doors to open. After spending a few thousand dollars on new photos for headshots and acting class five days a week, the money I brought to L.A. had all but evaporated. I'd managed to stay somewhat afloat with the twelve-hundred-dollar monthly allowance from my parents and a series of part-time jobs, but with the constant cost of trying to make it as an actress, the money didn't go very far.

I took a job as a salesgirl at the Guess Marciano store on Rodeo Drive. I hated it. My feet hurt from standing in heels all day long, and the pretension of the customers was nauseating at times. I quit after three weeks and moved on to a job in the client service department of a well established postproduction company in Santa Monica, making cappuccinos and ordering lunches for celebrity clientele.

My time outside of class and work at the production company was spent at Trader Joe's and talking on the phone to my parents and Cate in Washington for hours at a time. Daniel and I still spoke often.

One night after studying at Bonnie's studio, I left feeling in need of some real, human social interaction that didn't involve a phone and a thousand miles of separation. I called Daniel to see if he was awake and up for chatting.

"Lisette has been asking about you," he told me, completely out of the blue. "She wants to meet you."

"Who?" I asked. It had been months since he'd told me about her, when I'd dismissed his suggestion that we meet as bizarre and unwarranted. All he'd told me was that she was an heiress. That, combined with the stoic expression in the cell-phone photo he showed me, was enough for me to rule out any possibility of ever being able to relate to her.

"Remember, I showed you her picture before?" he said. "The Samsung girl."

"Oh, right," I said. "Yeah, I remember. Wait, how do you know her?"

"She's a friend," he said. "I met her when I was working for that director. She likes to say she stole me away from him. I work for her from time to time."

"What kind of work do you do for her?" I asked.

"Oh, you know, whatever she needs," he said. I marveled at how people seemed to have the strangest forms of employment in this town. "I told her about you, and she wants to meet you," he went on. "She thinks you sound like a cool girl."

"Really?" I asked. "I didn't think that she even knew who I was." I was shocked to hear that Lisette wanted to meet me. She was an heiress; she could meet anyone. How could she possibly think we would have anything in common?

"She's looking for new friends too, kiddo," Daniel told me. "She said she wants someone who isn't jaded by Hollywood. I told her I knew the perfect girl, someone who's FOB."

"What's FOB?" I asked.

Daniel laughed. "My point exactly. Fresh Off the Bus. You could learn a lot from Lisette."

Though I thought it might be exciting to meet this mysterious heiress, I found it all very strange. It felt like I was being set up on a blind date with someone who was way out of my league. I'd heard of an arranged marriage, but never an arranged friendship. Maybe it was an L.A. thing.

3

THE HEIRESS

My MySpace profile had a flowery background and a Jack Johnson song that played whenever someone opened my page, and it featured photos of my family and friends from Washington. With the exception of the occasional bogus profile for a marketing ploy, I rarely got friend requests from people I didn't know.

On a lazy morning in November, not long after my last conversation with Daniel about his heiress friend, I logged in to MySpace to find a new friend request from someone under the username ~Royal*Princess*007~. The profile was set as private. The user picture looked like an ad from a magazine. I recognized a familiar face. It was a young Asian woman modeling in a black tank top and holding up a hand to touch her windblown hair. She wore makeup with shades of pink and deep purple, and two beauty marks were barely visible against her porcelain skin, one on her cheek and one next to her pouted pastel lips. I accepted the friend request and opened up the profile belonging to Lisette Lee.

She'd chosen a hard-core rap song to be the sound track of her page, much in contrast to the slow strum of beach music on mine. Where I had photos of my family and friends on my profile, she had glittery Clipart of diamonds and cars that had been animated to sparkle in motion on the computer screen. There were modeling stills of Lisette all over her site, and her online photo albums showed pictures of her in what looked like various modeling campaigns. No photos of friends or family. No photos of anyone, actually, except for Lisette. I returned to her main page and noticed one Clipart icon that seemed to stand out among the others—a bejeweled pink handgun. This struck me as more than a little different, but then again most things I'd heard about this heiress were quite a distance from anything I'd considered normal. She seemed to be an outlier in all regards.

I looked through the comments that had been posted on her wall, more like love letters from fans rather than notes from friends. Many of the comments addressed Lisette as "Princess" and "Darling." They all seemed to hero-worship her. I wondered why Lisette would seek out a new friendship with an outsider who knew nothing about her when she already had a pool of sycophants at her disposal. Just as in the first photo Daniel showed me of her on his cell phone, Lisette was stoic and unsmiling in every one of her pictures on MySpace. Seeing her profile here only added to my initial concerns about her, but I still didn't have any close girlfriends in Los Angeles yet and I had to admit that Lisette Lee was a fascinating creature.

A few hours later, Lisette sent me a message on MySpace to introduce herself. I opened the message in a hurry, eager to see what the "Princess" had to say.

Her message read:

> Meili, I understand that we have a few things in common. We share Daniel as a dear friend, and I believe that we also share a desire to spend time with someone who isn't typical of this Godforsaken town. In that, you and I apparently share common sense. I've grown up in Beverly Hills, but I've been lucky to do my fair share of jet-setting around the world with my family. I'm sure that Daniel has already told you a little about me. You'll get to know me and find out for yourself that I'm not what you might think. People misjudge me simply because I'm an heiress. Unfortunately, my former schoolmate Paris

Hilton has given heiresses a bad name. We are not all
like that. I don't only like to hang out with other rich
people, and I care about more than just money. I'm tired
of being around people who think that way. From what
Daniel has told me, you sound like a true breath of fresh
air. I can't wait to finally meet you.

XO,

LL

I reread her message. I hadn't expected Lisette to be so charming
and *nice* to me. I felt a little guilty for assuming that she would be a
total snob. I was just another person judging her. I told myself that I
ought to be more open-minded. How could I expect to make genuine
friendships here if I didn't give people a chance?

I wrote her back, and she suggested that we go shopping together.
I was slightly anxious at the thought of going to Rodeo Drive to watch
her drop thousands of dollars on designer clothing, while I wondered if
I'd have enough money to buy a latte if we stopped for lunch, but I was
excited to meet Lisette and willing to do so on her terms.

I DROVE TO LISETTE'S CONDOMINIUM in West Hollywood, making
sure to arrive early. I wore my only pair of expensive jeans, uncomfortable but new-looking heels, and a black lacy T-shirt. My hair was
curled tight and my makeup had been carefully applied. It had taken
me an exorbitant amount of time to get ready, but I wanted to feel
confident and try to make a good first impression. I stopped at the
address Lisette gave me and waited in my freshly washed Jetta for
a few minutes, next to a corner building that looked like a fitting
place for a young heiress to live. The neighborhood was moderately
upscale, but her building was by far the nicest one on the block. It
reminded me of a small French villa.

Suddenly a long purple Mercedes cruised down the sun-soaked
street toward me. I could see that the driver was a woman with long
dark hair and large sunglasses that hid much of her face. Beneath her

sunglasses, pastel lips pulled up into a confident smirk and Lisette waved at me from behind the steering wheel. She seemed giddy to see me. I never would have imagined that the woman Daniel showed me in that cell-phone photo months ago would have been capable of giddy. I waved back at Lisette, mirroring her excitement.

She pulled her shark of a car up to the parking entrance of the building and motioned for me to follow her into the structure. The garage was small and full of Range Rovers, Porsches, and other Mercedes. Upon Lisette's instruction, I pulled my Jetta into a guest parking space. I got out of the car and walked toward her. She was thin, a little taller than me. Her hair was very long, down to her waist and full. It looked as though she'd just come from the salon, as every thread of hair was perfectly styled into loose waves. She wore a lavender velour lounge suit of drawstring pants and a matching tank top with tiny straps that looped over her petite shoulders. Her pedicured feet were lifted by Chanel wedges with tiny logos on the buckles.

As I walked to greet her, I noticed glints of jewelry around her neck and a massive rock of a ring on her right hand. She paused outside of her car for a moment and took in my appearance. She had a smug, approving smile that gave me the confidence to walk a little taller and let go of some nerves. Lisette suddenly let out an ingratiating shriek of enthusiasm as she threw her arms out to welcome me in a hug. She pulled back from the hug to look at me again. "Well, well. At last, I get to meet the girl Daniel has told me all about," she said, surprising me with her voice; feminine, yet spoken from a lower octave than most women. I detected a hint of a British accent.

We settled into the pristine leather seats of Lisette's Mercedes. She started the engine and turned up the radio, playing hip-hop. "So, Meili, sweetie, the Jack Johnson tribute on your MySpace page was cute, but please tell me that's not all you listen to," she said, shooting me a playful grin. "No, I like this," I said. "I mean, I like all kinds of music." A throwback Tupac song rumbled through the speakers. She nodded her head to the beat in perfect rhythm. To join her and show her that I wasn't exclusively into campfire music, I nodded my head to the music also. My rhythm was terrible at best, but Lisette didn't comment. She just laughed and said, "All right! That's my girl! I have a feeling we're going to get along just fine."

Lisette drove us to Melrose Avenue and parked at a meter in front of a generic-looking storefront. Melrose was known for its shopping, but what it offered was a far cry from what a shopper would find on the marbled streets of Rodeo Drive. People went to Melrose for cool vintage apparel, quirky smoke shops, and secondhand stores. There was only a short stretch on Melrose that could accommodate serious upscale shopping. I assumed that was where she was taking us until we flew past Fred Segal, marking the last chance to stop for designer labels and overpriced T-shirts.

"I just want to get a few things," she said. "You don't mind, do you, sweetie?" She turned off the car. "Not at all," I said. At this point I was equally surprised and curious about what we were doing here. It appeared that, in fact, she didn't always have to shop at the "best of the best" after all. Perhaps I'd been wrong again about this mysterious heiress.

I followed Lisette into the store. It was far from fancy, but cute, a place I could see myself stopping in to look around if I found myself with any spending money. The small boutique had a modest selection of clothes and a few accessories. Some of the styles were a bit too glittery for my taste, but they were fun to look at. I noticed a variety of velour pants much like the pair that Lisette was wearing and I wondered if this was where she usually shopped.

A friendly salesgirl approached Lisette. "Can I help you with anything?" I held my breath for a moment, afraid of what Lisette might say to her. I remembered vividly how rude some women were to me when I worked in sales on Rodeo Drive. Some of the clientele seemed to feel that just because they had money and I had a name tag, it was okay to treat me like I was beneath them. Some customers would act like I didn't exist at all.

I'd been worried that Lisette might have similar behavior, a deal breaker for me.

Lisette looked up from browsing to acknowledge the salesgirl, gave a warm smile, and said, "No, we're fine. Just looking. Thanks, sweetie."

Lisette was different. The girl I thought I saw in all her pictures was not the girl I found myself spending the afternoon with. She wasn't dry and unlikable at all, as I'd thought she must be from her photos; she was one of the most charming people I'd met. I felt special knowing that she had actively sought me out as a friend, though I couldn't grasp her reasons for doing so. There was something almost disarming about her; she was beautiful and poised enough to be intimidating to most people, and though her MySpace page suggested that she might use that to her advantage, that didn't seem to be the case. I wasn't sure exactly what she'd seen in me that drew her in, but just the idea that she'd seen it and deemed it worthwhile was enough for me. After feeling invisible in a town where everyone wanted to be seen, I found myself a little smitten with her. I felt like a freshman in high school who had been befriended by the senior prom queen.

As Lisette and I perused a rack of colorful tops, she held up an especially revealing tank top and said, "This one would look good on you." I looked at it and cringed, imagining myself wearing it, and the image of a large sausage wrapped tight with butcher string came to mind.

"Ha, no," I said. "I don't . . . think that one's for me." Lisette looked struck by what I'd said. I went on. "I just think it looks a little . . . um, small."

"You don't think it would fit you?" she asked. I confessed that I'd like to lose a few pounds for acting. She nodded. "Well, you don't have much to lose. It shouldn't take long. If you want to lose it fast, I can tell you how."

I perked up. "How?"

She walked around the clothing rack, stood a little closer to me, and spoke quietly, almost in a naughty whisper. "Blow."

"What's that?" I was desperate to know what this secret weight-loss tip was.

She looked surprised, then amused, and said, "Yay? Nose candy?"

"What?" I was confused.

Lisette got a little closer to me, glanced around the store, then whispered, "Coke. You know, *coke*? Like cocaine?"

"Oh," I said. "I got it now. Yes, duh, sorry. Yeah, I know what that is."

Lisette took the material on a furry-looking sweater and casually rubbed it between her thumb and forefinger as she talked to me. "Well. Have you done it before?" Her eyes focused on the sweater.

"No, I've never done any drugs," I said. "I mean, I've smoked pot, but only a couple of times. I don't think I'll ever do any other drugs. I don't judge anyone who does, but I personally don't want to try them."

I was taken aback by her suggestion; Lisette didn't seem like the sort who did heavy drugs. Then again, I'd never been around drugs, so I was a little out of my depth. She'd grown up in a whole different world than I had, and maybe coke was common here in the way that pot was common where I was from. I supposed there must be quite a difference between a "cokehead" and someone who only dabbled occasionally, especially if the person was doing it for a specific purpose like losing weight. Lisette seemed savvy enough to know where to draw the line. I held my breath a moment, hoping I hadn't offended her. She turned away from the sweater to face me.

She studied me and said, "Well, that's fine if you don't want to try it, but if you want to lose weight quickly, I'm telling you I do it every time and it works like a charm."

"It really makes you lose weight that fast?" I asked.

"Oh yeah."

After we finished browsing, Lisette bought a pink velour pantsuit almost identical to the one she was wearing. Back at her car, she proclaimed, "I think that drinks are in order to celebrate us finally meeting!" She stopped. "You do drink, right?" I told her there was no need to worry about that one. "Thank God," she said, looking relieved.

LISETTE'S CONDO WAS ON THE top floor of her building. A heavy wooden door opened to a long entry hallway with a thin black table along the wall. Lisette tossed her bag of new clothes onto the table as she passed and hit a switch on the wall, bringing dimmed light into the condo. The kitchen at the end of the hallway was full of dark wood and stainless steel appliances, with a few bottles of wine sitting around on the polished granite countertops. "Do you live by yourself?" I asked.

"No," she said. "My boyfriend lives here too. He's at work." He was one of the owners of an upscale wine and spirits store on the West Side.

She added, "Don't worry, he won't be home for a few hours. We can have girl time until then."

Everything in Lisette's home was clean, as though a maid had just been in. Gold-striped curtains were drawn shut in the living room, blocking out the afternoon sun. "Should we let some light in?" I asked. "No," Lisette said. "I'm a vampire." The wall color was one of the only elements of her decor that wasn't dark. There were shades of gray in it that appeared almost lavender in the right light. I followed Lisette into her master bedroom. Her king-sized bed frame was covered in mirrors, as was the vanity next to it. Lisette sat down and looked at her reflection. I stood behind her a few paces, watching her in what appeared to be something of a routine. She opened a drawer and pulled out a makeup compact. I recognized the signature Chanel emblem on the front of it. She dabbed her face a little, then put the compact back in its place. She let out a breath and turned to me, looking suddenly excited. She clapped her hands together and said, "Okay! Drinks!"

Back in the kitchen, Lisette assured me that she was about to make me the best Bloody Mary I'd ever had in my life. I sat at her granite countertop while she poured Belvedere vodka and pulled olives and pepperoncinis out of the fridge. The refrigerator was largely empty, with only a bottle of champagne, a few Fiji water bottles, and a small collection of jars and hot sauces on the inside of the door. Lisette saw me looking.

"I can pour a drink like a pro, but cooking, not so much," she said. "I'm barely here anyway. I have dinner meetings almost every night, so this kitchen doesn't see a lot of action." She shot me a coy smile and shrugged. "It functions more like a bar, really. I spend most of my time at the main house in Bel Air when I don't have to run around for Samsung or be at a photo shoot. Trust me, having an afternoon off like this is a rarity. I just needed a break from work today."

Her parents owned a massive home in Bel Air, and though they were usually out of town for business, whenever they were in Los Angeles they lived there. Lisette's mother was Korean and the granddaughter of the founder of Samsung; her father was Japanese and ran casinos in Japan. She told me that he was a respected, if not feared, businessman who had a significant hand in "making Sony what it is today."

She had Sony on one side of the family and Samsung on the other—my ability to comprehend or relate to any of her life was non-existent. I just listened in amazement. I'd never met someone who so readily gave me a full, and almost unbelievable, story of her life. Everything she told me was so outrageous that I felt I could either choose to believe nothing she was saying or everything she was say-ing. After all the other oddities I'd heard about her from Daniel, a trusted friend, I couldn't help but be absorbed in her stories and cap-tivated by the charisma with which she told them. If they'd come from a perfect stranger whom I had no prior introduction to or reason to believe, I'd have been skeptical. But Daniel's reassurance backed up everything she was saying.

Lisette handed me a Bloody Mary. "Ready?" she asked. I took a sip. "Wow. You weren't kidding." I raised my glass to clink with hers. She clinked back and sat down at a dining table. I joined her.

There were a few dozen books on a shelf near the table. I didn't see anything I'd read, but I recognized some of the titles, including *The Prince* and *The Art of War.* "Have you read all of these?" I asked.

"Oh, a million years ago," she said. "I think everyone has read the classics." She told me about her education: how she skipped two grades when she was in a private prep school called Buckley in Beverly Hills, how she went on to finishing school in London (which I decided was an acceptable explanation for her hint of an accent) before studying criminal law at Harvard University. She added that there was a fountain on the Harvard campus that was dedicated to her family. "I was only sixteen when I went, and it was pretty boring," she said. "I left after two years because my dad told me that I didn't need a degree to make money."

After two Bloody Marys, Lisette announced that her boyfriend would be home soon and that I ought to leave. We made plans to see each other again soon. Less than an hour later, I got a text from her:

MEILI~ YOU TRULY ARE A DIAMOND IN THE ROUGH. I CAN SEE
THAT AFTER MEETING YOU ONLY ONCE. TODAY WAS SUCH A
WELCOME CHANGE FOR ME. I THINK YOU'RE EXACTLY WHAT
I'VE BEEN NEEDING IN MY LIFE. TODAY IS THE FIRST TIME
I'VE LAUGHED IN OVER A MONTH, I SWEAR TO GOD. WE OWE
DANIEL A DRINK FOR INTRODUCING US. I CAN'T WAIT TO SEE
YOU AGAIN SOON SWEETIE. XO

After our first outing, I visited Lisette at her condo whenever her busy schedule permitted. She told me that she was one of the highest-paid models at the Elite Modeling Agency in Beverly Hills, and that she spent a great deal of time going back and forth from the agency. But mostly, she said, her life was consumed by answering to family obligations for Samsung, living under constant expectation to be present at local meetings to represent the family. Lisette was the only person I'd met whom I could imagine holding her own at board meetings for one of the biggest companies in the world. She assured me that I wouldn't recognize her demeanor when she sat in those meetings, that she always kept a "business face" when she was there, that some of the executives thought she was "scary" and didn't dare question her because they knew her connections to the family. She seemed to almost begrudge her obligation to dedicate so much of her life to serving Samsung and what her parents expected of her.

I felt terrible for her because she seemed so sad when she talked about it, like she never had a choice about how she wanted to spend her life. She told me that she didn't even want to be with her boyfriend, and that she only went out with him in the beginning because someone dared her to. "I was rebelling against my parents," she said. Now, it had been almost four years and she was still with him, living with him. "They've never approved of him, never even met him." She said that once she moved in, she felt locked into it.

"Why don't you leave him if you're not happy?" I asked.

"Babe, it's a lot more complicated than that," she told me with sad eyes. "Sometimes it feels like you're the only bright spot in my life now."

"Do you think that your parents would like me?" Lisette asked after a thoughtful moment.

"Of course they would! They would love you," I assured her. "I've already told them all about you." My parents thought it was wonderful that I'd found a friend in Los Angeles, and they were happy to see me so excited. They found the stories I'd told them about Lisette to be fascinating, though they said, "We've just never heard of anybody who lives like that."

Lisette and I were bonded into an intense friendship within weeks. She didn't like to go out and be around people much because "most people are so goddamn boring." So we usually just hung out at her condo. When her boyfriend was out of town for work, we stayed up all night in her kitchen drinking yummy cocktails and talking about anything and everything we could think of. We shared jokes and funny stories we'd heard since last seeing each other. We never stopped talking. It was like a girly, childhood sleepover, only with fewer pillow fights and a lot more vodka.

Lisette said it was "kismet" that we'd found each other; that we were like yin and yang, seeming opposites in nature, yet beautifully compatible. She told me, "You're friendly and outwardly nice, and people will take that kindness for weakness. They'll believe that you're stupid. But *I* know that you're not. And people think I'm just a coldhearted bitch, but you see a different side of me. People don't understand our friendship because they don't understand *us*." Maybe Lisette was exactly right. I wondered if it was possible that she knew me better than anyone ever had, though we'd only known each other a short time. I wondered if she knew me better than even Cate, my dearest friend since first grade.

One night, after a few drinks, I confided to Lisette that I used to be bullied when I was in elementary school, that some of my closest friends had a part in it. It was difficult and embarrassing for me to admit, but I wanted her to know me. "Where was Cate during all of this?" she asked. "These people make me fucking sick. They were never your friends. I would never do that to you."

"We were all just kids," I told her. "It's okay."

She was not as forgiving. "If I ever see any of these so-called friends of yours, I'm going to clock them in the fucking face. No one messes with my girl." I asked her not to speak unkindly about my other friends, though her defensiveness was somewhat endearing. She looked at me and said, "Listen, I don't play second fiddle to anyone. Ever. If we're going to do this, I need you all in. I will never hurt you like they did. If I say I'm going to do something, I do it right." I felt conflicted, defensive of the friends I'd grown up with and whom I still loved like sisters through thick and thin, but Lisette's argument for my defense was something I'd longed for my entire life. I fantasized about her having been there with me in grade school, how she would have protected me. From her words, I knew that she would have come to my rescue if she'd had the chance. And though she wasn't able to do so then, she was coming to rescue me now. Lisette and I vowed to be "Best Friends Forever."

I was delighted to know that I understood Lisette in ways that no one else did. She didn't want to have her guard down and let people see how secretly wonderful and kind she was. She was more comfortable letting them think she was a bitch who ought to be feared. I felt like I was the safekeeper of an incredible secret, as though I was the only one who got to turn the key and see that side of her. It was hard not being able to see her often due to her busy work schedule, but sometimes she texted me at the last minute and told me to come over for drinks.

BABE, I CANCELED MY MEETING! COME OVER ASAP! XO.

If ever I had plans with another friend and Lisette became available, I felt torn. She'd sound defeated and say, "Can't you just cancel? I'm your best friend, and I never get to see you." I even called off work at the production company to see her sometimes. She loved it. "Ha! I won!" she said. I knew that she would do the same for me. My family and friends, including Cate, said that our friendship sounded strange, but I knew that it was the best thing that had ever happened to me. I'd never felt a part of something this special in my life. No one, not even Cate, could possibly understand what Lisette and I had together.

Lisette continued to insist that cocaine could help me lose the small amount of weight that I'd been struggling to shake off. She said that the experience would be fun and meaningful for us to share because it would be my first time—"And who better to do it with than your best friend?" she asked me. "Just try it once. See if you like it. And if you don't like it, fine. Then you never have to do it again. Life is too short, babe."

Stress eating had made it especially difficult for me to stay trim recently. I had become financially unable to continue with regular classes at Bonnie Chase's acting studio. I hadn't heard from my agent in months, and my self-submissions on casting websites weren't attracting many auditions. When I did get the odd audition for a commercial for a product I'd never heard of or for a movie that seemed entirely without financial backing, I felt self-conscious when I went in. I'd been eating my feelings lately, and I was afraid it was beginning to show. Those feelings had come in the form of various pints of Ben and Jerry's, large pizzas for one, and hefty bags of fast food, all of which was usually consumed in solitude and seasoned with shame. The actresses here were so thin and "bikini ready." It affected my confidence at auditions, which killed any small chance I would have had of booking even the most nominal part. Maybe it was because I was holding on to an old childhood image of myself, but the last ten pounds seemed to be stubborn, and I binged to compensate whenever it felt like I might be on the verge of losing weight. It was a damaging cycle that I was desperate to break. I told Lisette my frustrations. "Coke eliminates hunger," she swore. "I'll barely eat for days, and at the end of it I'll have lost almost five pounds. Works like a charm."

I decided to try cocaine for my first time, with Lisette. She was bubbling over with excitement when I arrived at her condo. She told me to get to her place early so that we would have plenty of time to experiment before her boyfriend arrived home in the evening. As ever, every curtain in Lisette's condo was drawn shut, hiding us from the outside world. She opened a bottle of sparkling dry rosé and filled two champagne flutes with pink bubbles. She held up her glass and said, "To trying new things, to us, and to you, my beautiful girl." We tapped glasses and shared a giddy hug. "Okay!" Lisette jumped up from her seat and disappeared into her bedroom. She returned a moment later looking happy and holding something in her hand. She set it on the table. It was the smallest plastic bag I'd ever seen, at about one inch by an inch and a half. It was a little more than half full of a white powder that looked fine like flour, yet slightly more crystal-like. Lisette grabbed the bag off the counter and smelled it. "Babe, this is some of the cleanest coke you can get in L.A. You know I don't fuck with anything but the best."

Lisette placed a black Chanel hand mirror on the kitchen table. "You can never do it on wood. You have to have a dry, flat surface," she warned. She took the plastic bag and poured a nickel-sized amount of the powder onto the mirror. It looked like a tiny pile of baking soda, with much of it sort of clumped together into mounds. I watched with fascination as Lisette worked on the mounds with a small razor, breaking up the chunks, then cutting them into loose powder. She divided the coke into six thin lines, spaced about half an inch apart from one another. She took a cut-off straw about two inches long and bent down. "What you want to do is plug one side of your nose and put the straw just barely inside of the other nostril. Then move the straw directly over the line and breathe in through your nose. Like this." In one quick and smooth motion she leaned over the mirror, inhaled, and the line of powder was gone. "Make sure you don't breathe out through your mouth though because the coke will blow everywhere. Your turn." She handed me the straw. She put her finger on a small amount of excess cocaine on the mirror, then rubbed it on the inside of her mouth, onto her gums. I did the same. My gums instantly began to feel numb. The coke had a chalky, slightly acidic taste, but it wasn't repulsive. It was strong and shocking to my senses. Lisette studied me intently as I tried to mimic what I'd just seen her do with the straw. I leaned down to the mirror. I could see the reflection of my face between the lines of coke. My green eyes stared back at me. I breathed out a little and accidentally blew a bit of the powder around, messing up the straightness of the lines. "Careful," Lisette said.

"Sorry, sorry," I said, breathing in and then turning my face away from the mirror to exhale as much as I could. I plugged my nose and tried to hold the straw steady as I moved it jaggedly over the line, then popped up and touched my nose to prevent some of the powder from spilling out. Very messy work compared with Lisette's experienced woofing minutes earlier. She sat forward on her chair and stared at me like Dr. Frankenstein at his new creation, eager to see the effects of this experiment. "I don't think I got much," I confessed. We both looked at the mirror, where the line I'd been aiming at had been partially consumed, though mostly just scattered around the mirror as though I'd ripped through it with a leaf blower.

"No shit," she said. We both laughed.

Lisette coached me more on how to properly do a line. The next one hit me. My head felt light, like a balloon. My lips were dry and pouted out from contact with the drug. My gums were numb all over. There was a bizarre current running from my nose, inside my head, and all around my body. I tried to straighten my posture. My heart was racing. My arms were up, elbows lifted above my chest like I was about to clap or do a squat. Lisette marveled at this. "What the fuck are you doing?" I looked at her, then at my elbows.

I swallowed and thought for a long moment. "Um," I said. "Ha, I don't know. I can't put my elbows down." I took another line and caught my reflection again in the mirror. I paused for a moment over the glass. My pupils were huge now, making my eyes appear dark. I looked away and I sat back in the chair. Over the next two hours, Lisette sipped sparkling rosé and enjoyed my unusual behavior. She said she'd never seen anything like it. My arms were sore from holding them up, but the impulse to keep them there was more powerful than my will to lower them. Lisette was thrilled by my reaction to the drug.

"Babe, you are a fucking drug lightweight." She laughed. After we'd gone through about half of the bag, she looked at the clock and announced that it was time for us to stop because her boyfriend would be returning soon and I'd best be on my way. "Are you okay to drive?" she asked.

"Uh, yeah," I said "I think so. I mean, is it weird to drive on this?"

"You're good," she said. "I wouldn't let you drive if you weren't." She offered me a Valium to take before I went to bed. "It'll help you sleep," she told me. She gave me a tight hug at her door. "Text me when you're home safe," she said. "Love you." I left the privacy of Lisette's condo and wandered off into the evening to find my Jetta.

I never thought that I would try cocaine. I never even wanted to try marijuana. The only reason I ever did try pot in my senior year of high school was because I found myself looking down on people, even my friends, who did it. I thought I was better than them, but I hated that I felt that way. I didn't want to spend my life with my nose in the air and riding around on some smelly high horse. I couldn't help the way I felt, so I smoked pot with my friends in the group limo on prom night. I didn't feel guilty, and I never again judged anyone who liked to get high. My motivations for trying cocaine were slightly less noble, but to hell with it. I'd been a "good girl" my entire life and it had never gotten me very far. It felt good to be a little bad for once, to do something just because *I* wanted to try it. So what if I experimented? I was sick of asking permission from the world. Experimenting with cocaine was the first of many secrets and inside jokes that Lisette and I would come to share.

AFTER NEARLY A YEAR FILLED with countless giddy sleepovers, spicy Bloody Marys, and obsessively affectionate text exchanges, I left Lisette and Los Angeles to spend a weekend in Las Vegas. I flew to Sin City to meet Cate and celebrate our mutual friend's twenty-first birthday. I'd seen Cate only once, during Christmas, since her visit to L.A. the year before. We'd fallen out of the habit of talking every day since I'd moved, which I supposed was to be expected. I'd told her about Lisette. I mindfully omitted the words *best friend* when I described her to Cate, but it was clear I'd found someone new in L.A. and Lisette wasn't "playing second fiddle." Cate seemed oddly quiet when I told her about Lisette. She'd simply said, "I'm just glad you're meeting people." I suspected there might have been some feelings of jealousy on her part, but surely she'd made close friends in Seattle since leaving Bremerton to attend college in the city. She couldn't blame me for making friends in a new place where I didn't know anyone.

At the Las Vegas airport, I looked for the girls around baggage claim. I'd lost more than fifteen pounds since I'd last seen any of my friends from Washington, including Cate. I'd been running every day and taking good care of myself, except for the occasional coke binge with Lisette. The cocaine hadn't seemed to do much for dieting, but exercising every day and eating well had certainly helped. I'd done coke only a few times since my "cherry-popping," as Lisette had affectionately deemed it. She was sorely disappointed the second time, when my involuntary elbow-raising proved to be a fluke, one-time reaction. Despite her disappointment, she had recently given me a bejeweled Louis Vuitton necklace as a token of our friendship, and I was proudly wearing it today as I waited at the airport. I'd also brought one of Lisette's Chanel purses. She'd expressed displeasure with the old purse I'd been using, and one day she handed me a black-and-white Chanel bag from her collection and said, "Sweetie, it's yours." I couldn't believe how generous she'd been to give it to me.

I spotted Cate with the birthday girl, Reigh, and Reigh's mother, Lisa. I'd known all three of them since I was in first grade. As I ran up with my luggage, they turned to me with shocked expressions. "Meili! Holy shit. You're so skinny!" We all exchanged hugs and "I've missed yous." As we were waiting for Cate's last bag at the carousel, I noticed her staring intensely at my necklace. "What?" I asked her. "Nothing," she said. "It's just weird. I didn't even recognize you." I decided to take that as a compliment and ignored the fact that her eyes were once again burning into my necklace from Lisette.

The four of us settled into a room at the Treasure Island Hotel and Casino, throwing our bathing suits on and heading to the pool. We found some lounge chairs and set our things down. I took my swimsuit cover off, feeling confident in a bright blue bikini, and couldn't help but beam after the reaction from my friends. "You look like you lost half a person," Lisa remarked, staring at me.

I'd turned twenty-one in the beginning of the year and I'd barely been to any bars around L.A. I'd never been in the habit of drinking much in public, but today I decided to let loose and buy myself one of the tropical-looking drinks I'd seen people holding around the cabanas. I thought that ought to be sufficient for the afternoon. However, having little experience with the over-twenty-one scene, I wasn't prepared when a group of friendly, shirtless men started buying us drinks and passing them to us as we floated around in the pool.

The first gaudy cabana drink went down quick, and before I knew it I couldn't count how many I'd had. In fact, I probably couldn't have counted anything at this point. The drinks just kept coming to me in the pool and they were free. I couldn't say no. The water was warm and I floated in a dazed euphoria, comfortable and happy like a seal. I closed my eyes and slowly let go of all control. My body went limp, moving wherever the water took me. It felt so natural, so easy.

"GET HER OUT OF THE POOL!" The lifeguard blew his whistle. "Jesus." He shook his head. It was the second time in five minutes that I'd started to sink, unaided in the pool. I was still daydreaming about seals with my eyes closed when I felt someone lifting me out of the water.

I woke up hours later near the pool on a lounge chair that was fully reclined. It was almost completely dark outside now. Someone was talking to me, but I didn't want to open my eyes and let them know they'd had any success at waking me. Maybe they would leave me alone. I played possum for a moment longer until a still-drunk Cate jumped on top of me and shook me by the shoulders and I heard her scream, "OH GOD! Meili! Are you dead?!" I opened my eyes just enough to offer her some proof of life. I wanted nothing more than to go back to sleep, but it seemed that my invitation to do that had expired. I lifted my head a little to look around and assess my situation. I was freezing, and I had no idea where my swimsuit cover was. The hundreds of party people who had surrounded me earlier had been replaced by an old cleaning lady giving me judging eyes as she swept around the pool.

I turned to my side to see Reigh on the lounge chair next to me, only slightly more alive than I was. There was a bucket filled with vomit between our two chairs. The evidence was damning. Cate informed me that Reigh and I had been alternately adding to the pile throughout the afternoon, and that the act was so gruesome that no one dared make an attempt to clean it while we were still present. It was an active splash zone, too dangerous to come near.

Suddenly, two well-built security guards were hovering over me. "Okay, time to go," one told me. "Get up." After an honest effort, I was unable to meet his request. I tried to, but I immediately gave up and deferred to curling back onto the lounge chair to rest more. It became increasingly obvious to everyone present that I was physically incapable of standing at this point. Out of the corner of one squinted eye, I saw the security guards walk away. Relieved, I rolled my face into the plastic of the chair and covered my head with my hands, unsuccessfully trying to hide, and making deep red imprints on my face from the plastic. The security guards returned a few minutes later with a wheelchair. I groaned in agony as they hoisted me onto the cold leather. "Noooo."

Still without my swimsuit cover, I wore nothing but a tiny bikini and a sunburn as security wheeled me through the casino. Gamblers and tourists gave me odd looks and children in families pointed at me as I rolled by, slouched over with my head in my hands and resisting a strong urge to vomit on myself. The journey back to our hotel room was endless and humiliating.

After an hour of trying to sleep off the booze, intense hunger pangs set in, nearly drowning out the nausea. By some small miracle, we found the strength to trudge downstairs to the casino diner. A hostess looked bored at the front of the busy restaurant. "It'll be a few minutes, ladies," she told us, barely looking up. We plopped down on a bench and prepared to wait. A waiter walked by and noticed us. He stopped in his path, grabbed four menus, and approached us to say, "Ladies! Right this way! Let's get you some food!" Without questioning our good fortune, we followed him to a table. "How about a big order of fries to get you something in your stomach right away," he promised before rushing off.

"Wow," Cate said, "what a nice guy." We all agreed. We were pleased when a sizable portion of french fries was promptly delivered to our table with encouragement to "Eat up!" The four of us inhaled the free appetizer and perused the menu for more food.

I lifted my eyes from the food options and looked around the restaurant. I stopped short when I saw that one of the walls was made of glass. It was a one-way glass wall that allowed restaurant patrons to see out, without allowing anyone on the other side to see in and know they were being watched. Directly on the other side of this glass was an uninterrupted view of the lounge chairs that we'd been sitting in all afternoon. I stopped chewing my fries for a moment and stared out, mouth open, absorbing the facts. Cate, Reigh, and Lisa all looked at me. I raised a fry to point to the glass wall. After a quiet moment, Cate said, "No wonder the waiter wanted us to eat something. He probably thought you had another round left in you." With equal parts embarrassment and amusement, we gorged on greasy food until we rolled ourselves back to the room.

Cate and I were too exhausted from drinking at the pool to go out. Reigh and her mother left us to go down to the casino to gamble. Cate flopped down barefoot on the queen bed. She looked deep in thought, staring at the ceiling. I took a similar position on the other bed in the room.

"Whatcha thinkin' about?" I asked her.

"Did Lisette give you that necklace?" she asked me.

"Yeah," I said.

"And that ugly purse?" she continued.

"Hey," I said, "it's not ugly. And, yeah, Lisette gave it to me."

Cate got up from the bed. "Well, if that's your taste now." She grabbed a brush from the dresser and pulled it through her hair. I watched her, pissed that she would say that about Lisette.

"You told me you were happy that I finally had a close friend in L.A.," I said. Cate tensed, then shook her head, getting angrier.

"She's trying to buy you, Meili," she said quietly, through gritted teeth. "You shouldn't wear something that you couldn't afford to buy yourself."

"That's ridiculous," I said. "You're just mad because it's from Lisette." Cate abruptly threw the brush at the wall and faced me, tears erupting from her eyes. I was startled by her level of emotion.

"You're right. It is ridiculous. Fine. I AM fucking jealous! I fucking hate her and I've never even met her!" Cate crumbled to the floor and sat hugging her knees, sobbing almost into hyperventilation. She lowered her voice and cried softly, "I hate her because she stole my best friend. And I hate L.A. for the same reason. You broke my heart. More than anyone has in my life, you broke my heart." I didn't know what else to do, so I sat down on the floor next to my friend. I said nothing and laid my hand on her shoulder as she broke down.

I left Vegas thankful that our stay had been planned for only two nights. The argument with Cate pushed each of us to threaten to fly home early, but we decided to put our feelings aside and stay to support the birthday girl. I was disturbed by what Cate had said, and it pained me to watch her be so hurt. I guess I'd never realized how much she cared. It must have been hard for her to know that I'd met someone in L.A. who cared about me just as much as she did. Lisette swore that she would never accept being second best as my friend. She was all or nothing, and I needed her in Los Angeles. In time, I believed that Cate would learn to accept that Lisette was in my life to stay. At least I hoped so, because I knew who I'd be forced to choose if it came down to it.

4

"AND THE EMMY GOES TO . . ."

Lisette's life was a balancing act. I was in awe of how she was able to juggle so many things at once—she was constantly needed at meetings around town for Samsung, and on top of that she'd been hired as the face of an international modeling campaign for an Asian makeup brand. Unfortunately, the campaign would only be in Asia, so I wouldn't get to see it in advertising here in the States. Lisette didn't seem to get much joy out of modeling, only excited when she showed me edited photos of herself from recent shoots. She'd often text me from a photo shoot, bored and wishing she could be with me instead. I always assured her that whatever was going on at the photo shoot was more exciting than anything I was doing. Even so, it felt good to know that she would rather be with me.

In the evening, Lisette's boyfriend was usually home and his hardly concealed jealousy prevented me from spending a great deal of time with her. He knew that she adored me, and she never treated him with the affection she so freely gave to me. Lisette said it was driving him mad. She confessed that she'd never cared about a man the way that she cared for me, joking that if we were lesbians, we would escape together to another state and get married.

Lisette told me that she'd been recording music at Sony Studios and was preparing to release a pop album in Asia. Apparently it would be her second release, following a debut album that had multiple number one songs in Korea. She showed me a video of a live performance that she'd done at "the Asian version of the Video Music Awards." The video was a little distorted on her BlackBerry, so it was difficult to get a close look at her on the stage, but she sang beautifully and seemed to have incredible stage presence. I was proud of her and encouraged her to be less modest.

"I can't believe that you didn't tell me about this earlier. This is a big deal and you should take pride in it," I told her.

"My parents think my music career is silly, so I guess I don't talk about it much," she said. "They even took down all my music videos on YouTube."

I asked where I could read about her career online: I wanted to be supportive and also to send links to my family so that they could see how talented my girl was. Lisette told me that she used a Korean stage name that I "wouldn't be able to pronounce" and that her family had blocked all her career information on the Internet so that it wasn't searchable in the United States. I found this more than a little odd, but I was willing to believe that people in positions of power could do things that most people wouldn't think were possible. I was saddened by the thought that Lisette wasn't able to enjoy her success and have it embraced by her family. It seemed that the only way she would ever gain their support was through success in the business world.

One night during a sleepover at Lisette's place, we decided to order delivery—sushi from a restaurant and coke from Lisette's dealer. The coked arrived first, but Lisette set it aside for "dessert." She began shuffling through kitchen drawers, looking for the take-out menu for her favorite Japanese restaurant.

"Babe, can you go look in the drawer in the hallway?" she asked me. I walked to her entry hall and faced the table that ran along it. There were three drawers. I opened the one closest to me. I lurched back when I saw what was inside. A black handgun was visible from opening the drawer only a few inches. Lisette called out to me from the kitchen. "Did you find it?" I considered closing the drawer before she could see what I'd found. I felt like I'd been snooping through her things and seen something I shouldn't have. Before I could decide whether to attempt to cover my tracks, Lisette appeared in the hallway. "Wrong drawer," she said.

"Is that . . . real?" I stammered.

"Of course it's real," she said, casually reaching into the drawer to grasp the gun. She broke a tense silence with a laugh. "Calm down, I'm not going to shoot you. Here, hold it."

"I'm good. Guns freak me out." I stared at it. "Is it loaded?"

"Well, it wouldn't be much use if it wasn't, now would it?"

"Why do you have that?"

"For protection. We have a lot of valuable stuff in here." She motioned with the gun as she talked. "If someone tries to rob us, I can kill him before he gets past the front fucking door."

My father was a hunter, so I grew up with a small arsenal of hunting guns in the house. But I'd never seen up close a gun that was designed to hunt humans.

"Honestly, you should feel safer here knowing that I could protect you if it came down to it," Lisette said, putting the gun away. After a moment, I realized that I *did* feel safer knowing that she would be willing to kill someone to save me.

AS TIME WENT ON, I left my job at the postproduction house in Santa Monica to work freelance for a catering company. Like every aspiring actor I'd met in L.A., I needed a side gig to support myself while I pursued big dreams. Most of the "side jobs" actors took involved some form of food service. After a busy summer of tray passing at private parties in Malibu, the catering company offered me a regular position at the *Jimmy Kimmel Live* late-night talk show, as a caterer to the green room. I moved into an apartment in Hollywood, close to where the show was being filmed. I found the apartment and my roommate, a handsome young chef named Mike, on the website Roommates.com.

I was busy with work and had no time to buy any bedroom furniture, so my new roommate allowed me to sleep on his couch in the living room until I got set up. Mike was around my age and we got along as friends. In the first few weeks I was living with him, we often had a drink together when I came home from work. We'd sit on our balcony and talk about life and our respective plans for it. Mike also wanted to pursue acting, but he paid the bills by working as a personal chef. After a week of me sleeping on the couch, he began what I saw as a very thoughtful routine of waking me up with a plate of gourmet breakfast that tasted like it had come from a five-star restaurant. I told Lisette that I thought I'd gotten lucky with this one. "Not only is he an amazing cook, he's *really nice.*"

Though he was classically attractive and in impressive physical shape, I wasn't attracted to Mike. It soon became clear that he felt differently about our potential for romance. Two weeks after I moved in, he told me that he had strong feelings for me. I tried to politely evade his suggestion without damaging his ego by saying that we shouldn't date because we were roommates and we'd be destined to fail.

I spent the next few days staying away from our apartment as much as I could. I'd been uncomfortable since Mike's confession, and I wanted to give him some space to rethink his affection for me. On the third evening of trying to avoid him, I came home from a long day of working on the show to find Mike standing in our kitchen holding a bottle of vodka. He was obviously drunk and seemed to be in high spirits. He greeted me as I came in the door. "Welcome home, roomie! Do a shot with me!"

I laughed and said, "Okay, let me just get my shoes off." He handed me a shot and we threw them back in unison after a "one, two, three" count.

"More!" he said. We did another.

I made a sour face and set the glass down, choking, "Water, water."

He got me a glass of water. "Pussy." He did another shot by himself and made a yelping sound. "Woo! We need Sinatra!" I began to wonder how much he'd had to drink before I'd come home. His face was flushed and trickled with sweat.

Mike turned on his computer speakers to blast a Frank Sinatra song so loud that it felt like an assault. Before I could ask him to please turn it down a little, he rushed over and grabbed me by the waist, facing me head-on. "Dance with me," he said. I tried to be playful with him, but I could see that he liked to play rougher than I did. As we danced, moving in awkward circles around our living room, I could see that his eyes were severely bloodshot. He stared into my eyes with an intensity that made me break eye contact. I noticed a reddish bruise under his eye and a scratch above his eyebrow.

"What happened?" I asked him as he drunkenly tried to sway us around to the music. I felt like I was shouting over the sound.

"I got in a fight at the bar last night," he said. "Total assholes." He gave a silly grin.

I'd had enough of this weird, aggressive dance routine that he'd pulled me into. I backed away from him and walked into the kitchen to pour myself another glass of water. I told him I was tired and wanted to go to bed. I knew I'd have to sleep in my bedroom on the floor tonight. There was no chance that he'd leave me alone if I tried to sleep in the living room, as I would usually do.

Without saying a word, Mike turned off the music. Silence. Standing at his computer, he took his shirt off and tossed it on the carpet. He paused for a moment, suddenly appearing to be consumed by something. When he turned around, I could see through the dim light in our apartment that he had tears in his eyes. "Meili," he said, his voice strangled by emotion, "I love you." I felt uneasy and even a little afraid as he once again confessed his affection for me. He seemed to have come unhinged from all rational behavior. I reminded him that it was best that we stay only friends because we were living together as roommates. I didn't know how to say, "I don't like you *like that*," without damaging his already fragile self-image.

Mike pounded two more shots of vodka in quick succession. I sat on the floor next to our coffee table. It was almost three in the morning. I was exhausted and wanted nothing more than to go to bed. I thought that if I gave a few more minutes of trying to comfort him that the situation would dissolve and we could end the evening in peace. I was wrong. Seeing that I was getting nowhere with calming him down, I gave up and stretched out on the carpet. I closed my eyes. In a matter of seconds, Mike was on the floor beside me, turned on his side, with his naked, muscular chest moving toward me where I lay on my back. I opened my eyes, becoming more alert.

"What are you doing?" I asked him. He stared at me, and I saw something wild in him, something threatening.

"Can I take you?" he whispered as he moved his body closer and began to press his weight on top of me. I quickly darted out from under him.

"You're scaring me," I said. "You're drunk. I'm going to bed."

I closed my bedroom door and locked it. I realized that my hands were shaking as I turned the lock and checked it. Mike was on the other side of the door a second later, so obliterated he couldn't put a sentence together. He banged on the wood and muttered something to the effect that I needed to be "outta here" in the morning. Finally, he left me alone. I pulled my single blanket over my face to try to hide from the first glow of sunrise that was already spreading across my room.

At five o'clock in the morning, I heard a loud crashing sound that I'd later learn my neighbors had mistaken for an earthquake. The crash was startling and broke the quiet of the morning for our entire neighborhood. I awoke only for a moment. Though I was barely conscious, I knew somewhere in my gut that this sound had to do with me and with Mike. I rolled over and fell back to sleep.

My phone started ringing at 7 A.M. It was my dad. He called twice in a row. I immediately put my phone on silent, as if to hit a snooze button. At around 10 A.M. I woke up and scrolled through my missed calls. Dad sure seemed eager to get ahold of me. Before I could call him back my phone rang. It was my brother, Nick. "Are you okay?" he asked me.

"Yeah, just really tired. Why?"

Nick said Dad had received a call earlier in the morning from my car insurance company. They told him my Jetta had been totaled. This explained the loud noise from the street at sunrise. Mike must not have made it very far if he managed to destroy my car within a block of the building. I knew that the natural reaction to this information should be anger, but somehow I didn't feel angry. I knew that I should be, but I wasn't. I was preoccupied with thinking about how my father and brother had spent the early hours of the morning knowing that my car had been totaled and that I was unable to reach. I felt their joint relief when I spoke with Nick, giving the family proof of life and assuring them that I was perfectly fine and uninvolved in any accident.

I got up and smelled something burning the moment I opened my door. The stove had been left on, beneath a now blackened and smoking pot full of what looked like scorched macaroni and cheese. My phone rang again, this time with a call from Mike's father on the East Coast. He asked me what had happened with Mike last night. I didn't tell him everything, but he read between the lines. After a long pause, he asked me a straightforward yet unnerving question. "Did Mike make any unwanted sexual advances toward you?"

"Um, yeah," I told him. "I mean, kind of." It struck me as a truly bizarre thing for a father to ask about his son. I wondered what behavior in the past could have prompted him to think of such a thing. He told me that Mike had called him from the police station. Mike was being charged with a DUI. As roommates we had shared two tandem parking spaces and I'd given him access to the spare set of keys for my Jetta. It seemed that after he'd stopped pounding on my door last night, he'd taken my car for a ride to a nearby store. When he made it back to our street, he was driving fast and spun out of control. My Jetta flipped into the air about a block from our building and met its untimely end as it smashed onto the pavement and into three other parked cars. No wonder the neighbors mistook the sound for an earthquake. Two of the parked cars were also totaled. Mike had somewhat miraculously come out of the crash unscathed, save for a few minor injuries.

His father was terribly worried, and I felt some sympathy for both of them. It was clear that Mike had a lot of inner demons, but I'd seen how nice he usually was. All the breakfasts he'd cooked for me, how hard he'd tried to make me feel welcome in the apartment. Anyone who shows that sort of kindness can't be a monster.

His father told me that Mike would be home in a couple of hours. I hung up the phone. I couldn't imagine what it would be like to be stuck in a jail cell, hungover and alone with regret. What a terrible feeling, to know that you've caused so much damage. I had every right to be pissed if I'd wanted to, but I didn't have it in me. Getting mad wouldn't undo anything. I wasn't the one who had a burden to bear, it was Mike. He must have thought that I would hate him after what he'd done. I didn't hate him, I just didn't understand him. I believed that he meant well, and I wished that I could help him. He needed help from someone, and his parents were across the country.

I texted Lisette as I walked to the grocery store a few blocks away. I was planning to get some fresh bagels and coffee to have ready for Mike when he came home from the police station. I wanted him to know that I forgave him and everything would be okay. Lisette had told me that she was going to be in meetings all day, but I wanted to let her know what had happened. I sent her a series of long-winded messages, explaining everything in detail. I was surprised when I heard back from her immediately.

ANGEL WHERE ARE YOU? ARE YOU OKAY?

I told her that I was at the store getting bagels for Mike. Lisette then called me and said that she was canceling her next meeting and asked me what the cross streets were to the grocery store.

"YOU DON'T BUY FUCKING BAGELS for someone who just stole your car, totaled it, and practically tried to rape you. I don't give a shit how good his omelets are!"

I sat in the passenger seat of her new ivy-green Bentley, listening in silence as she lectured me. I couldn't argue with anything she was saying. It seemed so obvious hearing it from her. I felt a little embarrassed for having been too naive to see these things on my own. I nodded obediently and said, "Yes, you're right," as she went on.

"This guy is fucking crazy. Can you not see that? You're fucking lucky that it was your *car* he killed and not *you*. I honestly don't know how you live, babe. You're going to get eaten alive if you don't wise up. I'm not always going to be available to save you."

It was times like this when I was grateful to know that I had at least one person I could trust in Los Angeles.

I MOVED OUT OF THE apartment the following day. I kept the bagels for myself. With money from Mike's car insurance and a little extra from his parents, I bought a used Volkswagen Beetle.

The director of the indie film I'd acted in allowed me to crash at his apartment until I could find something more permanent. One night he invited me to tag along with him to the official after-party for the Screen Actors Guild Awards. I'd never been to an event like this and I jumped at the opportunity to go with him.

I was impressed that he had access to such an exclusive party. "How did you get tickets?" I asked. "Don't worry about it," he told me with a confident smirk as he chain-smoked en route to the event. "I have my ways." Clearly we weren't exactly on the guest list for the party. I hoped that I wouldn't look like an imposter in my dress from Forever 21 next to all the famous leading ladies in couture gowns—my blue dress was basically an oversized silky T-shirt, and I'd wrapped a silver chain around my waist as a belt. I'd thought that might dress it up a little. Light makeup, loosely curled hair. My companion wore a suit and a ball cap for a touch of rogue flare. At least we couldn't be accused of trying too hard. If we did get kicked out, I'd look slightly less ridiculous being punted out of the party than I would have if I'd shown up in a ball gown.

He parked the car a few blocks away from the venue and we began to walk. I carried my clutch purse at my side. I felt a little silly and got a bad case of giggles. I was promptly shushed by my coconspirator ahead of me. "I don't know how you're going to pull this off," I told him, trying to keep my voice down. "There is security everywhere. Maybe we should just go." We were standing around the corner from the auditorium where the award ceremony had taken place. He put his cigarette out on the sidewalk and looked over his shoulder. "You worry too much," he said. "Follow me."

It was just after sunset, and the red carpet entrance was being dismantled by workers. Mere hours before we arrived, the area had been filled with actors, their publicists, and hordes of press and cameras. Two security guards stood idle near the sidewalk. One had his hands in his pockets, and the other was looking off in the opposite direction of us. My heart thumped in my chest as I followed my friend behind the turned backs of the security guards. I hurried to keep up with him in my heels. We didn't look at the guards as we passed. We kept our eyes straight ahead of us and walked directly through the red carpet as it was being taken down by people who didn't know or care who we were. "Just look like you belong here," he said when I caught up to him.

As we entered the building, I could tell that he was making quick decisions about where to go next, where would be our best chance of sneaking in without being noticed. People with official-looking earpieces passed us with clipboards, engaged in conversations with one another. My adrenaline pumped when my fellow party crasher made a bold decision. He opened a door to the auditorium where the ceremony had ended only half an hour earlier, and where the last of the invited guests had left their reserved seats only minutes prior to our arrival. "This is the best time to get here because everyone's heads are turned," he explained. We walked at a brisk pace down the long aisle of the auditorium, up the stairs where the winners went to claim their awards, then onto the massive stage itself. It was the biggest stage I had ever stepped foot on. I stole a glance behind us at the view of the empty theater seats. For a moment I was reminded of my days in community theater in Washington. Though the brief view gave me a rush of happiness, I was sick with nerves by the time we'd made it backstage and down a hallway to a pair of unremarkable double doors. "Ready?" he asked, giving me a satisfied smile. He opened the door to the official after-party for the Screen Actors Guild Awards.

It was as if I'd stepped through the looking glass and into a page of *Vanity Fair* magazine. The entire space was decorated top to tails in pure Hollywood glamour. Gold curtains fell beautifully against the walls. There were purple velvet couches set up all around for guests to sit on and sip cocktails from the open bar. I noticed that some of the people on the couches were holding awards from the ceremony. All the men were in suits with black ties, and all the women looked like they'd just drifted off a red carpet—which many of them had. Many of the faces I saw looked familiar. I recognized a few right away. Sally Field was sitting at the bar in deep conversation with a young man who was probably her son. I saw the ginger-haired actor from a new TV show called *Dexter* standing by himself, holding a drink at his side and gazing around the party. I wondered why no one was talking to him. *Don't they know who he is?* I guess everyone was *somebody* here. Well, maybe not everyone.

We looked for the smoking section. On our way to the elegantly decorated outside area, an attractive waitress handed us two glasses of champagne from a tray. I bummed a cigarette from my friend. With a drink in one hand and a smoke in the other, I puffed and sipped alternately as I took in my surroundings. Suddenly my companion saw someone and burst out, "Meili! I have someone I'd like you to meet." He spun me around, and in one slick motion we were facing an actor I recognized the moment I laid eyes on him, a handsome TV star I'd watched on a well-known cable series for years. My friend told me he knew the star from "back in the day," and based on the actor's reaction to him, this seemed to be true. My friend gave each of us a hardy pat on our backs and mediated an introduction. "Aiden, I have someone I'd like you to meet. This is the young and talented actress Meili Cady. Meili, this is Aiden." I blushed at his compliment, though he was just being playful.

"It's nice to meet you," I said. I looked down and realized that I couldn't shake Aiden's hand because I was still holding the drink and the cigarette. I felt like Bridget Jones meeting Mark Darcy. I hardly ever smoked, and of course I decided to pick up the habit the moment that I should be shaking hands with Aiden Cohen. He saw my dilemma. He had only a drink in his hand.

"You're too pretty to be smoking," he said. "What if I were to take you on a date and I wanted to kiss you? And then you tasted like an ashtray?" I looked back at him in horror.

"Um, I don't usually smoke."

"That's good," he said, looking me up and down as he sipped his whiskey. "Now why don't you put that cigarette out, and we can go out to dinner sometime?"

I snuffed the Marlboro Light out in the nearest ashtray. "I'm cured!"

When he was putting my number into his BlackBerry contacts, I started to volunteer the spelling of my name, but he waved his hand and said, "It's not important." *What an odd sense of humor he has.* I spelled it aloud for him anyway.

AIDEN CALLED A FEW DAYS later to ask me to dinner. I dedicated my entire afternoon to getting ready. With old-fashioned curlers in my hair and Jack Johnson playing on Pandora, I tried on every piece of attractive clothing in my closet. I finally decided on a simple black cocktail dress. I rewarded my hard work with a glass of wine while I waited for him to arrive.

He picked me up in a black Prius that had loose CDs scattered all over the floor. I opened the passenger door and greeted him with an enthusiastic-to-the-point-of-possibly-unattractive "Hi!" I felt my stiletto snap at least one CD in half as I settled into his car. I couldn't tell if he'd noticed, as his eyes were glued to his BlackBerry. I felt overdressed when I saw that he was wearing jeans and a band T-shirt. "I didn't have time to change," he said, still looking at his phone, his fingers texting wildly. "Traffic on Sunset was fucked." Finally, he asked me, "So where did you want to go?" On the phone, he'd asked me the same question and my answer had been "Surprise me." He'd said that he would. I supposed this *was* a surprise that he had planned nothing, just not the kind of surprise I'd been hoping for.

Aiden took me to Bar Marmont, an extension of the famous Chateau Marmont on Sunset Boulevard. There, we sat at a long table with six of his male friends. I use the term "friends" loosely. One of the men was named Alec and did seem to be a close friend of Aiden's. The rest of the men, all British and all in suits, had either never met Aiden or met him only once. I sat next to Alec, across from my date. By the end of the first hour, Alec and I had exchanged life stories and developed quite a rapport. My interaction with Aiden had been limited to listening to him talk about acting roles with the other men, though at one point he did address me to ask how many drugs I'd done and what my astrological sign is. He told me that his sign was "known for being great in bed" with a wink.

I'd never seen anyone act this way; it was like he was playing a role, only a movie-of-the-week, two-dimensional, and unlikable character kind of role. This was not at all how I'd imagined my date with Aiden Cohen going. Part of me wanted to walk out and leave immediately. I wondered how long it would take for him to notice, or even if such a mild disturbance could pull him away from talking about his fame with total strangers. As I contemplated this, Aiden ended a conversation with one of the men and leaned across the table to get closer to me. Finally, my date was giving me some attention. I felt very forgiving when he flashed me a handsome smile. "Are you going to finish your wine?" he asked, indicating the three full glasses of wine in front of me. The British men had been ordering bottle after bottle, and everyone was passed a glass whenever a new one was opened. I'd been trying to stay relatively sober so that I didn't risk having one too many and making a fool of myself.

"I already had some," I told Aiden.

"Aw, come on," he said. "You need to catch up." Another wink. I'd never seen anyone wink so much in my life. The wink may not have been charming, but Aiden himself possessed the charm of a TV star, and it was enough to convince me to make all three glasses of wine disappear in a matter of minutes. Based on what I could remember the following morning, it's safe to say that this decision did not add to my own charm.

I woke up with a throbbing headache and an intense feeling of nausea. I opened my eyes and looked around me. The vague familiarity of the room suggested that I'd stayed the night on a friend's couch. The details were fuzzy, but I thought I remembered calling her when things went south at Bar Marmont. From what I could recall, everything had turned into a fiery train wreck after I chugged that wine. The combination of alcohol and subsequent rants from me to Aiden about how "just because you're famous doesn't mean you can treat people this way" had led to an uncomfortable and rather abrupt "adieu" when Alec's private driver named Stavros was asked to take me "wherever I needed to go," which ended up being to my friend's nearby apartment to sleep. And vomit, apparently, from what I could gather from the horrible taste in my mouth. I was mulling over every humiliating detail that I could remember when my phone rang. It was Aiden.

"Hello?"

"How are you feeling this morning?" *Oh, no. It must have been worse than I thought.*

"Um, fine."

"You were pretty upset last night."

"I was?"

"Oh yeah. I believe that you called me an asshole." I cringed.

"Sorry."

"No," he said, "it's okay. I have a habit of infuriating people. I just wanted to call to apologize."

Aiden said that he had an incoming call and needed to go, but told me to "feel better" before he hung up. Somehow I suspected that the purpose of that call wasn't to make *me* feel better, but perhaps to make *him* feel better about the possibility of an unflattering story about him getting out. I tossed my phone on the coffee table. Part of me wanted to throw it at the wall instead. I believed him when he said he had a "habit of infuriating people." His call hadn't made for much of an apology; it was simply an acknowledgment of the fact that he'd treated me poorly. I seriously doubted he felt any guilt about it. And why was *I* apologizing? I called him an asshole because he acted like one. I wasn't sure if his celebrity had gotten the better of him or of me. I'd like to think that I wouldn't usually have tolerated this kind of treatment from anyone, but clearly I allowed myself to be blinded by something. Maybe I was just starstruck, a common misstep among young, aspiring actresses in this town.

I spent the next evening with Lisette and told her everything. She fumed over her glass of wine. "What a fucking idiot. He's ugly anyway, babe. You can do so much better." Lisette consoled me, then shared stories of her own dating escapades with other actors like Channing Tatum and Leonardo DiCaprio. Every story of hers ended with the actor falling hopelessly in love with her though, much unlike my experience. "You just haven't met the right guy yet, sweetie," she assured me. She vowed revenge if she ever crossed paths with Aiden. "If I ever see that fucking Smurf face, I'm going to bury him alive. No one messes with my girl." She always had a way of making me feel better, even when it was through unwarranted threats of violence.

On more than one occasion, I saw Leonardo DiCaprio in VIP sections when I ventured out with other friends to nightclubs. I contemplated approaching him to say that we had a "mutual friend," but I never did.

SINCE MOVING TO LOS ANGELES I'd signed up for what is called "extra work" a handful of times. "Extras" are essentially warm bodies positioned in the background of movie and TV scenes to make them appear more realistic to the audience. Most extras are struggling actors who need a paycheck, but there is also a mix of retired folks and non-actors who do it because they like the feeling of being on a set. I've heard that a lot of ex-cons sign up because the job doesn't require a background check, which I've never been able to confirm, but it makes sense. The gross pay for nonunion extra work is around sixty dollars for an eight-hour day.

The first time I worked as an extra was for a Rob Zombie music video. I was one of about twenty-five girls dancing around a stage that had been built in the middle of a field. The video was filmed on a farm, and the way that the extras were literally herded around on the grass gave new meaning to the common comparison of extras to cattle. I'd had friends in acting class warn me that if casting directors saw me as an extra, they would never take me seriously as an actor. This scared me off at first, but the fact remained that extra work was the best way to get into the union. And if you wanted to be a professional actor, you definitely wanted to be in the union.

To be eligible to join the Screen Actors Guild, or SAG, an actor needed to earn a minimum of three union vouchers. These coveted vouchers were given to nonunion actors only under certain provisions. The one other way of becoming eligible for SAG was called a "Taft-Hartley." If a producer decided he or she would like to hire a nonunion actor for a union project, then the producer had to justify to SAG why that particular actor was needed, as opposed to someone who was already a dues-paying member. Getting Taft-Hartleyed into the union was rare because it only happened when someone really, truly wanted to hire you.

Central Casting was the main office in town for background work, where people went to register to be considered for jobs. After giving a photo and all relevant personal details, the information was kept on file and actors could be called on if work was available and appropriate for them. I'd practically forgotten that I was still registered at Central Casting when I got a call from their offices, from a woman asking me if I'd like to work on the set of *Californication* the next day. It was going to be a large call, filming at the Rainbow Room on Sunset, and they needed "all their girls" to be there to fill the restaurant while David Duchovny did a scene with a guest star. I didn't like the idea of working for sixty dollars before taxes were even taken out, but I knew that it could be a chance to get a union voucher. I had only one voucher to show for my more than two years of being in L.A., and I needed to get two more before I could pay my dues and join the Guild. I agreed to work the next day, determined to somehow earn a voucher.

In the morning I woke up two hours early to get ready for work. It took me three failed attempts, but I was finally able to glue fake eyelashes onto my eyelids. They looked a little wonky, so I globbed mascara on to compensate. I hadn't had my coffee yet and I was barely conscious, but I knew that I had to make myself stand out today to have a chance of getting a voucher. I carefully packed the sexiest, most revealing wardrobe I had into my rolling suitcase. The extras coordinator had instructed all the girls to bring lingerie and anything that would be fitting for fetish-driven rock-and-roll groupies to wear at the Rainbow Room, a landmark on the Sunset Strip and a legendary hangout for rock stars.

I arrived at the top of a parking structure a full half hour before my 10 A.M. call time, my suitcase thudding along behind me. I walked toward a sun tent with folding tables and chairs where two production assistants were standing around looking sleepy. I approached one and he told me to get some breakfast at catering.

After waking up a little over coffee and eggs, I walked my suitcase over to the wardrobe trailer. I was greeted by a woman named Caroline who was in charge there. She seemed pleased that I'd brought so many options of clothing to pick from. "This is a nice one," she said as she examined a lacy cream-and-black bra. I laid out a few skirts for her to look at.

"We need the Rocker Girls to wardrobe!" one of the production assistants called out. Caroline told me that there was a preselected group of eight union actresses who needed to get ready to be presented to the director. "I'm sorry," Caroline said with what seemed like genuine apology. "You'll be first after them." I gathered my items and moved them aside as the selected girls crowded ahead of me in line. I had a sinking feeling that there would be no SAG voucher for me today. If casting had gone to the effort of organizing a group of girls to get especially gussied up, that likely meant that someone was going to be chosen for a featured role, and it was clear that they wanted someone who was already in the union.

I sat down at a folding table for a while until it looked like the girls were done. I walked back and asked Caroline if I should get my things. "We're still working," she said sympathetically. "Are you sure you're not in the group?"

I shook my head. "No, I wish."

"Why don't you ask him?" She nodded to a production assistant. This had never occurred to me. "Tell him I told you to ask." I rushed over to the assistant.

"Caroline told me to ask you if I could be one of the Rocker Girls." I held my breath, waiting for his response. He rolled his head back and looked at Caroline.

"Get over there," he said.

"Thank you!" I ran back to Caroline.

"See?" she said, thumbing through my suitcase. I beamed as I showed her what I thought might work well for the scene.

In my experience, the people working in wardrobe on movies and TV were understandably pressed for time and didn't often give special attention to extras beyond what it took to get everyone ready for set. Every hopeful actor wants special attention, but you're likely to be sorely disappointed if you actually expect it. I knew better than to expect it. But over the next hour, much to my surprise, Caroline poured unusual kindness and effort into putting together a truly standout ensemble for me. She excitedly handpicked the most extreme, provocative pieces of wardrobe that she'd carefully preselected for the shoot. She instructed me to wear the cream-and-black lace bra that I'd brought from home with a tight black corset that stopped right below my breasts so the bra was fully visible. I wore a six-inch leather skirt with a slit over ripped fishnet stockings. The slit in the skirt was held together by two safety pins.

"Is it too much?" Caroline asked with slight hesitation. "I love it," I told her. "It's crazy and perfect." As I examined my new look in her full-length mirror, she walked up to me with a pair of long boots. "Wear these." She held the boots close to her chest, as though she were a museum curator about to show me her most prized piece of art. She handed them to me and I saw that they were lace-up, knee-high pleather boots with eight-inch stilettos in the style of Marilyn Manson. I laced them up with some effort and stood as though on stilts. "Can you walk?" Caroline asked. "I'll make it work," I told her, grateful. She eyed her creation and hugged me. "You look great," she said. "Good luck."

All the fiftysome extras were shuttled to the set at the Rainbow Room. Extras "holding," the designated area where extras were kept when they're not needed on set, was in the upstairs of the neighboring building. Instead of waiting there, I stood at a polite distance from set and watched all the goings-on with fascination. The outside patio area of the restaurant had been set up to look like a different location, and the crew was filming an unrelated scene from the show with two of the main actresses at a table. I could see the screen of the monitor from about fifteen feet away, and I watched as the actresses performed their casual dialogue.

I wanted to be on the other side of that camera like the actresses I saw on the monitor, and I felt that much closer to it today—I couldn't believe my luck in having been invited to be one of the Rocker Girls. Even if I wasn't chosen to be featured, it was worth it just to be here.

As I stood near the cameras, I was aware that everyone who passed was staring at me. Caroline did a masterful job in wardrobe, and her work was reflected in everyone's stunned reaction to my appearance. Instead of looking in the other direction, I said hello to every person who looked at me. David Duchovny strolled by on his way inside the Rainbow Room. "Hello," he said, glancing down at my boots. He looked much younger than I'd expected and strikingly attractive in his jeans and black T-shirt. Another man passed by in a white T-shirt and a ball cap. He also looked at my boots and seemed genuinely shocked by my entire ensemble. "Hi, how are you?" I said in a quiet voice so as not to disturb the filming. "Good, good," he said before walking inside.

After an hour or so, my feet had lost almost all feeling, and I found a place to sit where I could still see the monitor. The production assistant who'd given me a break earlier appeared and called out, "Rocker Girls to set! The director needs to see you guys." The other girls came down the stairs from holding, and we gathered near a booth inside the Rainbow Room. The man with the ball cap who had passed me earlier walked up to our group. The production assistant introduced him. "Girls, this is Dave, the director." Dave studied the nine of us. He pointed to a blond Russian girl and said, "You." My heart fell into my stomach. He continued to look at each of us, thinking. His eyes slowly landed on me and paused for a moment. "And you." He walked off.

The rest of the Rocker Girls were led away while the blond Russian and I were each given paperwork to fill out. She leaned in to me and said in a heavy accent, "Dun't sign nahtink until you oounderstahnd vhawt it is. I'm not sign till I know. I muz know vaht I'm ask to do." I ignored her entirely. I couldn't fill it out fast enough. I scribbled out everything I knew the answer to in the paperwork. I soon heard her in a discussion with an assistant director nearby. By the time I looked up from the paperwork, she was nowhere in sight. The assistant director came up to see if I was done. "I have to tell you something," I said. "I'm not in the union." He looked surprised. "Oh . . . Okay. Um, we'll see what we can do about getting you a voucher, but I gotta tell ya, Showtime is pretty strict about this stuff." I told him thanks and he disappeared.

I was told to wait on the patio. A makeup girl came with her kit to touch me up. As she patted my face with powder, I couldn't stop smiling. I knew that I must look silly to her, but I was so happy that I felt like I might explode into pieces.

When the makeup artist left, I noticed a middle-aged man in a light blue button-down shirt standing about ten feet away from me. He looked serious and he kept glancing at me and nodding while the assistant director spoke to him. I knew just from looking at him that he was a producer from Showtime. After I'd confessed to not being in the union, I was told that it might be necessary to call a producer to set. I smiled at him. I couldn't help it. After a moment, he walked right up to me. He didn't introduce himself, but he looked at me in a fatherly way and put his hand on my shoulder. "We're going to do something a little special for you," he said, and before I could come up with an appropriate response, he walked off.

"They're ready for you." I was ushered to set by the assistant director. The director, Dave, was standing in front of a booth where David Duchovny sat with another actor. "Meili, hi," he said as I walked up. "Have you met David and Callum?" I shook hands with each actor. Dave directed me to crouch underneath the table until Callum patted my knee as a cue for me to crawl up into the booth and kiss him. "Okay," I said. Dave put his hand on my shoulder in the way that the producer had. "Meili, when you come up to sit in the booth, I'd like you to *say* something. Maybe 'Anytime,' or whatever you feel like saying. Okay?" In this moment, it dawned on me what the producer had meant when he said that they were doing something special for me. Dialogue was a whole other ball game. That wasn't just being a "featured" extra. Dialogue meant an acting credit, not to mention about seven hundred dollars up from sixty. Far more meaningful, it meant a scene with dialogue on a major TV show *and*, as it turned out, a Taft-Hartley into being eligible to join the Screen Actors Guild. I wouldn't be getting a voucher today, or ever, because I wouldn't need it. I was getting a formal invitation to join the union.

A FEW WEEKS LATER, THE episode aired on Showtime. I hadn't told many friends to watch it because I knew there was always the chance that my scene would get cut. Of course I'd told Lisette everything, and she said that she couldn't be happier for me. "Fuck that Russian broad," she said when I told her the story. "Thank God she got out of the way and gave my angel some room to shine."

The scene opened with Callum Keith Rennie, portraying the record producer Lew Ashby, and David Duchovny, as the womanizing writer Hank Moody, sitting at a booth having drinks after Lew had just bailed Hank out of jail.

Lew: Smell the history. This was Led Zeppelin's table. Jimmy fucking Page used to get under-the-table oral from Miss Pamela right here. I bet you could still scrape some of his DNA off the floor.

Lew asked Hank if he'd like a blow job.

Hank: I don't know. I think it might ruin the friendship.
Lew: Take your pick. I'll hook you up. Her? Her? Her? (He points to girls around the room)
Hank: No, I'm good. I had a big breakfast.

The conversation continued as Lew spoke with a suspicious and increasing shortness of breath. Suddenly, he stuttered and breathed out. Hank stared at him. Then, Hank realized what had been going on beneath the table when I crawled out from under it and nuzzled up to Lew. "Thanks, sweetheart," Lew said. I kissed him and said, "Anytime." My next line was "You're welcome," but it was inaudible as I walked off camera. Lew added, "Job well done." Hank looked under the tablecloth to see if anyone else was hiding there. "Cool," he said. "Very cool." And thus ended my television debut.

When the episode aired on Showtime I was bombarded by e-mails and calls from friends and acquaintances who had seen me on TV. Someone wrote on my Facebook wall, "And the Emmy goes to . . ." Everyone was supportive, and we all thought the scene was funny, if a little crude. My parents went to dinner at a restaurant I'd worked at in high school in Washington, and the manager came to their table and whispered, "Um, did I see Meili on TV last night . . . ?" My folks just laughed and said, "Uh, yeah, you did." Though the scene was ultimately a "blow job scene," it was done in a humorous and tasteful way. My parents were happy for me because my dream was finally beginning to come true: at last, I was granted qualification to join the Screen Actors Guild.

I wondered if my aunt Wanda ever had to crawl out from under a table for a SAG card. My guess was probably not. Either way, I was sure that I wasn't the only girl in Hollywood who could say that she got into the union because of a blow job.

5

DOWN AND OUT IN ENCINO HILLS

At the top of the Great Recession in the winter of 2007, the Writers Guild of America began a strike. *Jimmy Kimmel Live*, along with practically every other television show on the air, halted production. After months of negotiations, the writers' issues were settled and the strike was over in early 2008. When filming resumed for television, to my surprise, the company that had given me a job as the caterer at *Jimmy Kimmel Live* did not invite me to return. I was unemployed and running out of what little money I had left in savings.

After my brief appearance on *Californication*, I thought that my acting career would gain momentum and take off. But it felt more like a ship that was rapidly sinking in the harbor after one short "bon voyage" toot of a horn and a golf clap from vaguely interested passersby.

When I chose to move to Los Angeles, I knew that it would be a challenge to make it as an actress here, but I never expected that I would find it a challenge to pay rent. I hadn't realized how quickly the odds could stack up against me, how quickly they can stack up against anyone trying to make it in Hollywood. I made a conscious, and in retrospect very foolish, decision when I got to town that I would only accept part-time work so that I would be available for auditions. The reality that followed was a tough pill; auditions were scarce, to say the least, maybe once or twice a month. I felt my dream slipping away from me, right in front of me and all around me.

My parents were generous to give me an allowance of twelve hundred dollars a month for my first two years in L.A. But those years were behind me now, and with them any financial crutch. My mother and father had been nothing short of remarkable and supportive of me my entire life, but I didn't want to keep asking them for money when they were facing potential hardships of their own in a failing economy. I was in my twenties, and I should be able to take care of myself. I was lucky to get any help from them to begin with. A lot of people here never have that.

Lisette had always encouraged me to "just ask" if I ever needed money, and even told me once that if she found out that I'd needed her help and I hadn't asked for it, she would be deeply insulted. Before I got the job at *Kimmel*, I'd been struggling, and I asked her if I could borrow a thousand dollars; she usually kept a few times that amount in cash in her purse and I knew it wasn't much to her. I was sure she'd say yes; I was her best friend, after all. But I'd never intended to actually take her up on the offer she'd made. I was nervous when I asked, my palms sweating as I held my phone. It was a blow to my pride to admit to her how bad things had gotten.

To my amazement, she'd answered me with a cold refusal and no explanation, despite her offers in the past. "It's not a good time right now." She seemed annoyed and judgmental—she had never wanted for anything in her life, and she couldn't relate. I'd rarely spoken of money woes around her, in part because I hadn't wanted her to think that I was asking for a handout, and in part because I was embarrassed. I never expressed to her how much it hurt me that she turned away when I'd asked her for help.

When I simply could no longer afford rent at the apartment I'd been sharing with the director of my first independent film, I moved in with a friend from acting class who lived with her family in Encino Hills. They had a spare room in a house, and generously didn't charge me any rent while I looked for more part-time work and struggled to make money. I tried my hand at being a club promoter at a small but trendy venue on the Sunset Strip, but I didn't like being in the chaotic atmosphere of nightclubs. Beyond the first nightclub event or two, it was difficult to get people to show up, and I knew I wasn't cut out for it.

Finding little success with the clubs, I made the difficult but necessary decision to step away from acting and find my first full-time job. I needed to survive, and part-time work wasn't cutting it. If I couldn't afford rent, I certainly couldn't afford to pay a photographer for new headshots, let alone the twenty-five hundred dollars I'd need for union dues. I hadn't had the money to officially join yet.

Desperate for work, I scoured Craigslist, where the effects of the down economy became painfully obvious and close to home. I e-mailed my résumé in response to every post that I could conceivably be hired for. I applied in person to a Jamba Juice on Ventura Boulevard, wearing a blazer and a dress. A pimple-faced teenager wearing a visor seemed confused and bewildered as I forced a smile and handed him my résumé. He stashed it behind the register and asked me if I wanted to order anything, but I said I was good. I couldn't afford it. Even Jamba Juice didn't give me a call back.

At last, I was hired by a marketing company to sell discounted spa packages door-to-door in the Valley. It was by no means a dream job, but it was a job, and I was grateful to finally have one. The company's hiring process was quite a departure from the norm; the managers hired anyone who was willing to work for them. The pay was purely commission based, so anyone who wasn't willing to cut their teeth in the trenches wasn't going to last more than a day or two. I woke up at 5 A.M. every morning and came back to the house after 7 P.M. every evening. The full-time sales position was grueling, with daily, often demoralizing rejection, but my hunger to climb out of a financial hole and return to pursuing my passion gave me the strength to endure the long hours and dedication that came with the job. I put money aside every day toward my goal of a fresh start.

Lisette told me that she wished she could buy a house for us to live in together, but that now wasn't a good time because she was still living with her boyfriend. She had never made a habit of being faithful to him, but she stayed his girlfriend nonetheless for reasons that I didn't understand. I was glad that I wasn't living with Lisette. I didn't want to lean on her, or anyone. I wanted to be independent and prove that I could take care of myself.

Within weeks I was one of the top sellers in my new position at the marketing company. I felt a sense of pride and self-worth that I hadn't had in quite a while. I made enough money there to move out of the house in Encino Hills and look for an apartment in town with a friend named Brie.

Brie was a fashion designer from the East Coast who looked more like a model than a designer with her thin frame, almond eyes, and mane of auburn hair. She was one of the most genuine people I'd met since moving to Los Angeles. I wish I'd met her sooner. We found a corner apartment above Sunset Boulevard that had hardwood floors and an abundance of natural sunlight: to us, it was perfect and symbolized a new beginning. In the throes of the recession, Brie had also struggled to find work, but she had recently been offered a job as a wardrobe assistant on a popular TV show. She designed jewelry in her spare time and hoped to one day develop her line into a successful business, so Brie and I were both artists in our own right. We talked constantly about our respective dreams and how we planned to reach them.

After signing the lease and giving a deposit, Brie and I couldn't afford to buy any furniture to fill our new home, but we spent countless nights after work sitting on the floor in our empty living room, sharing cheap wine and talking about how we wanted to decorate when we could afford it. Brie was a wonderful roommate, and we became close friends in our corner apartment. Lisette had no interest in meeting her, just as she had never wanted to meet anyone in my life outside of my family, who she made time to see whenever they came into town. "I can't blame you for keeping yourself busy when I'm not around," Lisette would tell me with a playfully pouty face, "just as long as no one tries to steal you from me."

ONE AFTERNOON IN THE SUMMER of 2009 Lisette asked me to come with her to the home of a music producer who wanted her to "lay down a track." She'd never met him before, but he'd come recommended to her by a friend she'd known for years named Petey, whom I'd met with Lisette a few months back. Lisette described Petey, a soft-spoken and pale white boy with a shaved head and a thin frame, as a "trust fund baby" whose parents had "helped build Vegas." He had an openly elitist attitude and enjoyed talking about money and his connections to the hip-hop community and various celebrities. He was enamored with Lisette.

Lisette and I arrived at the producer's house in the Hollywood Hills. She linked her arm with mine as we walked to the entrance and rang the doorbell. Petey greeted us. "Hiii," he said in a low voice that dripped with lust for Lisette.

The music producer was a man in his forties with shoulder-length hair and an excess of energy. He seemed nervous to meet Lisette, perhaps intimidated by the reputation that had surely preceded her. I knew well that Lisette would never agree to meet anyone without some information about her already being known, namely her ties to the Samsung dynasty. She had a huge ego, which she readily admitted, but I always kept my suspicions that she had secret insecurities to myself. I found the fact that she wasn't perfect, as none of us are, to be endearing, but I never let on to Lisette.

The producer treaded lightly around Lisette. It appeared that Petey had already regaled him with stories about the Samsung heiress and warned him that if he said the wrong thing to her, he was likely to get a verbal evisceration that would make his balls shrink back into his body—though possibly make his dick hard too, if he was anything like Petey. Petey loved it when Lisette acted like a bitch, and she rose to the occasion whenever she was around him.

I was uncomfortable in this environment, and I didn't understand why Lisette wanted to be here. If she had a contract with Sony Records, why was she bothering to come to this house to record something? It didn't strike me as the way things were usually done, but she'd always preferred to make her own rules and I respected that about her. Here, she was encouraged to act the part of the "Mafia princess" that she'd always joked about embodying. Guys like Petey and the producer loved the act and hung on her every word; meanwhile, it made me nauseated. I'd always felt as though she wasn't really being herself when she carried on that way, like she was putting on a front because she believed that was what people expected of her. Just another expectation she felt she had to live up to, I supposed. It had never been my favorite side of her personality, and I rarely saw it when it was just the two of us. I knew the giddy, sympathetic, and even silly side to Lisette that was practically never seen by others, and that wasn't invited to the party today. Though I was annoyed when she seemed so different around other people, I felt secretly lucky that she saved her best side for me, the way she really was at her core. I'd come today strictly on best friend duty, because she'd asked for my support, and I was ready for the show. I knew I was in for an afternoon full of it, and I braced myself.

After Lisette and the producer entertained some vague discussion about music, Petey announced that someone called "Freddy" was going to "come by." I soon gathered that Freddy was a drug dealer who was coming over to deliver a few grams of cocaine. "You gotta try Freddy's coke," Petey told Lisette. "He's got some sick shit."

I would later learn that Freddy's real name was David Garrett. "Freddy" was a pseudonym that David used when he dealt drugs.

David, a.k.a. Freddy, showed up with the coke. His appearance was shocking. I couldn't remember ever seeing someone with so many tattoos. David's body was covered with ink, all the way up to his neck. When he walked in the door, all eyes turned to him, including Lisette's. He was a well-built Hispanic man with a shaved head, who looked to be in his late twenties and walked with the kind of "hustler" swagger that I knew Lisette would find attractive. There was something handsome about him. He wore expensive jeans and a black polo shirt, revealing that his arms were also covered in tattoos. Lisette didn't get up from her chair when he came in, but stayed seated at the head of the dining room table, taking in his appearance while establishing her dominance in the room. David set the coke down on the table and introduced himself to Lisette. She shook his hand and said in her ambiguously British accent, "I hear you've got some good shit." David nodded and said, "Yeah, I like to keep it clean." Lisette smirked. "I'll be the judge of that." David seemed intrigued. "Be my guest."

Lisette asked Petey for a razor, but he didn't have one. "Goddamnit,

Petey, of all the people to not have a fucking razor. I need a knife."
Lisette stormed into the kitchen and pulled a large butcher knife out
from a wood block and examined the blade. "This knife is filthy," she
said. "This is disgusting. It's like you butchered Lizzie Borden's parents
and put it right back." After rinsing the knife in the sink, she poured the
cocaine on a plate and chopped it with the now clean and dried knife.
Once she was done, Lisette sampled David's product and gave him her
approval. "Well done," she said. "You should know that I'm not easily
impressed." She offered David a line.

"Nah, I'm not into that," he said. "I'm a businessman. I don't like to
mess around with that stuff." I could tell that Lisette liked his control.
Though I was on the sidelines of their exchange, I respected David for
not partaking. It was obvious he wasn't a typical drug dealer, and it
appeared that this was more of a side gig for him. I knew about taking side gigs and having plans for something greater. I didn't give any
thought to what his greater ambition might be.

David stayed for a drink. I sat in a chair across the room, playing
with my phone in silence while Lisette talked with him at the dining
table. I tuned in to bits of what they were saying, but I mostly zoned out
because I was uncomfortable and wanted to hightail it out of there as
soon as possible. What I caught of their conversation was agonizingly
boring and easy to ignore.

Little did I know that Lisette meeting David here would come to
drastically change not only both their lives forever, but mine as well.
Had I paid attention and been more aware of my surroundings, maybe
things would have turned out differently for me. But I was too busy
texting and fantasizing about getting home to my cozy apartment.

I did hear Lisette and David speaking about Commerce Casino, and
several names of people there who they knew in common. I'd been
aware that Lisette's work took her to Commerce Casino often, but I'd
never asked her for details. Her father was a heavy hitter in the casino
world of Japan so I understood that Lisette's role in the local casino
industry was somehow connected to her family. I didn't know the first
thing about that kind of business, and I was frankly not interested. If
Lisette wanted to tell me about it, I would have listened, but if she didn't

volunteer it, then I wasn't going to pretend to be curious. It was one of the few things that Lisette seemed to actually enjoy. I was happy if she was happy.

It was hours after nightfall by the time we left the producer's house in the hills. Lisette never "laid down a track." The idea was barely even discussed. When she told me it was time to go, I practically jogged outside and climbed eagerly into her Bentley, though at this point I would have accepted a ride in a shopping cart from a homeless person if it meant I'd be on my way.

I HADN'T SEEN LISETTE IN more than two months when she unexpectedly texted me on the morning of her birthday. She'd been disappointingly absent from my life recently. I'd tried to make plans with her, but she said she was busier than ever with work. This wasn't the first time she'd gone off the radar, always with the same vague excuses. Before, I'd written it off as the busy life of a businesswoman heiress, but after four years of inconsistencies in our friendship, it had finally caused some distance between us.

I read her text message:

ANGEL, DO YOU HAVE PLANS TONIGHT? I WANT TO SPEND MY BIRTHDAY WITH YOU. THERE IS NO ONE I WOULD RATHER BE WITH TODAY. I MISS YOU. I CANCELED FAMILY PLANS IN THE HOPE THAT YOU'LL BE ABLE TO SEE ME. CAN YOU STAY WITH ME TONIGHT AT THE RITZ IN MARINA DEL REY? DINNER IS ON ME. I KNOW YOU'RE BROKE. I NEED TO SEE YOU.
~LOVE ALWAYS, YOUR SETTA

Lisette was the one in the beginning who was dead set that we commit to each other in this "ride or die" kind of way, with an intensity rarely seen in platonic relationships. She'd insisted on the title of "best friends," which now felt a little juvenile as we were both adults well into our twenties. It had all felt romantic when it started. I didn't know anyone in L.A., and it was as though Lisette had swept me off my feet, there to save me from the world! But our honeymoon was over. I'd since developed other, healthy relationships with people in L.A., and I couldn't deny that what I had with Lisette was abnormal and severely imbalanced.

But we'd always said we were different, hadn't we? That no one would ever understand us except for each other. I tried to understand her, and I believed that on some level I did. The imbalance dug at me. Over the years I'd known her, she'd make plans with me only to cancel at the last minute, while I'd always dropped plans to see her at a moment's notice. She regularly took a long time to respond to my texts or phone calls, but she acted profoundly hurt and offended when I didn't respond to her right away. She allowed months to go by without making time to see me.

The only thing she'd never wavered on, however, was telling me how important I was to her and how much she loved me, how much she needed me. She said once that she would rather burn in Hell than not have me in her life. I couldn't bring myself to cast her aside when I believed in my heart that her intentions were good, though her follow-through was often nonexistent.

I reconciled the changes in Lisette's behavior in my mind by thinking of our relationship in more of a familial way, as if she were my older sister. If your sister lets you down, it doesn't make you love her any less, because that kind of love is unconditional. I believed that was the kind of love Lisette and I shared.

When I got Lisette's invitation, I told her that of course I'd meet her at the Ritz. Thankfully I'd already bought her a birthday card. I didn't have any money to buy her a gift. I'd left my job at the marketing company a few weeks back, when I got burned out and couldn't sell anymore. I'd become distracted. I'd signed with a new acting agency and paid to update my photos, and I was starting to get calls again, so I'd stop work in the middle of the day sometimes to sneak out to auditions. I tried for weeks to get back into a sales groove, but something was off and people could smell it on me when I pitched them. I'd come home after a full day of work and have sold fewer than five spa packages, sometimes zero, though when I started there I was selling up to twenty packages a day—I'd lost whatever magic touch I had in the beginning.

I'd been looking for work again but found it to be just as difficult to get hired as it was before, and now I had rent to pay every month. The effects of the recession were still painfully evident in the job market. I told Lisette the gist of my circumstances, and she said that she was sorry to hear I was having a hard time.

From the Ritz-Carlton, Lisette and I went to dinner at a seafood restaurant on Ocean Avenue, next to the waves in Santa Monica. Lisette had a Lincoln Town Car pick us up, which was odd because in the four years we'd been friends she'd never paid for a driver when it was just the two of us. Come to think of it, she'd never paid for a hotel room for just the two of us. There always had to be someone else there when she did something showy, like her boyfriend or one of her boys on the side. I'd routinely been the third wheel when she stepped out on her boy-friend to be courted by some poor sap who was about to have his heart run through a garbage disposal. Tonight felt like a special occasion that extended beyond just her birthday.

Back at the hotel, Lisette and I sat on queen beds in the oceanfront room. I gave her the birthday card. She read my message and appeared moved. "Thank you," she said, setting my card aside. "Thank you for being here tonight. I wasn't sure you'd come." She looked at me in a rare moment of humility. "I know that I haven't been a very good friend to you—"

I cut her off. "I know you've been busy."

"No," she said, "you've always been there for me, and I know that I haven't been there for you in the same way. But you never left me. You stayed with me when no one else in their right mind would have. You'll never know how much that has meant to me." She pulled me into a hug. "You deserve better. I promise I'll make it up to you."

Lisette told me that she and her boyfriend had broken up but were still living together. I wondered why she wouldn't want to move out and get a place of her own. With her family's wealth, she had plenty of money to support herself. She announced that David, whom she'd been seeing since they met at the music producer's house, was coming to the hotel to meet her soon. I wondered where she'd found time to see him when she hadn't made time for me in two months, but I held my tongue.

I'm sure it would have shocked a lot of people to see Lisette with David, a drug dealer with tattoos up to his neck, but it didn't surprise me. Lisette had told me that her father's entire body was covered in tattoos, even more so than David's. Her father wore suits every day, so no one could see his tattoos when he was working. I knew from the way that she spoke about him that Lisette admired him enormously. She said that he had "built an empire" in Asia, and that she would like to one day build an empire of her own. Lisette had always been drawn to ambitious men who had the "bad boy" persona, but who were driven by a business mind-set. To Lisette, that was the definition of a hustler.

"Sweetie, can you wait in the bar downstairs for David?" she asked. "I told him that my family is throwing me a party in a suite, but that I rented this room to see him."

I laughed. "Oh God."

"What?" Lisette said playfully. "It's fun. It'll keep him on his best behavior. Can you wait for him downstairs? Just order a drink and put it on the tab for the room."

I ordered a dirty martini and read a book by the fireplace while I waited for David to arrive. Being here with Lisette gave me a giddy feeling that I hadn't had in a while, like an old spark coming back. It was just the two of us staying here tonight. Whenever we spent time alone, we almost immediately reverted back to existing in our own little world, like childhood playmates who'd make up silly games and inside jokes together. I loved that feeling, and I needed it right now with all the stress and uncertainties in my life. It was like returning to a time when things were much simpler, and all you needed to do was play with your friend.

I noticed David right away when he walked into the lobby. He seemed to be the only person at the Ritz tonight with neck tattoos. "Meili," he said as I stood to greet him. "Nice to see you. How's the party?"

"Er, great," I said. I led him upstairs to Lisette's room. After I returned downstairs, I had time to read almost an entire chapter of my book while he was up there. He stopped into the bar to say bye to me before he left. I went back upstairs and knocked on the hotel room door. Lisette opened it with a naughty smirk. She looked sweaty and her hair was tussled. "Have fun?" I asked her as I stepped inside.

"Can you meet Henry in the bar?" Lisette dabbed her face with makeup.

"Who's Henry?" I asked, a little surprised.

"I never told you about Henry?" She explained that Henry was a valet at the new building she lived in. That's how he'd met her: parking her Bentleys on Wilshire Corridor. "He's really sweet. I think you'll like him," she said. "I told him that my parents were throwing me a party, but he asked if he could stop by to wish me a happy birthday."

When I met Henry in the lobby, he looked like a college kid, around my age, much younger than I'd expected. He was built like a football player and wore a button-down shirt and jeans. He was Mexican, but when he spoke, it was clear that he was raised in L.A. "Lisette's told me so much about you," he said, shaking my hand as he gave me a warm smile. "It's nice to finally meet you." He cleared his throat.

He spent almost an hour in the hotel room with Lisette. I'd nearly fallen asleep next to the fireplace in the bar when Lisette texted me.

COME UP ANGEL! HE JUST LEFT!

When I reentered the room, the air inside was hot and balmy. Lisette was sprawled out on the bed looking like a Tijuana hooker after a rough shift. "Holy shit," I said as I walked in. The bed comforter was piled on the floor a few feet from the bed, and Lisette lay on a mess of sheets. "Henry might seem shy," Lisette said, out of breath, "but that boy is a fucking animal in the sack." I silently thanked God that there were two beds in the room, and I gratefully plopped down on the one that appeared untouched.

Lisette broke into the minibar and mixed makeshift cocktails for us since the bar downstairs was now closed.

"Angel, I want to talk to you about something serious," she said as she sat next to me on the bed. "I'm sorry for not loaning you that money before." I put on a confused face, like I wasn't sure what she was talking about, but she stopped me. "I know it hurt you. I'm sorry. I hope that you can forgive me and that we can move past that."

I was stunned that she would bring up the loan—we hadn't spoken about it since it happened. The memory was still a painful one, and I needed a moment before I could accept her apology. I sucked my emotions in enough to look at Lisette with a straight face. "Thank you" was all I could say. Apologizing wasn't her style, and I knew that it took a lot for her to do it tonight.

"I know that you need a job," Lisette said. "I've never been in a position to hire you before because I've always worked for my family. But I have an opportunity to help you now. I'm starting a new business with David."

"Isn't he a drug dealer?" I asked. Lisette shook her head.

"Sweetie, that's just a side thing. David is smart, and he doesn't want to do that forever. Our business is going to be a private one, so I'm going to need someone I can trust. I have to be honest; you're not qualified for the job. I'm willing to stick my neck out for you, but you'd have to just keep your head down and trust me. How would you feel about being my executive personal assistant?" She glowed with happy anticipation, as though she'd just told me that I'd won a prize.

"What is that?" I asked.

"It's like a personal assistant, except that I can send you to work when I'm not there, so you can represent me if I can't make it. Are you interested?"

"Well, yeah, of course. I need a job."

"I can pay you in cash, and I'd give you time off whenever you have an audition."

"That would be amazing," I said.

"You'd have to travel with me on a private plane. But you *cannot* act like you've never been on a private plane before. Just act like it's nothing; otherwise, it will be too obvious that you're green and underqualified. Don't act too excited, because you'll be working. The best part is that I'd finally be able to see you more often. You'll be working for your best friend."

I remembered the conversation I heard between David and Lisette when they met, and I assumed that her new business would involve casinos. The casino industry was a foreign world to me, but one that I knew Lisette was passionate about. She'd confided to me many times that if she could choose to do anything with her life, she would want to run casinos, like her father did in Japan. Lisette was a member of the Samsung dynasty, so if there was anything she understood, it was business. I trusted her judgment.

When Lisette asked me to work for her, I felt as though she was once again coming to my rescue. With her help, I could continue to pursue my dream. I'd be able to afford my apartment, pay my bills, and escape the guilt of potentially asking my parents for more money. I told her that I was interested in her offer, though I still had no idea what the job would entail. All I knew is that it was a job, and I definitely needed one.

6

TEAM LL

Less than a week after our stay at the Ritz-Carlton, Lisette asked me to meet her at the bar of a quiet Beverly Hills hotel. She texted me beforehand with explicit instructions to park my Volkswagen Beetle around the corner from the hotel, "a few blocks away"; she didn't want anyone we would be working with to judge me for driving such an inexpensive car. "It's none of their fucking business," she said. Her request didn't surprise me. When I first met Lisette, she told me to tell anyone she introduced me to that I had known her since we were children, and that I'd initially met her when I traveled to Los Angeles with my family many years ago. I wasn't comfortable going along with a fake story, but her argument for it was compelling. It was to protect me from people in her life thinking that because I was a "new friend" I must only be "after her money." She'd said it would be "cruel" to subject me to such unfair suspicion. "Friends since childhood" had been our story ever since.

The hotel was located just off Wilshire Boulevard in Beverly Hills. I was struck by how deserted it looked when I walked into the air-conditioned lobby. From the entrance the only other people I could see were a receptionist and one lone bartender who was wiping down already clean glassware behind the bar. I passed the front desk and followed a dangerously polished floor into the lounge, where Lisette was waiting for me in a booth. She looked more like a madam than an entrepreneur, with her shimmering purple eye makeup and form-fitting black tank top. A bejeweled medallion was woven into her shirt, drawing attention to her chest beneath an already plunging neck-line. Her B cups had been pressed together by the godlike effect of a push-up bra. Lisette's hair was perfectly styled as usual and fell down over one shoulder. "Sweetie!" She got up and hugged me. "Frankie and Henry should be here any minute." *Henry?* She saw my confusion and explained that she had invited him to work for her as "kind of like a second bodyguard and driver, someone to carry luggage." "It's better than being a fucking valet," she said, sipping her Bombay Sapphire gin and tonic. "When David gets here, I am seriously going to die laughing. You have to help me because this shit is too much." She could barely contain her excitement about watching them meet for the first time. I was happy to see her enjoying herself, but I tried to keep some dis-tance from thinking about the hearts I knew she would likely break. It's like when a dog owner sees that his beloved pet has bitten the head off a mouse. The carnage can be disturbing, even if you always knew it's in the dog's nature.

From what Lisette told me, it seemed that David and Henry had each fallen for her, hard. David didn't know about Henry, and Henry only knew that David liked Lisette. He had no idea that David had been seriously dating her for months. Lisette was delighted that the two men would be forced to work together, oblivious to the web that she had spun them into. The mere thought of it gave her a childlike joy, enter-taining and impressing herself with her ability to play with men as if they were toys.

I'd had friends who had cheated on their boyfriends in the past, but Lisette took it to another level. Her sommelier ex-boyfriend who still shared a condo and a bed with her didn't know about either of her new lovers. I imagined that he'd be surprised to learn that one of the valets at his building had been making house calls upstairs.

Henry arrived and sat next to Lisette in the booth. Frankie, Lisette's

Samoan bodyguard, was the next to show up. He was about forty years old. In his twenties he was a semiprofessional basketball player in Europe. He had the height and bulk to make you believe it. When we saw his six-foot-eight frame walk into the lobby of the hotel, Lisette whispered quickly in my ear, "Angel, remember what I told you." I nodded.

I got up from the table and met Frankie with a big hug. "Frankie!"

"Ah, Meili," he said, "nice to see you, girl. You, uh, ya been good?"

"I've been great!" I said. I sat back down and glanced at Lisette. She looked satisfied, which told me I'd done my job. I had never met Frankie in my life, but Lisette didn't want anyone to know that. "Frankie has been a bodyguard for my family since I was five years old," she explained to me before the meeting. "If anyone finds out that you two haven't met, they'll find it pretty fucking hard to believe that you've known me since we were kids. Don't worry, sweetie, I already told Frankie what to do when he sees you."

David and Ko were the last to join our meeting. Ko, David's close friend, was a Korean man in his early forties who had been starstruck by Lisette since hearing from David that she was the Samsung heiress. Samsung has enormous power in Korea, and to Ko, Lisette was like royalty. Whenever he was around her, he anxiously tried to make conversation. This tended to irritate her, which led him to talking more to try to appease her, which usually led to Ko getting his ass handed to him when Lisette silenced him with some kind of verbal venom. But her insults always seemed to bounce off Ko. I think in a way he enjoyed their routine. Maybe he liked to get a rise out of her.

Since Lisette started dating David the four of us had gone out to a few dinners together. I'd heard from Lisette that Ko used to be in a Korean gang; he kept the nails of his pinkie fingers long. I asked him once what it meant and he said, "It means I can get down." His response didn't entirely answer my question, but it did stop me from asking him anything further.

David walked a step ahead of Ko into the lounge. Lisette introduced them to Frankie. She kept a straight face as David shook Henry's hand. Soon after this meeting our group would come to be called "Team LL," for Lisette Lee, a nickname thought up by LL herself.

Our time at the hotel was short, and halfway through the meeting Lisette asked me to step outside with Henry. "Sweetie, go sit by the pool. I'll text you when to come back." I got up from the booth and leaned over to share a kiss on the cheek with her. She smiled at me and said, "That's my girl."

Henry and I sat idle on lounge chairs outside by the pool. I still didn't know what it was that we would be doing on the upcoming "trip," and it seemed that Henry didn't either. I didn't even know where we would be going, beyond a brief mention from Lisette that it would be "east."

Henry and I got along, maybe because we were the same age, twenty-three, and perhaps because we shared a similar adoration of Lisette. Neither of us had much in common with anyone else here. We were also both apparently not invited to be in the know with regard to Lisette's new business, but I don't think either of us really cared. We were just happy to be a part of Lisette's orbit, however unusual it was.

COME INSIDE ANGEL.

When I received Lisette's text, I returned to the meeting with Henry. David was ready to wrap things up with the "need-to-knows." "Okay, we leave on Friday," he said. "We meet at my place downtown. Ko is gonna fly with Henry and Meili on the jet, and I'm gonna meet them over there. The next morning, Meili and Henry fly back to L.A. on commercial and we take care of everything from there."

After the men left, I stayed at the table to talk with Lisette for a few minutes.

"Wait, so, you're not coming with us?" I asked her. This was not how I thought this would go. She'd said that we'd be traveling together.

She frowned and said, "No, sweetie, I can't. I wish I could, but I have meetings in town I have to attend. That's why I need you to go for me, to make sure everything runs smoothly and to keep an eye on the boys."

Lisette told me that David was going to hand me two thousand dollars in cash before I flew back to L.A. "Wow," I said, "that's a lot. I don't know what to say. Thank you."

She smirked and said, "You deserve it. What did I tell you? You're working for your best friend. You'll never have to worry about money again." She warned me not to talk with any of the guys about how much I was being paid.

"I just don't want anyone getting pissed because you're making more than they are," she explained.

"Yeah, that makes sense," I agreed. Lisette knew that I wouldn't say anything if she told me not to. She could count on me for that. If I had gone against her wishes and found out what the other guys were getting paid, maybe it would have been enough to make me leave, or at least wise up about where I stood with her. Many details like this I would only learn years later from the pages of an article in *Rolling Stone* magazine.

"I need you on the flight," Lisette said. "We're going to have a lot of luggage, and I don't want anyone to bother us. It's no one's business. David can't be on the plane because he looks like a goddamn gangster. But if it looks like the bags are yours, it will make more sense, and no one will harass us. You need to play it up like a diva. You can do it. You're a good actress. This could be the role of a lifetime for you."

When I left the hotel, I had a different feeling about Lisette's new business than I'd had before the meeting. At the Ritz, when she'd first spoken about offering me the job, I hadn't put much thought into it because I honestly didn't think she would follow through with the offer. I thought I'd literally never hear about it again. She'd been so flaky in the last year. I was surprised when she turned out to be serious about it. Pleasantly surprised, mind you, because God knows I needed the money.

When she told me that she'd be working with David, I assumed that she just wanted to bring one of her new "boy toys," as she called them, on board to expand some casino work she was already doing for her family. She'd said for years that she constantly went back and forth to Commerce Casino in L.A. for family business, so it seemed logical that this operation would be tied in some way to that.

I'd never questioned what Lisette did in business because she was bred by the founding family of one of the most successful companies in the world. Samsung was a company of such stature that it was in everyone's backyard. Half my friends owned Samsung electronics. If the people who ran the company had been using certain methods for years, as Lisette said, it was likely commonplace in that pocket of society. When Lisette first told me that I shouldn't "ask any questions" about what we'd be doing, I'd initially thought that she was following some business protocol by not divulging "confidential" information. Now I wondered if she was trying to protect me from knowing something that I wouldn't want to know. It was like when I found that gun in her condo. She felt that she had a logical reason for having it, but it made me uneasy to find it in her drawer. I was beginning to think that she must have very specific reasons why she wanted to keep me in the dark about the details of her work. Probably because, as she'd said, I wouldn't understand a lot of things that were typical of the world she'd grown up in, the world of "big business."

Lisette had spoken casually about her family using a hit man in certain areas of work when "it comes to that." She'd told me that they called the contract killer "Angel," which I found mildly disturbing because Angel was also her pet name for me. She joked that she had Angel "on speed dial" but said that he was called upon only in "extreme cases," and that usually it wasn't to kill someone, only to "rough them up," like breaking bones. When I heard this from her, I was stunned. I didn't know how to process the information coming from my best friend. It sounded like something out of a Martin Scorsese movie about gangsters. It was difficult to find a place for it in my perception of reality. It would be one thing if it seemed *real* and it was in front of me, but when you hear that kind of thing over cocktails during a sleepover, it lands on you differently.

Lisette had always reveled in being mysterious and secretive, but this was a step beyond that, even for her. I was her closest friend and even *I* didn't know what she was planning. I just knew that I was to be a part of her plan.

ANGEL I NEED YOU TO COME TO THE BANK WITH ME TODAY. THIS WILL BE YOUR FIRST OFFICIAL JOB TASK ;).

On the Wednesday before our first trip, I didn't know what to expect as Lisette drove us to a bank in Beverly Hills. When we parked, she opened her Chanel purse to show me that she'd brought what appeared to be a substantial amount of cash, neatly stacked and rubber-banded. "This is what forty thousand dollars looks like," she told me before we got out of her Bentley. "That's incredible that it all fits in there," I said. "I would have thought it would take up more room." Lisette had always carried large amounts of cash, but I was sure this was the most I'd seen her with. It didn't surprise me that she would want to handle everything in cash, as she'd often joked about being partial to it, but I'd never seen her pull it out of her purse and tell me the amount that was there.

In line inside the bank, Lisette whispered to me as we waited for an available teller. "Just follow my lead, sweetie," she said. "You'll do this on your own from now on, so pay attention. I come here all the time, so this should be easy for you once they know that you work for me."

This was already unlike any job I'd ever had, but I'd suspected that working for Lisette would be just as unconventional as she was. She delighted in mystery and keeping things playful in a sense. I liked that about her, like she was always holding the cards but would give me a wink to tell me it's all okay and it's just for fun. She was the kind of girl who'd exude an air of mystery even when she told you what she'd had for breakfast, and somehow you'd be intrigued.

Lisette greeted the teller in a high tone. "Hi, sweetie, how are you?"

He looked happy to see her. "Good afternoon, Miss Lee. I'm good. What can I do you for today?"

Lisette motioned to me, placing her hand on my arm. "Have you met my assistant, Meili? We need to do a wire transfer to JetSetter Charter. We're flying to Miami for a party on Friday. Just a weekend. I need a break." Lisette pushed a smile, along with her lie. Her British accent was particularly heavy today.

"Man, I'm jealous," the teller said as he took her cash and filled out a form.

"Maybe we can take you with us one of these times," Lisette told him. He blushed. When he handed Lisette the slip of paper with a pen, she slid it over to me. "Just put all your information down," she told me. "Hmm?" I asked, trying to be subtle about my confusion so that the teller didn't pick up on it. Lisette pointed to the paper. "Fill it out." She turned back to the teller and continued their conversation. I was uncomfortable putting my name on something that I didn't understand, especially when attaching it to a large sum of cash that didn't belong to me. With the teller as a witness, I tried to act like this was business as usual.

Why couldn't this be in Lisette's name? I didn't like lying to anyone, even strangers. This didn't feel right, but I didn't want to fail at my very first job assignment from Lisette. I didn't want to risk Lisette's faith in me that I could do the job, let alone risk losing the payment to come that I desperately needed.

"Just always tell them we're going to Miami for vacation, or something like that," Lisette said once we were outside of the bank. "And if you can, make sure it's a teller who has seen us in there before. It's better if they already know us."

"Okay," I said. "So I'll be doing that before every trip then?"

"Unless you can find us a jet company who will just *give* us a plane for free," she said, a little irritated.

"Sorry, I just want to make sure that it's okay. I mean, isn't it bad to have a bunch of money go through my account? Like for taxes?" Maybe Lisette felt protected by Samsung when it came to finances, but I knew well that my banking history was full of overdraft fees, and that it would seem beyond unusual to anyone if I suddenly put forty thousand dollars, in cash, no less, under my name for anything at a bank.

"The money doesn't register if it's only in your account for two minutes, babe," she said. I could tell that I was annoying her, but I needed to understand this. I needed some reassurance going forward. I needed some reason to believe that everything my gut was telling me was wrong and overcautious. I wanted to believe that this was all okay.

"Wouldn't it be better to do it through your account?" I asked. "I mean, obviously I'll do it, but I'm just wondering if it looks weird to the bank to have that much money going through an account that's been overdrawn like ten times this year."

I'd hit a nerve with Lisette. She rolled her eyes in frustration, then looked at me with a tight jaw. "Okay, do you want to work or not?" She underlined every word with direct hand gestures. "Because I'm not going to pay you for doing nothing. Other than riding on a fucking private plane, this is your only job task. Do you have any idea how many girls out there would kill to be in your position? I'm doing you a favor and you're already complaining."

I decided to back off. She'd offered me a job I needed, and I'd immediately questioned her. "You know that I'm grateful to have this job," I said. "I didn't mean it like that. Of course I'm willing to work. I'm just still learning what it is that you want me to do."

"Okay," Lisette said, calming herself. "*This* is what I want you to do. It's not rocket science. A monkey could do it. Trust me, you'll be fine." Lisette knew more about these things than I did, but I couldn't shake the feeling that what I'd done wasn't necessarily "on the up and up."

When I came home after the bank, my roommate, Brie, was sitting on the couch with her sketchbook. "Hey, love!" she said. "Sorry about the mess, I'll clean it up later." Brie had the day off, and judging by the colorful crystals that were spread across our coffee table, she'd been working on her jewelry line. "Don't worry about it," I said. Brie knew what a clean freak I am, and she was always considerate about keeping things nice around the apartment. We were able to finally get a couch and a little bit of furniture recently from a friend who was moving, so the place was starting to look more like a home.

"Oh, I like this one," I said as I picked up a necklace from the coffee table. Brie had filled a long tube of crin with purple crystals, and they sparkled through the black mesh like fish scales in the water. "This is gorgeous." I held it in between my fingers. "It's squishy too! I love it!" Brie ran into the kitchen and came back holding a bottle of Two Buck Chuck from Trader Joe's in one hand and two glasses in the other. "I bought some wine to celebrate your new job!"

Brie and I took our wine outside and talked while we shared a cigarette. I told her about the money transfer at the bank today. "I don't know, Miles," she said. "I think that it gets reported if you deposit more than ten thousand dollars at once."

"But it wasn't really a deposit," I said, ashing into a coffee cup. "It was a transfer, and she said it won't get reported because it was only in my account for a few minutes."

Brie thought as she took a drag from the cigarette. We both watched as the sun disappeared into the smog of the Hollywood skyline. Brie blew a final puff of smoke into the air and tossed the cigarette in the coffee cup. "Well," she said on our way back inside, "Lisette would know a lot more about this stuff than I do, but I'd just say be careful because that's a lot of cash. I know she's your friend and she's looking out for you, and I know that she wants to keep her work private and all—which I still think is weird, but whatever. I'm just saying be careful."

EARLY FRIDAY MORNING I DROVE downtown to meet David, Ko, and Henry at David's penthouse on Wilshire Boulevard. Per instructions from David, I left my car in guest parking in his downstairs garage; I'd be back to collect it tomorrow night, Lisette had assured me. David's building was surprisingly fancy. It was just as nice as the place Lisette lived in, only more modern. Lisette's building was stuffy and reeked of old money.

After leaving my car, I went to the lobby to wait for an elevator. Henry showed up next to me and we took the ride together. Wearing a black suit with a tie, he looked like a groomsman at a wedding.

Lisette told me to wear my hair down and "dress like a diva." I wasn't sure what a diva would wear, so I just went with jeans, boots, and a basic black top. I'd also brought a scarf and a black-and-white-speckled winter coat because David told me that it would be cold where we were going. I packed my toothbrush in a plastic baggie inside my purse, but I wasn't able to bring a change of clothes, however, because Lisette told me that I couldn't bring any luggage—there wouldn't be room for extra bags on the plane. I saw that Henry had no luggage either, so I guessed that he got the same note from our girl.

"How are you doing?" Henry asked me as the elevator carried us up. "Good," I said. "A little tired."

"Yep," Henry said, "it's pretty early. At least I guess we'll be back by tomorrow night." Henry definitely seemed to have the same level of security clearance as I did with this whole arrangement. I wondered if he knew where we were flying to today, but of course I didn't ask him. Lisette told me not to engage in much conversation with any of the men and to keep talk about my personal life to a minimum.

Henry knocked on David's door. We heard someone check the peephole, then the door swung open. Ko looked sweaty and out of breath as he greeted us. "Come on in, guys," he said. There were about seven suitcases standing around the kitchen of the penthouse apartment. Ko was lining them up near the door, struggling to move them, as though they were extremely heavy. I wondered what could make them so heavy. After seeing how easily forty thousand dollars fit into Lisette's purse, it was difficult to believe that it could be all money in the suitcases; maybe it was coins, or perhaps casino chips. I wondered for a moment, then I brushed it off. If Lisette didn't want me to know, then I wouldn't spend time racking my brain about it.

We were on the seventeenth floor with an impressive view of downtown Los Angeles. David walked in from one of the bedrooms, his eyes glued to a cell phone in his hand. He nodded to us and said, "What's up, guys? It'll be just a minute before the limo gets here. Chill for a second." He disappeared back into the bedroom. Henry and I stood in silence in the kitchen. In the living room the television was turned on to a football game. A tall, bulky Mexican man with a shaved head and dark, stoic eyes walked into the living room from another area of the apartment, wearing jeans and an oversized T-shirt. He looked at Henry and me, intently observing us as he sat down on David's couch in front of the television and propped his bright white sneakers on a coffee table and grabbed the remote. Before turning his attention to the game, he tilted his head to acknowledge us. I wasn't sure how to respond to this gesture, so I attempted to tilt my head back to him in a similar manner, though I probably just looked like I had a neck cramp.

I texted Lisette. She told me to keep her posted along every step of the trip. "I want to know everything as it's happening," she said. "Text me when you get there, when you're leaving, everything." In my text message, I let her know that I'd made it downtown and that I was waiting with the guys for the limo.

Lisette wrote back.

PERFECT, ANGEL. ENJOY YOUR FIRST RIDE ON A PRIVATE PLANE! TEXT ME WHEN YOU'VE LANDED. LOVE YOU ALWAYS.

David returned from his room and announced that the limo was downstairs. Indicating the man on the couch, David turned to Henry and me and asked, "You guys meet Jose?" Henry and I shook our heads. The man on the couch glanced up at us from the game. David said, "Jose, this is Meili, Henry." Jose gave us a head bob, then went back to watching the television without uttering a word. I'd never heard Lisette or David mention anyone named Jose before. He could have been uninvolved and merely a friend of David's who just happened to be at his apartment this morning, but it seemed unlikely for a total outsider to be present today, given how secretive Lisette was.

Jose stayed on the couch as Ko, David, and Henry rolled the suitcases through the hallway to the elevator. I helped by holding the door open for them as they passed, all of them struggling with the weight of the bags. We took the suitcases downstairs and outside to the back of David's building, next to the valet and the entrance to his parking garage. There was a side street in the back where a stretch limousine waited for us at the curb, the driver standing at attention by the limo door. He immediately offered to help with loading our luggage into the limo. The trunk had limited space, so most of the bags were placed on top of the leather seats inside.

The suitcases were loaded and it was time to head to the private airport in Van Nuys. David stayed at the curb as Ko, Henry, and I climbed into the limousine, cramped inside because the luggage took up most of the available seating. David leaned over the open limo door and said, "Okay, guys, I'm gonna head to LAX soon for my flight. I'll see you later tonight." He closed the door and we were off. I texted Lisette to let her know. THE EAGLE IS IN FLIGHT, I told her. WHAT THE FUCK ARE YOU TALKING ABOUT? she responded. WHAT EAGLE? ARE YOU HIGH? I laughed out loud as I texted her back and looked up to see Ko and Henry staring at me. I stifled my laughter and set my phone aside, trying to maintain some form of professionalism. I looked out the window and watched the scenery pass by us as we drove from downtown L.A. to the Valley.

The Van Nuys Airport was surrounded by a residential neighborhood, separated from the community by a basic metal fence. We pulled up to the airport entrance and stopped at a boxy structure to the side of the entrance gate, just big enough to hold one overweight security guard, a clipboard, and a chair. The guard poked his head out of the structure as we pulled up. Ko opened the door and lifted himself out of the limo. "I'll be right back," he said. "Stay here." Henry and I watched Ko have a short conversation with the guard. The two men walked over to the limo. Ko opened the door so that the guard could see us sitting inside with the luggage. "Hello," the guard said as he acknowledged us. He told us to "go ahead" and "have a nice flight." The limo driver took us directly onto the tarmac, next to where a small plane and its pilot were waiting for us.

I was shocked at how easy it was for us to breeze through security. I could see why Lisette talked about how much she preferred to fly on private jets. I guess that's what forty thousand dollars gets you. It's not quite the same experience with a three-hundred-dollar commercial ticket.

I remembered Lisette's instructions: "Get out of the limo, walk up the stairs and onto the plane. Sit down and don't talk to anyone." The plane wasn't fancy, the way I'd imagined it would be; it basically looked like a miniversion of a regular commercial airplane, with enough seating for maybe six people to travel.

I grabbed a blanket from a seat and got comfortable while Henry and Ko boarded the plane. Henry looked around the cabin like it was all new to him too, but Ko bounced in confidently, grinning. He went to work eating his way through a snack basket before we took off. Once we were in the air, I closed the window to block out the outside light so I could take a nap. I wondered where I would be when we landed. New York? Florida? Perhaps we really were heading to Miami, like Lisette told the bank teller. Henry saw me snuggling beneath the blanket and said, "Good night."

When I awoke, it seemed I'd slept for hours. Most of the lights in the plane had been turned off. Henry and Ko sat ahead of me, quiet and possibly enjoying their own naps. I lifted the shade on my tiny oval window. If we were going east, there would likely be a three-hour difference, so I supposed I shouldn't have been surprised to see that it was almost nightfall.

After another hour or so, the plane began a descent. We landed in the dark on top of black concrete that glimmered with hints of frost and bits of snow on the ground, just outside of the tarmac. David was right, it looked cold out there. I wrapped my scarf around my neck and pulled on my coat.

This private airport was small, like the one in Van Nuys. A few hundred yards from our plane, there was a white building that read LANE AVIATION in huge letters, where a few airport employees directed the plane to stop. The pilot opened the door to the jet, and Ko, Henry, and I stepped outside onto the tarmac. Once we'd stepped down I turned to Ko and asked, "Do you guys need help with the bags?" Ko got close to me and said in a low voice, "No. Go inside. We'll meet you in there." The workers watched me as I hurried toward the Lane Aviation building. My nose and hands were already feeling bitten by the cold. I should have brought gloves.

I walked into a small room with yellowing travel brochures and limited waiting-room-style seating. It was about as fancy as a DMV, not like anywhere a "diva" would be likely to travel to. It reminded me of the office of the deep-sea fishing company that my parents took me to when I was a teenager, when we went fishing with my brother, Nick. I would have rather been deep-sea fishing right now, instead of waiting alone in this room for an unknown amount of time, in an unknown location, for an unknown purpose. I practically had to turn my brain off just to accept the terms of my employment with Lisette. It was mind-numbing to be left so in the dark—at least I'd be getting paid tomorrow. I had mounting bills that were past due, and I needed some room to breathe.

Ko walked into the building with his cell phone in his hand. "We need to rent a car," he said. "A shuttle is going to be here soon."

Henry, Ko, and I were shuttled with the suitcases to a desolate rental car company a few miles away. It was pitch black outside, and absolutely freezing. Many of the cars in the parking lot had snow on them. I rubbed my hands together for warmth while I sat on a folding chair in the back of the rental office, listening while Ko tried to convince Henry to put the rental car under his name because Ko didn't have a credit card. "I only deal in cash, man," he whispered to Henry. Henry was hesitant to let him use his card, so Ko went to me next. I reluctantly handed my debit card over. For some reason my card wasn't accepted when the clerk tried to run it. I cringed. *My account is probably overdrawn again.* "I don't know what could be wrong," I said with a shrug. I was relieved that the car wouldn't be in my name, especially since I probably wouldn't be the one driving it. I didn't even like to let other people drive the car I owned in L.A. because I was the only person on the insurance policy. It was too risky. Looking back, I might have been wise to choose my risks more thoughtfully.

After more than an hour of trying to rent a car and running into confusing delays, David showed up in a cab to meet us. He walked in wearing a bulky winter coat. The tattoos on his neck were visible just above his wool collar. "Yo, you don't have a car yet?" he asked. "Jesus fucking Christ, guys." David shook his head as he went to talk with the clerk. Finally, we left in a rental car that was big enough to accommodate the four of us, as well as the luggage.

We drove on an almost empty freeway, past dense forest, on our way to a hotel. Whatever town we were in was a far cry from Los Angeles. In the front seat, David turned on the radio and talked with Ko about "the drive tomorrow." Henry and I sat quietly in the back. I wanted to ask David where we were. It wasn't like I was brought here in some kind of hostage situation with a bag over my head. I wondered why no one had said anything about it, but I didn't want to be the first one to address the pink elephant in the room. If I'd had Internet access on my archaic cell phone, I would have found out fairly quickly through GPS, but I didn't have such luxuries with my budget at the time.

Despite my curiosity, I decided that it was best to keep my questions to myself. Besides, it was going to be pretty obvious what city I was in when I flew out of the commercial airport the next day.

We pulled into the parking lot of an old chain hotel called the Drury Inn, a tall building that looked almost haunted amid the weather and the night. I helped Ko and Henry wheel the bags into the lobby as David paid for two rooms from a thick envelope of cash he pulled from his coat. I found it physically impossible for me to lift one of the suitcases; it took some doing just to drag it along the carpet into the lobby. Now I understood why everyone had been struggling to move the bags all day.

All the suitcases were moved into the lobby and ready to be taken to David and Ko's room for safekeeping. David passed out access keys.

"We got two rooms. Both have two queen beds, don't worry. Ko, you and me are gonna share a room. Henry and Meili, you guys share one too. Sorry, guys, we got a budget. And I know this ain't the Ritz, but when you start a business, you gotta cut some corners."

All four of us helped take the suitcases upstairs to David and Ko's room. "I'm fucking starving, man," David said when we were done. "You guys hungry?"

As we walked across the street to a Rally's Diner, I got a text from Lisette.

ANGEL, ARE YOU THERE? CALL ME SO I KNOW YOU'RE OKAY.

I called her right away. She answered, "Does this mean you're alive?! Jesus, you had me worried! How is everything going, sweetie?" David and Ko heard me on the phone and turned around. It's Lisette, I mouthed silently to them. David smiled a bit. So did Henry. "How are the boys getting along?" Lisette asked me coyly. She was referring to her boys, of course.

"Oh, you know, it's . . . good," I said, aware that everyone could hear me.

"Let me talk to Henry," she said.

I handed Henry the phone. "Lisette wants to talk to you." David, a few yards ahead of us, overheard me and glanced over his shoulder to see Henry talking on my phone and grinning. Henry passed my phone back to me. David glanced back again, confirming that she had never asked to talk to him. I tried not to bring any attention to the tense moment. The last thing I wanted was for Lisette's love triangle to be discovered during a work trip, with me there to answer for it.

The inside of the diner looked like a set from *Happy Days*. We settled into a booth and ordered greasy food from sticky menus. David's phone rang, and he looked smug when he saw that Lisette was calling. "I'll be right back," he said.

I was uncomfortable spending time around David and Henry, especially both of them at once. I tried to keep a distance from Lisette's "boy toys." I'd never seen her with a man whose heart she didn't end up shattering, and I didn't like the idea of being in the splash zone of her emotional carnage.

By the time Henry and I got inside our room back at the dreary inn, we were both exhausted after a long day. I used my toothbrush from the plastic baggie in my purse, then crawled into bed with my clothes on. David was going to call us a taxi at sunrise, so there wasn't long to rest before we traveled again.

IN NO TIME, WE WOKE up to a prearranged and savagely early wake-up call from the front desk and met David downstairs.

"The cab is gonna be here any minute," David said as Henry and I stood with him inside the hotel lobby. Ko walked inside from the parking lot to join us.

"Shit, it's cold out there," Ko said. "David, I got all the bags back in the car, so we're good to go."

"Cool. Let's take off after we get them in a cab," David said. "It's gonna be a long fuckin' drive, man. And in the snow."

"You guys are driving a lot today?" I asked, curious.

David and Ko looked at each other. "Yeah," David said. "About ten hours."

Henry's eyes widened. "Wow," he said. "Well, have a safe drive."

"Thanks, man." David pulled out two white envelopes. "Before I forget, this is for you." He handed me an envelope. "And this is for you." He handed the other to Henry. Then he reached back into his coat to grab the thicker envelope I'd seen him with yesterday. He counted out a stack of hundred-dollar bills and handed them to me. "This should cover the cab to the airport and two tickets back to L.A. If there's change, keep it for food or something. Thanks, guys."

As the taxi carried us into the airport, I finally saw a sign: PORT COLUMBUS INTERNATIONAL AIRPORT. *Ohio?* I'd never heard of a booming casino industry in Ohio. Then again, I'd never been to Ohio, and I had no idea what industries were booming here. From the short exposure I'd had though, between last night and this morning, it looked like this place wasn't brimming with things to do. Gambling would be an understandable pastime. David had probably connected Lisette to people here, and she was bringing her expertise on to expand someone's business. It made sense. That would explain what was likely money or equipment in the suitcases.

It all still seemed dodgy, though; I had a feeling that whatever we were doing must be on the edge of legality, maybe some specific form of gambling. If it was in fact illegal, it was probably something that was commonly done in the "big business" world that generally flew under the radar. I couldn't imagine Lisette doing something far outside what her family would support.

My mind stopped wandering through possibilities as Henry and I walked into the airport. It was time to focus on getting home, which we were both eager to do. I bought us two tickets on the first available flight back to Los Angeles. In the two hours before our flight, we walked around the airport gift shops, talking about everything except work. We laughed easily together. This was probably more conversation than Lisette would have liked us to be having, but what do you expect when two people are forced to spend so much time with each other? I enjoyed Henry's company. We'd graduated from high school the same year, 2004, so we would have been in the same class. I thought that we would have been friends if we'd been in school together. I hoped that Lisette would be kind to this one. And, for Henry's sake, I hoped that David never found out that they were sharing Lisette. As Lisette had said, "He would kill him if he found out." I didn't take David for a killer, but love and lust can make people do crazy things.

IN L.A., HENRY AND I shared a taxi back to David's apartment to collect our cars. "See you soon," Henry said when the cab left us in front of the building. "I think we're leaving again next week. Lisette said something about that."

"Oh." I nodded. This was new information to me, but I didn't let on. "Yeah, see you then."

When I got home around midnight, Lisette texted me.

ANGEL I AM SO PROUD OF YOU! DAVID SAID THAT EVERYTHING WENT SMOOTHLY. I NEED TO HEAR DETAILS FROM YOU. DRINKS TOMORROW? I MISS YOU. XOXO

"It was pretty uneventful," I told Lisette the next day at her condo. "We just kinda went there and came back."

"Excellent, sweetheart," she said. "That's all you need to do. Best job ever, right? You're going to fly out again in about a week. Same routine. I'll give you cash when I need you to do the wire transfer."

A FEW DAYS AFTER MY first trip to Ohio, I caught up on all my bills and went shopping for groceries. I couldn't remember the last time my refrigerator had been full. I got my car washed. I bought wine for Brie and me, and some tea candles for our apartment. I put fresh flowers out on our dining room table, in a vase that hadn't been used in months. Things were turning around, I could feel it. My parents were happy and relieved that I'd found work; my struggle to support myself had been a constant source of concern for them since I'd moved to L.A. It felt fantastic to finally be able to tell them that "I'm fine" financially and mean it.

My mom had met Lisette in Los Angeles a few times, during semi-annual visits. Lisette always insisted on making time to see her, which meant a lot to me. I loved Lisette like a sister, and I wanted my parents to view her as an honorary daughter, to recognize her as an important part of my life, and hopefully grow to love her. My mom was friendly with Lisette the few times they'd met, but she was nice to everyone. My dad never met Lisette, but he was a good listener with an open heart. "It sounds like you girls are having fun, and I'm real glad you met someone you enjoy so much," he said. My parents always just wanted me to be happy. They never understood why I'd want to live in Los Angeles when I could live in their beautiful Northwest, but they still supported my decision to do so. If they'd had any serious doubts about my friendship with Lisette, they would have had a hard time voicing them. The few times that they raised questions like "Wait, what exactly does she do for a living?" that were tinged with skepticism, I blew up in Lisette's defense. "You have no idea what her life has been like," I'd say. "No one understands her because no one can relate to her. Everyone is always judging her." My parents knew that she was a hot button for me, and that anyone who criticized her in my presence would wish that they hadn't.

Lisette asked me not to tell anyone, including my family, even the most menial details of my work for her. "It's no one's business," she said. "You know how private I am." She was furious when I told her that I'd asked Brie what she thought about the money transfer. "Why the hell would you even tell her that?" Lisette asked, heated. "Do you think Brie is some kind of expert on banking?" I should have known better. I just wanted some outside advice. Lisette pointed out that I tended to overshare, so we agreed that it would be easiest for me to keep things to myself if I told everyone in my life that I'd signed a confidentiality agreement. Figuratively speaking, there was some truth in it.

ON THE MORNING OF OUR second trip, we met at David's apartment. Frankie would be joining us this time. Ko greeted me at the door looking exhausted and sweaty, just as he had on the morning of our previous trip. The kitchen was once again filled with suitcases. The Mexican man named Jose, whom I'd met here last time, drifted in and out of the room with a casual swagger. When he saw me, he gave a silent greeting with a slight lift of his chin before sitting down to watch a game on David's couch. *Just another day at the office. And these are my coworkers. This is completely normal.* As I waited by the door for Henry and Frankie to arrive, I watched Ko as he struggled with a suitcase. He was trying to zip it shut, but from his efforts it seemed as though his goal was nearly impossible. Beads of sweat were visibly dripping down his forehead, so much that he wiped them away before they could obstruct his vision. He stopped, breathed out like he'd just finished a marathon, then bent forward to rest with his hands on his knees. He paused there a moment, then decided on a new approach. He moved the suitcase against a wall and used his foot to hold it in place as he tried again to zip it. I was only a few feet away from him, and I had a clear view of what he was doing. The bag was so overstuffed that where the zipper was undone, I could see six inches inside of the suitcase. I wanted to look away, but I couldn't.

All I saw inside was cash; dollars that had been stacked and rubber-banded the way that Lisette's forty thousand dollars was when she took me with her to the bank. Forty thousand dollars fit into Lisette's purse.

From where I was standing, it looked like cash was the *only* thing filling the suitcase. When I went backpacking through Europe after high school, my backpack weighed thirty pounds. As a fit eighteen-year-old, it was heavy to me, but I was still able to carry it for five weeks. Now Ko, a grown man, could barely lift this suitcase. I couldn't imagine how much it must weigh. Sixty, maybe a hundred pounds? Maybe more? And it was all money. *I was right. I knew it was money.* There was an audible strain on the zipper as Ko was finally able to yank it up all the way. "Hooo!" He let out a sigh of relief. I immediately turned my back to him, hoping that he hadn't seen me staring.

A limo driver took Ko, Henry, Frankie, and me to Van Nuys Airport. With the help of a pilot, the men loaded the half-dozen or so suitcases out of the limo and into the luggage compartment of a chartered G3 jet that was waiting for us. We arrived in Ohio in the evening and checked into another dreary hotel. David met us there. After he checked us into rooms, David paid me with an envelope containing two thousand dollars cash. He gave me a second, smaller stack of money for one plane ticket back to Los Angeles. "Keep the change for food or whatever," he said. "We need Henry and Frankie for the drive this time. There should be enough money in there for a cab to the airport tomorrow and one back to your car once you're in L.A." In the morning, I flew home to Los Angeles by myself.

"DID YOU OFFER TO HELP with the suitcases?" Lisette stared at me from behind her Bloody Mary as we sat at a booth in the lounge of a Beverly Hills hotel, waiting for the team to assemble for a meeting.

"Um, I think I offered to help them when we landed," I said. "I didn't want to just stand around while they worked."

"Jesus, Meili." Lisette shook her head. "That's what I heard. I heard that you were 'very sweet.'" She used a mocking voice and gestured quotations with her fingers. "How do you think that made us look?"

I was stunned. "I don't—I don't know."

"Babe"—Lisette sighed—"I love you because you *are* so sweet. You're nice. And that's great to be a nice friend. But when you're my *employee* who I've asked to act *like a diva*, that's not going to help me."

"Sorry," I said.

She went on. "Anyone who would travel with seven suitcases, *with a fucking bodyguard*, would never offer to help with the bags. Do you follow me?"

"Lisette, I didn't know. You never said—"

"This should have gone without saying," she said. "It's common sense. I thought this would be so easy for you. I mean, you're an actress for fuck's sake. All you had to do was say nothing! I can't afford mistakes like this."

"I won't offer again," I said.

"It won't matter now," Lisette said. "Now I have to clear my schedule and go with you because no one believes you as a diva."

"You mean you're coming from now on?" I asked her.

Lisette cracked into a smile. "Well, yeah, I have to, since your dumb ass couldn't keep a lid on it. Jesus"—she laughed—"you'd think that you'd know how to act like a diva after four years with me."

I couldn't stop myself from smirking a little. "Okay, I'm sorry that I messed up, but I'm really excited that you're finally coming with us."

"I'm excited too, sweetheart," she said. "We'll have fun."

Her smile faded as she took a sip from her cocktail. "Angel, I need to talk with you about your pay. Now, I don't know how this happened, but someone found out how much you've been getting paid. I won't say who, but they're pretty upset. They said that it's not fair for you to get two thousand dollars when you don't really *do* anything for it. David knows not to tell the guys, so I don't know who the leak was."

"I never told anyone," I assured her.

"I believe you," she said. "But this puts me in a tough position because I can't play favorites just because you're my best friend. I can't show that weakness. I'm sorry, but I have to lower your pay to fifteen hundred dollars a trip."

"Okay. I respect your decision," I told her.

I felt relieved. For a moment I'd thought it was going to be much worse than that. Fifteen hundred dollars was still a lot of money to me, and Lisette said that we would be making trips every week or so once things got organized, so that could add up to quite a bit.

"I knew you would," she said. "This doesn't have to be permanent. We'll see how things go moving forward, and hopefully we can get you back up to two thousand."

"Thanks."

"Of course," Lisette said. "You know I always look out for my girl."

Frankie, Ko, David, and Henry joined us in the lounge. Lisette announced that she was going to be coming to Ohio with us from now on. She lifted her glass and said, "And we won't be flying in those goddamn cargo planes you've been using. You're going to see what it looks like to travel in style, with a *real* diva."

PART TWO
A BAD HIGH

7

MY DOUGH, MY SHOW

ANGEL, GO DOWNTOWN TO SEE DAVID. HE'LL GIVE YOU
CASH FOR THE WIRE TRANSFER TODAY. COME SEE ME WHEN
YOU'RE DONE.

After reading Lisette's text, I drove downtown to David's apartment building. I pulled my car up to the curb in front of the valet station, where the limos usually picked us up before we flew out. I put my car in park and craned my neck to look around for David, but I didn't see him. A valet dressed in a vest and tie approached me. From behind my closed window, I waved him off and tried to gesticulate that I was waiting for someone. *Come on, David, where are you?* After a minute, my phone buzzed with a text message. It was from David.

NOT THERE. GO AROUND THE BLOCK AGAIN AND STOP JUST
BEFORE THE VALET AREA.

I pulled out from the curb and went around the block. Great, now this is going to look like a drug deal. Every day on this job feels shadier and shadier. Perhaps David had held on to some of his old habits from his days as a cocaine dealer, and doing business out of sight was one of them; but it was bizarre and made me uncomfortable. When I'd agreed to work for Lisette, I envisioned tagging along with her to board meetings and picking up dry cleaning—not hiding from the valet while I waited for her business partner.

I stopped my car along the side of the building, just short of where it would be visible to the valet staff. *This is ridiculous.* I was startled when my passenger door was suddenly opened. "Yo," David said as he climbed into my car. He handed me a shoe box with some weight in it. *Oh God. Please tell me that isn't the money.* "There you go," he said. "Later." He got out of my car. Once he'd disappeared, I slowly lifted the lid of the cardboard box. Money. *Shit.* Tens of thousands of dollars, stacked and rubber-banded. *Shady, shady.* It wasn't all neat, crisp hundreds like what Lisette had given me for the past two trips. The denominations of bills appeared to have quite a range this time. I saw some twenty-dollar bills, some fifties, and even a few tens in there.

How the hell am I going to keep a straight face walking into a bank with a shoe box full of money? I'll look like I'm there to exchange a pair of basketball sneakers, not charter an airplane.

I parked at the bank in Beverly Hills. I turned my car off and looked at the shoe box in my passenger seat. *I can't do this.* I grabbed my purse and rummaged through it. It was decently sized. *This could work, as long as I don't try to zip it shut.* To make room for the money, I took out some hand sanitizer, a pack of gum, and some lotion from my purse and set them aside. I stole a quick look around the parking lot to make sure that no one was watching me, then I grabbed the money from the shoe box in handfuls and stuffed my Chanel purse like a Thanksgiving turkey. It was absurdly full by the time I'd shoved the last stack of dollars inside. *Oh well. It's better than a shoe box!*

Standing in line inside the bank, I was relieved to see that the teller whom Lisette had introduced me to was working today. Maybe he worked here full-time. He'd been here when she'd sent me by myself for our previous trip.

"Hi!" I said as I stepped up to his window, setting my purse on the counter.

"How are you?" he greeted me.

"Oh, good," I said. "We're just . . . Lisette and I are going to Miami again." *No, we're not. That's a lie.*

"Again?" he asked me. *Nope! I've never been to Miami.*

"Yeah!" I said. "We just, we love it there. Great, beautiful place."

The teller nodded as he filled out the form for the wire transfer to JetSetter Charter. "Yeah," he said, "she said she has a brother who lives there?" *I doubt that.*

"Uh, yeah, her brother, yes," I said. "He lives there." *I hate this. Get me out of here.*

I felt guilty when I left the bank, after looking the teller in the eye and lying to him. He'd believed everything I was saying, and he was so nice to me. All the while, I was betraying his trust and breaking a code of human decency.

I didn't understand why we needed to lie about everything. Lisette thought that it was a fun charade, but when I lied, it made me feel sick to my stomach. I didn't know how she could do it without feeling anything, to lie and actually enjoy it. And I still didn't understand why the money had to go through my account. Why couldn't it go through her account?

I met Lisette at her condo nearby on Wilshire Corridor. She greeted me at the door wearing her signature lounge attire—a lavender velour tank top and matching drawstring pants. As always, her makeup was a thick application of purple and lavender eye shadow with long, fake eyelashes.

"I just came home from a god-awful meeting," she said. "I swear these people are trying to kill me. Did everything go okay at the bank? Was our favorite guy there?"

"Yeah," I said.

She smiled. "Excellent. He is such a sweetheart." She looked off for a moment in thought. "I should drop him a little something extra for helping us."

"Lisette?" I asked.

"Yes, sweetie?"

"Um." I breathed out. I was already nervous, remembering her reaction to this question last time, but I needed to ask again. "Are you sure that it's okay for me to be wiring the money? I just wonder about taxes and whatnot. I wonder if the IRS would think that the money is mine or that it's income, you know?"

Lisette pursed her lips and said, "I thought I already explained this to you." She was pissed. "Were you just not listening? You know I don't like repeating myself. I'm exhausted enough as it is. It has to go through your account *for* taxes. We're going to get you on the Samsung payroll at the end of the year, so you'll be square on taxes. Stop freaking out about it. We need a paper trail to prove that you work for me; otherwise, you don't exist on paper!"

"What?" I asked. "Babe, that doesn't really make any sense."

"You are not going to have to pay taxes on it!" Lisette rarely raised her voice like this. I braced myself. "It's not even your fucking money!" she yelled. "Why the hell would you have to pay taxes on money that's not yours? Any idiot could see that."

"Sorry," I said. "But I just still don't understand. I don't know how these things work."

"Well, I do know how these things work, and that's why I'm telling you. You should try listening to me," she said. "Honestly, babe, I could throw a stick down Sunset Boulevard and hit some other dumb broad who would do this for half the money. David already said that he has friends who would do it for five hundred dollars. You're making three times that much. I stuck my neck out for you when I hired you. If you can't grow up and handle the responsibility of being a professional, feel free to walk out the door."

I sat in silence for a minute. I didn't want to look at Lisette because I knew how angry she was. This was why people say you should never do business with your friends. I knew she had a temper when I'd agreed to work for her—I was just not used to having it directed at me. I usually tried to avoid upsetting her at all costs because I knew how vicious she could be, and she always knew what to say to get to someone. She'd given me the job because she was my friend and wanted to help me. I had to remember to be grateful for that, even when she acted like this. At least I knew that she was ultimately trying to help me, for the benefit of both of us. She wanted me to learn to be better.

"You're not going to regret hiring me," I told her. "I really am trying to do a good job."

"Well," she said, "then stop asking stupid questions. I don't have time to hold your hand every time I ask you to do something. Okay?"

"Okay," I said.

AS IN THE FIRST TWO trips, we assembled at David's penthouse in the morning before our flight. Lisette would drive separately and meet us at the airport. The men took the suitcases downstairs and loaded them into a limo and a black Escalade along the curb—more suitcases this time, maybe ten. Lisette said that we would be staying a few days, so I could bring one personal bag. On the ride to the airport I was anxious to see her and finally travel with her. I had been sad to not be able to see her often due to her busy work schedule, but now that I was her employee and would be traveling with her, our problems would be solved. We would be with each other constantly, as we'd always wished that we could; I'd be able to pay my bills and work with my best friend. I was going to show her that she hadn't made a mistake in hiring me. No more questions. She knew what she was doing when it came to business, and it had probably been insulting when I'd questioned her.

When we pulled up to the airport entrance, I saw Lisette's new pearl-white Bentley passing through security ahead of us. Perfect timing. She had given her new ride the pet name of Diablo, after lyrics in a Notorious B.I.G. song.

Lisette cruised onto the tarmac and parked Diablo a few yards away from the chartered jet that awaited her. She stepped out of the car "dressed like a diva." She wore a fur-trimmed winter coat, a vanity drawer's worth of diamonds, tight designer jeans, and leather boots with stilettos long and sharp enough to rip a man's throat out. She collected one small item of Louis Vuitton luggage from her trunk before passing her keys to a skycap. "Hi, sweetie. Take good care of her for me, okay?" The skycap smiled as he accepted a tip.

Her British accent was in full force this morning. She'd told me that her mother was in town this week, which would explain it. Lisette said that her half-Korean and half-Italian mother spent a great deal of time growing up in Britain, and she spoke with a heavy British accent.

Lisette learned to speak with an English accent from her. Whenever she spent time with her mother, it became more pronounced.

I stepped out of the limo and joined Lisette. "Hi!" I rushed up to greet her. "Hi, sweetheart," she said under her breath. She gave a small smile that told me that she was excited too but wanted to maintain a professional demeanor until we got on the plane. She handed me her purse. "Babe, can you put this up on a seat for me?" she asked. "Go ahead inside. I'll be up shortly." Another skycap took her Louis Vuitton into the cabin of the plane.

As I walked toward the jet, I could hear Lisette instructing the men exactly how and where to load the bags into the luggage compartment in the back of the aircraft. She was in her element. The moment she'd arrived this morning, everyone knew that she was in charge. She didn't need Diablo for that, though I was sure it didn't exactly hurt.

Lisette commanded the attention of anyone whose path she crossed. It was far more than just her smoky bedroom eyes and designer attire; at first glance, everything about her suggested that she was the walking epitome of a snobby, entitled bitch, but when she opened her mouth, people were stunned because she wasn't what they expected. Her appearance got people's attention, but she fascinated people because of her contradictions. No one would look at her and expect that she was whip smart and spoke five different languages, was extremely witty, and could hold her own at any board meeting in the world. When she spoke, everyone listened to her. She carried herself with such certainty and imperial confidence that people were afraid to question her, even grown men.

Just before I entered the cabin, I looked back and saw that Lisette was chatting with the chief pilot and the copilot, already charming them with her knowledge about the inner workings of this specific kind of Gulfstream jet. After knowing her as long as I had, she still never failed to impress me with her depth of knowledge of things I knew nothing about. I felt proud of her. She had always complained about being forced to work for her family, and now she was finally running her own business. For the first time in quite a while, she seemed happy.

I was the first passenger to board the plane. As I climbed the steps, I felt like the first kid to see the tree on Christmas morning. I smiled as I carefully placed Lisette's purse down on a cushiony seat near the front of the cabin. Now *this* looked like a private plane, with lacquered wood grain and buttery leather covering the interior. At least ten people could comfortably travel in this jet. There were rows of oversized, overstuffed chairs that reclined, in addition to leather benches filled with decorative throw pillows and folded blankets. There were snack baskets, as in the other planes, but these were larger, with more variety. In the middle of the aisle a bottle of champagne on ice waited for us with a greeting card, courtesy of JetSetter Charter and signed by someone named Carol. I'd heard Lisette talk about Carol as being her contact point at the jet company. A catering spread was ready at the back of the cabin in a small yet elegantly lit kitchen area. There was fresh coffee and orange juice, as well as a refrigerator stocked with sodas and booze. I noticed a bottle of Bombay Sapphire in the kitchen, Lisette's favorite. There were two large plastic catering trays. One was filled with fruit and berries, and the other was stacked with panini sandwiches.

Once the suitcases were loaded, the rest of Team LL boarded the plane and settled into seats. Lisette took the champagne and walked it back to the kitchen. She put it on ice in the sink. "That was so sweet of Carol," she said. "We'll pop it after we're in the air." Lisette and I sat close to each other in a row near the front of the plane that was separated by the aisle, each with two seats to ourselves. She instructed us to wait to help ourselves to the catering until we were stable. "Jesus," she said, laughing. "I think you guys can wait five minutes. Meili, sweetie, can you serve it to everyone in a little while?"

"Of course," I said, grinning. I couldn't help it. This was fun.

As we sat waiting for takeoff, Lisette leaned over the aisle that separated us and whispered to me. "So, Angel, what do you think?"

I leaned in to her and said, "Um. Yes. I think this will have to do . . . *Holy shit.*" We both laughed. "Do you want to say hi to the pilots?" she asked.

"Yeah, sure," I said.

Lisette walked me up to the front and knocked on the folding door that separated the cockpit from the main cabin. A pilot opened it with a friendly smile. "Well, hello!" he said.

"Hi," Lisette said. "This is my assistant, Meili. Would you mind if she sits in the jump seat for takeoff? This is her first time in a G5." I looked at her, surprised.

"Sure," the pilot said.

"Go ahead, sweetie," Lisette said. She seemed genuinely delighted to see me so excited. A few feet behind the pilots, she pulled down a small seat from the wall. "Sit down."

I sat down against the wall and she helped buckle me in. She looked at me with an almost motherly affection and said, "Have fun." I was touched by her kindness as she returned to her seat in the main cabin.

"All right!" the chief pilot said. "You ready?" He looked back and smiled at me from behind athletic sunglasses. I had butterflies in my stomach as the jet moved down the runway, gaining speed, preparing to fly. I was so close to the front of the plane that it felt like I was helping them fly it, though in reality I was hanging from the wall like a useless sack of potatoes. The wheels lifted off the concrete, and I had an instant euphoric rush of adrenaline. As I stared out at the vast sky ahead of me I felt alive, like I was lucky to be experiencing this. All the confusion since I'd started working for Lisette suddenly faded away and everything seemed worth it. She was right; in ways this was a dream job. I'd just been too hung up on the details to see it before now. Once we were stable in the air, I sensed that it was time to thank the pilots and rejoin the team in the cabin.

"Well?" Lisette said as I closed the cockpit door behind me.

"That was amazing," I said. "Thank you so much for doing that."

She smirked. "I thought you'd like that. It would have been wasted on me since I've done it so many times."

As promised, Lisette popped open the bottle of champagne and handed out crystal flutes to the team, with the exception of Frankie. "No drinking on the job," she told him. "You know my parents would murder you if they knew my bodyguard was drinking when he's supposed to be protecting me."

Frankie nodded and said, "Yeah, I know." We raised a toast to "having the best boss in the world," then broke into the catering. I passed out plates and utensils and then came around with the catering trays.

After a little while, I came back around to offer seconds to everyone. "Want some more?" I asked Lisette.

She handed me her plate and waved away the offer. "I'm good, sweetie," she said. "I eat to live, I don't live to eat."

We touched down at Lane Aviation in Columbus. As we taxied in, we could clearly see a mammoth-sized stretch SUV limousine waiting for us. It was the kind of obnoxious, neon-lit limousine that was rarely seen outside of the Vegas strip or en route to a school dance. Lisette pulled her coat on and looked out the window of the plane. "Oh God," she said. "Tell me that's not our limo." I stifled laughter because I knew that the thought of being seen in this car was nothing short of horrifying to her. "How the hell was I supposed to know they'd send a goddamn tour bus to get us?" she barked. We both laughed a little, despite ourselves. If we had to ride in it, at least we'd be doing it together.

The giant limo pulled into the parking lot of the Hilton in Columbus. *Yes. Finally, a hotel that doesn't look dreary or haunted.* I pulled my decrepit, off-brand suitcase toward me, eager to get out and explore the amenities.

Lisette opened the door nearest to her and stepped out. I followed her out the limo door, struggling in an effort to yank my suitcase out. "No, no," she said. "Sweetie. We aren't staying here. David and Ko are. Come with me. Henry, wait here until we text you to bring the bags in," she said.

I frowned and hustled to follow her as she turned away from me to go into the hotel. "How come they get to stay here?" I asked. We stepped in line for the reception desk.

Lisette turned to me. "I don't know why David feels he needs to stay at the goddamn Hilton when we're working," she said. "We're staying a few blocks away. Don't worry."

Lisette reserved a room. "Text Henry the room number and tell him to bring the luggage up with Frankie" she said. We took the elevator to the third floor and waited for them. After they finished bringing all the suitcases up, we abandoned the room. On the way out, Lisette left the room key at the front desk in an envelope for David to pick up when he arrived.

A few blocks away, we settled into rooms at a modest hotel. It was no Hilton, but it was no Drury Inn, either. It seemed odd to arrive in a chartered private plane and stay at two-star hotels. It wasn't Lisette's style. In L.A., I'd never known Lisette to stay at anything short of a luxury hotel. Her budget for the trips must have been tapped out by the jets. If she was interested in avoiding questions about suitcases full of money, flying private was definitely the way to go.

Our hotel appeared to be in a prime location, right in the middle of a town center of sorts. Lisette had reserved two rooms: one for Frankie and Henry to share, and one for Lisette and me to share. From the window in our room I could see half a dozen restaurants and a Trader Joe's.

Lisette took the team to dinner at P.F. Chang's. Henry and Frankie, in typical form, refrained from alcohol, while Lisette and I, also in typical form, ordered cocktails. We drank Chinese 88 gin martinis served in sugar-rimmed glasses and topped with sparkling wine. "I was thinking we could all go see a movie tomorrow, if there's time," Lisette said.

"That would be fun," Henry said.

"Yeah, man, I'd be in for that," Frankie added. It occurred to me that I wasn't certain how long we would be staying in Columbus.

"How many nights are we going to be here?" I asked Lisette.

"Three nights, probably," she said. "We have to wait for a few things to go through here before we can go home. Which reminds me, Meili; call Ko and see where the hell he and David are. It's unacceptable that I haven't gotten an update from them yet. David was scheduled to arrive an hour ago."

I got Ko on the phone. David was with him. "Yeah, sorry. We were going to call you soon," Ko said.

"Tell him to put David on the phone," Lisette said, looking serious and holding her hand out to take my cell phone. She excused herself and walked outside the restaurant to speak to David privately. When she returned a few minutes later, she looked irritated. "Let's get back to the rooms," she said. "Frankie, I need you to drive me to a meeting early tomorrow morning. Meili and Henry get to sleep in."

When I woke up in the morning, I had a new text from Lisette.

I'M GOING TO BE COMING BACK LATER THAN EXPECTED TODAY ANGEL. TAKE A ROOM KEY WITH YOU IF YOU WANT TO WALK AROUND OUTSIDE AND GET SOMETHING TO EAT. I'LL SEE YOU TONIGHT. LOVE YOU XOXO.

I guessed that meant no movie.

I grabbed a key and wandered aimlessly around the shopping center for a bit, then stopped by Trader Joe's to buy some food. I came back to the hotel and watched TV while I waited to hear from Lisette. I never saw Henry, but I assumed that he was doing something similar.

Lisette came back to the hotel room in the evening looking tired. She sent me downstairs with cash to buy "whatever snack food they have" at the front desk for dinner. "Text the boys to say we're not going anywhere tonight," she said as she changed into pink velour pajamas. We stayed in our room eating instant macaroni and cheese and watching a marathon of the true crime TV show *Snapped*.

THE NEXT MORNING LISETTE WOKE me up. I moaned and turned over. I saw her standing over me, fully dressed. "We need to go to the bank," she said. "Come on, I've been up for hours and already finished a meeting. When we're done at the bank, you can come back and sleep the rest of the day. I'm going to have Frankie drop you off afterwards anyway because I'll need him to drive me. This is the only thing you'll have to do while you're here."

I hurried to get dressed. "It doesn't need to be fancy," Lisette said. I slid on jeans and grabbed my scarf on my way out the door. Frankie was waiting for us in the parking lot next to a rented Escalade. He wore a long black wool coat. I could see his breath blowing a cloud of heat into the air when he said, "All right, let's do this," before climbing into the driver's seat. It was surprisingly bright outside, given how cold it was. There were few clouds in the sky today, and the sun was melting some of the frost on the ground. Today Columbus had a charm that reminded me of Washington.

The drive was quick, as the bank was only a few blocks away. "Frankie, wait in the car," Lisette said after we'd parked.

"Is it cool if I go through a drive-through while you guys are in there?" Frankie asked. "I need some food."

"Oh God," Lisette said. "Okay, go. Stuff your face if you must. As long as you're back by the time we're done." As we crossed the parking lot to the bank, Lisette instructed me to let her do the talking.

The bank building was relatively new, or at least remodeled, and the crowd inside appeared to be made up of predominantly middle-class customers. A well-dressed banker greeted us as we came in. "Welcome, ladies. What can we do for you today?"

Lisette smiled at him and said, "Hi, yes, I need to do a wire transfer." He pointed us in the direction of a stout middle-aged man sitting at a desk in the corner. The man behind the desk stood to give us a jolly greeting as we approached him.

"Hello!" he said. "How can I help you today?"

"We need to wire some money," Lisette said. She looked down at his desk to see a nameplate that read BARRY. "Barry, is it?" she asked.

"Sure is," he said, sitting back down behind his desk. "Have a seat, ladies."

"I'm Lisette and this is my assistant, Meili," Lisette told him. In a short span of minutes, Lisette explained to Barry that she was in town to visit some close friends who had recently moved out here. She told him that she was a pop singer with a successful career in Asia, and that she was considering buying a house in the area for vacation. "It really is a beautiful part of the country," she said. "I hope to spend more time here." Once Lisette had developed something of a rapport with Barry, she told him that she needed to wire a sizable amount of cash to the jet company that she was chartering planes from for her travels. Barry's eyes widened when she told him how much cash she wanted to wire.

"Well, now," he said, "aha, boy that's, uh, that's quite a bit of cash there." Lisette took out stacks of dollars from her purse and set them on his desk. After staring for a beat, Barry scooped the stacks of cash up in an awkward handful and stood up. "I'm just going to run this through a counting machine in the back real quick here. We'd be here all day if I started countin' it on my desk." He chuckled to himself as he waddled away with the money. After it had been counted, Barry wired more than thirty thousand dollars through my checking account to Jet-Setter Charter.

When the transfer was complete, Barry stood to shake our hands. Lisette gave him a charming smile and said, "Barry, do you work here full-time?"

"Yes, ma'am, I do," he said.

"That's perfect," she said. "We'll make sure to ask for you next time." Lisette accepted Barry's business card before leaving the bank.

ON THE THIRD DAY OF the trip I woke up to find that I was again alone in the hotel room. I spent a few hours watching more episodes of *Snapped*. It was one of the few shows that Lisette and I watched together. I'm sure neither of us could have fathomed that one day we'd be the subjects of multiple true crime series like this.

I began to feel cooped up and walked around outside for some fresh air. I took the opportunity to call my dad. I would usually have talked with him every day, but I felt a little weird doing it when I was in Ohio. When Lisette was around, she didn't like me to be on my phone. I couldn't tell my parents where I was, and I was used to telling them everything. They'd been respectful of the fact that Lisette didn't want me to share information about her business with other people—just one more thing that they didn't understand about "people in L.A."

In the evening, the door to the hotel room swung open. Lisette walked in with Frankie and Henry close behind her. "We got the paper-work settled," she said, dropping her purse on a queen bed like a comedian dropping a microphone onstage after a crowd-winning set. "That's great!" I said, pretending to understand what that meant.

I didn't know it at the time, but "paperwork" referred to money, and it had likely been "settled" in exchange for what was in our suitcases.

"Ko and David are going to drop it off with the bags in the morning before the limo comes to get us," Lisette said. "And it won't be a goddamn bus this time. I ripped the owner of the limousine company a new asshole for sending a parade float to welcome us at the airport. He's got a real sick fucking sense of humor. It's my dough, my show, and I'm not going to pay someone to make me look like an idiot."

LISETTE PAID ME FIFTEEN HUNDRED dollars at the end of our trip. "We'll be leaving again soon, Angel. Be ready," she told me. She said that she wanted us to fly out about three times a month soon, so I knew that I would be making a lot more money. I decided to treat myself to some shopping and a new haircut for the first time in over a year. I had a new job, so it seemed fitting to revamp my appearance. Why the hell not? I could afford it, and I was ready to embrace more positive change. I felt different. Since catching up on my bills and starting work again, I'd gained confidence, no longer feeling like a dumpy nobody begging people to buy spa packages or begging a casting director to hire me. I didn't need approval anymore. Not from those people anyway. Now, Lisette's approval was all that mattered.

I got my hair cut and dyed a deep mahogany brown. My bangs were trimmed and formed just above my eyebrows. "This will make the green in your eyes pop," the stylist said. I went shopping for clothes and bought new boots and a black leather jacket.

When I came back to the apartment, Brie was home. I did a little fashion show for her to show off my new stuff. "Wow, Miles," she said, looking me up and down with her expert eye for fashion. "You look amazing. I barely recognized you when I walked in. You look like a badass."

The next day I went to the Grove, an upscale outdoor shopping center in L.A. I wore my new leather jacket, high boots, and skin-tight shiny black American Apparel leggings, which made me feel like Sandy in *Grease* after the Pink Ladies transformed her for the school carnival.

When I passed by the movie theater at the Grove, I remembered that I'd forgotten to get my parking validated. I decided to try to run in and out quickly to get the ticket stamped. As I was weaving through the lines of people, I unintentionally slammed right through the middle of a young couple, separating them. They both stepped back, startled by my charge. I stopped and turned around to apologize for bumping into them. Before I could start, I heard my name spoken in a familiar French accent.

"Meili?" I looked up and found myself staring into handsome brown eyes that I recognized immediately—they belonged to a Frenchman who'd taken me on two dates two years ago, and who then unceremoniously dumped me for a ballet dancer with a great ass. Before I allowed myself to get too lost in his brown eyes, I remembered that he was with a date, and that I'd just literally run between them and punted her out of the way. *Perfect.* "Meili," he said, "wow, hello." *Oh no. No, no!* It must have looked like I'd done this on purpose.

"Uh," I said, "hi!" I turned to acknowledge his date. "Hi! Sorry, that was an accident. I didn't, I mean, ha! Whoops!" His date looked horrified. And he looked . . . at me. He was staring at me and laughing along at my stupid jokes that didn't make sense. He couldn't keep his eyes off me. And his date was jealous! *Ha! I win!*

"You look great," he said. "Wow. I almost didn't think it was you."

"Well, nice seeing you," I said, and then I turned on the heel of my sexy new boots and walked away. Something told me that was a first date, and that it would probably be a last date now, too.

He'd never looked at me like that when we were dating. I had secrets now and apparently it was attractive. The night air felt exhilarating as it breezed through my open jacket. As I walked through the outdoor mall, something dawned on me. Not only were people looking at me differently, I realized that I was looking at everyone else differently than I had before I'd started working for Lisette. I'd gone through the wardrobe. Only this wardrobe didn't lead to Narnia, it led to Ohio. And instead of dwarfs and centaurs, there were private planes and suitcases full of money. I was now a part of a whole other world, and I couldn't tell a single soul about it. I was living a double life. I didn't feel as able to relate to other people as I used to, and in ways I was sad to feel so distant. But I embraced the feeling of being a part of something unique and daring. Most people would have never dived into a situation like the one that I was in without knowing what they were doing—most people weren't best friends with someone like Lisette. Sometimes I felt like Ray Liotta's wife in *Goodfellas*, when he handed her the gun to hide and she said that it turned her on. It was exciting to shed my inhibitions and be a part of Lisette's world, to get to experience some of the action. I still didn't know the details of her business, but at this point it was safe to assume that she wasn't selling Girl Scout cookies.

8

LOVE IN THE TIME OF FELONIES

As I transitioned from friend to employee, I had some tense moments with Lisette. When she told me that I was "underqualified" for this position, perhaps she'd been right in that I was unprepared to be exposed to a different side of her. I hadn't enjoyed being reamed when I'd questioned her, but I was reassured to see that when she wasn't stressed about running her new business, her claws retracted and I recognized my friend again. Spending time working with her meant a great deal to me, beyond just being able to keep a positive balance in my checking account.

For four years Lisette had been a rock in my life, someone I went to for comfort when times were tough, and someone I wanted to celebrate with when they were good. I knew that she looked at me in the same way. She'd always said that I was like her wife, and she was my badass husband. Right now, we were both happier than we'd been in a long time. It felt right that we should experience that happiness together.

One night, Lisette asked me to stop by to see her before she had to leave her condo for a dinner meeting. She texted me to wait for her in the lobby of her building. I sat down on a couch surrounded by marble floor and potted tropical plants. Classical music played quietly through-out the lobby. A gentleman working in the valet stood at the front desk. "Welcome. May I help you?" he asked. He'd seen me here before, visiting Lisette.

"No thanks, she's coming down," I said. The valet nodded.

An elevator dinged open and Lisette appeared. Under the ambient lighting in the lobby, she looked as though she'd just stepped off a page in a fashion magazine. Her dark hair waterfalled down over a high-collared designer coat. She wore black Paige skinny jeans and stiletto heels.

"Wow," I said. "You look gorgeous." We threw our arms around each other in a hug. She pulled back and flashed a mischievous grin.

"Hold out your hand," she said.

"Why?"

"None of your beeswax," she said playfully. "Just do it."

"Okay."

"And close your eyes!"

"Okay, okay." I closed my eyes and held my hand out in front of me. I felt Lisette's hands on mine as she pushed something tiny into my palm.

"Open your eyes," she said.

I opened my eyes to see what appeared to be an emerald-cut dia-mond ring in the center of my palm. The diamond was huge, as big as some of the ones I'd seen Lisette wear. There was a thin platinum band around it, emphasizing the size of the stone. "Oh my God," I said. I looked up at Lisette. She smiled, taking in my reaction.

"It's two and a half carats," she said. "I thought it was time for you to have a diamond. I'm giving this to you as a symbol of our friendship." I felt my eyes start to tear up. "Oh God, don't cry, you wa-wa crazy actress," she said. "I want you to know how proud I am of you. I know how much you're trying, and you're doing a good job."

"Thank you so much," I said. I'd been waiting to hear those words from her. Perhaps I'd been waiting to hear them from anyone, for a long time.

"Let's see it on," Lisette said with excitement. I tried to put it on the middle finger of my right hand.

"Oh no," I said, "I'm not sure it's going to fit."

"Try the other finger," she said. I slid it onto the ring finger of my left hand. It fit perfectly. "It looks beautiful on you," she said. "Do you like it?"

"Are you kidding? I love it." We both admired it on my finger. I laughed a bit. "If I wear it on this finger, people are going to think I'm engaged."

"Oh, who cares?" Lisette said, rolling her eyes. "I wear rings there all the time. Besides, we're practically married anyway, so it's not far from the truth."

As I linked arms with Lisette to go say good-bye at the elevator, I noticed that the valet at the lobby desk was staring in our direction with wide eyes. When I turned toward him, he immediately looked away and pretended to be suddenly interested in a nearby wall. Lisette saw this too. "He must think we're total dykes," she whispered to me, giggling.

Lisette told me that she wasn't sure when our next trip to Ohio would be. "Soon," she said. We were already well into November, and Christmas was right around the corner. My parents had bought me a plane ticket to go home to Washington on December 18 to spend the holiday with them. In the meantime, I found myself with no work to tend to for Lisette and an unexpected open schedule.

IT WAS ALMOST ONE IN the morning when I got a text from a friend, asking me to meet her at a nightclub. She was with a group of people at a small but trendy venue on Hollywood Boulevard, walking distance from my apartment. I didn't usually go to clubs, but when she texted me, I was on my way back from the Valley, where I'd been sitting in on a late-night acting class at my old studio. I agreed to meet her, knowing that the club would close soon anyway, so I wouldn't be sequestered in a boxy room and forced to listen to house music for very long. I'd gotten to know quite a few promoters when I worked for a place on Sunset a while back, so it was likely I'd be familiar with whomever she was with tonight.

I spotted my friend right away when I walked into the club. She was dressed in full hipster attire, with high-waisted pants and a crop top. She was swaying around to house music. "Meili!" she screamed when she saw me. "You made it!" We greeted each other and walked to the bar to catch up. Someone brought her a drink from nearby table service, and she immediately passed it to me. "Take it," she said. "I'm already too drunk." We had to practically yell over the music, and after a minute or so we gave up trying to talk. She headed back to the dance floor and melded into a group there. I stayed at the bar. I'd never been much for dancing.

My attention was grabbed when I noticed a familiar face walking through the crowd. I was sure I knew this person, but I couldn't place him. He stared back at me as he walked by, as though he knew me too. *He must be one of the promoters.* He was classically handsome, tall, with blue eyes and light brown hair that curled slightly. He wore a simple black T-shirt and jeans. *Who is that?* I racked my brain. I would have thought I'd remember such an attractive face, but then again pretty faces were common in Los Angeles. Our eyes stayed locked until he passed me. I saw him walk up to a girl standing near my friend on the dance floor. He joined the group, then glanced back at me.

The DJ began to play the usual send-off mash-up of old-school hip-hop blended with a few current hits. Then, as was tradition at every club I'd been to, the DJ played Oasis's "Wonderwall." I went to stand with my friend in her group on the dance floor. All around the tiny venue people were throwing their hands up and singing along to the music, with some of the more inebriated clubgoers practically shouting the words. *"Maybe you're gonna be the one that saves me / And after all / You're my wonderwall . . ."*

The lights came up in the club. We shuffled out with the crowd and walked to an after-party at the Roosevelt Hotel a few blocks away. There were about ten of us, only a few whom I'd met before. The guy I noticed in the club came with us. I still hadn't figured out how I knew him. On our way to the after-party he came up to walk beside me.

"Hey," he said. "Do I know you? You look familiar."

"What's your name?" I asked. "You're a promoter, right?"

He laughed and said, "My name is Ben and, no, I'm not a promoter. I don't even like going to clubs. I'm just here with some friends from UCLA. You ever go to SC? I know I've seen you somewhere."

"No," I said. "I've never even been on the campus. Have you ever been to an acting class? Maybe I met you at one."

"Not even close. I grew up in L.A. and I have zero interest in acting. Okay, so you're an actress. What else do you do? There's always something else."

"I work for my best friend as an assistant," I said.

He nodded. "I've known a lot of girls who do assistant work. Is your friend famous or something?"

"She's an heiress."

"To what?" he asked.

"Samsung."

He noticed the ring on my finger. "Are you engaged?"

"No," I said. "That's from my best friend."

"Wow," he said. "That's a nice friend. Well, since you're not engaged, you should have dinner with me this week."

BEN AND I WENT OUT two days later. I passed Brie in the living room as I left to meet him downstairs. "Have fun!" she said as she sat on the couch behind her sketch pad.

A gray BMW idled on the street outside of our apartment. Ben got out of the driver's side and walked around to open the car door for me. "You look beautiful," he said.

"Thanks." I was wearing new clip-in hair extensions to give my hair more volume; they were a recent, impulsive purchase. I thought I'd done a fair job of concealing the clips to make it look natural. Lisette had given me a spare set of fake eyelashes to try on a while back. They always looked so glamorous on her, so I thought I'd use them tonight. It took some doing to get them glued onto my eyelids, but with Brie's assistance I was able to make them stay. I had fun getting ready for tonight. I felt like I was playing dress-up.

Ben drove us away from my street. "So where are we going?" I asked him. "You'll see," he said. "It's a surprise." *Not another surprise.* I shuddered remembering how Aiden Cohen "surprised" me with the worst date of my life a few years back.

We drove toward the Hollywood Hills and turned to go up a road.

Along the way, we passed the Magic Castle, the clubhouse for the Academy of Magical Arts. At the top of a hill, we arrived at a sushi restaurant that overlooked the city, surrounded by elaborate Japanese gardens and pagodas. We sat at a table next to a window with a view of the hills.

Over dinner we exchanged polite and limited life stories, as with most first dates. Ben grew up in Calabasas, was twenty-seven years old and a senior studying communications at UCLA. Though his family had money, he'd paid his own tuition by working a high-paying job after high school in lieu of going to college right away. He admitted that since he'd left the job and gone back to school, he'd been a little insecure about being much older than most of the students. I admired his decision to go back and told him that he shouldn't be embarrassed. His humility was endearing.

Ben and I tried again to think of how we might know each other, but finally conceded that we'd never actually met, despite our initial feelings otherwise. "It must have been in a past life," Ben joked. After dinner he suggested that we buy Christmas decorations and take them back to my apartment. I found his request oddly charming.

We stopped by a drugstore and wandered through the aisles of holiday decorations to buy the gaudiest selections we could find. Ben grabbed two boxes of colorful lights. "We'll need these," he said, dropping them into a shopping basket. He chose a bottle of chardonnay, and we headed to the register to check out. When he pulled out his wallet to pay, I stopped him and put my credit card down. He looked stunned. "Are you sure you live in L.A.?" he asked. I shrugged and said, "You got dinner." It felt good to be able to pay for things.

Brie was surprised when Ben and I came barreling into the apartment with armfuls of decorations. After introducing her, Ben and I took the decorations into my room. We drank wine and played Christmas music while we twisted a string of lights around the headboard of my bed. Ben found an outlet and plugged it into the wall. "And now, for the full effect," he said. He got up and hit a switch to turn off my overhead light. He came back to the bed and we lay side by side under the glow of my new Christmas lights, listening to "Jingle Bell Rock" on Pandora. "I love it," I said. "This was a great idea." Ben turned on his side toward me and looked into my eyes. He leaned in and reached his hand out to my face. I began to close my eyes, ready for a kiss. "I'm not judging you," he said, "but this is falling off." He lifted an already detached fake eyelash from my face. I was mortified. "I seriously don't care," he said. "But just so you know, you don't need these." He kissed me and put his hand behind my head, running his fingers through my hair. I was lost in the moment when suddenly he stopped. I cringed as I felt his fingers examining one of the clips of fake hair I'd fastened to my scalp. "What the . . . ?" he said. "Okay, what else do I need to know?"

I OPTED OUT OF WEARING my hair extensions and any fake eyelashes for our second date. I'd told Lisette about Ben and asked her to meet him. I'd never asked her to meet anyone I'd dated, so she took the request seriously and made herself available on short notice. "I'm bringing David," she said. "We'll make it a double date. But, sweetie, don't use David's real name. Tonight, just call him Freddy." She told me that it was okay for Ben to know that I worked for her, but that it was best if he didn't realize that he was meeting her business partner as well. "What did you tell him about me?" she asked.

"A lot," I said. "I told him that you're my best friend and I work for you. All good things. He thought the ring was pretty crazy."

"Ha," she said. "Good. Let him feel a little threatened."

Before we met Lisette and David, Ben took me to a basketball game at UCLA. We left at halftime to meet them downtown at a beer and wine bar called Bottle Rock. I was anxious as we walked into the bar to find them waiting for us at a high-top table. Lisette's approval meant so much to me that if she didn't like Ben, I might choose to never see him again. I'd know after tonight.

As we sat down at the table, I realized that I'd forgotten to warn Ben about David's neck tattoos. I decided it was probably best Ben didn't know I was working with this person. He probably would have wondered what the hell line of work we were in. Lisette, a wine connoisseur in her own right, ordered wine for the table. Everyone seemed to be in a good mood tonight, and conversation flowed easily among the four of us. David was personable and friendly to Ben. The two men actually appeared to get along well. Lisette excused herself to the restroom. I took the cue to join her. The moment that the bathroom door closed behind us I started in. "So?" I asked her. "What do you think?" She laughed at my eagerness. "Well," she said, "I mean, I just met the guy. And, sweetie, you barely know him either. But I think he's cute for you."

With the approval I'd been craving from my best friend, I felt free to explore things with Ben. After leaving the wine bar, Ben and I decided to go somewhere else for another drink by ourselves. "I just need to grab a jacket from my place first," he said as we drove to a residential neighborhood near the UCLA campus. "You can come up if you want, but it will only take a sec."

"That's okay," I said. "I want to see your place."

He lived over the garage of a typical college house. I followed Ben into his bedroom. I stopped short in front of a dresser in his room. It was covered in prescription pill bottles, at least seven of them. I could see tiny capsules of unknown content inside each bottle. I didn't recognize any of the labels offhand from a glance. Ben walked up holding a black fleece jacket.

"Yeah," he said, "these are my crazy pills."

"Oh," I said, unsure of how to respond.

"I know it looks like a lot," he said. "Listen, I really like you, and I want to be honest with you if we're going to date."

"Okay," I said.

"Most of this is just for normal stuff like depression and anxiety. The rest is mostly for sleeping. Some nights I don't sleep at all, and my doctor is experimenting with some different prescriptions."

"Oh. Oh, okay," I said, forcing a supportive smile, though I didn't know how to process what he'd just told me. I'd never known anyone who took pills like these. Lisette took what she called "crazy pills" too, because she said that she was diagnosed as bipolar. But I'd never seen her with a veritable pharmacy of drugs on her boudoir.

It wasn't like I walked in and found a meth lab in his bedroom. I brushed off my initial shock and enjoyed the rest of our evening together. I also enjoyed the night with him, the next morning, and the entire following day. Our second date turned out to be more than thirty hours long. With no sense of time, we bounced from bars to all-night diners, and then to his bed, where we stayed warm and close under his covers for most of the next day. I lost track of how many times we made love. As I lay naked and half asleep in his arms, Ben asked me to be his girlfriend. I turned over and answered him with a deep kiss. It was all happening so fast, but nothing had ever felt so right and so natural to me. When he dropped me off at my apartment, the main reason for our departure was to shower and get ready to see each other again.

A WEEK LATER, ON A trip to Ohio, I told Lisette all about my new relationship during an evening alone with her in our hotel room. At first she seemed curious, but when her questions subsided and I continued to talk about him, she became quiet.

"I really like him," I gushed.

"Jesus," she said, "he sure moved up the ladder quick."

"What does that mean?" I asked.

"It means that you just met this guy and suddenly he's important," she said. "You don't even know him."

"But I'm getting to know him," I told her. Lisette looked deep in thought.

"You know, it just makes me wonder," she said.

"Wonder what?"

"Let me ask you this," she said. "And you better be honest. If Ben and I were each standing on the edge of a cliff and you had to choose to push one of us over the edge to our death, who would you push?"

I stared at her for a moment in stunned silence. "I—that's not fair," I said. "That's terrible. I'm not going to answer that."

"Answer it," she said, her irritation building.

"But," I said, "I mean, you're my best friend and what we have is forever, but what if hypothetically, I have children with Ben someday. Then you'd be asking me to choose between you and my unborn children and my entire hypothetical family." I could see that Lisette was unwilling to accept this answer. She stared dead into my eyes, waiting. "But," I said, giving in, "that's all unknown, and what you and I have is known, so I'd say that I would choose to push Ben."

"You hesitated," Lisette said. "I'm not going to lie. That really hurt me."

I tried to console Lisette and assured her that her position was not threatened by Ben, and that he understood that she was a permanent fixture in my life.

"You didn't tell him anything about work, right?" she asked.

"No, nothing," I said. "He just knows that we fly to the East Coast. I told him that I signed a confidentiality agreement with you."

Lisette looked satisfied. "Good girl," she said.

AS OUR TRIPS TO OHIO became more frequent, we developed a familiar routine in Columbus. We usually drove from the private airport straight to a cheap hotel. Frankie, Henry, and I waited in the hotel parking lot while Lisette went into the lobby. Once she had secured a room, we'd meet her at a side entrance, and then the four of us loaded anywhere between ten and seventeen suitcases inside, using a luggage cart. Lisette left the key for the room at the front desk of the hotel. She never said who would be picking up the key and accessing the room, but it was clear that the bags would be collected after we were long gone and settled into another nearby hotel.

We'd stay three nights and four days. I hung out in my pajamas in a hotel room while Lisette went to and from meetings. I never knew details of her meetings, who they were with or what they were concerning.

Though court documents and news articles have since shed light on many areas of LL's operation, what exactly she did those days in Ohio is still a mystery to me. My guess is that she was meeting with local drug dealers who had connections in the area for distribution.

My only job tasks in Ohio remained doing wire transfers at the bank and grabbing cheap snack food from the front desk for Lisette and me to have on hand when we didn't go out for dinner, which was more common than not. Once we stepped off the jet, our stays in Ohio were far from fancy. On the evening of the third day of the trip, or sometimes on the morning of the fourth day, Ko and David would bring back some of the suitcases to our hotel room. The bags were always fewer and much, much lighter than when we'd arrived in Columbus. The jet that we chartered from Los Angeles would wait for us at the private airport while we were in town, and once Lisette said that we were ready, we'd return to the airport and fly home with the remaining suitcases.

AS CHRISTMAS NEARED, BEN WENT on a trip to Miami for his winter vacation from UCLA. He texted me from Florida saying that he missed me and wanted to cut his vacation short and come back to L.A. early if I'd be in town. He left after only a few days in Miami.

After I picked Ben up from LAX, we went downtown and walked hand in hand around an outdoor entertainment complex next to the Staples Center. Elaborate Christmas decorations and lights had been put up all around the complex. A large ice-skating rink had been built in the middle of a courtyard, and we stopped to enjoy the simple pleasure of watching skaters glide around on the ice.

We went to dinner at Bottega Louie, a dimly lit Italian restaurant downtown. While we waited for our food, Ben told me that he'd been very curious about what kind of business I was in with Lisette. "You know I can't talk about it," I told him, trying to mask my irritation that he kept bringing it up. I didn't yet know the exact nature of what I was involved in, but I knew not to divulge any details at all to third parties. I suspected Lisette's whole operation was on the edge, if not over the edge, of legality, and I didn't want to stir the pot. If she said it was all okay, I wanted to believe her. I'd been nervous enough about everything as it was, and I didn't need to be thrown into a panic by other people asking probing questions that I didn't know the answers to. I finally had a job that was working out, and I wanted to keep it that way. No one had ever understood my friendship with Lisette, and I couldn't expect them to understand my employment with her.

"I know, I know you can't tell me," Ben said. "But I had some time on the flight home, so I made a little list of guesses." He pulled a crumpled piece of paper from his jean pocket. He cleared his throat and grinned at me before he began. "Now, these are just some possibilities, based on what I know," he said. "Okay, here we go." He settled down in his chair and leaned over the table. "You're married, and Lisette is flying with you to the East Coast to handle your divorce." He playfully raised his eyes to gauge my reaction after each guess. "You're really a call girl. Lisette is your madam, and she pimps you out to international businessmen."

"Ooh, you're getting warmer," I joked.

"Okay, last one," he said. "Money laundering. I just put that one down because it would explain a lot." This made me nervous because I suspected that it couldn't be far off from what we were really doing. I wasn't sure exactly what would define money laundering, but I knew that serious cash was involved in Lisette's operation. I didn't let on that I thought he was close to the truth. I just laughed along with his wild suspicions.

"You're good at keeping a secret," he said as he crumpled the list and tucked it back into his jean pocket.

"Well, it's Lisette's secret," I said. "I mean, it's her business and I know that she wants to keep it private."

"That's weird," Ben said in a more serious tone now, shaking his head as he took a sip of wine.

DURING THIS TIME, LISETTE TOLD me to be ready and available to fly out on a day's notice. "We're leaving soon," she kept saying. Days passed with no work and no money coming in. I spent all my time with Ben. It was like we were addicted to each other. He introduced me to his family. After having dinner with them in Malibu, we visited his mother and stepfather at their gated estate in Calabasas. His stepfather sent us home with six bottles of wine that had been purchased from Lisette's ex-boyfriend's wine shop. The day after we visited his parents, Ben said that his mother had given him her approval of me. "She said that you're beautiful, well-spoken, and smart," he told me on the phone. "And she said that I'm lucky to have you. Nothing I didn't already know."

Lisette maintained that I needed to remain in town for now in case she needed me to work for her. I was frustrated because that was what she'd been saying for some time, and no work had happened. I could have been home celebrating the holidays with my family this entire time, possibly with Ben. He'd said that he wanted to come home with me. My parents were upset that I wouldn't be using my ticket they'd bought me to fly into Seattle on the eighteenth of December. I'd been planning to use it, but Lisette told me that she needed me to stay in town to be on call for her. "Well, when are you coming home?" my mother asked me. The day before Christmas Eve, my parents had had enough. "You're coming home, sweetheart," my mom said. "There is no way that Lisette is going to need you for work between now and Christmas. I'm sure that Lisette's parents are going to want her home too." I told Lisette that I was leaving. THAT'S FINE, she texted me. WE'RE FLYING OUT THE FIRST WEEK OF JANUARY. I was incredulous at the thought that she might have let me stay in Los Angeles through Christmas without ever telling me that it was okay to go home. Maybe she was preoccupied with her own agenda running a still-new business, but such callous disregard seemed unusually selfish, even for her.

Ben and I exchanged holiday gifts at my apartment before he took me to the airport to fly home for Christmas. My twenty-fourth birthday was a week away, and he surprised me with an early birthday present. He noticed that the wallet I'd been using was old and tattered, and he replaced it with a brand-new Gucci wallet, made with the smoothest leather I'd ever felt. It was entirely black and had tiny metal circles on the corners. He presented it to me in the signature bronze bag from the store with a gift receipt, which I'd seen in the back of his car for almost two weeks now. "Yeah, I kinda suck at wrapping . . ." he said with a boy-ish smile as he watched me take the wallet out of the bag.

"It's beautiful," I told him, shocked by his thoughtfulness and gener-osity. "It's exactly what I would have picked out."

Ben seemed relieved and said, "I thought so. The sales guy on Rodeo was trying to get me to buy a wallet with 'Gucci' written all over it, but I told him that's not your style. I mean, it was the same price, but he just couldn't believe that you'd want this one instead." I was stunned by how well Ben knew me after dating me for less than two months. Anyone else would have thought I'd want something emblazoned with flashy logos, but Ben saw that wasn't me. Lisette had known me for four years, and every purse and piece of jewelry she'd given me had had the name of the designer visible all over it. I'd never had the heart to admit to her that I thought it was tacky. I set the wallet aside on the coffee table and lifted my dress up to straddle my boyfriend where he sat on the couch. "Thank you," I whispered as I sat down to face him. He leaned in to me for a long kiss, then picked me up and carried me to my bedroom, where we made the most of the last hour we had together before he drove me to the airport.

9

HIGH TIMES

Lisette drove Diablo through the gate of the private airport in Van
Nuys, a Tupac song thundering out of her sound system. She whisked
through the security kiosk on her way in, nodding a familiar greeting
to the guard. I was moments behind her in a limo with Frankie, Henry,
and an armada of suitcases. Our driver waved at the security guard as
we rolled past the kiosk, but the guard's attention seemed to be linger-
ing on Lisette and her Bentley. "Team LL" was no doubt an anomaly
here, but no one more than LL herself. "This isn't our first rodeo," as
she liked to say. This was our fifth trip, but the airport employees still
gawked at us in wonder every time we flew. I could only imagine what
they thought we were up to.

As the limo followed Lisette in, the thought crossed my mind that
a person would have to show more ID to rent a pair of roller skates
than they would to board a flight here. You can't drive a two-hundred-
thousand-dollar car into a skating rink. If you could, Lisette might be
more of a skater.

Lisette parked her Bentley near the plane, as usual, and oversaw
as the bags were moved into the plane. I stood by for a moment while

Frankie and Henry assisted with the luggage from the limo. I didn't really have anything I was supposed to be doing here, but I stood around with a straight face, like it all made perfect sense. Two pilots emerged from inside the plane to greet us. We'd flown with these pilots before, though I didn't recall their names. "Good morning, Miss Lee. Nice to see you. How would you like the bags arranged?" The younger pilot's eyes drifted down to Lisette's cleavage, which was bolstered by a push-up bra and a bejeweled top.

The suitcases looked as heavy as ever. Even Frankie, who towered over the group and was built like a redwood, was sweating through his suit as he lifted the bags into the back of the jet. He grunted under his breath, "Goddamn," as he hoisted a bag over his shoulders to hand it to one of the pilots.

"Angel, go ahead," Lisette told me. She handed me her purse to take into the cabin.

Inside the plane, I grabbed a cup to pour myself some coffee when a blond woman appeared in a uniform. "Good morning!" she said. "Can I get you some coffee?"

"Hi. Good morning," I said. "Um, yeah, sure. Er, no! I mean, I can get it. Thanks though, thank you. No, I can do that. No problem." I poured myself a cup. I wasn't used to having an attendant on the flight.

The rest of the team boarded the G4 and settled into the cabin, ready for takeoff. Lisette claimed a bench of creamy leather and throw pillows near me, after giving me a hug and announcing her plan to get some rest on our way to Ohio.

The attendant served the catering after we were in the air, complete with champagne from JetSetter. Lisette and I leaned across the aisle to clink champagne flutes for a "cheers" before she disappeared underneath a blanket.

Suddenly I was consumed by a familiar smell. It smelled like marijuana—like a lot of marijuana. It was overwhelming. I felt like I was stuck inside of a flying blunt. Someone must have been smoking on the plane before we boarded today—perhaps some touring musicians had chartered it last, and the smell hadn't come out yet. I looked to Lisette to share my theory, but she appeared to be knocked out asleep beneath her blanket.

This is too funny. I have to share this with someone.

The flight attendant was headed down the aisle, about to pass me. Maybe she would be able to tell me who'd used the plane last. I caught her attention, and she paused in front of me, leaning down to hear me as I spoke quietly to be careful not to wake Lisette.

"Hey," I said. "Um, do you . . . smell that?" I was hoping that she'd say something like, "Yes! Snoop Dogg flew with us this morning and he decided to hot box the plane." Instead, she looked at me with what appeared to be genuine confusion.

"Smell what?" she asked.

"Uh, it kinda smells like . . . marijuana. Do you think that someone was smoking it on the plane, like maybe the last people who flew with it?" She seemed unamused and rather concerned. "Oh. No. I don't know. Would you like me to turn on the air-conditioning? That might help."

"Er, no, that's okay," I said. "Thanks. It's fine."

It occurred to me that the smell could be coming from our group, and that someone was probably carrying a dank dime bag or something. I immediately felt stupid for asking her. I sank into my seat and turned back to look around the cabin. I prayed that no one on Team LL had heard me.

I managed to sleep a little during the flight. Lisette shook me awake before we landed. "Sweetie. Sweetie. Good morning, sunshine. Aw, did you sleep okay? We're almost there."

We touched down in Columbus and loaded the suitcases and ourselves into a limo and a black Escalade. Lisette would ride with Frankie in the Escalade. I climbed in next to Henry in the limo, wedging myself against the suitcases that filled the inside of the vehicle. We sat in silence, waiting for Lisette to dispatch her instructions.

I looked at Henry. There was no way that he was the one carrying pot. He'd never smoked it in his life. Frankie? I'd never even seen him drink alcohol. Lisette almost never smoked. I wondered why she wouldn't tell me if she'd brought some. Wherever she got it, she was packing some powerful plant.

I sat with the door open. Lisette walked over to me. "Where's your phone? Tell Ko we're on our way. Get the address." She went to the Escalade. I texted Ko. He said, OK. WE WILL BE THERE IN AN HOUR, and gave me the address of a local hotel. I passed it along to Lisette. **THANKS ANGEL,** she wrote back. The Escalade led the way. I decided to wait until we were alone to ask Lisette about the smell.

We drove to the address where Ko had presumably arranged for the bags to be picked up later. Once the luggage was secure in a room, Lisette left a key at the front desk and we headed to another hotel a short distance away.

Lisette checked us into the hotel. She reserved two rooms as usual, one for Frankie and Henry and one for Lisette and me. Frankie walked with Lisette into our room. I went to the bathroom to freshen up and change, then came back in to hear Lisette and Frankie talking. It looked heated, and though I was in the room and could hear everything, I minded my own business. Lisette was boiling over.

"It smelled like a fucking Cypress Hill concert up there," she said. "We need to take some goddamn precaution. This can't happen again. The pilots were probably catching a contact high. I swear to God, I was waiting for them to say something."

Frankie nodded. "Yeah, I mean, I could smell it. It was pretty strong. I was thinkin', 'Shit, man, we got a problem.'"

"Next trip we have to be careful," said Lisette. "We can't afford to be amateurs."

Frankie nodded again. "No doubt."

I tried to busy myself with my luggage, but my heart raced. I realized that I wasn't moving.

In an attempt to look more natural, I pulled out a sweater and refolded it, hands shaking. Was it possible that all the suitcases we'd been bringing to Ohio had been full of marijuana, and not money that Lisette didn't care to be moving through a bank account? But I'd seen Ko zipping that suitcase full of money on the second trip. I hadn't wanted to see it, but I did. Did that cash go toward paying some drug dealer, in exchange for egregious amounts of pot? I never imagined that Lisette would break away from Samsung to launch a drug operation. This was definitely illegal. How could this not be illegal?

Frankie left. I kept my face to my luggage.

"Babe, what are you doing? I need a fucking drink," Lisette said.

How was it possible that I'd never smelled it before this morning, on the plane? Who else knew about this?

"Ha. Yeah," I said. I turned to face her. "I could use a drink too. It's been a long day."

She rolled her eyes. "Long day? Babe, honestly, you have the easiest job in the world. If you need me to stop paying you to ride on a private plane and feed you champagne, tell me now."

There's no way that Lisette could have believed that I knew about this. She never told me. She just said it was "business." She intentionally kept me in the dark the whole time, knowing I'd go along with almost anything she asked me to do. Now I knew what had been discussed at all the meetings after she'd told me to step out. There could have at least been some conversation that went like, "Hey, want to smuggle some drugs with me? Because that's the plan. That cool with you?"

I found myself eerily disturbed that Lisette would knowingly lead me into such a precarious situation. And now that the secret was out, instead of addressing it and making sure I was okay, she made no apologies and looked me straight in the eye as if to challenge me. Her brazen behavior made me uncomfortable and even a little afraid.

"I know that I'm very lucky to be here," I said, forcing a smile.

"Good," she said.

Bad. This is bad. Oh God. I'm a drug trafficker. What?! No. This can't be as bad as I think it is. Lisette must know something that I don't. She's in charge. I should just forget I ever heard any of it . . . or smelled any of it. I know that she would never lead me into anything that was actually dangerous. But how could drug trafficking not be dangerous?

Lisette stood and slipped back into her Chanel wedges. "Text Frankie. We need to run to the store." I reached for my phone and my shoes.

The Escalade parked at the Giant Eagle. It looked like a hardware store to me, but apparently this was the grocery store in Ohio. I walked in with Lisette, Frankie, and Henry. "Man, I'm starving," said Frankie. Lisette and Henry flirted ahead of us. I wondered if Frankie knew that she was sleeping with him. Lisette turned back to Frankie, laughing. "You're always starving. This is probably the longest you've ever gone without food in your life." Frankie laughed.

Frankie pushed the shopping cart as we talked about what to get. "The Giant Eagle." It sounded so American. I noticed people staring at us, especially Lisette wearing her fur-lined coat and diamonds. *Don't worry, folks. We're just a few of your fellow Americans here, in search of food in this great country of ours. We're just like you. No reason to be alarmed. It's not as if we've just brought a Range Rover's worth of illegal drugs into your community. Carry on.*

The woman at the checkout offered a warm greeting as we approached the register. She scanned our items. Beep. Vodka. "So where are y'all comin' from?" she asked. Beep. Beef jerky. "Don't look like you're from around here." Beep. Mac and cheese. Henry was friendly and answered, "We're from L.A." Lisette was at his side and chimed in. "We're in town visiting some friends. We just love it here." The woman stopped scanning for a moment and raised her eyes to our group. All four of us faced her with reassuring smiles as Lisette pulled out her wallet to pay.

We left the store with enough groceries and booze to carry us through our four-day stay in Columbus. Team LL returned to the hotel. Frankie and Henry carried the shopping bags into the room that Lisette and I would share and they took out their dinner, though Henry looked like he wanted to stay. He said to Lisette, "Are you going to bed?" Lisette said, "Yeah, sweetie, we're pretty tired. You two go to your room and we'll see you in the morning." She gave him a look. He nodded with a boyish smile and said, "Good night." Henry was sweet. I wondered how much he knew. The door shut behind them. I changed into a matching flannel sleep suit, courtesy of my parents last Christmas. They give me one every year.

Lisette burst out, "Aha! Finally, some alone time with my girl. Time for those drinks." She rummaged through her purse and took out a small bag of cocaine. "I'll be out in a minute." She set the bag on a table and left to the bathroom to change.

I stared at the coke a minute. Out of Lisette's presence, questions pounded in my head and tightened in my chest, followed by dread. Reality sank in like a poison. I swallowed the thoughts, then swallowed vodka to bury my nerves. If I said nothing, if I did nothing, maybe it would all just turn out okay. I leaned against a cupboard, focusing on the stitching pattern on the back of an aging couch in front of me. In my mind, I rehearsed how I was going to ask Lisette to fill me in on what the hell was going on. I was lost in thought by the time the bathroom door reopened.

Lisette came out dressed in a pink velour tank top with matching drawstring pants. She didn't look at me as she scanned the room to find the coke on a table, still in the bag. "Babe, give me your credit card," she said. I breathed out. It was always my card. I hated getting coke on my card. She'd insisted that we use my blood donor card a couple of times. That might have been the reason why I stopped donating—I couldn't face those people again without feeling the eyes of God on me. I got a debit card from my purse and handed it to her. "Thanks, Angel." She opened the bag and poured white powder out on a table.

I passed her a strong pour of vodka and sat down next to her as she cut the coke. She did it like a pro. She'd been doing coke for years before she met me. I only did it when I was with her, save for the occasional late-night bump at parties in Hollywood. Coke seemed to be a staple at any after-hours in L.A., and it was starting to become a staple in our trips to Ohio as well. Lisette and I routinely indulged once we were alone and had bid adieu to the boys for the night.

She formed the drug into six small lines on the glass table, set my debit card aside, and said, "Okay. Time for a toast. To us, and to my girl. You have really stepped up your game for this. I wasn't sure you could do it. Cheers, Angel." She took a drink, then leaned down to snort up a line of blow with a severed plastic straw. She popped back up, inhaling through her nose and touching her nostrils to make sure she got it all.

I set my drink down. My palms were sweating already, before I'd even touched the cocaine. *Okay, here we go.* "Lisette," I said, "can I ask you something?"

"Of course," she said, "Just let me say this first." She went on. "I am so proud of you. You're getting savvier. I had some reservations about hiring you, but you haven't let me down. You're finally growing up, babe. You should be proud of yourself." I didn't feel proud. I felt confused. I decided I needed more than just alcohol before I could ask my questions. I grabbed the straw from the table and held my hair back to rip through a line. *Woo! Strong stuff.*

I looked into Lisette's eyes. Purple contacts today. I thought it was cute that she wore them and never addressed it. My face melted as I felt a bubble of emotion rising. This was my best friend, after all. My mind drifted for a moment in a daze. She looked back at me, completely sober. She never got high. She was like a machine, able to consume in excess but unable to feel anything. She said, "What did you want to ask me?" The words weren't coming. It was all blocked up. I didn't know how to say it, especially now. Cocaine made it hard to talk.

I don't want to get yelled at again. What if she kicks me out of the room? What if she doesn't let me fly home with them? I can't afford a plane ticket! This is the first trip in over a month. I'm almost overdrawn in my account again . . .

"Thank you for giving me this job," I said. "It's made my life a lot better. It was getting really rough there. It's good to finally get to spend some time with you."

In the last year, Lisette had been so consumed with work that I'd barely seen her, but since she'd hired me I felt as though I had my friend back. She'd had her unpleasant moments recently and was obsessed with work, but I knew that beneath her designer sunglasses and scalding temper, there was a good person, someone I still cared about. My friendship with her had been one of the few things that I'd believed to be permanent in my life since moving to Los Angeles. We'd been together for four years, and I wasn't ready to lose her. I wondered if saying anything that could risk my job might also be risking our friendship.

I grabbed my debit card and moved the mound of excess coke around on the glass, making patterns, then swishing them away like waves over sand. I tried to inhale deeply. The coke made my breaths shorter.

Just bring it up casually. Somehow . . .

I looked up toward her, but I struggled to begin. I was distracted by what she'd said before. "You really think I'm growing up?" I asked. She'd always told me I was very "young" for my age, so saying that I was anywhere near "grown up" was high praise coming from her. She nodded as she came up from woofing through another line. "Mm-hmm," she said, touching her nose. "Absolutely. You're taking work seriously. You're showing real commitment. You've never been late to meetings, nothing. I'm impressed. And happy that I don't have to make excuses for you to the rest of the team. You know that no one thought you were cut out to work. No one wanted you here. They all thought you were just some dumb, idiot broad, but you're proving them wrong. I had to fight for you to stay, and thank God I did, because you know I don't like spending time with people, especially chicks. There aren't many people I could stand to be with for four days in a row in bum-fuck Ohio, so I'm happy that it's working out with you. Just keep it up."

So I'm a dumb, idiot broad when it looks like I might be an overcurious outsider, but I'm savvy and grown-up when I'm on time and don't ask any questions?

Her logic dumbfounded me, and I wasn't sure what made sense anymore.

I combined two small lines of coke and leaned down to take them in. I popped back up. I undid the top button of my sleep shirt.

"Is it hot in here?" I asked. "It feels hot to me." Lisette gave me a once-over.

"You do look a little sweaty," she said.

"I'm going to put a tank on," I said as I got up and moved to my luggage. It was so much easier when I didn't know. I'd felt so much safer then. Now I didn't know what to do with this information. I felt as though I was imploding and there was nowhere for the debris to go, so I had to keep it inside me.

I closed my eyes and pulled my tank top on.

Just breathe. I don't have to talk about this, not right now.

"Was Henry okay tonight?" I asked Lisette as I returned to sit with her at the table. "He seemed like he wanted to stay up with us. Are you guys still . . . ?"

Lisette was cutting more of the drug. "Oh, sweetie, I'm sure he's just fine," she said. "And yes, I am still sitting on his face every now and then. He's so quiet, but I swear to God that boy fucks like a champion."

"Well, I'm glad that he's taking good care of you," I said, pleased that I'd successfully changed the subject. "What about David?"

She rolled her eyes and said, "Ergh. He's pissing me off lately. He thinks this is supposed to be some vacation out here, and he's using street mentality for bigger business, which doesn't work. He expects me to swoon when he's acting like some thug."

"Do you think he knows about Henry?" I asked.

"Ha, no, he'd lose his shit if he found out," she said. "Thank God for you. Can you imagine me being stuck out here with everyone, by myself? Jesus." I let out a nervous laugh.

That last line of coke hit me hard. Good.

"Your hair looks so pretty," I said, admiring it.

"Aw, thank you," Lisette said.

"I'm so grateful to have you," I told her.

Lisette smiled. "You'll probably never know how much you mean to me," she said. "No guy has ever meant as much to me as you do. Guys come and go, but we're forever. You're fucking priceless, and I'm keeping you."

We stayed up talking for hours. Before the sun rose over Columbus, Lisette gave me a Valium and a kiss good night on the cheek. "I love you," she whispered. "Sleep in tomorrow. Frankie is going to drive me to a few meetings, but I'll be back in the afternoon. Get some rest, Angel."

I never asked her about the pot. I knew she was looking out for me and everything would be okay. I told myself this as I tried to lie still in bed, trembling and waiting for the Valium to kick in.

10

#008

After that trip to Columbus, I wondered if Lisette would sit me down and say something like, "Well, now you know, so let's be open about what we're doing." But she didn't address it. She never came out and admitted that her plan all along was to smuggle drugs. This was not in my job description. But there *was* no job description. I'd foolishly thought little of it when Lisette told me not to ask any questions about her business. She'd always reveled in unnecessary mystery and preferred practically everything she did to be "cloak and dagger." Perhaps I was twice the fool for saying nothing after I'd found out the truth, but I saw no way of backing out. I didn't imagine that I'd have the team's blessing if I'd tried to politely excuse myself from the operation and assure them that their secret would be safe with me. Lisette told me that everyone was uneasy about my working with them in the first place, and that she'd had to vouch for me. She knew that I wasn't going to look like a smuggler to the team or to anyone, including pilots on chartered flights and tellers at banks. I'm sure it helped that I didn't know that I was a drug mule. No need to even pretend! Perfect. So many things made more sense now. That was why she wanted me on the plane. No one would think that I was traveling with a quarter ton of pot in my carry-ons.

Long after our arrest, I would come to have a much greater understanding of the plan I'd been a part of. At the outset, David told Lisette he knew a supplier who could provide tons of weed on a regular basis, and that he could get buyers in Ohio. I met his supplier twice, before each of the first two trips, though I didn't know who he was at the time. He was Jose, the eerily quiet Mexican man with the new white sneakers on at David's apartment. Jose lived in Arizona and had connections to a Mexican cartel. David could buy pot from him at $500 a pound and then sell it in Ohio for at least $1,000 a pound, making a 100 percent profit margin. David wanted to move on the opportunity, but the missing piece was transportation. Finding a discreet way to move thousands of pounds of pot across the country is a tall order, even for experienced drug dealers. Lisette was their answer.

Lisette flew only on private jets; she said she'd never flown on a commercial airline, save for a trip to Cabo with me a few years back. Her showy appearance and entitled demeanor on a private flight were unlikely to raise questions. And "divas" like her were expected to have too much luggage, which would explain the hoard of suitcases.

For Lisette's part, she was intrigued by the cloak-and-dagger nature of such an operation. She'd always said that her gangster father ran casinos in Japan, and perhaps getting into business with David seemed like a fitting venture for a "Mafia princess." I don't think she ever really considered the potential consequences. She and David agreed to be partners, with Lisette responsible for travel logistics and David responsible for buying and selling the weed. I was the first "staff" member Lisette recruited.

Part of me was glad that Lisette didn't talk about the fact that we were smuggling drugs, and that no one did. I didn't want to hear it. If I didn't say it out loud and if no one else did, then it didn't feel entirely real to me. After I heard the conversation between Lisette and Frankie, it became an open secret, the pink elephant in the room. A big, smelly elephant that got stuffed into suitcases before every outbound trip to Ohio.

Ben still had no idea about the nature of my work for Lisette. I couldn't tell him. Thankfully, his curiosity took a backseat to studying during his final semester of UCLA. He asked me fewer questions about work when he was busy. Between trips to Columbus, I spent as much time with him as possible.

More of my friends and family were asking what it was exactly that I did for work. My parents didn't understand why I couldn't at least tell them which state I traveled to. "We worry about you," my mother said. "We just wish we knew where you go. I don't like all these secrets." I told them all that it was Lisette's private business, and I stuck to the story about having signed a confidentiality agreement. I hated lying to everyone, especially my parents, but it was the only way to prevent further questions. It wasn't just for my own good; it was for the good of the people I cared about. Things had changed, and my secrecy was no longer just out of respect for Lisette's privacy. My loyalty for her blurred with self-preservation, and I could no longer tell the difference. I had potentially dangerous information now, and if people in my life knew what I was doing, they would almost certainly interfere. I couldn't be sure of anyone's safety if that were to happen. I'd gotten myself into this rabbit hole, and I refused to pull anyone else into it with me, no matter how far down I was spiraling.

LISETTE WASTED NO TIME IN beginning to plan for our next trip. She sent me to the bank with another bushel of cash, and she arranged for our flight through Carol at JetSetter Charter.

Since I'd first become close with Lisette, she'd had a habit of asking me to answer her cell phone for her when we were together. When it rang, she'd often pass it to me and say something like, "Sweetie, answer this and say, 'Ms. Lee's phone, this is Alice.'" She wanted me to pretend to be one of her "many" assistants who were assigned to her through Samsung. I would answer to "see who was calling," then tell them to wait "one moment please" before I pressed the mute button and passed the phone to Lisette. She especially loved whenever I used a fake British accent to answer. She would egg me on as her phone rang, saying, "Babe, do the accent. Oh, come on, you're so good at it!" The first couple of times she asked me to answer her phone, I was uneasy because I didn't want to lie to whoever was on the other end of the line. But after she reminded me that we were just playing a harmless joke on people who were calling her, I decided to play along whenever she handed me her phone as it rang. Lisette always found it amusing, and I liked being able to make her laugh.

A month or so after she hired me, I was with Lisette when Carol from JetSetter Charter called her. "Answer it and say you're Stephanie," she said. "That's the name of my assistant in New York. Carol knows her. No accent." With no time to ask for a further explanation, I answered the phone with "Miss Lee's phone, this is Stephanie." Carol was very friendly and certainly seemed familiar with Stephanie. She said things like, "What a pleasant surprise! It's so good to talk with you." I was instantly uncomfortable and passed the phone off to Lisette after sidestepping the conversation. It had been one thing in the past to pretend to be a made-up assistant during a four-second greeting, but the idea of actively impersonating a real assistant and deceiving someone who knew her was far outside of my comfort zone.

"Carol will never know," Lisette said. "She's never even met Stephanie in person. They just talk on the phone because Stephanie takes care of the details for our flights." I'd spoken with Carol only one time since, and the conversation was equally brief and uncomfortable on my end.

Two days before we were scheduled to fly east again, Lisette texted me saying that I needed to come to her condo after sunset. **LEAVE YOUR CAR WITH THE VALET,** she wrote. **YOU'LL RIDE WITH ME.**

Lisette drove us to meet the rest of Team LL at the edge of a park in Beverly Hills. The coast was clear and the neighborhood was dark. Lisette bumped gangster rap as she pulled Diablo to a spot at the curb. We shared a Djarum cigarette while we waited on the sidewalk of the park. She hadn't told me why we were here, just that we "needed to meet." I didn't ask questions as I took drags from the clove cigarette and stared through the darkness looking for headlights.

Familiar cars pulled up behind us over the span of a few minutes. Radios silenced and engines powered down. The only sound that could be heard was the closing of car doors as everyone got out to assemble on the grass. Once we were all standing in a close circle, David handed out packs of what looked like small walkie-talkies. As I stared at the device in my palm, David whispered, "Okay, guys, the numbers are already in there. The contacts are all three-digit identification numbers, and yours is written on the pack." I noticed "#008" scribbled in black marker on the package I was holding. I glanced at Lisette's and saw "#007" written on the back of hers. Something told me that she'd been given "double o seven" by special request. David went on to say, "One thing we have to be clear on, guys. No names. Ever. You want to talk about somebody, don't use the name. Use their number. We all got them. Okay?" David instructed us that from now on we were to carry these "burner phones" with us at all times.

I used the new phone only when Lisette asked me to contact someone we worked with to give or receive information. It was meant to be our "safe line," as long as we said no names. I kept it zipped in a pocket inside a Chanel purse Lisette gave me. The idea of a burner phone is that it can't be traced back to the person using it; the minutes are all prepaid, and no personal information needs to be given to a wireless company. David told us that we would need to trash the phones in two weeks, at which point we would be given new ones.

Team LL now strictly included Lisette, Frankie, Henry, and me. Lisette had emphasized this, as well as the necessity of our allegiance to her and not to David. "He's not your boss, I am," she said. "He has Ko and I have you three. You work *with* David, not for him. I am your only boss." Tension had been building between Lisette and David regarding how to run the business. She said that he was unprofessional and sloppy. There were a few fake hundred-dollar bills found in the money that David brought back from Ohio during the last trip. Some of the money was used to pay the team. Lisette was furious. As her romantic relationship with David landed on the rocks, Henry rose in her favor.

David's attitude toward Lisette had also changed. It seemed that he was starting to think that she was crazy and unrealistic. The term "crazy bitch" had made its way through the grapevine, apparently from David. I'd never heard him call her that, but I could imagine that he would. Lisette had never taken kindly to criticism. She told me that she wanted to cut him out. "I just need to get in touch with his contact," she said, "some guy named Jose." The quiet guy who was at David's apartment before the first two trips. Lisette was surprised when I told her, "I think I met him."

Lisette informed us that we would no longer be meeting at David's apartment in the morning before flights to Ohio; now the operation would be centered at Lisette's place on Wilshire Corridor. The evening before our trip we met her there for "Wardrobe." I never had any idea why Lisette called it that, as it had absolutely nothing to do with clothing or physical attire, but no one questioned her about it. At the time, when I believed that she had a career as a pop singer, I wondered if it had come from some kind of industry term for dress rehearsal. During Wardrobe, we assembled in Lisette's unit and waited for David to "chirp" one of us on a burner phone to let us know he had arrived. He showed up behind the wheel of a truck full of suitcases. He parked around the corner. We helped take the suitcases up and line them around the inside of Lisette's condo. I wasn't much help during Wardrobe, as it was impossible for me to lift any of the bags. My presence was just a formality in Lisette's eyes.

Lisette told me that she was tapping cell phones now. Henry, David, Ko. All their personal phones were being tapped, she said. She told me that she'd even had surveillance cameras installed in David's apartment, unbeknownst to him of course. She assured me that she wasn't tapping my phone, but who knew? From then on, I could never shake the feeling that my phone might be tapped.

During meetings at the hotel bar in Beverly Hills, it became increasingly less common for Lisette to ask Henry and me to step out while sensitive information was being discussed. Henry and I sat at the table in silence as we listened to the others talk. It wasn't as though we could excuse ourselves. We could leave only if Lisette excused us. Anything else would have gone against the unspoken rules of the world we lived in now—her world.

I GOT A TEXT FROM Lisette early one morning before Team LL was scheduled to assemble at her condo.

BABE I NEED YOU TO PICK UP SOME AIR FRESHENER ON YOUR WAY HERE. WE MAY NEED A FEW BOTTLES.

I had a feeling I knew what this was for.

I walked into a drugstore wearing a black pencil skirt and a matching blazer. Lisette had told me that I needed to stop dressing so casually when we traveled. "You're working," she'd said. "You should look like it." I perused an aisle full of cleaning supplies until I found myself standing in front of an assortment of air fresheners. Lisette hadn't specified which scent she wanted me to get. I stared blankly at the selection. Ocean breeze? Citrus delight? I picked up a pink bottle and sprayed a cloud of mist into the air. It smelled like tropical fruit. Delicious! But which scent would be best for concealing the smell of marijuana? This was probably not an appropriate question for me to ask the sales clerk. I grabbed three bottles of varying scents and headed to the register.

In Lisette's condo the suitcases we'd brought up the day before were now lying open around the living room. This was the first time I'd seen any of the bags unzipped and completely opened. Inside each suitcase there appeared to be four massive bricks of marijuana that had been sealed with thick plastic. I'd never seen so much of the drug in my life, not even on television. I paused for a moment at the entrance of her penthouse to adjust to the situation and breathe. This was different from merely smelling something on the plane and witnessing a conversation. Even then, there had still been some shred of possibility that I was wrong, however slight. Now, looking around the room at what must have been hundreds of pounds of the drug in front of me, the truth was undeniable. My involvement was undeniable too; I had just bought air freshener to cover up the smell. Everyone on the team saw that I knew now. The room was heavy with the smell of the plant. I continued to be amazed that I'd never smelled the marijuana during our first four trips. Perhaps it had been packaged differently. I wondered where the plant was coming from anyway, and who else was involved. And who else knew that I was involved.

Frankie and Henry were kneeling around the bags, laying dryer sheets on top of the bricks. Lisette greeted me where I stood at the entrance. "Hi, sweetie! Did you get it?" she asked. I nodded and forced a smile, trying to appear unfazed by what I'd just walked into. I handed her the bag from the drugstore. "What the fuck?" she said as she pulled out the air fresheners.

"Er, the pink one smells really good," I said. "I wasn't sure what you wanted, so I brought a selection."

Lisette cracked a smile. "Well, A for effort, sweetie. Okay, guys!" she said, addressing the boys. "Fire away! Just unload these onto the bags."

My eyes widened. "All of them?" I asked.

Lisette shrugged. "Yeah, why not?"

The boys laid swathes of cloth over the pot bricks, then zipped every suitcase closed. We followed our boss's instructions and sprayed until the entire contents of each bottle had been emptied onto the outside of the bags.

WITHIN MINUTES OF BOARDING OUR chartered flight to Ohio, a pungent smell drifted into the main cabin from the cargo hold. The odor combination of tropical citrus, ocean breeze, and marijuana was comically overpowering. I tried to avoid drawing attention to it as I slowly looked around to see if anyone else wished they were wearing a gas mask. Lisette looked back at me with a mix of amusement and horror. She smelled it too, no doubt. It was sickeningly strong and there was nothing we could do about it at this point. We both stifled laughter watching Frankie's face as he caught a whiff, glanced toward the back, then shook his head and said, "Nah, man, that shit is nasty," under his breath. Henry just smiled and said quietly, "Hey, at least it's better than last time."

I couldn't help but wonder what Henry's reaction had been when he'd first realized that we'd been moving pot. How had he found out? Had he smelled it on the plane before our last trip? Had Lisette told him? Somehow I got the sense that he'd found out around the same time I had. I didn't believe that he would have signed on to work for Lisette if he'd known in the beginning, regardless of his affection for her. Henry had never used drugs in his life and maintained that he had no desire to. I seriously doubted that he would feel okay about knowingly smuggling them.

In Columbus, Lisette took me to the bank with her to transfer money through my account. Per usual, we made the transfer with the help of our trusted banker there named Barry. After Lisette handed him an armload of cash, he headed off to get it counted and transferred. My wallet sat on Barry's desk. I had taken it out to present my ID. When Barry walked off, I grabbed my wallet to put it back in my purse. Lisette eyed it and said, "Is that the wallet that Ben gave you?"

"Oh, yeah, it is," I said. I lightened up at the mention of his name.

"Let me see it," Lisette said, grabbing it out of my hands. She felt the leather, then opened the wallet and examined the interior of it. "Huh," she scoffed.

"What's wrong?" I asked her. She closed the wallet and handed it back to me.

"This is a fake Gucci wallet," she said. "I can tell by the zipper."

"What?" I said. "I don't think so. Ben gave it to me in the bag from the store. He even had a gift receipt. I mean, I didn't accept the receipt because I wanted to keep the wallet, but he offered it to me." Lisette rolled her eyes.

"Anyone can get a bag from the store," she said. "I can't believe he did that to you. That's very déclassé, babe."

"It's not fake though," I told her. "Feel the leather." She felt it and shook her head.

"It's okay," she said, "but I've seen better fakes."

"Well, either way, it's a quality wallet and a sweet gift," I told her. "I still love it." I was quite sure that the wallet was authentic, but I didn't want to insult Lisette by insisting that her judgment was wrong.

Lisette sighed and said, "I'm telling you, I know a fake when I see one. If I were you, I'd be pissed."

AFTER FOUR DAYS OF WHAT had become our routine in Ohio, we headed home. During the flight back to Los Angeles, I was in the middle of telling a story to Frankie that involved Ben when Lisette whipped around in her chair in front of us to address me. "Seriously, Meili, enough!" she said, her voice raised and seething. "Everyone here is sick of hearing you talk about some loser who is strung out on prescription pills. I seriously doubt that half the things he tells you are true, but you believe anything. If you want to waste your time on him, fine, but I'm not going to let you waste our time any longer." Frankie and Henry looked on in silence.

"Sorry," I told her. "Jesus. Okay, I'll stop talking about it."

Lisette gave me a cold stare. "No, we're past that," she said. "It's completely unprofessional to be talking about your love life during trips, and I've warned you about this. You're too obsessed with your boyfriend now to be useful anyway."

"That's not true," I told her.

She shook her head. "I think you should focus your attention on what you really want," she said. "And it's pretty obvious what that is." Lisette refused to speak to me for the remainder of the flight back to L.A.

11

I AM STEPHANIE

My best friend fired me. You know you're an incompetent employee when that happens. I'd promised Lisette that she wouldn't regret hiring me and I'd managed to let her down. I'd disappointed the person whose opinion had essentially validated me for months, and perhaps far longer. She'd said I was proving myself, and now it seemed that I had only proven myself to be unfit for employment. She was proud of me, but not anymore. It made me sick to my stomach. I felt worthless.

Not only was she angry with me as an employee, but she felt that I'd chosen a man over her, and I knew she was hurt. When she fired me, Lisette said that she probably wouldn't have much time to see me from now on. I never would have imagined that my friendship with her, which was supposed to last forever, could become contingent upon my employment by her. She was testing me with this job because she saw potential in me and I'd failed miserably. In one fell swoop I'd hurt my friend, offended my boss, and lost my job.

At least I still had my boyfriend, but love wasn't going to pay my bills. I didn't know what I was fit to do anymore. Acting had obviously been a wash: when the highlight of a five-year attempt at a career is an under-the-table blow job on Showtime, it's safe to say things haven't exactly taken off. I'd failed at the dream I'd had since I was a child, and now I didn't know what to dream about. I'd felt so far removed from normal society since I'd gone deeper into working for Lisette. My perception of reality had skewed, and I was becoming paranoid, always on edge now; I would have needed to readjust if I tried to move on with my life as it was before all this. The occasional coke binge with Lisette probably wasn't helping my paranoia and anxiety. When I was in public, I often wondered if people could sense that something was off, that I was hiding something. It was like wandering into the streets high as a kite and trying to act normally.

Maybe Brie was right when she told me that Lisette's firing me could be a good thing. I was sitting on the floor of our living room with my legs crossed and my arms wrapped around my knees, too upset to eat. Brie could tell I'd been crying, so I told her what had happened.

I have always leaned on my friends and family for advice, even for relatively minor decisions. One of the drawbacks of lying to your friends is that it's impossible to get informed advice from them. How can anyone advise on a situation that they know only the half of, especially when the half they don't know concerns a secret life of drug smuggling? Brie thought things would all work out and I hoped she was right, but in reality she had no clue what was going on. It was so foreign to me to be unable to call on anyone for guidance. I certainly couldn't call on Lisette, who'd gotten me into this.

On top of everything, my relationship with Ben had been affected by my work with Lisette. Since I found out what was in the suitcases, I'd had trouble sleeping. My mind was always racing, and at night I was left alone with my thoughts, which were often terrifying. Ben's insomnia was ever present, and after he took a sleeping pill and put earplugs in, he didn't want to be disturbed until morning. He was particularly desperate for rest since he needed energy to study for finals. Nothing seemed to help him sleep.

It pained me to see him look so pale and stressed, so I tried not to interfere with his routine when we went to bed. Sometimes I got up after he was asleep to go to the kitchen to drink. Alcohol was one of the few things that helped to drown my thoughts and carry me to sleep.

I wondered if it was for the best that Lisette fired me—I was never particularly useful at the job, and I never wanted to be involved in that kind of business anyway. I wasn't cut out for it and everyone involved knew it. I'd just wanted to pay my bills and hang out with Lisette. Her rejection and insults hurt like hell right now, but at least I was out. I felt some peace that the decision had been made for me. Lisette's ego would never have allowed me to walk away without some sort of personal shaming, or worse. I'd seen new, darker sides of her lately, and I wasn't sure what she was capable of. I didn't want to find out.

IT HAD BEEN A WHILE since I'd relaxed enough to enjoy something as simple as having a night in with my boyfriend. After finishing some homework one night, Ben invited me to come over. We walked to the Ralphs near his apartment to pick up a bottle of wine. As we browsed the selection, we were in constant physical contact, both eager to return to the privacy of his apartment. Every touch, every kiss on my forehead and arm around my shoulders from Ben was a shot of euphoria to me, a reminder of what it was to be happy. It made me forget about everything bad in the world, and I wanted to hold on to this feeling forever. Ben leaned in to kiss me but I held back, smiling. He smiled back and said, "What?"

"Nothing," I said coyly.

"No, what?" he said. "You have to tell me."

I bit my lip, then said, "Well, the lease is almost up on my apartment. I was just wondering what you would think about us moving in together . . ."

He paused for a moment, then said, "I wouldn't mind coming home to you," and pulled me in for a kiss.

OVER THE NEXT FEW DAYS, Ben and I discussed getting an apartment together in a few months, after he graduated from college. It made me sad to be planning such a big step without Lisette's blessing, when she'd said that she one day expected to be the godmother to my children. It didn't feel right to be moving forward in a relationship without her approval. I had hoped that she would come to like Ben and respect my affection for him, but perhaps I'd pushed the issue too soon. I was still reeling from Lisette's rejection, and I was hurt that she hadn't returned my texts in almost a week, since our last trip to Ohio.

Finally, Lisette responded to me in a text message.

I'VE HAD SOME TIME TO COOL DOWN, I'M WILLING TO TALK ABOUT THIS IF YOU CAN COME OVER SOON.

I rushed over to her condo. It was early afternoon, so there was little traffic and I got there fast. She gave me a reluctant hug when she met me at her door.

"Hey," she said, "okay, come in."

"Thanks," I said.

"Don't thank me yet," she said. "We need to talk first."

I took a breath, then started. "Lisette, I apologize that I wasn't acting in, well, a professional way during trips."

Lisette looked stern and unflinching as she said, "Listen, I know that you have it in you to rise above your immaturity, get smart, and be responsible. I am willing to give you another chance, but I need to see your commitment."

Commitment to her or commitment to working for her?

It seemed they were one in the same in her eyes now. I was taken slightly aback when she immediately began talking about work. I hadn't come here expecting to get my job back. I thought that ship had sailed, and part of me was glad. It hadn't even crossed my mind on my way over to her condo, though I was still out of a job. All I could think about was trying to save our friendship. But if she wanted me to work for her again, I'd do it. She might have been a "crazy bitch" as David said, but she was *my* crazy bitch. I still loved her and would do just about anything she asked of me.

"I won't let you down again," I told her.

"You need to grow up and learn fast, babe," she said. "Can I count on you?"

"Of course you can," I assured her. I was relieved to be back in Lisette's good graces. Trying constantly to please her was exhausting at times, and I had to fight an urge to be defensive or angry when she regarded me with a condescending tone. I still believed that there was a lot I could learn from her. She could be harsh, but I was grateful to have someone around who wanted to push me to grow and be stronger.

"I'm glad you said that, because I need you tonight," she said, looking pleased. "It's actually the perfect way for you to prove your commitment."

"Sure, absolutely," I said. "What is it?"

"The owner of JetSetter Charter is coming into town from the East Coast today and he is bringing Carol," Lisette said. "They want to have dinner tonight and meet me in person. I've made a reservation for four people at the Ivy."

"Fancy," I said. "I'm sure that'll go over well."

"I'm one of their biggest clients, and they're very curious about me," Lisette said. "As you know, Carol has been our contact point for every flight we've chartered."

"Yeah, I remember," I said.

Lisette went on. "Carol is expecting to meet my assistant Stephanie at dinner tonight. You might remember that she's developed quite a rapport with her over the phone. They've never met, and Carol has been excited to finally get to meet her."

"Nice," I said. "That'll be fun for them to meet."

Lisette looked at me straight on and said, "Yeah, well, there's been an unexpected problem. Stephanie wasn't able to fly into L.A. at the last minute. But it's in our best interest to make sure that Carol gets to meet 'Stephanie,' regardless."

"What do you mean?" I asked, confused. "Can't Stephanie just fly in tomorrow for lunch or something?"

"No. Carol is only available tonight," Lisette said. "If Stephanie isn't at the dinner, it could send up a red flag to the company, and we need them for transporting. I need you to come with me and pretend to be Stephanie."

"What?"

"Just be yourself," Lisette jumped in. "You don't need to act any differently. Just answer to a different name. It'll be easy."

"You want me to straight up act like I'm the person she's had dozens of phone calls with? What about the next time Carol talks to the real Stephanie and Stephanie says she was never in L.A.?"

"Obviously I would tell Stephanie and she'd play along with it," Lisette said. She was getting agitated. "This is serious. We need this."

I grasped for some thread of logic that would talk Lisette out of this. "Doesn't Carol know who I am, anyway, from the flight records and the wire transfers?"

"Of course she knows your name, but that's all she knows," Lisette said. "She has no idea what you look like."

"What if I just called her? Like before! You said that my voice sounds similar to Stephanie's. I could just tell her that I got sick and can't make it. Or the real Stephanie could do that. But I can do it if you want! I'm sure that Carol would understand."

"Meili, you're an actress. You should have no problem pretending to be someone you're not. Think of it as a job. Wait, this *is* your job."

I saw no way out of this one. My choices were to either do this or lose my best friend and my job. Lisette had made it pretty clear that if I stopped working for her, she would be upset enough to cut me out of her life completely. I was intensely anxious about meeting Carol. Lisette seemed to notice.

"Oh Jesus, it'll probably be fun," she said. "It'll only be for a couple of hours, and we're going to the goddamn Ivy in a limo. You'll survive."

I went home to get dressed and ready for dinner. Lisette told me to come back to her as soon as I could. Brie was home when I arrived at the apartment. She emerged from her room to greet me. "Looks like I got my job back," I told her as I hurried into my room to decide what to wear to dinner.

"That was fast," Brie said, coming up to stand in my doorway. "How did you get it back? Did Lisette calm down?"

"Uh, yeah, basically," I told her.

She watched me as I selected a black cocktail dress from my closet. "Where are you going?" she asked.

"I'm meeting Lisette for dinner. Sorry, I'm kind of in a hurry." Brie stepped aside so I could pass her on my way to the bathroom. Nerves were building in the pit of my stomach as I took out my curling iron to style my hair. Brie stayed nearby in the hallway. I could feel her studying me.

"Are you okay?" she asked me.

I turned briefly in her direction and nodded. "Mm-hmm, I'm good. I just . . . I'm worried about traffic. I don't want to be late."

LISETTE GREETED ME AT THE door of her penthouse draped in diamonds and a fur coat. "Hi, sweetie!" she said. "Are you ready?"

"Yeah, I think so," I told her.

"You'll be perfect," she said. "Nice necklace."

I was wearing a crystal-studded Louis Vuitton necklace that she gave me. The ring she gave me was on my finger, as usual. Even through the tension in our friendship, I had worn the ring every day as a symbol of our bond.

A black limousine waited for us downstairs. The driver took us a few miles away to the front of a hotel in Beverly Hills. "All right, here we go," Lisette whispered to me as the limo pulled up to a sidewalk. "I told Carol to meet us outside. The owner of JetSetter will be with her. His name is Steve. Here they come." Through the tinted limo windows I saw a blond woman in her early forties walking out of the hotel alongside a tall, dark-haired man of the same age. He wore a suit, and Carol wore a business-style dress. She was beautiful and reminded me a bit of Heather Locklear.

"You get out first," Lisette said, ushering me toward the door. "Go hug Carol and say how good it is to finally meet her or something. Remember, you're Stephanie and you've talked with this woman a hundred times, so don't act like a stranger or it will be weird. Treat her like a long-lost friend."

I took a breath as the driver opened the door for me.

I can do this.

I stepped out of the limo and immediately found myself face-to-face with Carol. She looked excited with a huge smile. "Carol!" I said with a grin to match hers.

"Aw, Stephanie!" she said. "You look just like I imagined!" We embraced warmly.

"It's so good to finally meet you in person," I told her, just as Lisette had instructed.

"I'm just so happy that you were going to be in town while we're here," Carol said. "Great timing, huh?"

"Aha, yes! I know!" I said, laughing along with her.

I can't believe I'm doing this.

Within seconds of meeting her, I already had a sense that Carol was a kind, genuine person. It made me sick to look into her eyes and tell her Lisette's lies.

I noticed that Lisette was out of the limo and standing at my side, waiting to be introduced. "Carol, this is Miss Lee," I said.

Lisette smiled as she shook Carol's hand. "You can call me Lisette," she said.

Carol gestured to the dark-haired man in the suit. "This is Steve," she said.

"What a pleasure it is to meet one of our favorite clients," Steve said, looking Lisette up and down. I didn't imagine that they had many clients who looked like her.

After Carol and Steve had been thoroughly filled up with dinner and lies, we dropped them back off in front of their hotel. I hugged Carol good night, then climbed back into the limo. I sank into my seat. I felt ashamed for having been so dishonest with her. She seemed so open and sincere, and I was the opposite tonight. I was acting like myself most of the evening, but it was all done under a false pretense, so essentially everything that came out of my mouth was a lie.

Lisette was the first to speak once we were alone in the back of the limo. She smirked at me, then said, "A job well done, sweetie." I forced a smile back at her. "Babe, I have to tell you, I'm impressed," she said. "That was quite a performance."

"I should say the same for you," I told her in a drier tone than intended.

"Well, I've had more practice," she said. "But seriously, you did a great job tonight. You really stepped up your game. I'm proud of you."

I was back on the team.

12

THE CRIMINALS

There was a disruption in our plans when we arrived in Ohio for our next trip. It was the dead of winter in the Midwest and snow was heavy on the streets.

We drove from the private airport to an aging Extended Stay hotel on the outskirts of town. This time, rather than leaving a key at the front desk and abandoning our luggage in a room, Lisette said that we needed to wait at the hotel until the merchandise was collected. Frankie, Henry, and I waited with Lisette in a cramped, dingy room containing seventeen suitcases. "Meili, go outside and chirp David," Lisette told me. "They should be here soon. Take the room key with you so you can lead them in."

I called David on my burner phone once I was outside. "Hey," he said, "so there's gonna be a white van comin' any minute. They said they're close by. They got delayed because of the weather. Man, no one can drive in this shit. I already told 'em you'd be there so they know to look for you."

"Okay, thanks," I said. I could see my breath as I spoke. I wasn't used to this kind of cold, not even in Washington. I stood in the dry winter air, moving around to keep some feeling in my legs. I paced and looked out on the parking lot in anticipation of the white van that David had instructed me was coming.

Come on, come on. Let's get this over with so we can check into our hotel and I can get into a hot shower.

After twenty minutes of waiting, I saw a rusty white van creep into the lot. It moved slowly over the icy concrete and blew filthy exhaust in its wake.

This can't be them. I don't want to wait any longer, but please don't let this be who I'm waiting for . . .

The decrepit van stopped in front of me. Just from looking at it, my instinct was to turn away and go inside, but I had a sinking feeling that this was the van I'd been instructed to greet. Two black men sat in the front of the vehicle, both wearing faded black hoodies and looking skittish. They looked at me, sizing me up from inside their van. I lifted my chin to give them a subtle acknowledgment. I'm sure they were just as surprised to see me. Two sets of eyes stared blankly back at me, then they exchanged a look with each other. They pulled the van into a parking space and got out. They walked toward me with their heads down, glancing around them on their way across the lot. The van scared me at first, but these men scared me more. There was something wild in their eyes. I wondered what they saw when they looked into my eyes.

Without a breath of exchange between us, I turned around to access the side entrance of the hotel. I felt exposed and vulnerable with my back to them as I used the key. My hands were shaking. I got the glass door open, and they followed me down the hall to the room. I used my key to enter and was startled by what I saw when the door swung open. The room was dark, save for one floor lamp that cast dim light over the shadows. Lisette and Henry were nowhere to be seen. They were hiding in the bathroom with their ears pressed to the door. Frankie sat facing the entrance in a chair at the back of the room. His six-foot-eight body of muscle was dressed in a full business suit, and he held a stare so menacing that one would have expected him to have his trigger finger on a gun. His massive frame was silhouetted in shadow. He tilted his head to the men. He didn't need to say a word because his message was already loud and clear: *Get what you need, then get the hell out.* I could feel the energy shift behind me.

Thanks, Frankie.

In silence, I assisted the hooded men in hurrying the luggage into their van through a side door down the hall. We never spoke a word to one another.

I watched with intense relief as the van turned out of the parking lot, disappearing into the night as quickly and strangely as it had arrived. I was shaken by what I'd just experienced. I'd tried to keep a stiff lip when they were in the room so as not to show weakness or fear, but with them out of sight I felt both intensely. The men hadn't shown up in a limo, wearing suits, like we did. I don't know what I'd been expecting, but this wasn't it. They came dressed like burglars, with shifty demeanors. These were criminals. But so were we. We were all criminals. This unnerving idea began to sink in. Wearing fancy suits and chartering private jets didn't change the fact that we were just like them in this operation.

I never wanted to be a criminal. I wanted to be an actress. All those scenes from famous crime films that I'd performed at Bonnie Chase's acting studio hadn't prepared me for the real thing. Lisette told me when she hired me that this would be the role of a lifetime. I didn't understand what she meant. It all felt like an innocent game then. Maybe what she said could be true, but I didn't want it to be the role of *my* lifetime. Someone else's, not mine. But the fact remained that I was now actively and consciously working in a criminal enterprise. When I decided to shed my good girl persona and "live a little," I'd planned on wearing tighter pants and partying with Lisette, not smuggling illegal drugs and risking my life ushering thugs into shady hotel rooms to collect suitcases of contraband. I was trapped by decisions I'd already made. I'd built my own cage and I knew it. I'd ridden this slippery slope from the top like a water slide at Magic Mountain. I didn't know what might be waiting for me at the bottom, but I knew that's where I was headed.

LESS THAN A WEEK AFTER we returned from our trip, Lisette sent me to Ohio by myself. "I just need you to pick something up," she said. "We have to get this done before we can leave again." She told me that I'd be collecting money there and wiring it to JetSetter Charter through a local bank. She gave me a ticket for a commercial flight to arrive in Columbus in the afternoon and be on a flight back to L.A. before sundown.

I got a taxi from the airport in Columbus. I went to a suburban shopping area. Once the cab left me, I called David on my burner phone for instructions. "Yo, you there?" he asked me.

"Yeah, I'm here," I told him reluctantly, glancing around me to make sure no one was paying attention.

"You see a parking structure across the street from a little hotel?" he asked.

"Uh, hold on," I said. I walked half a block and turned a corner to see a hotel and two giant parking structures right across from it. I walked up to stand in front of the one closest to me. "Yeah, I got it. I'm right in front," I told him.

"Go inside." David spoke slowly into the phone as he gave me coded instructions. "On the first level there is gonna be a yellow Volkswagen Beetle on your right. It'll be unlocked. The driver just walked away so you guys ain't gonna see each other. You need to pop the trunk from the driver's seat, then grab a bag from the back. The bag is gonna have paperwork in it, and Seven wants that moved through the bank. Call me when you got it from the trunk."

"Right," I whispered into the phone. "I'll talk to you in a minute." I walked into the parking garage and looked around for the car. No yellow Beetle. I walked to the other side of the lot. I called David again.

"You got it?" he said.

"No," I told him. "I can't, um . . . I can't find it."

"The bag's not there? Yo, look again. My guy said it's there."

"No, the car," I told him. "I can't find the car."

"Oh shit, really?" he said. "Hold on, let me call him. Keep lookin'." David called back a minute later. "Are you sure you're in the right garage?" he asked me.

"Yeah, pretty sure," I said. "I mean, it was the first one."

"There's two?" he asked.

"There's another one next to it, yeah," I told him.

"Shit," he said. "Okay, let me call him."

As I stood in the middle of the top level of the garage, I watched a yellow Volkswagen Beetle drive past the entrance and head for what I realized was a third parking garage in the shopping center. I called David. Finally, he said, "Okay. Eight?"

"Yeah?" I said.

"Look, usually we wouldn't want to do this in such an open spot, but this shit is getting complicated. Just go to the parking lot of the hotel. Be fast, though. My guy just left the car."

When I got there, the Volkswagen was unlocked, as David said it would be. I sensed someone watching me from nearby. I glanced over my shoulder before opening the front door to pop the trunk. There was forty thousand dollars in cash ("paperwork") inside of a small duffel bag. I took it and slammed the trunk.

I flagged down another taxi. "Hi, I need to go to the bank," I told the driver. I couldn't remember the exact location of the bank Lisette usually took us to when we'd see Barry. I'd never been the one driving or giving directions, so I didn't have a good sense of where I was in relation to where I'd been. I didn't want to ask Lisette to text me such specific information over the phone, so I winged it.

It can't be that big of a difference to just go to the first bank I see.

The taxi driver took me to a seedy part of town that was completely unfamiliar to me. He pulled up to a bank. "Can you wait for me?" I asked him. "I need to go to the airport right after this."

It's probably good that I didn't use the same cabdriver to and from the airport. That could have raised some suspicion.

The driver reluctantly agreed to wait for me after making it clear that I would be charged for his time. "That's okay! No problem, I'll pay it," I said. "I'll be back soon. Thanks!"

I walked into the bank with the duffel bag. The vibe was tense from the moment I stepped inside. Everyone was looking at me. They were staring. They could tell that something was off. It must have been obvious in every move I made, every cautious step I took, every nervous glance as my eyes darted around the bank.

The teller raised an eyebrow when I told him that I needed to wire forty thousand dollars in cash by the end of the business day. "Ma'am, typically that would require at least a full business day for the funds to be transferred . . ."

Something isn't right.

A bank manager appeared behind the teller when he saw that tension was building. I noticed eyes of other employees peeking out from over their cubicles around the bank.

They're listening.

"I need to wire this to JetSetter Charter," I told the manager with a straight face. He looked at the bag of cash and furrowed his brow.

"I'm just wondering why it needs to be done so quickly," he said. "That is an unusual request, and that's an unusual amount of cash for a young lady to be walking around with. You have to understand. We're not used to seeing this kind of thing. It's . . . unusual." He blinked at me, waiting for a response, but I couldn't think of anything to say. He went on. "Is this your money?"

"It belongs to my boss," I told him, trying to keep myself collected. He could tell that I was nervous. I wasn't used to being asked so many questions. I wanted to take the money and run out of the bank.

I wish that Barry were here. Why didn't I get the address for his bank?

"Who is your boss?" he asked me.

"She's, uh, an heiress . . . to Samsung."

"Samsung, like the phones?" he said.

"Yes, Samsung electronics," I said. "I'll just go ahead and ask her what she'd like me to do." I stepped to the side of the line. He watched me carefully, then whispered something to one of the tellers. The manager disappeared into the back of the bank.

He's going to call someone. What is he doing?

I texted Lisette for help.

WHY DIDN'T YOU GO SEE BARRY? she asked. She was livid, and I could see why. THAT IS THE ONLY BANK WE GO TO THERE. I DON'T KNOW ANYONE AT THE BRANCH YOU'RE AT. SHIT. GIVE ME THEIR PHONE NUMBER. I'LL CALL IN.

The bank manager reappeared and looked at me expectantly.

Maybe he didn't call anyone after all.

I didn't know who he would call or what he would say, but I knew that he found my behavior "unusual," which meant that he didn't believe a word I was saying. "She is going to call," I told him.

"Wonderful," he said. A phone rang behind him. A teller answered, then handed the manager the phone. It was Lisette. I couldn't hear much of their conversation behind the glass. He was doing a lot of nodding.

Is that good?

I could hear the employees whispering about me.

This is taking too long.

My heart pounded.

God only knows what Lisette said to him, but it worked. She'd always known how to persuade people; I had to give her that. By some small miracle, the manager let me complete the wire transfer to JetSetter. I walked out the door with my mission complete. I resisted an instinct to sprint into the parking lot and tell the cabdriver to hit the gas.

I had sweated through my blazer by the time I climbed back into the taxi to return to the airport.

PART THREE
CRASHING

13

LOST IN COLUMBUS

Team LL was scheduled to be in Ohio on February 14, but we would be returning to Los Angeles that evening, just in time for me to see Ben and celebrate my first Valentine's Day with a boyfriend. I'd always been envious watching girls be given stuffed animals by their valentines, and though it was a petty, adolescent wish, I was secretly hoping that Ben would give me one. I didn't care what kind of stuffed animal it was. I would have been happy with a Beanie Baby, as long as it was from him.

On the eve of the Hallmark holiday, Lisette and I were ready for bed in our shared Columbus hotel room. As Lisette sat cross-legged on one of our queen beds in her pajamas, I showed her the greeting card that I'd bought for Ben. "I looked at a ton of cards in the store, but I thought this one was perfect," I told her. I'd never bought a card for a love interest on Valentine's before, and I'd spent an egregious amount of time trying to pick the right one. I lay on my stomach and rested my elbows on a pillow as she examined the card in her hand and read the front of it aloud.

"Okay, here we go. 'I have fallen in love many times,'" she read. Her expression went from vaguely curious to amused. "Oh," she said, laughing, "that's a great thing to tell someone. Make the boy feel special. I'm liking this card more and more."

"No," I insisted. "Read the inside." She frowned.

"Okay. 'I have fallen in love many times . . .'" She opened the card to read the continued message on the inside. "' . . . always with you.'" She closed the card and tossed it away from her on the bed. "That's very . . . romantic," she said. "I'm sure he'll love it."

I got up and grabbed two sealed envelopes from my suitcase. "And of course I got a card for my girl too," I said. "Okay, maybe two."

Lisette's eyes lit up. She grabbed the cards and said with a smug grin, "Well, shit, I hope so, after that mush you made me read. My cards better be mushier."

I bought two Valentine's Day cards for Lisette instead of one, as I'd usually get her, because I didn't want her to feel sensitive about my plans with a boyfriend this year. She appeared alternately moved and entertained as she read my messages on each card. The message in one of them was a heartfelt, wordy profession of sentiments, and the other card was meant for humor. Lisette finished reading both and gave me a hug. "Thank you, sweetie, those mean a lot to me," she said. "Now you have to open your card!" She looked excited as she went to her purse and took out a large pink envelope.

"Aw! It's so big!" I said, gently opening it. On the front of the card there was a colorful picture of Tinker Bell smiling and sprinkling glittery dust into the air. I opened the card and read Lisette's handwritten message:

> *Angel,*
>
> > *Because to me you are a magical little fairy that flew into my life and sprinkled your glitter of love, friendship, loyalty, laughs, our tears, our hugs, our sneaky times, and so much more into my heart and soul, I got you this card. I thought I had it all before you, but after experiencing true love and heartfelt do-or-die friendship with my "alter ego" BFF, I now know what I was missing. Your place in my heart is forever and primary till my last breath.*
>
> > > *I love you my Angel love,*
> > > *Allegra-Lisette Lee Morita*

I looked up from her card with tears in my eyes. "Thank you," I said. "That was beautiful." Lisette appeared to be near tears too—a rare side of her that almost no one saw. I felt blessed whenever I saw her like this. We set our cards aside and stayed awake talking and giggling from our respective beds until we drifted into sleep.

In the morning, Team LL hustled to get ready to head to the private airport. I woke up beaming, knowing that it was now officially Valentine's Day and I was going to see Ben tonight. Lisette got ready before me. She left our room and went into the adjoining room where Frankie and Henry had stayed. I dressed and packed up my personal suitcase. I took a pair of earrings from the bedside table that I'd placed there the night before. With the earrings on, I looked around the bedside table for my diamond ring. I wore it every day, but it was too big to comfortably sleep with, so I always took it off and set it aside before I went to bed. I didn't see it on the table. I'd been drinking with Lisette last night, so I might have put it somewhere else and forgotten. I couldn't remember. I could have sworn I'd put it with my earrings. I leaned down to see if perhaps it had fallen behind the table. It wasn't there. Panic began to rise in me. I dropped to my knees and crawled around on the stale hotel room carpet, lowering my body to look underneath both beds. I frantically prayed that I'd find it before Lisette discovered that I'd lost it. I stood up and scanned the floor in the room. I rushed to the bathroom to check if I'd left my ring by the sink. It wasn't in the bathroom.

Where the hell is it?

My phone beeped with a text message from Lisette. **BABE COME TO THE ROOM. WE HAVE TO LEAVE,** she wrote. Adrenaline and despair came over me in a sickening wave. The door between the adjoining rooms swung open and Lisette walked in. "Babe, what are you doing?" she asked me. "We have to go." I faced her, frozen for a moment. "What's wrong?" she asked.

My heart sank as I told her, "I can't find my ring." Her eyes widened. She stared at me in silence for a moment. "I'm still looking for it," I said. "I thought I left it by the bed, but it's not there. I looked everywhere in the room. Do you think maybe it's in the guys' room?" Lisette stood with her arms stiff at her sides. She looked away from me and took a deep breath.

"I don't know," she said. "I guess we should check." She looked pissed. Lisette walked into the guys' room. I followed her. "Meili lost her ring," she announced to Frankie and Henry, who were standing among ten suitcases with their shoes on, ready to leave for the airport.

"Are you fucking serious?" Frankie asked. I could feel tears filling my eyes, threatening to fall down my cheeks. I nodded.

Frankie, Lisette, and Henry helped me search around both adjoining rooms until Lisette finally said, "We have to go. I guess it's gone forever." She wouldn't look at me. It broke my heart to leave our hotel, knowing that my beloved ring must still be there somewhere.

On the drive to the airport Henry and Frankie both gave me the cold shoulder. Lisette seemed wounded and indignant. On the plane, I sat in shame. By the time we were airborne and en route to L.A., I unraveled, sobbing into my hands. I couldn't help it. I was overcome with guilt. The pilots could hear me, and their discomfort only added to the already heavy tension on the plane.

I'd never been more devastated over the loss of something material. I would never have pawned the ring or had it appraised, so the monetary loss was beside the point. I couldn't believe that I'd lost the ring that Lisette gave me. It was a symbol of our friendship, and I'd carelessly lost track of it. The symbolism was obvious to everyone on the plane, and to none more than Lisette. She came to stand by me where I sat, pressing my face into my palms. "Stop crying," she said. "We left our information at the hotel. They're going to call us if it turns up. Though I doubt anyone would turn it in if they found it."

"I don't even know what to say," I told her, trying to breathe. She stared at me behind a stoic expression.

"I know it was an accident," she said. "Accidents happen. But the thing that gets me, what really hurts . . . is that I can't help but wonder if you would have lost the ring if Ben was the one who'd given it to you."

Her words cut me. "What?" I said, looking up. "No, Lisette, if I lost the one you gave me, then I'd just as easily have lost it if it had been from him or anyone." She watched me as I began to collect myself.

"I'm upset," she said. "I'll be honest, I'm really hurt . . . But I forgive you." This choked me up even more.

"Thanks," I said, rubbing my now puffy red face with my hands. "I think I'm going to cancel my plans with Ben tonight."

"Don't do that," Lisette said. "I know how much you've been looking forward to it." She abruptly turned away from me and walked back down the aisle to her seat.

I was completely deflated and emotionally exhausted by the time we arrived back in Los Angeles. I went home with a heavy heart to wait for Ben to meet me at my apartment. I was no longer excited about celebrating now, but I wanted to make some effort to be in a better mood to avoid ruining not only Lisette's Valentine's Day, but Ben's too. If a girlfriend were to ever cancel on a guy, it shouldn't be on Valentine's Day. I changed into a dress and sat on my bed to wait for him. I opened his card to fill it out before he arrived. I'd planned to write him a thoughtful, long message, but I didn't have it in me right now. I simply wrote "I love you" and sealed the envelope. Brie was home, and when there was a knock on our door, she offered to let Ben in. I breathed out, trying to overcome my devastation about losing the ring and put on a happy face for my boyfriend.

Ben walked into my bedroom holding a bouquet of a dozen red roses, a card with my name on it, and a stuffed teddy bear with a red bow around its neck. "Happy Valentine's Day," he said as he set everything down and wrapped his arms around me.

In lieu of a fancy dinner with a reservation, we walked to the late-night diner at the Roosevelt Hotel to get grilled cheese sandwiches and tomato soup. I hadn't thought it was possible after such a disastrous morning in Ohio, but against the odds, Ben and I shared an incredible Valentine's night together. When he left my bed in the morning to go home and study, the teddy bear took his place in my arms. I slept in after he left, holding the bear close to me like a security blanket. I may not have had the ring anymore, but I had the stuffed animal I'd always wanted, and at that moment it was worth more to me than any diamond.

14

NO REST FOR THE WICKED

After the ring debacle, Lisette told me in an impersonal message that we wouldn't be flying to Columbus that week, but that I should be prepared to leave "soon," as always.

Lisette refused to pay anyone in advance of trips to Ohio. I'd been overdrawn in my checking account more than once while we'd flown out on a private jet. The irony weighed heavily on me—the in-flight champagne doesn't taste as good when you know you're broke. I drank it anyway. What else was I going to do? At this point, I was so shell-shocked by everything that had been happening that I doubted I could keep my wits about me in another job. I felt such a departure from normal society now that I was uncomfortable when I was in it.

I couldn't come to terms with the reality I'd created for myself. My decisions stared back at me every time I looked in the mirror, and I had nothing to say for them. I had never openly discussed what was happening with Lisette, and I couldn't go to anyone else at that point. Every opportunity to turn back was behind me now. I drank every night just to try to sleep, and when I did finally sleep, I had nightmares. I dreamed that I was being chased. The people chasing me varied from police officers to Mexican gang members. I usually woke up right before they caught me, or, in the case of the gang members, right before they were going to kill me. I had a haunting dream one night that I was hanging by my fingers on the edge of a cliff and Lisette was looking down at me as I screamed out to her for help. She turned and walked away casually, leaving me there to die. I woke up from every nightmare covered in sweat and frantic to check my phone and see if Lisette had texted me.

AS MUCH AS I DIDN'T want to go on more trips or smuggle more drugs, I needed cash. I was running out of money. Weeks had passed since the last trip to Ohio, but Lisette continued to instruct me to wire large sums of cash to JetSetter Charter. She said that the money would go toward future jet rentals, but I suspected that trips were happening without me. I wondered if, on some level, she wanted to punish me for loving someone else. She knew that I was almost broke again. Was it possible she was intentionally punishing me by depriving me of income? Whenever I brought up the idea of getting a second job, she discouraged me from doing so, saying that she needed me to be available, that we'd be leaving again "any day now." I felt a little guilty for thinking she might be hiding things from me. I tried to kick my suspicions, but my gut feeling was becoming hard to ignore—hard, though not impossible. I was already in a habit of disregarding any gut feelings that weren't in line with my employ or friendship with Lisette.

Brie had witnessed my erosion in stability and any notable joy. She watched me pacing the hardwood floors in our apartment, paranoid of cryptic texts from Lisette and anxious about the increasing fragility of my romance with Ben. The new prescription drugs he was taking had changed him, and our relationship had taken a sad, sharp turn for the worse. His once constant adoration and affection for me had diminished to what seemed like apathy, and I didn't know if it was the drugs or if he'd finally tired of my secrets. Anyone would have tired of them eventually, and perhaps his new prescription cocktail had merely sped up the inevitable. I knew I would never be the one to leave him; I was still holding on to the memory of the happiness I'd experienced. But our relationship was doomed either way. Lisette had never approved of him. I'd sworn years ago to spend my life with Lisette, and without her blessing I could never feel entirely content with someone else.

The dozen roses that Ben had given me for Valentine's Day were on their last leg of life in a black glass vase in our dining room. I hadn't heard from him for hours one afternoon, and I was paranoid that he'd purposely been ignoring me. Brie was home, sketching in her bedroom with her door open. An Edith Piaf song played through her computer speakers, and a glass of red wine sat at her bedside. I'd been nursing a bottle of Seagram's since noon, but it hadn't done much to calm my nerves. I went outside to smoke a cigarette and finish a vodka soda. When I came back in, I set the now empty glass down and took one last look at my cell phone. Still nothing from Ben. And still, nothing from Lisette. What the hell was I waiting to hear from either of them anyway? I stared at the phone like it was going to tell me something that could make everything okay. But everything wasn't okay, and it wasn't going to be.

Anger swelled inside of me, momentarily eclipsing my anxiety. I wanted to hurt something. I wanted to make something broken, the way that I felt broken.

I went to my room and snatched from my bed the teddy bear that Ben had given to me. Brie glanced up from her sketch pad as I passed her door. I carried the bear into the kitchen and tossed it into the center of the tile floor. I lifted the dozen roses from their vase in the dining room. I took them into the kitchen and dropped them over my beloved bear, like tossing flowers onto a casket before it's lowered into the ground. Adrenaline pulsed through me as I returned to my room and took two cards from a box in my closet: the card that Ben had given me for Valentine's Day, and the card that I'd given to him. He'd left the card I bought for him at my apartment after he read it. I'd tried to ignore the way he seemed to scoff at it. I assumed he was offended that I'd only written "I love you" as a message. I'd thought that said it all. He, on the other hand, had a veritable novella inside of his card to me. I paused for a brief moment and reread his card.

Where the wordy prefixed message ended, a handwritten one began, and Ben added his own effusion of affection. In the bottom right corner, he wrote, "I love you." It made me queasy to read this and know that our relationship wouldn't last, as I'd hoped it would. It all seemed unreal now.

I left my room to add both cards to the pile in the kitchen. Brie watched me as I passed her door again, with Edith Piaf's romantic croon drifting out from behind it. The kitchen tile was cold under my bare feet. I calmly opened a drawer and grasped the biggest knife I could find. I knelt down in front of the pile, took in one short breath, then lifted the knife in the air. The blade struck down blindly into the pile. Blood rushed through me as I stabbed faster, harder. I heard a scream bellow out of me as I brought the knife down through the pile and onto the dense tile. Again, again. I couldn't destroy everything fast enough. I set the knife down for a moment so that I could rip into pieces the card that I'd given to Ben. I snapped the stems of the roses in half and ripped off their crimson petals. Their beauty seemed to mock me, tempting me to believe that the beautiful moments in life would last. But they had all died, just like the roses in the vase. I wanted to destroy them before the last petal could fall. I grabbed Ben's Valentine's card to me and began to cut into the center of it, nearly tearing it in half. Suddenly, I took the knife out and set the card aside, disturbed by the thought of destroying what might be the only existing testimony that Ben had once loved me. I spared the card and picked up the teddy bear. In my hands the bear felt so soft, so comforting. I'd slept with it every night since Ben had given it to me. But holding on to this bear would mean holding on to false hope. I laid the bear on the tile, on his back, and I began to stab into him. His unchanging, woven expression stared up and at me as I dismembered his body, beginning with his ridiculous, fluffy legs. The legs and arms came off easily with the help of the blade, but removing the bear's head took some doing. Brie heard the commotion, and she walked into the kitchen just as I was sawing the bear's head off with a now dull blade. Without a word, she stopped at the doorway and watched me from a safe distance.

After the bear had been taken out and the roses shredded, my hysteria turned from cries to laughter. Then silence. I sat down on the tile, drunk on hard liquor and desperation, and stared at my work. The tip of the knife in my hand was bent from blows to the floor, and my palm was white and red from holding it. I released the knife. It made a loud clanking sound as it hit the tile. Brie leaned against the door frame, sipping red wine from her glass. I looked up at her. She stared at the bear's detached head on the kitchen floor. "I think he's dead," she said in a dry tone. We both let out an uncomfortable laugh.

When Ben called me in the evening, I told him that the bear was gone. "I've been so stressed," I said. "I don't know what to do. I don't know what's wrong with me. I feel like I'm losing my mind."

"What happened to the bear?" he asked.

"Uh . . . the bear met a rather untimely and . . . er, violent end . . ." I said.

"Oh God." He laughed, lightening the mood. "Do I even want to know?"

"Probably not," I said, cringing at how crazy my behavior seemed in retrospect. "But I miss the little guy now, for what it's worth. I'm in mourning."

"You must have been really pissed if you hurt the bear," he said. "You loved that thing."

Ben came to my apartment late in the evening after studying for an upcoming test. He said that he wanted to go to bed immediately, in the hope of getting some sleep before another long day of studying. He gave me a quick kiss when he walked into my apartment, but he seemed preoccupied with other thoughts. He went straight to the bathroom to get ready for bed. After a few minutes, the bathroom door opened and he came out. "Is my contact solution in your room?" he asked.

"No, I don't see it," I said. Ben put his shoes on at the door.

"What are you doing?" I asked, with a terrible feeling in my stomach.

"I think I have some solution in my car," he said.

"Okay," I said, "I'll come with you."

"No, no," he said. "You don't have to do that. I'll be right back."

He walked out the door and into the night. Something inside me said that he wasn't coming back, but I tried not to listen to it. Brie wasn't home, and the apartment was deathly quiet. I was alone with my thoughts. Minutes passed. I sat still, waiting.

Where is he? It shouldn't take this long to get something from his car. Was that just an excuse? Did something snap in him and he realized that he didn't want to be here?

Another minute passed. I couldn't stand the idea of waiting any longer to find out. I ran to the door and put my Ugg boots on. Wearing only a flimsy, pale nightdress, I hurried down the stairs of my apartment and sprinted down the street toward where I knew he'd parked his car. I was out of breath by the time I reached the spot. His car wasn't there. He did leave. It wasn't in my head.

I turned around and walked straight back to my apartment. I took my shoes off at the door and went into the bedroom. I sat in shock, motionless on my bed.

I heard some noise at the front door. Someone was trying to get it. It occurred to me that I'd left it unlocked. I heard the door open and a man's shoes walking on the hardwood floors of our living room.

Ben appeared at my bedroom door with a grocery bag in one hand and a fuzzy stuffed animal, a rabbit, in the other. "I didn't find any contact solution in my car," he said, "so I went to the market." He held up the stuffed animal in his hand. "And I figured you needed a new one of these." He smiled at me with tired eyes. I got up and threw my arms around his waist.

A SHORT TIME LATER, LISETTE invited me to her condo to have drinks and discuss an upcoming trip. "Are you still seeing Ben?" she asked.

"I thought you didn't want to hear about him," I told her.

"Oh, come on," she said. "It's just us right now. You can tell me." I said nothing. "It's not like I don't know," she snapped. "I'm not stupid. I know you're still seeing him." She took a drink of Bombay Sapphire on the rocks. "It's okay. It's your life."

"Yeah, well, we'll see what happens," I said.

"*I'll* see what happens," she said. "I don't trust him. I've asked my PI to tail him for me. Just for a while. I want to see what he's up to."

"You put a private investigator on Ben?" I asked her.

"Don't get too excited," she said. "It's not like I went out of my way.

You know that I keep a PI on retainer. I thought he needed something to do anyway; otherwise, what am I paying him for? You should be glad I'm doing this, sweetie. Now you'll know if Ben starts seeing someone else. You never know what people are capable of."

"I appreciate the thought, but this is completely unnecessary," I told her. "You don't need to do this."

Lisette shrugged and said, "I'll be the judge of that. It's just a very basic tail, sweetie. It's nothing to freak out about."

ON ST. PATRICK'S DAY, BEN came over to my apartment late in the evening. I'd expected him earlier, and I'd become increasingly anxious as I waited for him to arrive. Almost two hours after he said he'd be here, he walked in the door in a gruff mood. "Sorry I'm late," he said. "Can we please just go to bed?"

"Where were you?" I asked.

"These chicks asked me for a ride when I was at the market," he said. "They said their car wasn't working or something."

"And you gave them a ride?"

"Yeah."

"Did you know them?" I asked.

"No. I mean, it wasn't that far away."

"But it took you two hours . . ." I said. "You would have been here two hours ago."

"Listen, I don't want to talk about this," he said. "I'm so fucking tired."

"I'm not," I told him from where I sat on the couch. "I couldn't sleep at all if I tried to right now. I've . . . got a lot on my mind."

"Just do a shot or something," he said. "That usually seems to work for you . . ."

"I'm out of alcohol," I told him.

"Let's walk to the liquor store," he said. "After that we can come back and go to bed."

At the liquor store, I bought a handful of minibottles of vodka. Shortly after returning to the apartment, Ben took his nightly sleeping pill and lay down in my bed. I stood by him in a white satin nightie and drank through the tiny bottles of liquor. He frowned as he reached out and pinched the side of my stomach. "You're so skinny right now," he said.

"Okay . . ." I said, not sure if this was meant to be an insult or a compliment.

"You've lost a lot of weight . . ." he said. "At least ten pounds since we started dating." I ignored him and opened another minibottle. "Were you trying to lose weight, or . . . ?"

"I don't know," I said. "Not really."

"Geez," he said, "you think you're drinking those fast enough?"

I glared at him. "You're the one who was in such a hurry to go to bed."

"I still am," he said. He put his earplugs in and settled down into the covers.

I couldn't help but wonder about the girls Ben gave a ride to. I wouldn't ask him any more about them, but I had a feeling that there must have been some interest there. Ben was an okay guy, but I'd never call him philanthropic. I couldn't imagine him going out of his way to give a stranger a ride, especially so late in the evening, if he didn't have some ulterior motive. I crawled onto the bed and sat upright next to where Ben was lying, turned away from me now. The alcohol was taking effect. I wondered if it was possible to ever go back to the way things were, if we were ever going to at least try. I started to cry. Ben heard me and turned over. He was instantly irritated. "What?! Why are you crying? Seriously, I need to sleep!"

"What are we doing here?" I asked.

"I don't know what you're doing, but I'm trying to sleep," he said.

"Can we please talk about this?" I asked him.

He took one earplug out and said, "If you wanted to have this talk, you could have done it earlier. I have to get some sleep. It's the one thing I want right now."

"I just don't know what to do," I said. "I'm scared. Lisette said that she's having a private investigator follow you. I don't know what she wants. She might be bluffing, but I don't know."

Ben looked at me incredulously. "This is crazy. This shit's getting out of hand," he said. "I don't know what to say when you tell me stuff like that."

"What am I supposed to do?" I asked him.

"I don't know what to tell you," he said. He lay back down and turned away from me. "All I know is I'm tired and I don't want to talk about this or anything right now. I just want to sleep."

I tried to wipe my tears away, but more streamed down my face. "Ben, please," I said. "I just want to talk for a few minutes. I can't sleep otherwise." He said nothing back to me. "Ben?" I leaned in to see that he was wearing both earplugs again.

"Go to sleep," he said. Unable to contain my emotion, I got up from the bed.

"I'm going to sleep in Brie's room," I said.

"Don't," he said, a warning tone in his voice. "Don't be stupid."

"No, I can't sleep right now," I said. "I'll leave you alone."

In the morning, I woke up alone on top of the covers of Brie's bed. I felt a sick sadness in my stomach from the moment I opened my eyes. I stared up into the whiteness of her ceiling. My eyes were swollen from crying, so much so that it obscured my vision. I shuddered as I remembered the way Ben had looked at me as I sobbed. He was angry. He thought I was pathetic. He saw how weak I had become, and of course it was repulsive to him. He watched with disgust as I sucked down minibottles of vodka before bed, desperately seeking tranquillity. As if he had any right to judge me. He had his sleeping pills and his earplugs and his harsh words to me before he fought for sleep. I was fighting for the same thing, but my weapons were alcohol to drown my awareness and tears to exhaust myself into rest, like a child who needed to be rocked to sleep.

I walked quietly back to my room where Ben was asleep in my bed. Morning light cracked through the blinds of my window, but the air inside remained cold and lifeless. I took great care not to disturb Ben as I crawled back into bed next to him. I knew that I'd deprived him of sleep last night, and I didn't want to wake him abruptly. I lay on my side in the fetal position. His body was turned away from me. I reached my hand out to gently touch his back to let him know that I'd returned. His skin lacked any warmth, as did his reaction to my touch. I could feel now that he was only pretending to be asleep, and that his muscles were tense and determined not to acknowledge me.

I wanted him to understand that I hadn't slept in Brie's room to be cruel to him. It was somehow less painful for me to sleep there. I was able to take some small comfort in knowing that he was in the other room. That way it was easier for me to pretend that it wasn't over between us and that he still felt some affection for me. I could still imagine that if I'd been next to him that he would have made love to me, or even just held me in his arms the way he used to, not long ago. Next to him, I would have known that all this was merely a fantasy I was clinging to.

In the beginning of my relationship with Ben, I saw incredible happiness in my future. As the months went on, though, I'd watched with a breaking heart as life and love faded from our relationship. In blind desperation, I'd hung my last hope for happiness on my future with Ben. But I knew that he would leave me. If I'd had the choice, I'd leave me too. I couldn't stand what I'd become. I was stuck with me and this bizarre, unbearable reality that was suffocating me.

I carefully slipped out of bed and walked to the bathroom to begin getting ready for work. I washed my face and dabbed concealer on the deep circles under my eyes. I heard the door of my apartment slam shut. I dropped my makeup brush onto the linoleum floor and ran out of the bathroom. Holding my breath, I threw open the door to my apartment and looked below me to see Ben walking away, toward the street. I shouted his name, but he didn't respond. "Ben!" I called after him again, my voice shaking. "Where are you going?" Without turning to look at me he called back, "I'm going. I have to go."

I watched from the top of my stairs as he turned the corner and walked out of my life. I didn't have time to run after him, and no time to cry. I went back inside to finish my makeup.

As I applied foundation to my face, I felt as though I was painting a cadaver. I couldn't look distraught when Lisette saw me, so I buried everything I was feeling. I dabbed pink blush on my cheeks to give the illusion of liveliness. I zipped up my black pencil skirt and grabbed my blazer, then drove to meet Lisette and the rest of Team LL at her penthouse.

15

WRITTEN ON THE WALL

In the spring of 2010, David left the operation, with Ko shortly to follow. Lisette and David's relationship, both personal and professional, had soured. They'd lost whatever trust they'd had in the beginning. Lisette had accused David of mishandling money and lying to her, and he responded by calling her a "crazy bitch" who thought this was "all a game." I wasn't present when any of this went down, but vague details were filtered through Lisette. I didn't know what to believe since I was hearing only one side of it, and frankly I didn't care about the details. It was all done behind closed doors, and I never knew the full story on anything anyway, so I stopped trying to keep track. Lisette had somehow managed to get ahold of David's weed supplier, Jose, and she had every intention of carrying on without David. In a time when she might have counted her losses and folded the entire operation, she was adamant about moving forward without David as a partner. Now she was working with Jose, who in her eyes was more powerful than David, and closer to the "gangster" fantasy she'd seen play out in her favorite movies. She told everyone on the team to delete David's phone number.

Henry was the next to go. Team LL was falling apart, after less than six months since our first trip to Ohio. Lisette had broken off her romance with Henry a few weeks before, but he'd continued to work for her. During our recent trip, it had occurred to me that perhaps I wasn't the only one on Team LL with a broken heart. I can't speak for him; I can only guess what he might have felt. Watching him try to keep his distance from her when we were traveling, I wondered how he was handling everything. She was snappy and impersonal toward him, but he remained strong and kind in return. He seemed to genuinely care for her. It was almost as if Lisette enjoyed the possibility that she'd made him miserable. I'd developed a kind of camaraderie with Henry, but to abide by Lisette's expectations, I tried not to engage in conversation with him. Shortly after we returned to L.A., Lisette announced that Henry had been fired.

Maybe he was fired, maybe he left voluntarily. I don't know. I'd like to think that he caught wise and left. Henry always seemed like a smart guy, and he certainly deserved more than Lisette was offering him.

IT WAS TWO WEEKS AFTER Ben walked out of my apartment, and I'd been given no work to do for Lisette. Again, I wondered if trips were happening without me. I'd seen how much she'd enjoyed watching Henry in pain, and I couldn't kick the thought that maybe she liked to see me suffer too. I couldn't believe I was thinking these things about the person I'd called my best friend for years. But I'd seen her betray other people. Why not me next? I didn't feel protected the way I used to. I still saw her socially, but only when she invited me. I hung out with her now more out of obligation than genuine interest; she had never taken well to rejection, and if I didn't have a very good reason for not seeing her, it could cause problems that I didn't have the energy for. Part of me, the part that had never listened to reason, still loved her as I always had, but another part of me feared her and saw her as a dangerous stranger. I tried not to let her see how conflicted I was, but she could tell that my affection for her was circling the drain. I never asked when I could see her because I hardly cared. I felt very little. Numbness was a welcome change for me. I secretly wished that she would fire me for good, though I didn't know what I would do if she did.

Around that time, I was invited to a party on a small, private yacht in Marina del Rey. It was the first time I'd gone out and felt like a part of the living world in quite a while. The fresh air in the marina was invigorating from the moment I stepped off the dock onto the tethered yacht. The drinks were cold and the company was welcoming. I was halfway through my first beer when I got a text from Lisette.

HI ANGEL! GREAT NEWS! I CANCELED MY MEETINGS TODAY AND YOU'RE COMING OVER! WE'RE GOING TO BED BATH & BEYOND TO GET SOME STUFF FOR MY NEW CONDO! WHEN CAN YOU BE HERE? I MISS YOU XOXO.

Lisette had recently moved into an even more expensive, more regal-looking building on Wilshire Corridor. Her penthouse was enormous and as of yet unfurnished, save for her mirrored bedroom furniture. I texted her back saying that I couldn't join her because I was at a party in the marina. I knew she wouldn't like hearing this, especially the fact that I was with other friends, but what the hell did she want me to do? Drop everything I was doing, everyone I was with, and go to her? No. It wasn't like that anymore. She responded to me ten minutes later, saying **NO PROBLEM**, and telling me that she had already assigned one of her "army of skanks" devotees to join her instead. I'd never met any of these other friends she'd said she grew up with, her army of skanks. I wondered sometimes if they even existed. The pictures on their MySpace profiles never changed, not in four years. Unless every one of them had packed on eighty pounds and didn't want to update their photos, it didn't make sense. People change their photos, they just do. It was difficult to imagine that Lisette would create such an embarrassing lie to make it seem like she had other loyal friends, but who knew?

I remembered once, years ago, when I was present for a fight between Lisette and her sommelier ex-boyfriend. I was on the sidelines of their screaming match, and her boyfriend said something that truly shocked me. He called her a liar. He'd turned to me and said, "Meili, you do know that she's a pathological liar, don't you?" I was so taken aback by that. I thought he was just throwing out unfounded accusations. I'd never thought of her as a liar, and I'd forgotten that he'd said that until recently. Now, in these past months, the memory of his words had come back to me. I had never caught Lisette in a lie, but I wondered sometimes if maybe her ex-boyfriend had legitimate reasons for saying that.

I was enjoying perfect weather on the roof of the yacht when I got another text from Lisette.

OMG BABE—GOOD THING YOU DIDN'T COME WITH ME TODAY. MOTHERFUCKING BEN IS HERE SHOPPING WITH SOME DUMB BROAD NEW GIRLFRIEND. UNBELIEVABLE. THEY ARE TWO PEOPLE AHEAD OF ME IN LINE RIGHT NOW. I'M FIGHTING A STRONG URGE TO PUNCH HIM IN THE BACK OF HIS HEAD.

I excused myself from a conversation with a friend and went downstairs to sit by myself on the lower level of the boat.

I just breathed and looked out on the water, taking a moment by myself before I texted Lisette back.

ARE YOU SURE IT WAS HIM? I asked. DID HE SEE YOU?

IT WAS DEFINITELY HIM, she said. I'D KNOW THAT FUCKING SHIT FACE ANYWHERE. HE DIDN'T SEE ME. HE'S TOO DUMB, AND HE WAS FOCUSING ALL OF HIS ATTENTION ON HIS NEW WHORE. IT WAS DISGUSTING.

My stomach twisted with nausea at the thought of Ben's hands on another woman, especially so soon after we'd broken up.

ARE YOU SURE THEY WERE TOGETHER? I asked her.

POSITIVE, she wrote. IF YOU WANT TO KNOW MORE, YOU CAN MEET ME FOR DINNER TONIGHT WHEN YOU'RE DONE WITH THE PARTY.

I did my best to have a good time during the remainder of the party. Getting Lisette's texts had brought up a wave of feelings, but I was determined not to let myself be swept away by them. When the sun began to sink in the watery skyline of the marina, the guests on the yacht reached for their sweaters. I took this as my cue to leave.

Lisette told me to meet her in the valet area of her building so that we could ride together to a nearby Indian restaurant. She appeared to be in an unusually chipper mood when I climbed into her shimmering white Bentley. "How was the party?" she asked me as she drove.

"It was fine," I said, distracted by a head full of questions about Ben's mystery girlfriend at Bed Bath & Beyond.

I walked into the restaurant wearing shorts and a sweatshirt, with an uneven sunburn and a layer of salt on my skin from the ocean breeze. Lisette was her usual put-together self, with thick yet skillfully layered makeup and shiny, dark hair falling elegantly down her back. When the waiter came to our table, Lisette ordered a sizable variety plate from the menu. "I'm starving," she said. I ordered a hot tea that I didn't plan on drinking.

"So what do you want to know?" she asked me from across the table.

"Um," I said, "I don't know . . . what did she look like?"

"She was blond, looked kind of like a cheerleader type," Lisette said. "She looked like that Hayden Pannaberry actress from TV, whatever the hell her name is. Really annoying."

"Was she pretty?" I asked.

Lisette thought for a moment, then said, "Babe, I mean, do you want me to lie to you?"

"No," I told her.

"She was pretty. Annoying though. She kept laughing really loudly."

The waiter brought me my tea. I took the tea bag out of its package and put it into the hot water. Lisette studied me.

"I'm surprised you're taking this so well," she said. "Usually you'd be on the floor by now."

"I know," I said. "I guess I'm out of tears for this guy . . . Time to move on." Lisette pursed her lips and nodded.

"I'm trying to think of what else," she said. "I know how you're obsessed with details, so I don't want to leave anything out."

"What else is there?" I asked. The waiter brought Lisette's meal. She dug in right away, taking in hearty forkfuls of Indian food. My fully steeped tea was untouched in front of me on the table. "What were they buying?" I asked.

"A bunch of stuff, like household stuff. They were so cheesy—they had His and Hers bathrobes and a bunch of scented candles. Made me want to yak."

"When you say 'household stuff,' what do you mean?" I asked. "Like stuff for an apartment?" I felt my heart pounding faster in my chest.

Lisette nodded with a mouthful of food. "Mm-hmm." She swallowed her bite. "Yeah, like they were moving in together or something." My knees felt weaker by the second.

His and Hers bathrobes? Moving in together? I was supposed to be the one moving in with Ben.

Lisette stared at me. "Are you okay, sweetie?" she asked. "How does this make you feel?"

"Ha. Uh, not particularly good," I said.

"I'm really shocked you're not crying," she said. "You must have found your strength."

"Yeah, I guess. I just have one more question," I said, giving in to a masochistic curiosity.

"What is it?" Lisette asked.

"Did you hear either of them say 'I love you'?" Lisette set her fork down and looked at me, then turned away like she didn't want to say it. She nodded.

"Yeah, I think I heard that," she said, grabbing a piece of naan from her plate.

"Did she say it to him, or he said it to her?" I asked, on my last leg of strength.

"I heard him say it to her," Lisette told me. "She probably said it to him too. It was hard to hear everything. They were all over each other in line. That's probably why he never noticed me. He kept coming up to her from behind and putting his arms around her and kissing her neck. It was gross."

I stared at her and sat for a minute in silence. I could feel the meager wall of strength I'd managed to build beginning to crumble. "He told her that he loved her?" I asked.

"Yeah," Lisette said matter-of-factly. She casually dipped a piece of naan into a puddle of orange sauce on her plate.

I rested my elbows on the table and leaned onto them. I dropped my face into my hands, as if to try to block everything out and keep my feelings bottled. But it was no use. I felt a warm, salty tear come out against my palm. I immediately wiped it away and sucked in the rest that might have followed. Lisette swallowed a mouthful of Indian food, got up from her seat across the table, and came over to sit beside me. She put her arm around me. I looked at her and noticed wetness in her eyes. "It breaks my heart to tell you all this," she said, stroking my hair. "Maybe I shouldn't have told you . . ."

SHORTLY AFTER THAT DINNER WHEN I heard such devastating news about Ben, Lisette called a meeting for Team LL. We still rendezvoused at the same Beverly Hills hotel bar. It was quiet there, and no one asked questions. Lisette told me before we assembled that I'd be meeting a man named Richard who was going to replace Henry on the team from now on. "Who the hell is Richard?" I asked her.

"Richard. My assistant. Sweetie, I've told you about him."

"I've never heard you talk about anyone named Richard, ever."

"He's been my assistant for six years." She always seemed to have a lot of assistants that came and went casually out of the woodwork.

"What?" I asked. "How is it possible that I've never heard of him?"

"Well, he was my assistant when I met you, and then he left for a while to chase some girl. He's back now and working for me again. Oh, and, babe, when you see Richard at the meeting, I need you to act like you've met him before. Just in front of Frankie, otherwise it would look weird. Frankie has obviously known Richard for years."

At the hotel bar, I sat with Frankie and Lisette at a booth. Lisette's BlackBerry lay on the table. It lit up with a message. She'd installed a text tone that played a remixed version of Tony Montana's most famous lines from *Scarface*, set to music, every time she got a text. She looked at her phone. "He's here," she said. The man Lisette was calling Richard walked into the bar from the lobby. He was tall, standing only a few inches shorter than Frankie, and filled out a suit. Richard was white, in his late twenties, and judging by his slight accent, I'd say he was from the South. Richard smiled a lot, but you got the sense that he liked things to be dangerous. It was obvious to me that he and Lisette had a flirtation.

This is bullshit. They haven't known each other for six years. I can tell just from watching their body language.

After a few minutes of discussing details for the next trip to Ohio, Frankie left. Lisette, Richard, and I stayed at the booth. Lisette paid the tab for our cocktails, then suggested that the three of us get a hotel room upstairs and hang out for a while.

Once we settled into a room, Richard broke out a bag of cocaine and poured some of it on a horizontal mirror. "All right, mama, get ready to be impressed," he told Lisette.

"I'm ready to see what you have," she said.

"What should I use to cut?" he asked.

"Use a card. Just grab one from your wallet," she said.

"All right." Richard took a leather wallet out of his pocket. He plucked his driver's license from it and began to break the lump of cocaine down into a powder.

I was suspicious of Richard and his relationship to Lisette. I simply didn't believe that I was being told the truth, or at least not the entire truth. As Richard leaned over the mirror and cut, I took a closer look at his ID. I couldn't read it, but it sure didn't look like it said Richard. Once he stopped cutting for a moment, I read the name. His license said Christopher Cash. "Your name's not Richard," I said. He looked up at me nervously. He hadn't expected that and looked to Lisette.

"Yes, it is," she stammered.

"No, it's not," I said. They both appeared confused. I was sick of the lies. It was past the point of ridiculous. "Dude, come on. You used your driver's license to cut the coke. It says Christopher Cash." He looked down at the card in his hand.

"That's not his license," Lisette chimed in.

"Oh my God, yes, it is!" I said. "Stop lying to me. What the hell is your real name? Is it Christopher Cash?"

He looked at Lisette before saying, "Uh, yeah, it—I mean, that's my birth name."

"Richard is the name he uses for business," Lisette said. "Don't call him Chris in front of Frankie or anyone."

I said fine, though none of it made sense. My expectation that things should generally make sense had gone out the window a long time ago.

In all Team LL business going forward, I'd be alerted of our schedule via group text messages to the team that were coming from Chris, though every message would be signed off with the name "Richard." He was using one of Lisette's old phone numbers, she said. She told me that she gave him her phone to use for business.

A few days after the meeting, Lisette invited me to come over to her penthouse. When I came to her door, we shared a close hug. She was beaming.

"Babe, you have to see what my mum just sent me from France," she said.

She walked me down her entryway and stopped in front of a portrait. What looked like masterful brushstrokes had conjured the image of a woman in profile, sitting alone at a bar. She wore a bloodred cocktail dress, with shadowy hair swept delicately behind her neck. Her fair skin was illuminated by the glow of a jazz show, and she sat turned toward it, ignoring the untouched martini that waited at her side.

"It's beautiful, isn't it? It's a gift from a Parisian artist—very famous in Europe," Lisette told me. "You probably wouldn't have heard of him. He loves my family. He told my mum that he wanted me to have this."

"It's gorgeous," I said. "It looks like your mom."

The woman at the bar did look like Lisette's mother. In the four years that I'd known her, I'd never met either of her parents, though she spoke of them constantly, gushing about how much they adored her and when they might be coming into town next. She said that they traveled a lot for business and owned homes all over the world. She'd always seemed to keep a few photos of them, but I remembered one professional photo of her mother, sitting on an expensive-looking couch. She was striking and looked much like Lisette. The only photo that Lisette had shared of her father showed a handsome Asian man dressed in a full suit, standing almost as one would in a catalog for menswear. I'd never seen any candid photos of her parents, or pictures that she was in with them.

"Do you think that he painted this of your mom?" I asked. Lisette stared at the woman in the painting.

"I wouldn't be surprised," she said, without moving her eyes from the image. "Probably."

"You should ask her," I said. "I bet he did."

Lisette took me farther down the lengthy entryway to reveal a smaller painting. "This is another work from the same artist, babe. My mummy bought it for me," she said. It was a cityscape of what appeared to be some European metropolis at night. The tiny windows in the buildings stood out like stars against the dark canvas.

"Wow," I said. "That's really sweet that your mom sent these to you."

"I know," Lisette said, smiling dreamily at the artwork.

Less than a week later, I went to Bed Bath & Beyond to pick up some candles for my apartment. While I wandered around the store, I passed an aisle of home decor. As I glanced over the selection, something caught my attention and stopped me in my tracks. Sitting ahead of me on a crowded shelf, I saw exact duplicates of the works that I'd been in such awe of at Lisette's penthouse, looking slightly less regal and slightly more like mass-produced knockoffs than when I'd seen them hung so pristinely on her walls. They were priced at sixty dollars each. I gaped at the prints.

She lied.

It seemed preposterous to imagine her gussied up in Bed Bath & Beyond, strutting through the aisles with her phony priceless paintings sticking out of a rusty shopping cart. I couldn't fathom why she felt the need to lie about something so trivial, especially to me. It would've been humiliating for her if I'd told her that I knew. I was flushed with embarrassment for her just at the thought of it. I decided that it was best not to say anything, for now. I knew that whatever had compelled her to lie about such a petty matter had nothing to do with me, and I didn't want to put her on the spot and make her feel defensive. To me, it represented a greater issue that ought to be handled sensitively. I didn't know how or when I would ever address it, but I wasn't going to bring it up casually without being prepared for a full-on intervention.

I didn't want to think about the paintings anyway. It was a string I didn't want to pull on, for fear of what might unravel. After more than four years, finally catching her red-handed in a lie scared me. It gave me a valid reason, beyond just a gut feeling, to question everything she'd ever told me. I tried to ignore my growing suspicions. Denial was more comfortable, because if I allowed myself to believe that this was just one of many lies, that meant admitting to the possibility that our entire friendship had been a lie, and that working for her had put me in more danger than I could have ever imagined.

ON THE MORNING OF OUR next flight to Ohio, Team LL assembled on the tarmac at the private airport in Van Nuys. It was early and no one was in sight, save for the team and a few airport employees. I stood by Lisette as we watched Chris and Frankie help airport employees lift about a dozen suitcases into the cargo hold. Lisette kept her eyes on the men as mine drifted to something that caught my attention just beyond where we stood. About fifty yards away from our chartered jet, I saw a parked police car. It sat idle, directly on the other side of the airport fence, facing us. Two men were sitting inside. I couldn't see their faces from where I stood, but it seemed as though they were staring at us. "Lisette," I said in a hushed voice, trying not to show much reaction. I tapped her arm. "Lisette."

"What is it?" she asked. She followed my gaze to see the police car. Her full lips twisted up into a confident smirk. "Sweetie, this is one of those priceless moments in life," she said. She laughed. I laughed too, but it was all nerves. "They're not going to do anything," she said dismissively as she turned on her Chanel heel and walked away toward the plane. I stared back at the police car for a moment longer, then moved to follow Lisette.

16

THE OTHER SIDE

In the first week of June I went with Brie and a group of friends to the Art Walk in downtown Los Angeles. As we wedged through foot traffic and vendors on a crowded sidewalk, a young girl who couldn't be older than nine approached me. "Would you like a free palm reading?" she called up to me.

"What?" I struggled to hear what she said over the chaos around us. I stopped walking and craned my head downward a bit to hear her.

"She can read your palm if you want," the girl said.

"Who?" I asked. The child pointed a few yards away to a woman sitting behind a card table. An empty folding chair held a makeshift sign that read TAROT CARD AND PALM READING. I looked at Brie and our group.

"What are you doing?" Brie asked me, seeing that I'd stopped. Everyone we'd come with was hungry and set on going to eat at Bottega Louie, which held too many memories with Ben for me to want to rush over. I'd never been to any kind of self-proclaimed psychic before, but it seemed this might not be a bad time to try it out. I looked again at the little girl.

"Sure, I'll try it," I said. I turned to Brie. "You guys go ahead. I'll catch up." Brie watched me sit down at the card table.

Through a laugh, she said, "Okay, have fun!," before disappearing into the crowd.

A prediscussed twenty-five-dollar tip later, I agreed to have the "free" palm reading, as well as a tarot card reading. The supposed psychic who sat on the folding chair didn't strike me as much of an Edgar Cayce. She was distracted by her phone during the reading. She wore a gold Cartier bracelet. I wondered how much money she made from this gig. She told me not to say anything at all to her until the reading was over, which was fine by me since I didn't feel much like talking anyway.

To begin the tarot reading, she placed a card on the table. "This is the false face card," she said. "This means that there is someone in your life who is giving you a false face. They are acting as though they have your best interests at heart, but they don't. You've already started to see this, but it's about to be revealed to you tenfold."

She laid down a second card. She stared at it for a moment looking concerned.

This is so hokey.

She lifted her eyes to look at me. "Don't take this the wrong way," she said, "but in the next four weeks, your life is going to fall apart. Everything will come crashing down. You will hit rock bottom."

"Um, what do you—" I started.

"Please, no talking," she said.

Another card went down. "There will be something legal."

"Sorry, can I stop you?" I said. "Legal, as in what?" She blinked at me and said, "Well, I don't know. I only know what the cards are telling me."

"Okay . . ." I shifted in my seat. This reading wasn't giving me the sense of playful optimism I thought I had paid for. Who goes to a psychic to be told their life is only going to get worse?

The woman touched her cards and continued on in a casual manner, but not before checking her phone to read a text message. I tried not to be annoyed by how distracted she had been.

"Sorry," she said, setting her phone aside. "Okay, yes. As I said, in the next four weeks, your life is going to fall apart."

Well, I guess she hadn't lost her train of thought.

"When everything comes crashing down—and trust me, it's going to—that is when you should thank God. Because that will mean that everything is happening as it's supposed to. Because in six weeks, good things will start happening that never could have happened, had these other things not fallen apart."

As I walked to Bottega Louie to join my friends, I wasn't sure what to make of the reading. I decided there was no sense in forming an opinion of it now, because I wouldn't know if anything she said would ring true someday. I scribbled a few notes onto a scrap piece of paper and put it in my purse. I planned to look at it in a few months and see if anything she said had actually been right, or if I truly had paid for a common street performance.

A FEW DAYS LATER, I stayed the night at Lisette's penthouse on Wilshire Corridor. In the morning, I woke up beneath her lavender silk comforter feeling nauseated. I'd had only a few drinks the night before, but this felt a little like a hangover. Lisette was already up and dressed in black jeans, a plunging red tank top, and a triple circle diamond-and-platinum necklace that rested just above her cleavage. Her BlackBerry rang. "Babe, answer it," she said, holding the phone out for me to take. "Just say, 'Miss Lee's phone, this is Alice.'" I waved her off and sank into her Egyptian sheets. I shook my head.

"No, I can't today," I said. "I don't feel good." She frowned slightly, then answered the phone herself. When she finished a short call, she walked to the bedside.

"I'm sorry you're not feeling good," she said. "You can sleep as long as you want. There's some pizza in the fridge if you want some when you get up. Feel better, sweetie."

After sleeping awhile longer, I woke up still tired. Lisette hadn't installed blackout shades in her new condo yet, and the sun filled every inch of her bedroom with light, making it almost impossible to sleep. I lay on my side in bed and squinted at her alarm clock. It was 10:30 A.M. I closed my eyes to try to fall back asleep. I began to drift into the lazy calm of the morning when, out of nowhere, there was a bounce on the bed. It felt exactly as it did when a small dog jumped on it. It startled me and jolted me into hyperawareness for a moment.

I held my breath. There were no dogs here today. I was the only living thing in the penthouse.

I decided to ignore the strange movement of the bed. I had enough on my mind without adding things I couldn't explain.

Just as I was trying to forget the initial bounce, I felt it happen twice more in quick succession, rattling the entire bed and me in it. This was more difficult to ignore, but I was set on doing so regardless. I turned on my other side, spooked and desperately wanting to return to sleep and forget what just happened.

I lay facing Lisette's bedroom door. Through still-tired eyes, I watched as the image of a woman walked into the brightly lit bedroom from the hallway. I blinked twice, but her ethereal image remained. I didn't react; I just lay motionless watching. She was dark-skinned and wore a red dress with polka dots, in a 1950s style. Her presence was unthreatening, almost comforting. She stopped at the corner of Lisette's bed and sat down. She talked to me in a very casual manner. As I listened, I understood most of what she was saying, though I wouldn't be able to remember much of it after. It was something like, "Lisette is at work, but she'll be back soon. Don't worry." I stayed still, observing her in awe, tucked inside the covers and holding on to them for comfort.

After a minute, the woman in the red dress strolled out of the room and was gone. I didn't have time to process what I'd seen before the image of a second woman came in from the hallway. She wasn't like the other one. The moment she appeared, I felt like the air was being sucked out of the room. Whatever she was, it was evil. I'd never felt such a vacuous energy before in my life. This woman was blond and physically beautiful. She wore a light-colored, flowing 1950s-style dress. She stared placidly at me. "Hi, sweetie," she said in a barely audible whisper. "Are you feeling better?" My body felt frozen in fear. She spoke with the same intonations and had the same mannerisms as Lisette did. She wanted me to believe that she *was* Lisette. I felt tight in my entire body, including my throat, but I managed to say, "You're not Lisette," aloud. The words struggled to come out, like trying to fly in a dream.

Was I dreaming?

The woman's pale face twisted into a closemouthed smile as she started to climb onto the corner of the bed to get to me, making jagged movements with her elbows pointed out and her eyes locked on me. In defense, I put my hand out to block her face. As she launched in, I saw that her body wasn't sitting on the bed. She'd begun to disappear into thin air. Her neck was airy and transparent now, like smoke.

When my hand met her face, it didn't feel like a face at all. It was as though I was an inch away from her, and I was pushing against a heavy wall of energy, not actually touching her. As I pushed against it, her image changed entirely. It was as if her skin was burning off, unmasking her. Her eyes went black, and in an instant her face turned from a beautiful young woman into what looked like a rotting, half-alive skull, with a bony expression pulled back in a silent scream. The horrific image disappeared in front of me, against my open palm. The room was quiet. I had to remind myself to breathe. I lay still, eyes peeled.

The dark-skinned woman in the red polka-dot dress returned. She acted exactly the same as before, completely benign, and walked out after a minute or so.

I tried to escape into sleep again, and to my amazement, I was successful, regardless of the blinding light that still filled the room. Every part of me was exhausted. In my last breaths of consciousness, I told myself that what I'd just experienced was merely another bad dream.

I was awakened some time later by loud sounds of vomiting in Lisette's bathroom, which was about a dozen feet from the bed. She must have come home early from her meeting. She had a history of strange illness, so I wasn't alarmed. I knew the sound of her vomiting from sickness very well. I was relieved to know that I wasn't alone in her penthouse now. I considered going to her and asking if I could help, as I would have in times past, but instead I pretended to be asleep. I was fully rested now and I was ready to get up, but I knew that I'd be expected to help her if she saw that I was wide awake. I didn't feel like holding her hair as she hurled into the toilet this time. The vomiting stopped after a few minutes. Then nothing. I wondered what she could be doing in there, if perhaps she'd passed out.

I opened one eye to peer around the room. I didn't see Lisette's purse anywhere, and no high heels were tossed on the carpet. I got up and went to the bathroom to see what she was doing, expecting to find her applying makeup or thumbing through e-mails on her phone. But Lisette wasn't inside. She hadn't been back since she left in the early morning.

In two quick steps, I leaped back to bed and hid under the covers for protection, as I had when I was a child. I turned away from the door to face the window, hoping to return to some kind of numbness. I didn't want to see anything. I didn't want to hear anything. It was too early in the day for things to get this strange. I curled into a ball and closed my eyes.

Within seconds, I felt a heavy, draining energy inches away from my face, staring into me and demanding me to acknowledge it. I refused to open my eyes. I squeezed them shut as tightly as I could, trying to will away whatever might be in front of me.

Almost instantly, a concentrated shot of cold air was blasted directly into my face. I launched out of bed, sprinting as fast as I could out of the room and into the kitchen.

I grabbed my phone and called my dad. "Dad, some very, very weird shit just happened. I need you to bring me back down to earth. Just tell me about your day." I listened to him talk about his detailed plans to start an herb garden this year.

As he spoke, I stared at my hand. *This* was real. My hand was real, just like my phone, my father, and this floor I was standing on. They were all real. Back in that room, that wasn't real. It couldn't have been. I'd heard of people hallucinating from stress. I must have been hallucinating. Apparently my nightmares were no longer limited to times when I was asleep.

I ran back to the bedroom and threw the covers over to make the bed at least vaguely presentable for Lisette when she came home. I got my purse and left in a hurry. I texted Lisette saying that her penthouse had a strange energy, and I couldn't spend the night there again. She laughed and told me I was crazy.

17

A DRAMATIC EXIT

I returned to Lisette's penthouse a few days later on the eve of our next trip to Columbus. She'd asked me to come by to see her in the evening, and I'd reluctantly agreed. "I'm not spending the night," I warned her when she greeted me at her door. She rolled her eyes and walked into the kitchen to get two tumbler glasses. She poured us both Bombay Sapphire on the rocks. The days of mixers were all but over. We sat barefoot on her new Parisian-style white couch, the only piece of furniture in her massive living room, and sipped our liquor. The empty space and high ceilings made it feel a bit like a carpeted ballroom, with three walls covered in floor-to-ceiling windows. With all the lights turned off inside and the sun gone from the sky, the world below us was illuminated, as though we were floating above the city. Lisette brought the Bombay bottle into the living room and refreshed our drinks.

As we lounged on her couch, Lisette's cell phone began to play its usual *Scarface* remix, alerting her to a new text message. "He's here," she said, looking at her phone. "Angel, do you mind going downstairs to get it?"

"Sure," I said. I got up to accept a hundred-dollar bill from Lisette.

"Make sure he doesn't skimp this time," she said as I walked to her private elevator entrance. "Check the bags before you accept them. I want them to look like goddamn pillows of yay."

Downstairs, I passed through the baroque lobby to go outside to Wilshire Boulevard. A white Porsche waited at the curb. I did a quick once-over of the street to make sure no one was watching me. Lisette's coke dealer sat behind the wheel of the Porsche. He gave me a familiar nod as I opened the passenger door and climbed into his car. Our exchange was quick, as usual. Lisette generally sent me downstairs with a hundred dollars to get two grams. She always paid for it, and I always retrieved it. Tonight, for some reason, I felt uneasy about everything. I hadn't wanted to go downstairs when she asked me, but I didn't want to cause some exhausting conflict. "Tell your girl 'what up' for me," the dealer said before I shut the car door behind me and walked back to the building.

I returned to the penthouse with two grams of coke. We were stocking up for the trip to Ohio. Lisette examined the tiny baggies of powder. "Okay," she said. "This looks good. I swear to God, I'm going to bury him if he tries to fuck with me again. I know what a full gram looks like." She took one of the bags into her master bathroom. I followed her with my drink. "Let's have a tasting," she said in a playful tone. Lisette took a white hand towel off a rack and used it to wipe down her marble countertop. It was part of a set of towels she'd recently had monogrammed in lavender cursive with "L.L." With the countertop dry, she poured a small pile of coke onto it and cut eight lines with a razor blade.

After we woofed through the lines, she wiped the counter and picked up both baggies of coke. "Let's save some for the trip," she said. "Here you go, sweetie." She handed the baggies out for me to take. Immediately I had an overwhelming feeling that I shouldn't take the coke with me. With few exceptions, I'd always been the one to carry it to Ohio for Lisette and me. But I was paranoid tonight, viscerally, more than ever. I didn't want to drive with it in my purse.

"Um," I said, staring at the coke. "Do you mind if I leave it here tonight? Just so I don't have to drive with it. Since you're not going anywhere. I'd just be leaving with it tonight, then bringing it back tomorrow morning. It makes more sense to leave it." Lisette considered this.

"Okay, no problem," she said. She tucked both baggies into her crocodile purse for safekeeping.

I told Lisette that I was worried about getting any sleep before our flight. I needed to be back to her condo by 7:00 A.M. the next morning to report for work. "This will help," she assured me. She filled a Fiji water bottle with four fingers of gin.

I left her penthouse late. I could still feel the coke pulsing through my system as I drove. Nervous thoughts raced through my mind. *I shouldn't have done any. I'm still high. What the hell was I thinking? Shit. I wasn't thinking. I'm going to get pulled over. I'm going to get into an accident. Something bad is going to happen. I can feel it . . .*

I became overwhelmed with anxiety and quickly pulled my car off the main road to take side streets through Beverly Hills. When I got home, I chugged the gin from the water bottle, climbed into bed, and prayed that I'd get at least a few hours of sleep.

I WOKE UP WITH THE worst hangover of my life. After an almost sleepless night, I mechanically got ready and drove back to Lisette's penthouse. I couldn't be bothered to put on any makeup today. I could barely be bothered to stand up. To my amazement, I made it all the way to Lisette's condo before the urge to vomit came on in full force.

On the plane ride to Ohio, I ignored the catering. I was so physically ill that I crawled on my hands and knees back and forth to the bathroom. Lisette was delighted watching this routine. It seemed to put her in a good mood. She grabbed a colorful pack of candy from a basket. She took a seat behind Frankie and whipped little candies at the back of his head. After a moment, he noticed that they were accumulating in his hair. He flicked his hand to brush them off. "Aw, man, don't do that. Come on now. I'm serious," he said. Lisette giggled and fired off another round of neon sugar balls at him. She took a piece of gum from a snack basket and popped it into her mouth.

I sat with my head buried in my hands, trying to block all light. Lisette had been taking swigs from a now quarter-gone bottle of Bombay Sapphire gin, and she set it down to come up behind me and pat my hair. "Oh, sweetie," she cooed. "You poor thing." I groaned and folded over to put my head between my knees. Time to go to the bathroom again.

After dry heaving over the toilet for a few minutes, I stood at the sink and washed my hands. I rubbed my eyes and tilted my head. I felt something roll around in my hair.

Did Lisette put one of the candies in my hair that she was throwing at Frankie?

I rummaged through the sweaty mess of hair on my head and found something that felt like a soft pebble. I took it out and held it in front of me. It was gum.

Did she put her gum in my hair on purpose? No, that would be a stretch, even for her. Thankfully, the gum hadn't stuck in my hair. It must have fallen out of her mouth when she was talking.

Ew.

I returned to my seat and resumed my head-in-knees position. Lisette came behind me again and patted my head. "I'm sorry you're not feeling well," she said. She took her hand off my head for a moment, then came back and patted it with much more pressure. I felt her press something into my scalp. I jerked away from her immediately. "What the fuck are you doing?" I yelled. She jolted back, clearly caught off guard by my reaction.

"What?" she said. She looked at Frankie and Chris Cash, who were both staring at her now. I felt around on my scalp. Gum.

"Are you in fucking third grade? Really? You put gum in my hair! What the hell is wrong with you?" I said. Lisette laughed.

"Oh my God, babe, you *do* have gum in your hair!" she said. "It must have fallen out of my mouth."

"It didn't fall out of your mouth. I felt you smush it into my scalp." She tried to touch my hair, but I batted her hand away. "Don't touch me."

She laughed again. "Somebody's grumpy today. Babe, you know I would never do that on purpose. Come on." She turned to Frankie. "Frankie, you've known me my entire life. Tell Meili I would never put gum in someone's hair. Listen, I know I'm a bitch, but even I have to draw the line somewhere." Frankie looked like he didn't want to be involved in this.

"Man, I don't know," he said. "You were throwin' those damn candies at me. If you did put gum in her hair, that'd be some dumb shit. Y'all need to grow up. Come on now, this is embarrassing."

I took out my makeup compact and looked at my scalp in the mirror. Lisette had successfully attached the gum to the hair near my scalp this time. "Oh, it looks like it's stuck," she said.

"Yeah, you really got it in there," I said snidely.

"Here, let me see it," she said. I leaned to the side, trying to get away from her, but I was too hungover to be anything but a slow-moving animal today. "I'm not going to hurt you," she said. "Jesus." She took a closer look at my hair and grimaced. "Yeah. I think we're going to have to cut it out." She went to the back of the plane to get scissors. I couldn't get a good enough look at it to cut it out myself, so I begrudgingly allowed Lisette to do the cutting once she had sworn to cut only what was tangled in gum. When she finished, I felt on top of my head. Right above my bangs, there was now a chunk of half-inch-long hair that was sticking out like a cowlick. I sank back into my chair, pissed off and aching for sleep.

When we touched down in Columbus, I couldn't tell if I'd slept during the flight or not. My head was pounding. Slouched down in my seat, I squinted into a tiny makeup mirror to gauge if it was worth trying to hide my hangover. The damage appeared to be irreparable, at least for this morning. Dark circles were carved under my eyes. Unbrushed hair was matted to my skin from twisting around during the trip. My face was puffed and sweaty. I looked like a dead frog that had been fished out of a lake after a storm.

I stared ahead at the plush back of Lisette's seat. I couldn't see her, but I knew that she was buried in her own Chanel compact, touching up before we unloaded. She stood, and it was clear that she'd had more luck in this department than me today. My already futile chances of looking vaguely attractive had been put to rest by the gum incident. I tugged at my pencil skirt and buttoned my blazer. My hair went up in a clip. Presentable was the best I could hope for today, and even that was likely out of reach. I slid on a pair of crystal-studded Chanel sunglasses Lisette had given me as a birthday present a few years back. I didn't want to look at anyone. I just wanted to get to a hotel and crawl into a bed. Lisette owed me a Valium for the shit she pulled during the flight.

Two pilots climbed out of the cockpit and opened the door for us. I'd never seen them before this trip. They weren't as chatty as the others had been. I didn't know how Lisette arranged the staffing, but there had seemed to be a familiar rotation. Not too familiar; that could be dangerous.

As Lisette moved past the pilots, she complimented them on a smooth landing before stepping down onto the tarmac. Lisette wore a low-cut, billowy pink tank top, black stretch pants, and her signature Chanel wedges. I followed close behind her in my ancient Old Navy blazer and an oversized white Eddie Bauer button-up.

Chris and Frankie began unloading the back of the plane with the help of three Lane Aviation employees. Thirteen large suitcases were loaded into two SUVs and a van that were ready for us on the tarmac.

I watched as Lisette directed the men about how to distribute the bags among the three cars. She caught my eye and shot me a tense look. After greasing the airport guys with a fifty each and a "Thanks, sweetie," she walked straight to me and said, "Babe, come here." I followed her behind a wing of the plane. "This is bullshit," she said. "Something is off. Everyone is acting weird. I don't know where the fuck they got these pilots, but we're never using this crew again."

Lisette and I watched as the last bags were loaded. She instructed me to ride with the bulk of the luggage in the van behind the SUVs. Of course I was the one who had to ride in the van.

Lisette jumped into the first SUV with Frankie. Chris sat shotgun next to a hired driver in the second SUV, and I skulked into the shitty white van next to another driver. I settled in and gave him a polite hello as we waited for movement from the front.

The driver was awkward. He took long breaths, looking ahead for a signal. He cleared his throat. "So," he said, "what are you folks doing in Ohio? I mean, you're from L.A., right? That's where you're coming from?"

"Yeah," I said, looking up from a text message. "L.A."

As we started to move he let out a nervous laugh. "Well, aha, you know, it's none of my business what you're doing here. Your secret is safe with me." This was alarming.

What secret? How does he know that we have any secrets?

This guy was making me nervous. He was right. It was none of his business. No more talking. Back to my text message.

I was texting my father. I hadn't had a chance to call him yesterday. I needed to be quick if I wanted to get a text out.

HEY DAD. HOPE YOU'RE HAVING A GOOD DAY. LISETTE AND I ARE WORKING ALL DAY, AND I'M GOING TO TRY TO GET TO BED EARLY TONIGHT. I'LL CALL YOU TMRW. LOVE YOU.

I felt the van turning to face the exit gate of the airport. I was about to press send when Lisette called me. I put the phone to my ear and lifted my head to answer, but she hung up abruptly before she had a chance to speak. I looked up and saw why she was calling. Our caravan had been blocked by a wall of officers in bulletproof vests, half a dozen police cars with lights flashing, and a militia's worth of submachine guns. The officers wore blue uniforms with bright gold badges that read DEA in bold letters. Their guns were all aimed directly at us.

On instinct, I glanced to the driver. His eyes were locked straight ahead. We were set up. No wonder the pilots seemed odd. They must have known what was waiting for us.

"Put your hands in the air and get out of the vehicle." I looked to the side of the van and found myself staring down the black barrel of an MP5 submachine gun. The officer behind it said again, "Miss, put your hands in the air and step out of the vehicle." I was still holding my cell phone, and I lifted it into the air as I put both hands up. "Um, should I—er, can I put my phone down?" I asked the officer. I suspected I couldn't bring it with me.

He nodded. "Yes. Set it down and step out." I set my phone on the dashboard near my purse and stepped out of the van. "Are you carrying any weapons?" the officer asked.

"No," I said. It occurred to me that it would be reasonable to feel some sense of panic right now, but I felt apathetic and numb. My pulse had raised more over a parking ticket.

"You're sure? You're not carrying any weapons at all?" the officer asked.

"I'm sure."

"I'm going to pat you down," he said. "Stay still." He took his aim off me and patted me down with his hands. "Okay." He took a long look at me. "What are you doing in Ohio?"

I wanted very much to avoid answering this. They were about to find out anyway. Why continue this ridiculous charade? I really didn't want to say that we were filming a music video here. I knew that was a stupid idea, and it didn't even come close to adding up given the circumstances. It never had. However, I didn't want to be the first one to say what was really going on.

The officer stared at me, waiting for an answer. I broke eye contact with him, muttered something under my breath about a music video and cringed.

"What was that?" he asked. I wasn't going to repeat it. I hoped that he hadn't heard me. I just looked back at him for a moment in silence. His stare softened slightly. "You're not in charge here, are you?"

I let out an involuntary laugh. "No."

"I didn't think so," he said. The officer and I both looked around us. From a glance, I couldn't count how many dozens of officers there were, let alone how many guns. If this were a movie, Bruce Willis would have been lowered onto the tarmac via helicopter with a knife in his teeth and a machine gun slung over his back, saying something like, "We've got these bastards," into a walkie-talkie.

I saw Chris Cash up ahead, smiling and laughing next to an officer. Of course he would be laughing through this. There really is a lot of truth to the idea that people either laugh or cry in extreme situations. I couldn't see Frankie or Lisette. They were two SUVs ahead of me.

The officer at my side eyed me. "Do you understand what's happening?" he asked. I said nothing. I must have seemed catatonic to him. He pointed to the badge he wore over his bulletproof vest and uniform. "Hey, do you know what this is? This is a federal badge. I'm a federal officer." I nodded, unsure of how to respond. He went on, trying a different approach. "What's your name?"

"Meili. What's your name?"

"My name is Steve. Where are you from, Meili? Where's your family?"

"Washington State. My family's there."

"Washington? No kidding. I just spent six months working on the force up there. Beautiful area. Where in Washington?"

"Bremerton, about an hour outside of Seattle."

"You know anyone on the force there?"

I thought for a moment. "Yeah, actually. I've got a cousin in Belfair who is a police officer. You know Belfair?"

He shook his head. "No, I've heard of it, but I don't know anyone there. You go back often?"

"I try to. Maybe twice a year."

Officer Steve straightened his posture when he saw two other officers approach the SUV ahead of us with two German shepherds on leashes. The dogs eagerly sniffed around. "You know what kind of dogs those are?" he asked me.

"Uh . . ." I said. "I'm . . . you know . . . I don't, I don't know much about dogs."

He looked at me, a little frustrated. "I wasn't asking which breed they are. Okay, they're looking for something. What do you think they're looking for?"

I scrunched up my face as I considered how best to answer his question.

Well, Officer, my guess is they're after that pot in the suitcases.

"Something . . . illegal?" I said.

"Yes," he said, nodding. "That's right. Now, we're gonna wait here until we know whether or not they find anything."

Trust me, this won't take long.

I was amazed when it took more than sixty seconds for the dogs to give some kind of signal to the officers holding their leashes. The reaction rippled through the vast crowd of DEA agents on the scene. Steve turned to me and reluctantly reached for something at his side. "You know what I have to do now, right?" I saw him take out a pair of handcuffs.

I'm being arrested. This is really happening. There is nothing I can say, and nothing I can do, to stop those handcuffs from going on me.

My face dropped. He paused for a moment, recognizing fear in my eyes. "Hold your hands out. I'm going to put these on in the front, but just for right now." He slid the cold steel under my wrists, then bonded them. He looked at me. "I'll let you keep them in front for now, but just so you know, in a few minutes we're going to have to put them behind you."

"Thanks," I said in a low voice. Steve walked off to confer with another officer. The handcuffs were tight and uncomfortable, even wearing them in front of me. I supposed that was the point. I saw Chris Cash standing a few paces away from the SUV ahead of me. His wrists had been cuffed behind his back. He wasn't laughing now, and neither was I. I didn't feel like laughing or crying. It was all too surreal. Was I supposed to follow Officer Steve? I slowly walked across the pavement in handcuffs, taking hesitant steps to show that I wasn't trying to make a break for it. I had a feeling all these guns were loaded. Two officers walked by me as I went, neither acknowledging me. When they passed, I saw Lisette. She stood only a few yards away from me. Her tiny wrists had been pulled behind her in handcuffs. I stood with my hands cuffed in front of me. I wondered how Lisette was planning to make all this okay. Each of us stood motionless on the concrete. She was staring down at the ground. I watched her intently until she lifted her eyes to meet mine. I didn't recognize the expression on her face. It was one that suggested something I never imagined she was capable of: defeat.

An officer walked over to address Lisette and me. "My name is Agent Matt Heufelder. We're gonna head out in a few minutes," he said. He looked us up and down, clearly not yet sure what to make of us. "You two are going to ride in this car." He indicated a black SUV behind him. I got the sense that he was in charge here. He came up to me and took my handcuffs off. "We need these in back now, sorry," he said. Lisette watched as he pulled my hands behind me and bound them at the wrist.

Agent Heufelder instructed us to get into the backseat of the SUV. I quickly realized that it was impossible to climb into an elevated vehicle gracefully with handcuffs on. It took some doing, but I managed to flop myself up and into the backseat. It was extremely uncomfortable once I sat down, forcing a strain on the cuffs behind me. I could feel the steel digging into my skin on my wrist bones.

Agent Heufelder stood by the open car door as we got situated. "No talking," he said. "I'll be back in a minute."

Lisette and I sat side by side, handcuffed, in the backseat of a police SUV. I wanted to be able to talk with her and ask her what was going to happen to us. I wanted to know that she had a plan.

She got us into this. Now how the hell is she going to get us out?

Within a few minutes, Agent Heufelder returned to the SUV. He helped us buckle our seat belts, then shut the back doors and got into the driver's seat. A female officer sat next to him up front. As the car began to move forward, she glanced back at Lisette and me.

What must she be thinking of us right now?

I felt like a zoo animal. I never would've imagined that being arrested would be so . . . awkward. The officers in the front seat started a casual, friendly conversation with each other. For some reason this made me feel even more awkward. I arched my back and tried to reposition my hands behind me so that there was less strain on my wrists. The skin around the handcuffs felt like it was about to break. Lisette saw me writhing around. "What the hell are you doing? Stop," she hissed in a low whisper. "Stop doing that. Just sit still." The officers in the front ceased their conversation. Lisette knew she had everyone's attention again. In a notably British accent, she said, "This is humiliating. I've never been so embarrassed in my life." Agent Heufelder looked at Lisette in the rearview mirror as he drove. She fumed. "I don't know what my family is going to do when they find out about this," she said. "And Samsung . . . You know, Samsung?" They officers looked at each other.

"The electronics company?" Heufelder asked.

"Yes," Lisette said. "That's my family."

"Your family is Samsung?" he asked. "What do you mean? Your family owns the company?"

Lisette was getting irritated with him. "Yes." She stared out the window. "They're not going to be happy about this."

"Well, I'm sorry to hear that," he said.

The SUV took us through downtown Columbus, then pulled into the covered parking garage of what looked like a government building.

The officers opened the SUV doors and helped Lisette and me out of the backseat, starting by unbuckling our seat belts for us. We'd arrived at DEA headquarters for Columbus, Ohio. We were escorted inside the building and into a small, whitewashed, sterile-looking room with a folding table and two chairs. Lisette and I once again sat side by side in handcuffs, but this time only for a minute or so. An officer came into the room, told me to stand up, then removed my handcuffs. As I was led out of the room, I took one last look at Lisette. She was lost in thought, staring ahead of her. As I left the room, I wondered when I would see her again. It didn't occur to me that this might be the last time, ever.

I was taken to an almost identical room a few paces away. Two male officers followed in behind, closed the door, and sat down on folding chairs across a table from me. One officer looked gruff from first glance, and the other one looked vaguely amicable. The gruff one could have almost been considered handsome if he hadn't looked so rabid. I noticed an open, bloody gash on his shin, just below his cargo shorts. "What happened to your leg?" I asked him.

"One of your bags fell on it," he grunted. I knew this wasn't going to go well for me.

The agents told me that I had the right to consult with an attorney before any questions were asked, but I was also assured that no attorneys would be available until the morning, and that the DEA would be happy to provide me with a jail cell to sleep in until my counsel could get here. I opted for an interview instead. As the first hour of interrogation began, I was reminded of how hungover I was. The shock of the arrest had eclipsed my physical discomfort for a while, but it was all coming back to me now. Thankfully, I didn't have anything left to throw up.

The agents tried to pull the truth out of me; the gruff one was a real bastard. I told them I didn't know it was pot. Of course, we all said that. The officers asked me where I was born and how long I'd lived in Los Angeles. They asked me what my parents did for a living, what sort of jobs I'd had in the past. They went through my wallet and asked if I'd brought any drugs, then pushed again to see if I would admit to having any weapons with me. The gruff officer discovered three punch cards to various yogurt shops in L.A. inside my wallet and eyed me suspiciously as he asked if I enjoyed eating frozen yogurt. Everything was subject to scrutiny.

In a room two doors down from mine, Lisette gave her own version of events to DEA agents. She told them she was in Ohio to move supplies to a horse farm for a boyfriend in town. I don't know how far she made it with that story before she began to alter it, but it wasn't long. Before the end of the interrogation, she conceded that she'd been paid $60,000 to bring the suitcases to Ohio, and while she had no knowledge of their content, she suspected it was "weapons and money laundering or something." The agents listened as she explained to them that she was not only an heiress to the Samsung electronics fortune, but also a pop sensation in Korea. They were so befuddled by the interview she gave that they simply wrote "heiress" as her occupation in official police paperwork.

In her crocodile purse they found the baggie of cocaine, three cell phones, $6,500 in cash, and a piece of paper from a hotel notepad that was essentially a drug ledger tracking $300,000, with numbers representing weights and purchase prices. During my interrogation, an agent walked into the room with the piece of paper in hand. "Sorry, guys," he told the agents interviewing me, "I just have to ask her a quick question." He held the paper out for me to take. I recognized the hotel logo from a previous trip. I stared at it in disbelief. "Is this your handwriting?" he asked me stone-faced. I had to bite my lip in order to keep a straight face. While there were a few damning numbers scribbled on it, the majority of the paper was dedicated to Lisette practicing her signature in variations. "Um. No, that's not my handwriting," I said, and quickly handed back the paper. "Do you know who wrote this?" he asked. "Nope," I replied, shrugging. He nodded and walked out of the room.

I told the DEA the truth about everything, except about that paper—and the fact that I knew it was pot in the suitcases. I decided to leave that detail out. I suspected that if I didn't, I'd be offered that jail cell again, and I might not have the option to turn it down. It was true that I hadn't known at first, so I skipped over the part when it started smelling like a hot box on the plane and Lisette asked us to hose down the luggage with Febreze. The officers didn't believe me, of course. It seemed like they didn't believe a word of what I was saying, not even the parts that were true, which really was the vast majority of it. Everything I said sounded like lies because I was nervous and exhausted, and I was talking in circles. Both officers seemed frustrated and mystified by the entire arrest today. After what must have been two, maybe three hours, they left me alone in the room and shut the door.

I could hear voices in the hallway. They were talking about Lisette. Someone said, "They all believed her. All of them." Then I heard the gruff bastard's voice. He was talking about me. He said, "That has got to be the stupidest girl I've met in my entire life. I tell ya." I leaned back in the chair with my arms crossed. I would like to retract what I thought about him being possibly handsome underneath his horrible personality.

Thanks a lot, asshole.

A new voice joined the conversation. It was another male officer. "All right, guys," he said. "Parker won the bet. We just weighed it." A voice asked, "How much? I said four hundred." The other officer went on. "Nope," he said. "Five hundred and six pounds." The officers were talking about the pot from the suitcases. They had been making bets on how much was there.

After a few minutes, the voices faded and I heard nothing. I couldn't tell how much time had passed. There were no clocks in the room. With no watch, no cell phone, and no ability to leave, I felt a sudden pang of loneliness. I just didn't want to be alone in this damn room. I didn't know what was happening. I wanted to leave and be with other people, and I wanted to eat something.

I was startled when the door opened. It was the "good cop" from my interrogation. I was relieved to see another human. After I'd stopped hearing people in the hallway, I was afraid everyone had gone somewhere else and I really was alone. "All right," he said. "Come here." I was finally able to walk out of the room.

"You ready?" he asked me.

"For what?"

My initial feeling of relief turned out to be fleeting. "Your close-up," he said. He grinned at me and stood by something that looked like some type of camera. It was facing a white wall that had a box with black lines and numbers on it. I knew immediately what was about to happen, and my stomach lurched with the sinking awareness that I could do nothing to prevent it.

I had a terrifying flashback to the last time I'd looked in a mirror today. The damage had been irreparable before the arrest, and I could only imagine that it had gotten exponentially worse since then. But there was no way out. Three DEA agents gathered around and snickered as I stood in front of the camera. One of the men said, "Aren't you gonna smile?" The flash made me blink a few times. I could only pray that no one would ever see this photo.

I was sent back into the room to wait for what felt like an eternity. After ten minutes or so, the door opened. It was the "good cop" again. I looked up at him from my chair, hoping for some kind of update. He rubbed his hands together like he was trying to start a fire. "And now, for the moment of truth," he said.

"What?" I asked, fearing what fresh new hell he might have in store for me.

"Now we get to run your ID and do a little background check. We're gonna find out whether you're going home tonight." He flashed me a cryptic smile before backing out of the room and closing the door behind him. I didn't want to find out the alternative to going home. I was quite certain it would involve a jail cell. If I had a "clean record," then I got to leave. I'd never been arrested before in my life. I should have felt more confident right now, but my luck seemed to have started on empty today. I stood and walked a few paces around the room, then sat back down. My palms were sweating. I crossed my legs, then uncrossed them. Time passed. A minute, an hour; I'd lost any reliable sense of it. Finally, the door opened again. I held my breath as the officer returned with a grave expression on his face.

"So?" I asked meekly, a feeling of dread creeping in.

The officer looked stern. "You're under arrest."

"Am I really?" My voice cracked as I spoke. I began to go into a state of shock. I felt like someone had just punched me in the stomach.

"Nah, I'm just playin'," he said, breaking into a hearty laugh. "You can leave."

"Are you serious?"

"Yeah, you got no record," he said. "But, man, I totally had you goin'."

I was too stunned to speak for a moment. Then I laughed too.

"That was so mean."

"Yeah, but I got you smilin', though," he said. "Hey, at least you're not going to jail. Not today."

"Yeah . . . So we can go now?"

"Three of you can," he said. "Your homegirl is staying with us."

"What?" My emotion rose again on instinct in defense of Lisette. *They're keeping her?*

I took a deep breath, trying to process what he'd just told me. I raised my head to look at him. "Can I see her?" I asked.

"No," he said. "Of course you can't. She's being booked right now anyway. She's going to jail."

Booked? Jail? She'd always seemed so invincible. I couldn't imagine Lisette in some dirty cell, defeated, the way I'd seen her look today. The officer watched me as my mind raced.

"Let me ask you this," he said. "Why would you want to see the person who got you into this whole mess in the first place?" His words hit me. "Think about that," he said. "You got a lot to learn." He held the door open for me to walk out of the interrogation room.

IT WAS AFTER 11:00 P.M. when the DEA released us. An officer escorted me out of the building alongside Chris and Frankie. We'd been given our belongings back, and each of us towed a piece of personal luggage behind us. Outside, the streets of downtown Columbus were eerily empty and dimly lit. When the officer disappeared back into the building, the three of us let out a collective sigh of relief. After exchanging wide-eyed and dazed looks at one another, we stood in silence for a moment. "I don't know about you two, but I need a fucking drink," Frankie said.

Chris eyed the building. "Let's get out of here," he said. "Before they change their minds."

We checked into the first hotel we saw and left our bags in a room. We were eager to sit down with a drink and attempt to collect ourselves. Two blocks from the hotel was one of only two late-night bars in downtown. I sat on a bar stool next to Chris Cash. Frankie stood. We all ordered beers. Frankie took a few long pulls on his drink, then set it down. "Man, I haven't drunk in years," he said, shaking his head. "But I'm probably getting drunk tonight. I gotta call my wife and tell her about this shit first."

"You're going to tell her?" I asked him. I hadn't even considered telling anyone. From what I'd understood, Frankie's wife had been as informed about the details of Lisette's business as everyone in my life had. His wife knew that he worked for Lisette, but she didn't know anything past that. I'd never been sure whether Frankie knew what was going on from the beginning, or if he'd found out sometime before I had. I couldn't fathom the phone call he was about to make. He had to tell his wife, the mother of his children, that he'd just been arrested.

Frankie headed outside with his cell phone drawn. "Good luck," I said as he walked off.

When we'd left the DEA headquarters tonight, an officer said, "Bye, guys. We hope we never have to see you again!" What if they didn't charge us and it was possible that we could each just go on with the lives that we had before Team LL? We could start over. I had no doubt that Lisette's prominent family would get her out of jail soon. They'd figure something out. Maybe this would all go away.

"I'm doin' a shot," Chris said. He leaned one elbow on the bar in front of him as he tried to get the bartender's attention.

"I'll join you," I said. We each did a double shot of whiskey. It helped. "Hey," I said. "Lisette told me that you didn't bring your business phone with you for the trip. I should probably get your cell number so we can communicate about getting in and out of the hotel room and stuff until I can get a flight out of here tomorrow." Chris stared at me like I was crazy.

"Mama, I don't know what you're talking about," he said in an exhausted tone. He took a drink of beer. "I only got one phone."

"The business one," I said. "The one Lisette gave you for work." He looked at me and raised his eyebrows like he still had no clue what I was talking about. I began to get a little irritated. "The one you've sent me like a hundred texts from." It was probably more like hundreds of text messages, back and forth, giving information about work. This phone number had even sent me messages about how I should be more patient with Lisette as a friend and told me that she loved me and had never felt this way about anyone before in her life, that it was worth my while to hold on and have some faith in her. I had often wondered if maybe she'd been encouraging "Richard" to send me these kinds of messages, maybe even overseeing them; perhaps she needed someone else to express for her the things that she couldn't bring herself to say, which required being vulnerable.

"Listen," Chris said, also a little irritated now, "I've never sent you a single text message before in my life. I've never even had your phone number."

"You can't be serious," I said.

"I'm serious." Chris ordered another shot of whiskey from the bartender. "I don't know who's been texting you, but it ain't me."

It was Lisette the entire time. It was so brazenly obvious. It made me want to drink away my embarrassment for having believed her.

She'd said she'd given Chris her "old phone" to use for business, but in reality she must have kept it as a second phone. I instantly felt like a fool, imagining how hilarious it must've been for her every time she'd sent me a message, and how she must have laughed about how gullible I was. Chris eyed me. "Someone texted you saying they were me?" he asked.

I nodded. "I think it was Lisette. It had to have been. But every text always had a sign-off as 'Richard.'" Chris grabbed a handful of bar food from a small bowl and shook his head.

"Richard," he said under his breath. "Wow. You know, I don't even know why she called me that."

"You've never gone by Richard?"

"No," he said.

"You haven't really been her assistant for six years, have you?" I asked. Chris turned his head to fully face me.

"Come on. I met Lisette maybe, I don't know, three months ago," he said. "She wanted advice on how to run her business, and she asked me to help her." I found out later that Chris was a jet broker who had assisted her in arranging some of the flights, and then agreed to come along after a flirtation began between them and he figured out what she was up to.

"I knew you guys had just met," I said. I finished my second beer and ordered a whiskey on the rocks. "Why would she lie about that?" I asked.

Chris shrugged. "I don't know."

"You want to know how long I've really known her?" I asked Chris. He laughed a little and took a drink.

"Sure. I'm guessing it ain't since you were kids; otherwise she wouldn't treat you so badly."

"I've known her just over four years," I said.

"Well, I guess that makes sense," he said.

"You think she treated me badly?" I asked him. It had never occurred to me that anyone present had noticed, though in retrospect it seemed logical.

"Yeah," he said. "A couple weeks ago I was hanging out with her and she was sayin' she knew she treated you badly, and she didn't know why."

"She said that?"

"Yeah. She said she felt bad about some drama with your boyfriend or something. Some joke about him having a new girlfriend, I don't know."

"What?" I said, my pulse raising. "Did she say she'd lied about seeing him with someone?"

"Yeah," he said. "It was something like that. I wasn't really listening, to be honest. I don't think she saw it as a big deal or anything, but she said she felt a little guilty about it."

A little guilty. She'd gone out of her way to fabricate something that she knew would hurt me more than almost anything. She'd regaled me with every painful, made-up detail about her supposed encounter with Ben and his new girlfriend. I remembered what she'd said at the restaurant, "It breaks my heart to tell you this . . . maybe I shouldn't have told you . . ." Maybe it's possible that she actually meant that second part and she was already starting to regret it. I'll never know. It didn't matter now.

The revelations continued when Frankie came back after a long conversation with his wife. He told Chris and me that he hadn't worked as a bodyguard for Lisette's family since she was a child, as she'd always said that he had. Frankie had known her for only three years, and they met at a party. We were all floored by Lisette's deception and embarrassed for having allowed ourselves to be fooled. She lied to all of us, and she'd made us lie to one another. That was what the DEA officer was talking about when I heard him in the hallway saying, "They all believed her." During the interrogation, I was asked who else was on the plane and what I knew about them. I was sure everyone had been asked the same questions. We must have looked like idiots to the DEA. No wonder they'd kept Lisette. It was so obvious that she'd been pumping us up with lies, that we'd been her puppets in some sick game that only she knew the rules to.

As the three of us sat at the bar, Chris's cell phone rang. He picked it up. "It's Lisette," he said. He answered anxiously and walked away. I could hear him saying things like, "We're gonna get you out of there. Stop crying. Listen, mama, it's gonna be okay." Apparently the spell she had over him had yet to be broken.

As I sat alone with my whiskey, anger boiled inside me. Lisette, who'd claimed to be my best friend for more than four years, had actively tried to hurt me by making up some ridiculous story about my ex-boyfriend. I decided that crossed a line. For whatever reason, after everything else, this made me the angriest. It was my tipping point, when my feelings about Lisette changed forever. Perhaps I'd been waiting for something I could hold on to with conviction, something that I couldn't talk myself out of. From this, there was no going back. I pulled my phone out of my purse. I had one missed call. Lisette had tried to call me before she'd called Chris. I was glad that I hadn't heard it ringing. I needed to let all this sink in before I could think clearly. I knew that hearing her cries from jail would have melted my anger and forced me to surrender to having some compassion for her.

This was the first time I'd held my phone since I'd raised it into the air when I was at gunpoint. I'd been trying to text my father. Thinking about my parents made me want to cry—I missed them so much right now. I wished that I could snap my fingers and be with them in Washington, sitting at our family dinner table to one of my mom's gourmet home-cooked meals. I wished I could hug my mom right now. "I'll be right back," I told Frankie as he came back from outside to take a seat. I left the bar stool with my phone in my hand. My fingers shook as I dialed my home phone in Washington.

"Hello?" My father's ever-cheery voice answered the phone.

"Hi, Dad," I said, forcing a smile to try to make my voice sound less troubled.

"Well, hello, sweetie! I didn't think I'd hear from you today!" he said. "How are you doin'?"

"I'm okay," I lied. *Another lie.* "I'm just . . . I don't really have that much time to talk, but I just wanted to hear your voice . . . I really miss you and Mom."

"We miss you too, honey," he said. I heard my mom in the background call out, "Love you!"

"I was thinking that I'd really like to come home soon," I said. "I just want to come home and, uh, see you guys for a little while . . . I really miss you."

"Well, you know we'd always love to have you here." My dad's tone softened. "Are you sure you're okay?"

"Yeah," I said. "I have to go though. Love you." I took a moment to collect myself before I headed back to the bar for last call.

THE NEXT DAY, I SAT inside our shared hotel room on my computer, looking for one-way flights back to L.A. I had less than a thousand dollars in my bank account, and most of the flights cost about eight hundred dollars. I felt trapped in Ohio. I heard the hotel room door being unlocked. The door opened and Frankie and Chris walked in with their heads down and their eyes wide, like they'd just seen a ghost. "What's wrong?" I asked. Frankie didn't answer me and just shook his head while he paced around the room. I looked to Chris. "What's wrong?" I asked again.

"We're on the news," he said. "We were sitting at the bar downstairs watching TV, and then some local reporter started talking about the story."

"Holy shit," I said. "That's not good."

"No. It's not," Chris said, looking nervous for the first time.

"Man, I need to get out of here," Frankie said. "I need some air."

When the guys left to go on a walk, I turned on the TV. I flipped through news channels. It didn't take long to see the headline scrolling at the bottom of the screen: "Alleged Samsung heiress arrested with 506 pounds of marijuana." Lisette's face appeared in an incredibly unflattering mug shot as a news anchor gave the story. The reporter said that the self-proclaimed heiress to Samsung had been arrested with two assistants and a bodyguard, and that we'd been caught coming off a plane with a quarter ton of marijuana stuffed into thirteen Louis Vuitton suitcases. *Louis Vuitton?*

None of those bags was designer, let alone Louis Vuitton. More like something purchased from Costco with a few years of wear on them. These people just wanted it to be a juicier story. The only thing that was Louis Vuitton had been Lisette's small, personal bag. The reporter went on to say that Samsung had released an official statement saying, "Lisette Lee is not an heiress of Samsung and is not a member of Samsung's Lee family." I turned the TV off. I didn't know what to believe.

I had plenty of confirmation that Lisette was a liar, but I wasn't sure whether she'd made this one up entirely. She had some whoppers under her belt, but this one would take the cake by a long shot. Maybe Samsung was just trying to dodge the negative press. But if she really was a family member, why would they turn their backs on her?

As my vision of the Lisette I'd known disappeared, so did the net that I'd thought would catch me if I fell. If I was charged with anything, she wasn't going to be able to help me. She couldn't save any of us, perhaps not even herself.

When Chris and Frankie returned to the hotel room an hour later, Chris said that he'd spoken to Lisette again. "She gave me the PIN number for her card," he said. "She said you can use it to buy a flight back to L.A." The day before we'd left for Ohio, Lisette gave me seven thousand dollars in cash to deposit into a bank account in her name that was to be used for traveling expenses for the team. When we were arrested, I still had the debit card tucked into my purse. Earlier that morning I'd asked Chris to get the PIN number from Lisette and ask her if I could use it to buy a ticket home. With her permission to do so, I used the card to book a flight to Los Angeles. The plane was leaving in a few hours. Before getting into a cab to the airport, I gave the debit card to Chris. "Take it," I said. "I'm not going to use it." Part of me wanted to take the card with me, but it wasn't my money. I'd never stolen anything in my life, and now probably wasn't a good time to start. I didn't feel like adding another item to the list of things I've done that I wasn't proud of.

When the plane touched down at LAX just after sunset, I felt some small sense of relief. Every inch of my body was still wired from nerves, but I was trying to be optimistic about what was going to happen next. The past few months had been such hell that it was hard to imagine it getting worse. I wanted to run to the nearest cab to get home, open a bottle of wine, and start looking for jobs online.

As I stepped off the plane I could feel that the weather outside was warm. Another summer night in Los Angeles. I made my way through the airport and arrived at baggage claim to collect my suitcase. I turned my phone on as I waited at the carousel. I had one new voice mail. It was from an Ohio number I didn't recognize. My heart dropped into my stomach as I began to listen to the message. It was from the head DEA agent, Matt Heufelder. He wanted my address so he could mail me some documents. He was calling to inform me that I had been named a "target of investigation."

18

TARGET OF INVESTIGATION

I sat silently in the back of a taxi on my way home from the airport. The world outside the car passed by me in a dingy blur of palm trees and streetlights. The last time I'd been driven from an airport I was in handcuffs in the back of a DEA SUV. It almost didn't seem like real life, but hearing Agent Heufelder's voice mail made it impossible for me to believe it was just another terrible dream. I wasn't entirely sure what it meant to be a target of investigation. I was willing to bet it was a step beyond being a "person of interest," a term I'd heard in TV shows and movies when it was somebody else's fictional life that hadn't really happened, and when no one was going to really pay for those fake crimes. Our crime was quite real, and the consequences for it would be equally real.

The sun had disappeared completely by the time I arrived back at my apartment. I was relieved to find that Brie wasn't home from work yet. It bought me more time to think of how I was going to tell her what had taken place in Ohio. I wasn't prepared to tell anyone about this yet. It was slowly dawning on me that the arrest of Team LL, as well as the truth about our business, wasn't going to remain a secret. I couldn't yet admit it fully to myself, let alone anyone else. Once I got inside the apartment with my suitcase, I immediately shut the door behind me and locked it. Someone was missing 506 pounds of marijuana, and people knew I was involved. I was a target of investigation, and I could be a target of God knows what else.

I'd eaten only once in the past two days. My clothes were hanging on me. I'd been too wired to eat or even have caffeine. I texted Brie to let her know I'd come back into town early. I said that I needed to tell her something when she got home. She replied she'd be back within the hour. I opened a bottle of merlot and took out two glasses. I'd have some poured for Brie when she walked in. While I waited for her, I took my computer out of my suitcase and opened it on the dining room table. I checked my e-mail and found that I had a new Google alert on my name. I followed a link in the e-mail to a YouTube video. It was a news clip from a national television station. Our arrest was national news now. The media had nicknamed Lisette "the Pot Princess." The one-minute video was similar to the report that I'd seen on the news in Ohio, but then the anchor added something more. "Lee was arrested with a bodyguard and two assistants." I watched in disbelief as footage of my acting demo reel played on the news report. "One of Lee's assistants is an actress named Meili Cady." My name and face were on the news.

Who else has seen this?

At least they weren't using my mug shot—some small consolation.

After scanning YouTube to find three other news videos about the arrest, I heard the door to the apartment being unlocked from the outside. Brie walked in looking concerned. "What's wrong with our lock?" she asked. "I could barely get it to open. Did you put anything in the keyhole besides the key?"

"No, I just got home," I said. "I don't know, it seemed to open fine when I came in."

Granted, I had other things on my mind so I was more than a little distracted.

"The key didn't fit at first," she said as she took a closer look at the lock. "I had to jangle it around. I hope no one tried to break in." She looked at me. "Is that what you were going to tell me?"

"No," I said. "I doubt anyone tried to break in." I walked up to her with a glass of wine. "I already poured you one."

"Thanks . . ." she said, eyeing me as she took a sip.

"Okay," I said, inhaling a deep breath. "Um . . . I think the best way to do this might be to show you a video."

"A video?" Brie looked confused.

"It's . . . it's a news video," I said. "Er, you might want to sit down." Brie looked nervous as she sat at the table in front of my computer. I reopened the first video and pressed play. I took a step back and stood with my arms crossed as she watched it.

When it ended, she lifted her eyes from the computer screen to look at me for a moment. "Wow," she said with wide eyes and an open mouth. "That explains a lot." She took a sip of her wine. "I guess I'm not that surprised. I mean, I always thought something was off . . . but I never thought it would be drugs."

"Neither did I," I said.

"You didn't know what was in the suitcases?" she asked.

"No," I said quickly. "I thought it was money." I couldn't bring myself to admit that I'd known for months what we'd been doing, and that I'd continued to do it. I wanted to deny everything, even to myself. I especially didn't want to discuss anything here since I'd already been wondering for weeks whether our apartment might be wired in some way. Lisette said that she'd installed surveillance in David's apartment a while back. Why not mine too? I didn't trust my cell phone, either. I didn't trust anyone's phones. It was safest to assume that everything was being tapped. To have a safe conversation, Brie and I needed to speak outside of the apartment, and we needed to take the batteries out of our cell phones. Chris Cash told me that was the only way to make sure no one could hear you if your phone was tapped.

THE NEXT MORNING I WOKE up to a call from my brother, Nick. When I answered the phone, he asked me right away, "Meili? Are you okay?" I could hear in his voice that he knew what had happened.

"No," I said. His girlfriend had seen the story of our arrest headlining Google News and told him.

"Do Mom and Dad know?" he asked.

"No," I said. "I haven't told them yet . . . I'm kind of scared to."

"I can see why," Nick said. "Maybe it's best if I tell them."

My parents wasted no time in calling their attorney in Washington to get a referral for a federal defense lawyer in Los Angeles. They dipped into their retirement to pay the hefty retainer fee for my new lawyer, which by itself cost more than any car I'd ever owned. After years of discomfort whenever I'd had to ask them for money, it made me sick to my stomach to know that they were now literally paying for my mistakes. In the midst of the down economy and my father's challenges with the suffering real estate market, my parents were left with the decision to either hemorrhage money from their savings to try to save their daughter from years in prison, or leave me to lie in the bed I'd made for myself. They were rightfully mad as hell that I'd gotten myself into this and they were scared for my safety, but they decided to risk everything and stand by me. The two people who'd raised me with such love as a child and did everything they could to protect me were now trying frantically to catch me as I fell from something that they might not be able to save me from.

Michael Proctor was a partner in a fancy downtown law firm in L.A. Within hours of getting the referral from my parents, I drove to meet him for the first time at his high-rise office building on Wilshire Boulevard. After checking in at a lacquered wood reception desk, I was led into a huge, glass-walled conference room that overlooked the building next door. As I waited to meet my new attorney, I stared out the window. From the conference room at the offices of Caldwell, Leslie and Proctor, I was rattled to my core when I discovered that I had an unobstructed view of the building David Garrett used to live in, where it all began. I could see clearly the back entrance where the limos would park and be loaded with suitcases before we rode to the airport. The suitcases were kept in his apartment in the beginning, long before I knew what was in them. I remembered getting into the limo there on the first two trips, before Lisette started coming with us. I remembered her texting me as I waited inside the limo, telling me to have a good trip.

Little did I know she was just hoping that I wouldn't get arrested, because I was a guinea pig for her. If I'd been arrested, she would have probably left me for dead and claimed innocence. That must have been why she had all the money for the planes wired through my banking account. She was setting up a wall between her and the federal government, and that wall was me.

Michael Proctor walked into the conference room. He introduced himself and invited me to have a seat. He asked me what felt like an endless list of questions about my history with Lisette. He told me that Lisette was in big trouble, and so was I, bringing law books into the conference room to make me see what I was up against. The sentencing guidelines said that I was looking at between five and forty years in prison.

Mike furrowed his brow and studied my reaction to what he'd just read out loud from a thick book of sentencing guidelines that stated clearly that even one of the trips I'd made to Ohio could earn me a felony and up to forty years behind bars.

"Do you think I'm going to go to prison?" I asked him after staring at the open page and taking a dry swallow of air.

"I don't know," he said. "I don't know." He closed the book and looked at me intently. "I think that's enough for today."

As much as I couldn't imagine myself going to federal prison, it was equally bizarre to imagine Lisette there. She was already in a county jail now. I struggled to wrap my head around any of it. She had always seemed undefeatable. I kept thinking that her family would step in soon and get her out of custody. When I left Ohio, Chris told me that she didn't even have a lawyer yet, but she must have had one by now. It was strange that Chris was the one trying to get legal counsel for her, rather than her family. I wondered if she would ever come looking for me when she got out, which could be soon.

Questions raced through my mind: *If I tell the DEA that I knew it was pot in the suitcases, will she be angry enough to have me killed by the supposed hit man she has "on speed dial"? Is a plan like that already in action?* I knew that other people were involved in the business, and it was safe to assume that whoever was missing that quarter ton of pot wasn't happy.

If I admitted to everything and cooperated with the government, my attorney said that I'd get a more lenient sentence. That would mean telling the DEA everything I knew about the person I used to call my best friend and possibly pissing off some Mexican gangsters . . . but I was looking at five to forty years. I now knew that Lisette was never a genuine or loyal friend to me, so I didn't feel guilty about not going out of my way to protect her. I couldn't protect her at that point even if I wanted to. We never discussed having a consistent cover story for what we were doing. I was extremely grateful that I had never been privy to many details about the operation, as the "everything I know" in reality wasn't very extensive. I could only tell my own experience, and I wasn't sure if that would be enough.

When I left Mike's office that day, I was consumed by thoughts of the horror that might well be awaiting me in a decades-long prison sentence. Five years was the minimum sentence for just *one* trip. I went on maybe *ten* trips. I wasn't even sure how many; they could easily add up to more years in prison than years I'd been alive.

As I pulled out of the underground parking for the office building, I was on the verge of tears and in desperate need of some kind of comfort.

I took out my phone and stared at it for a moment. Ben and I hadn't spoken since he'd walked out of my apartment and left me two months ago. I called his number and held my breath as it began to ring. When there was no answer on the second ring, I wondered if I shouldn't have called. I was strongly considering hanging up when he answered. "Hello?"

"Ben? It's Meili." I prepared myself to hear an abrupt click, but he didn't hang up. His voice didn't sound angry or mean, the way it had when I'd seen him last. He sounded relaxed and almost happy to hear from me.

"Hey. How are you doing?" he asked.

"Uh, well, I've had better days," I said. "Have you seen the news?"

"For what?" he asked. When I filled him in on what had happened, he didn't seem surprised. "I knew that bitch was crazy," he said. I told him what my attorney said about my sentencing guidelines. "Wow," Ben said. "That's a long time . . . do you have a good attorney? Because if you don't, I know someone."

"Thanks," I said, "but I think he seems really good. He's smart. I think if I have any chance of not going away for years and years, he's probably my best shot at it."

"Okay, good," Ben said. "Let me know if you need anything. It's good to hear your voice."

"It's good to hear your voice too," I said, surprised by his sudden sentiment. "Um . . . are you home? I'm downtown, not far from your place . . . I could really use a friend." The line went silent for a moment.

"Uh," he said, "I'm actually not home right now, and I won't be for a few hours. Sorry."

"No, no worries," I said. "It's fine. I know it's been a while."

"Listen," he said, "I gotta go, but I'll call you tonight to check in on you."

"Thanks," I managed to choke out before hanging up.

Ben didn't call to check on me. The next day he sent me a text message that read,

LEAVE ME ALONE. I HAVE NO INTEREST IN ASSOCIATING WITH SOMEONE WHO IS BEING ACCUSED OF A FELONY.

His cold words referred to the undeniable fact that I would likely be convicted of at least one felony, and that I'd be a felon for the rest of my life. Felon. A word that was synonymous in our society with bad, dangerous people. I wasn't prepared to bear that scarlet letter, but my actions may have already sealed my fate.

My parents bought me a ticket to come to Washington and speak with them in private. The phone lines weren't safe, so I couldn't have an open conversation with them until we were face-to-face. I shuddered to think of their faces now, the once proud parents who'd had an honor student and a student body president for a daughter, the one they supported in all her big dreams that she didn't think our small town could fulfill. That daughter had become a drug smuggler since leaving home and was now on her way to being branded a felon.

I didn't tell anyone that I was going out of town except Brie. Paranoia consumed me as I waited in line for security at LAX. I kept looking over my shoulder. What I was looking for, I didn't know. As I turned around to see behind me, I noticed a tall and hulking Hispanic man in his thirties who was covered in tattoos and wearing a sleeveless red jersey. He bore an eerie resemblance to David and his weed supplier, Jose, both of whom I'd met during my involvement in the sordid world of drug smuggling. He was waiting in the same security line as I was, but he had no luggage or personal bags with him.

Who flies with no luggage?

I faced forward. After I went through security, I had a fairly lengthy walk to my gate. I kept my eyes straight ahead and took quick steps. After a few minutes had passed, I gave myself permission to check over my shoulder again. The man in the jersey was about a hundred feet behind me. Still by himself, still with no luggage. Panic shortened my breath. Chills trickled down my spine. With every step I took, I wondered if it could be my last step toward home.

Is he going to break into a sprint and grab me? He's big enough to take on most of the security guards here. Is he working alone? Is there some thug waiting for me around the corner, ready to block my path and assist in my abduction?

On an impulse I darted into an airport bookstore and attempted to hide myself behind a shelf. My chest rose and fell with every breath I took. I peered around the wooden shelving to watch as he began to go by. He casually slowed down in front of the store, looked around, then stopped walking entirely. He went to a nearby pay phone and dialed a number.

Who uses a pay phone anymore? Why isn't he using a cell phone? What's he doing? Is he going to try to kill me?

As he talked, I hurried to pull my cell phone out of my purse. My hand shook uncontrollably as I held it up just around the shelf and snapped a quick picture of him. His call lasted less than a minute. He hung up and strolled on. I tried to calm myself down in the bookstore for a minute. I'd started to attract strange looks from the clerk. I suppose from an outside perspective my behavior looked odd, but people didn't know what I was up against. I sent the picture to Brie with a message:

I THINK THIS MAN IS FOLLOWING ME. IF SOMETHING HAPPENS TO ME, PLEASE SHARE THIS PHOTO WITH THE POLICE.

At least the authorities would have a lead if things went south and I never made it to Washington.

After I managed to gain some semblance of composure, I left the bookstore and bolted for my gate. Hundreds of people were crowded in the boarding area. I had half an hour before I was scheduled to board. Half an hour in which anything could happen. I stood near my gate and frantically scanned the room to find the man in the jersey. I didn't see him. I spun around. He wasn't here. He had to be here . . . I didn't think he'd give up that easily. Suddenly, I saw a red blur in the corner of my eye. It was the red of his sports jersey. He strolled casually into the boarding area and took a seat.

Is he planning to fly all the way to Washington and take me once I'm there? Will he follow me off the plane and snatch me up before I'm able to get to my father? There are plenty of wooded areas around Seattle to hide a body . . .

I tried not to make any sudden movements as I kept my head down and walked into a nearby restroom. Once I was inside, I took out my phone and called a family friend who was an attorney. After telling him everything in a breathless whisper, he told me to calm down. "Tell the airline that you're a witness in a federal drug case and that you believe you're being followed." I said okay and got off the phone. I took the long way back to my gate so as not to walk directly past the man in the jersey. I approached a woman in a blue-and-white uniform behind a desk in front of where my flight would board. She was fussing with some papers in front of her. I walked up to the desk as close as I could possibly get to it. I rested both of my arms on it and leaned in to face her, anxiously awaiting a chance to get her attention. After a moment she looked up. "Hi, can I help you?" she asked me in a friendly tone.

"Hi, yes . . ." I answered her in a shaky whisper. "I'm a passenger on the next flight to Seattle. I'm a witness in a federal drug case, and I believe that I'm being followed." She looked at me with a grave stare and nodded.

She leaned forward to me and lowered her voice. "Who do you believe is following you? Is the person here right now?"

I nodded. "Yes," I said very quietly. The woman moved her head in to make sure she could hear me as I went on. "He's the man in the red jersey sitting over there." I indicated with my now watery eyes which direction I meant.

She looked confused. "Do you mean the man with the shaved head?" "Yes," I said.

She looked sympathetically at me. "That's Edwin," she said. "He works here. He's just here to pick up his son."

AT THE SEATAC AIRPORT IN Seattle, I got off the plane and rushed to where my father had said he'd meet me. He'd never opted to pick me up outside of the airport with a car at the curb, despite the convenience it could afford. He had always parked and walked in so he'd be there to greet me when I came out. I wasn't sure if I could expect the same greeting today, after everything I'd done. As I walked out, I saw my dad. His once black hair was speckled with gray and looked fresh from a barber trim. He stood wearing a tucked-in black T-shirt I'd given him for Christmas last year and belted khaki slacks. I held my breath as he looked up and saw me. I broke into a short run and knocked hard into his comforting chest as he swallowed me in a tight hug.

IT WAS MIDNIGHT AT MY family home in Bremerton, Washington. We were ten minutes from town, but every mile between was consumed by dense forest. Our house was up a gravel driveway, a short stretch from the highway. Here, after nightfall, there were no streetlights. It was black outside in every direction.

I sat in our living room by an unlit fireplace with my parents. We were whispering, though no one was within earshot by quite a distance. All our cell phones had the batteries out and were tucked under a pillow in my parents' bedroom. We were all dressed in pajamas. My mother was in her favorite plaid L.L.Bean nightgown. My parents were in shock at what had happened.

Our conversation was interrupted when an abrupt knock at the door broke the otherwise deathly quiet of our home. We exchanged alarmed glances. It was after midnight, and we weren't expecting company. No one knew I was here. There was no logical reason for an unexpected visitor. We'd heard no sound of a car pulling into our gravel driveway. I decided that it must be my aunt. Perhaps my parents had told her I was here and hadn't let me know. We must have been too consumed in conversation to hear her SUV coming in. I stepped quietly toward our front door to look through the peephole. My dad was close behind me, and my mom stood up white-faced in her nightgown a few paces behind him.

I looked out through the peephole. My heart fell. A stranger stood on the other side of the door to our home. He had jet-black hair and looked Hispanic, in his midthirties, and was wearing jeans and a white T-shirt. His deadpan expression offered no sense of reassurance. He held a red gas can at his side. I moved my face from the peephole and avoided my mother's frightened eyes.

I glanced back at my father. He looked through the peephole, then quickly leaned to the side of the door with his back to the wall. I leaned on the other side. My mom stood back. Dad called out, "Hello?"

The stranger responded. "Hi. Yeah, I ran out of gas on the road. Wondered if I can use your phone. Sorry, I know it's late."

"I'm sorry, but we can't let you in," my father said. "There's a gas station up the road a quarter mile." For a heavy moment, there was silence on the other side of the door.

I heard the stranger's voice say, "Do you mind if I just use your phone? I'll be quick."

"No, I'm sorry," my dad said, his back still pressed up against the wall. My mother stood behind us with her hands cupped over her mouth.

"Is the gas station still open?" the stranger asked.

"Yes, it should be open," my dad said. I watched through the peephole as the man left our porch and faded away into the darkness. I rushed to grab our portable house phone and dialed 911. My father disappeared down our stairs in his bathrobe and pajamas.

I stayed on the phone with the 911 operator while we waited for a sheriff to come check the perimeter of our house. My dad reappeared from the stairs holding his hunting rifle. He loaded it. Just in case. His movements were quick and efficient from a lifetime of hunting. He held the gun at the ready as he scanned the yard from our kitchen window.

There was a breeze tonight, and as I looked outside I saw the bushes moving with the wind. I blinked, expecting to see dark figures rising out of them, ready to invade our home in arms, like in the final scene in *Scarface*. In the twenty-six years my parents had lived here, only one other person had broken down on the road and come to the house. It was by no means a common occurrence, and the visitor's timing tonight was haunting. After fifteen minutes of waiting while my father held his loaded rifle, a police car pulled into our driveway. Having heard our report before his arrival, the local sheriff told us that he'd seen no car on the road and no man walking along the highway.

THE NEXT EVENING, MY PARENTS and I were talking around our kitchen counter when my mother suddenly froze where she stood and held up a finger to hush us. My father and I exchanged startled glances. "Do you hear that?" she asked with a tight face. Before we could answer her, she stormed off in a brave fury and threw open the front door. She stepped out on our porch to peer into the darkness of our gravel driveway. The motion-detecting light on our carport flashed on and illuminated the driveway. My mother spotted three shadowy figures scurrying away toward the bushes, trying to escape the light of the motion detector. "Who's there?" she screamed, her voice hoarse with a mix of anger and fear. "You tell me right now! Show yourselves!" My father and I hurried up behind her in defense.

The figures near the bushes broke into tipsy laughter. The three shadows crept into the light from the garage and revealed their identity. It was Cate, a face my mom instantly recognized after almost twenty years of my close friendship with her. She'd come with two of our shared childhood friends. They'd been tossing small pieces of gravel at my bedroom window to try to get my attention. Cate had been trying to get ahold of me for the past few days, and after I uncharacteristically ignored multiple messages from her, I finally answered her from my father's phone, writing simply, MEILI IS OKAY. My last-minute visit home was meant to be a secret, to ensure privacy with my parents. Practically no one in town knew that I'd been arrested yet. It hadn't been on the news much in Washington, and it was by sheer chance that my brother's girlfriend had seen the story on Google News during the short period that it was featured. With the exception of a very few, most news outlets hadn't used my name in their reports, only Lisette's, so unless someone who knew my relationship to her happened to see the story and put the pieces together, it was unlikely that many people would find out right away. Cate had no idea about my arrest, but when she received my foreboding message from my father's cell phone, she became suspicious that something was wrong and had a hunch that I was in town and hiding for some reason. After an evening of drinking at a local hub, she'd become increasingly worried and rounded up the gang to investigate. As it was late and my friends didn't want to risk waking my parents up, they parked at the end of our gravel driveway and snuck up on foot. Cate's suspicions that I was home were confirmed when they saw that my bedroom light was on, at which point they began to throw pebbles at it in an attempt to get my attention.

When Cate and my friends poured in our front door, Cate threw her arms around me in a sloppy hug. "I knew you were here!" she said. "You sneaky snake!" I hadn't seen Cate in almost a year, and her embrace, though drunken, was more comforting right now than she could have possibly imagined. I held on to her a little longer than I usually would, and she had to pry me off her. "Ha!" she remarked. "Are you drunk too?" "No," I said with a smile. "I'm just happy to see you. But next time, please just knock." She laughed heartily and went on to hug my parents. When my mother and father invited my friends in, we didn't tell them why I was there. Thankfully, most of them had had enough drinks to not ask many questions. I wondered how long it would be before they found out that I'd been arrested. Soon, there would be no more secrets.

IN THE MORNING, I AWOKE to a gentle knock at my bedroom door. I opened my eyes, and through foggy vision I tried to decipher the neon numbers on the clock beside my bed. It was about five hours earlier than I would normally get up. "Come in," I called out in a groggy voice from underneath the covers. When the door opened, my mother appeared in lavender-and-white nursing scrubs, holding a steaming cup of coffee. She set the speckled yellow mug down at my bedside table. "I put a little cream in it," she said as she sat on my bed. "Not too much, I hope."

"Thanks," I said.

"I made some scrambled eggs," she said. "I thought we could eat breakfast together before I leave for work."

At the kitchen counter, I sat on a tall wooden swivel chair between my mom and dad. I poured hot sauce over my eggs and tried to gain consciousness with a sip of coffee. A little too much cream, but I told my mom it was just right. It was Father's Day. I would usually have at least sent my dad a card, but I didn't have anything prepared to give to him. I had no money to get him a gift or take him to dinner. I deeply regretted not having mailed a card.

"What are you doing today?" I asked him.

"I'm going to do some work on one of the rentals on Fifty-Eighth Street," he said. My family owned a half-dozen rental homes in a low-income neighborhood in Bremerton. Many of them had been vacant in the down economy, and my father was trying to fix one of them up in the hopes of renting it soon.

"Do you want some help?" I asked him. "I can come with you if you want."

My father nodded before taking a bite of eggs. "That'd be real nice, sweetie," he said. "I can't think of a better Father's Day gift."

I forced a smile.

How about not having a daughter who has recently committed a series of felonies? That might be an okay thing to have for Father's Day.

I SAT IN THE PASSENGER side of my dad's 1983 rusted yellow Toyota Tercel as he drove us through Bremerton with a wooden utility trailer full of yard tools thudding around behind us. My father had taught me how to drive in this car. Stick shift had always terrified me, but I was glad that I'd learned how to use it nonetheless. This had always been the car he used for hunting trips, and when I was sixteen, I switched out the camouflaged seat covers for Hawaiian prints and added some baby-blue dice to hang from the rearview mirror. Now there were no seat covers at all, and the original, now fading brown-and-gold plaid was exposed.

I used to think this car was embarrassing, but as my dad drove us through the run-down neighborhood where the rental property was,

I felt ashamed for having ever stuck up my nose at what my parents offered me when I was teenager. One thing I knew for sure was that I would rather be in this car with my father right now than riding shotgun in one of Lisette's Bentleys.

The Tercel came to a slow stop in front of a tiny, broken-looking house with foot-tall weeds and growth consuming every inch of the yard. It looked like something I would see in an episode of *Extreme Home Makeover*, before Ty Pennington would come with an army of workers to assist in making it livable. It dawned on me that had I not casually offered to tag along with my dad today he would have had to do everything by himself, and that he usually did because I didn't live here now and he didn't have a team of workers at his disposal. My mouth gaped as I stepped out of the car and stared at the property. I hadn't expected it to look so dilapidated. I would have believed the house was condemned if I'd passed by it without knowing it belonged to my family. It had been years since I'd been to any of our rentals. My dad got out of the car and grabbed a Weedwacker and a metal rake from the trailer, along with a box of black plastic trash bags. He handed me the rake. "All right," he said with a smile, "we want to get most of it out of the backyard."

My dad put on goggles and held the Weedwacker steady as it chomped through tall growth in the back of the property. I swung the rake down as fast and hard as I could to collect everything that was left behind him as he worked. When there was enough to fill a trash bag, I pulled one out, filled it, and tied it off as quickly as I could. Something was driving me today that I didn't recognize. I immediately went back to swinging the rake. As I hurled it down onto the freshly cut weeds, I realized that I couldn't remember the last time I'd worked this hard. I was wearing old drawstring pants, a T-shirt, and a sweatshirt I hadn't worn since high school. In less than an hour, I pulled off the sweatshirt because I was too hot. Beads of sweat were pouring from my hairline. It felt good. It felt raw. It felt like real, honest work, and it was something I hadn't felt in a long time. As much as I'd thought that I'd been doing my best in Los Angeles and trying to make ends meet, I was reminded now of what real work was. It was what my father had been doing since before I was born. He had provided for our family and put food on our table and a roof over our heads by work that included this kind of physical labor.

I didn't want to be someone who shied away from the kind of work that gets your blood pumping. It makes a person feel alive and embrace a sense of self-worth, something I hadn't always had. It was different from the self-serving satisfaction that I'd felt after a hot yoga or spin class at a trendy L.A. hotspot.

After hours of raking overgrown weeds into a now mounting pile of trash bags, I stopped to take a breath. I had finally caught up and raked and bagged all the weeds my father had chopped down with the Weedwacker. As I leaned out of breath on the rake, my father walked up to me. He lifted his now grass-splattered goggles and gave a wide grin. "I think we'll be done in about an hour," he said. He looked at the trash bags that were piled against the side of the house. "You're doin' a good job," he said. He patted my back with his garden-gloved hand. "I'm proud of you." Hearing those words from my father meant more to me than I could tell him right now. I sucked in a whirlwind of emotions. It was Father's Day, and it wasn't about me. I went back to raking.

By the time we finished work on the rental and loaded the bags of weeds into the trailer behind the Toyota, the sun was beginning to set. This was the last night I'd spend with my parents before I would plead guilty to a felony in federal court.

MY FATHER DROVE ME TO the airport in the morning. I tried to appear in good spirits when he hugged me good-bye in the car outside of my airline, but we both knew that the next time we'd see each other would likely be many months from now, when I would be sentenced to prison in Ohio.

19

QUEEN FOR A DAY

Mike Proctor called me in to his office to discuss my case. We sat on cushioned swivel chairs inside his glass-walled conference room overlooking David Garrett's former building. He told me that the best chance I'd have at getting any lenience from the prosecution was for me to agree to something called a "proffer session," also known as "Queen for a Day."

"I have to tell you it's not a hundred percent safe," Mike said. "It's a type of plea agreement where we'll sit down in a formal, in-person interview with Agent Heufelder and the prosecutor in Ohio. They'll probably have a second DEA agent there too. And you'll tell them everything they want to know. Any new and incriminating information that you bring into the meeting will not necessarily be held against you."

"Not necessarily? What does that mean?" I asked. "That doesn't sound very safe."

"Well, it's not," he said. "For example, say they don't already know about your wire transfers, and you talk about it in the meeting. Then, after the meeting, based on the terms of the proffer session, they can't hold what you've said against you. However, what they could do instead is subpoena your bank records and use *those* against you in court."

"Oh," I said, "great . . ."

"The most important thing you need to do in the meeting is tell the truth," he said. "Even knowingly omitting information can be seen as dishonesty. Any Queen for a Day agreement is contingent upon absolute honesty, and if the prosecution or DEA agents feel that you've lied to them about even the smallest detail, you'll be discredited and they won't recommend any lenience to the judge. But if you're honest, they're likely to help you." Mike made arrangements for a proffer session to happen the next month in Ohio.

The news coverage of our case became increasingly difficult to watch. To my own personal horror, my mug shot was released to the media, and it was being splashed across the Internet alongside Lisette's. Her heavy eye makeup and large hoop earrings made her mug shot look like it might belong to a prostitute, and in mine I was completely without makeup and savagely hungover, looking like an exhausted butch mule after a long day of plowing fields. A short patch of hair was visible just above my bangs where Lisette cut gum out on the morning of our arrest. On a scale of one to Nick Nolte, it was tough to say which of our mug shots was worse.

Four weeks after being arrested, I flew back to Ohio with Mike to meet with the prosecution. We arrived late in the evening and checked into our respective hotel rooms in downtown Columbus. We met early the next morning in the hotel lobby. We'd be going straight to the airport after the proffer session, so we brought our suitcases with us to the meeting.

Mike and I waited at the ground level of a secure government building. The prosecutor was on his way downstairs to give us access to the elevator. Assistant U.S. Attorney Tim Pritchard appeared from behind a locked stark-white door to greet us. He was younger than I'd expected, in his forties, just like Mike Proctor and the lead investigator for my case, Agent Heufelder. I didn't know why I'd expected everyone to be old. Pritchard gave Mike and me a stern greeting as he shook our hands. This man had the power to send me to prison for years, so I was extremely nervous as we rode the elevator up with Tim. Mike was friendly and asked Tim how long he'd worked at these offices. Tim opened up in conversation but kept his tone fairly dry and impersonal, for the most part. He was still sizing us up.

Tim led us to a small, windowless conference room. We followed him inside and saw Agent Heufelder seated at a conference table beside a face I instantly recognized. "Steve!" I yelled out enthusiastically, feeling suddenly less scared. Officer Steve, the agent I'd met during my arrest at the opposite end of an MP5 submachine gun, was sitting in as the "other DEA agent" who Mike had said might be present during the proffer session. "I didn't know you were going to be here!" I exclaimed with a big smile. I resisted an urge to walk up and give him a hug. The relief of seeing a familiar face of someone I remembered as having been kind to me wasn't something I'd expected today. I couldn't keep a lid on it when I walked into the conference room. I was worried that the second DEA agent at the meeting might be the gruff bastard who'd interrogated me, and seeing Steve here instead felt like the opposite of that scenario. Tim Pritchard seemed baffled by my friendly reaction to Steve. Agent Heufelder was tapping a pen on the table and keeping a tight mouth as he watched my informal exchange with his colleague. He met Tim's gaze and explained, "Steve was Meili's arresting officer." Tim nodded politely with widened eyes, though it might have raised more questions than answers.

"Okay," Mike said, clearing his throat. "Why don't we take a seat?" Mike and I sat side by side directly across the conference table from Tim, Agent Heufelder, and Steve.

After four weeks of coaching from Mike, I was prepared to give a full confession. If the prosecution suspected me of dishonesty I'd be given no lenience, and the promise of a lengthy prison sentence seemed imminent. I had to lay my cards down at the beginning of the meeting and admit to knowing it was weed in the suitcases. It was the only way they'd believe the rest of my story, to admit my guilt right away. Once my confession hit the table, Tim and the DEA agents turned down the heat and started asking questions. The proffer session lasted more than five hours. During a break, Tim told Mike that he thought I was the most honest witness he'd ever interviewed, and that he'd never taken more notes in his career.

IN THE MONTHS FOLLOWING THE proffer session, more than twenty of my friends and family members wrote letters to the prosecution on my behalf, defending my character and asking for mercy. In court documents, Tim Pritchard described Lisette's influence over me as being "svengali-like."

I took nearly everything Lisette had ever bought me to a well-regarded consignment store on Melrose Avenue. Her gifts had once served as reminders of our bond, and now they only reminded me of how wrong I'd been about her. The only items not included in my consignment store hefty bag were a pair of Chanel sunglasses that were lost in Ohio during our arrest and a wool-and-cashmere Marc Jacobs sweater that I wore too often to part with. Incidentally, these two items were the only gifts that she'd given me with the tags still on. When I brought four Chanel purses into the upscale consignment store, the manager there examined them. Within a few minutes, she told me she was certain that at least three of the purses were knockoffs, albeit very convincing ones to an untrained eye. She said that only one of them was likely genuine, but that it was too worn to be consigned regardless. Feeling deflated, I handed her a Ziploc bag of Louis Vuitton and Chanel jewelry bearing the designers' signature emblems. The manager examined each piece briefly, and then handed them back to me, shaking her head. She slid off her fashionable tortoiseshell glasses and assured me that none of the jewelry was genuine.

I left with the hefty bag and dropped everything off at the closest Goodwill donation center.

I remembered the tangent Lisette went on about how offensive it was if someone gives a gift that's a fake. One of the few things I'd never taken her word on was when she insisted that the Gucci wallet, which Ben had presented to me with a gift receipt from the store, was a knockoff. It was almost laughable to me now to think about how I'd believed almost everything Lisette had ever said, just as I was sure it was laughable to her while she was saying it. Throughout our friendship, I'd watched her delight in people believing her lies. Ironically, as her lies were becoming exposed through court and media outlets, other people were getting a chance to laugh at them too.

When I first met Lisette, she told me she was one year older than me. Later on, she said she was two years younger than I was, and in reality she was four years my senior. Even her sommelier ex-boyfriend, who lived with her for four years, never knew her real age until it was revealed in court.

Buckley, the private Beverly Hills prep school Lisette boasted about attending with Paris Hilton, had no record of her ever being a student there. Some of her famous alleged former classmates were interviewed by the press, and no one could recall meeting her. Lisette's private school pedigree was an illusion. In reality, she attended public school in Los Angeles until eighth grade, when she enrolled in a homeschooling program.

Though Lisette spoke at length about studying criminal law at Harvard when she was sixteen, there was no record of her being there, let alone at such a young age. If it were true that she'd studied criminal law at an Ivy League school, she might have had more foresight into what she was headed for when she started Team LL, and she might have thought up a better cover story than moving supplies to a nonexistent horse farm.

Her list of mistruths seemed endless, and I became desensitized to hearing new revelations as they surfaced. Everything about her background came under scrutiny, but nothing more so than her claim of connection to Samsung.

Lisette wasn't born in London, as she'd told me. She was born in Seoul, Korea, under the name Ji Yeun Lee. "Lisette" was a name she chose for herself as a teenager, after trying on at least three other temporary identities. While Samsung denied any relation to her in two public statements, in court a far more complicated story emerged through testimonies by her aunt and godparents.

Based on those testimonies, Lisette was born out of wedlock to a Japanese casino mogul father and a Korean mother. Her mother was the daughter of Lee Byung-chul, the late founder of Samsung. Their union was frowned upon by the Korean side of her family, and Lisette was informally adopted by a respected martial arts instructor and his wife in Los Angeles, close friends of Lisette's biological family. The godfather who raised her testified that Lisette was sent around fifty thousand dollars a year by her father to support her. Lisette told the prosecution that he gave her up to one hundred thousand dollars a month. It was unclear what was true. Lisette's aunt was asked under oath what Lisette's father did for a living. With the help of a translator, she replied that he was a "gangster." The prosecution asked her to elaborate on what she meant by "gangster." The translator explained that meant he ran casinos in Japan.

This new, though muddied, information helped me understand more why Lisette never had more than just a few professional-looking photos of her parents, and no pictures of her with them. She'd spoken so often of them, and with such love and admiration. I wondered how often she had really seen them. Though I was upset that she'd lied to me about so many things, I couldn't help but feel sad at the thought that she wasn't raised by her parents, as I knew she would have wanted to be.

While I awaited my court date, I was required to report to the Pretrial Service Office in downtown Los Angeles once a month to meet with a probation officer who never failed to address me in a way that made me feel like she was anxiously awaiting my inevitable failure to comply with the system, when she would finally get to send off an e-mail to the judge, confirming my depravity and recommending that I be locked up with no delay. The women at the recovery center were always nice to me, but the officers in Pretrial didn't make a habit of hiding the fact that they were incessantly judging everyone who walked through their doors.

On one particularly muggy summer afternoon, I drove downtown for my monthly meeting with a probation officer. I parked in a lot a few blocks away and trudged up to the government building. When I exited the elevator, I walked to a door that opened into the bland, dreary atmosphere of Pretrial Service.

As I stepped into a waiting room that looked like it belonged in a free clinic, my knees locked. Henry was standing in the middle of the otherwise empty room. He looked up and saw me. I hadn't seen him since his last trip with Team LL. The moment he looked at me, I ran into his arms. He held me as I burst into uncontrollable tears in the middle of the probation office. He patted my hair. "It's okay," he said. His voice was kind, one the kindest I'd ever known. After I took a moment to breathe, I asked him what his lawyer was saying. Henry told me that his lawyer said he would be lucky to be sentenced to less than three years in prison. I cried harder. "I'm so sorry for what Lisette did to you," I sobbed, throwing my arms around him again. "I watched her do it and I never stopped her. I'm so sorry." He pulled back and looked at me.

"Meili, it's okay," he said. It was clear that he was staying stronger than I was through all of this. I wiped away tears that were cascading down my face.

"She lied to us," I said.

"I know, she fucked us up," he said. "I kind of knew she was lying about a lot of things the whole time. Like when she said she was a pop star in Korea."

"Yeah," I said, smiling a little at how silly that sounded now. Henry smiled back.

"I mean, those blurry videos she showed us of her performing in awards shows and music videos? I knew that wasn't her," he said. "I figured there was no point in saying anything about it though. She wanted us to believe her so I played along with it."

"Yeah . . . I guess I kind of fell for all of it," I said.

"I think they're looking at us," Henry said suddenly, indicating a woman behind the bullet-resistant glass of the Pretrial reception desk who was giving us eyes. "They're probably about to call me in . . . Hey, I feel like I should tell you something. You remember that ring Lisette gave you?"

"Of course," I said.

"Well, that morning in Ohio—I think it was Valentine's Day. You know, when you lost it and we all looked for it?" I nodded. Henry went on. "You didn't lose it. Lisette flushed your ring down the toilet. Frankie and I watched her do it when you were still in bed. I think she was mad about your boyfriend or something. She told us we better not tell you that she did it."

I stood in front of Henry with my mouth agape, speechless. Memories of that horrible day and the devastation I felt for losing the ring that was given as a symbol of our friendship swirled through my head and heart.

"You seemed pretty upset about it . . ." Henry said. "I just thought you should know that you didn't lose it. I'm sure it was fake anyway."

The door to the waiting room popped open, and a female officer in a black-and-gray pantsuit looked rigid as she tilted her head in our direction. She called out Henry's name in a dry, robotic tone. It was clear that the receptionist had alerted her to our profuse display of emotions in an otherwise emotionally impotent environment, and she wasn't happy about it. Though there was not a stringent rule against it in our case, Henry and I weren't supposed to be talking to each other because we were codefendants. He said good-bye to me and disappeared with the officer behind a door. In the months to come, he would be sentenced to nine months in prison and nine months of home confinement.

AFTER MORE THAN A YEAR of living in a legal purgatory with constant drug tests, degrading visits with probation officers, an uncertain future, and severe depression at the thought of going to prison for years, my case was finally scheduled for sentencing in the last week of August 2011.

I flew to Columbus two days before my court date. I met my family at a downtown hotel near the courthouse. My parents and my brother, Nick, had insisted on coming to Ohio to be with me when I faced the judge. I arrived at the hotel late in the evening. My family had already settled into a room with two queen beds and one roll-away bed. I volunteered to sleep on the roll-away bed, but Nick said I'd probably need the sleep more than he would. He had a point, though I didn't expect to get much sleep regardless. The four of us walked to a restaurant to get a quick dinner, then came back and sat for a while in a small courtyard to the side of the hotel. Nick left to go read a book in the room, and soon after he went, my parents called it a night as well. My dad got up from the outdoor couch he'd been sitting on. "You comin'?" he asked me.

"I'll be there in a little bit," I told him.

"All right," he said. "Probably not too late tonight."

As my parents went to get ready for bed and watch TV, I was feeling antsy. I needed some fresh air and alone time. I'd been smiling for my family and trying not to appear terrified about what the judge might say. It was becoming difficult to keep pretending. I wanted to sneak away from the hotel for a little while. It wasn't a bad time to look for a bar and drink away my last night of guaranteed freedom. This was the last night I'd be able to drink before I went to court, as I'd promised my parents I'd be sober tomorrow night for the eve of my sentencing.

I got up from the courtyard and left the hotel through the front door of the lobby. It was around eleven o'clock, and the streets were empty in downtown Columbus. I looked up and noticed dark clouds gathering in the sky above me, but the air was warm and muggy with the heat of the last week of summer. There were no bars in sight, only tall office buildings and hotels.

There's got to be a bar here somewhere. Where do people go to get a drink?

Nightlife appeared to be scarce here. I was three blocks from the hotel when I felt something wet splash onto my nose, then another on my forehead. It began to rain. A light drizzle turned into a downpour within minutes. My hair was soaked, and drops of water clung to my long-sleeved cotton shirt, making it stick to my body. Beneath the thin cloth of my shoes, my socks were wet from stepping through puddles. I didn't mind the weather. For some reason it felt right that it would rain tonight. Lightning struck across the sky and I heard thunder somewhere off in the distance. I hadn't seen a storm like this in a long time. It was beautiful.

The city was like a ghost town. I didn't know where I was or how far I'd gone from the hotel. I'd been wandering, lost in thought. The sights around me all looked vaguely familiar. This all used to be territory for Team LL, making it feel more like my own personal ghost town. I was haunted by memories of my time in Ohio. It seemed like everything had happened so long ago, but as I walked the streets and looked around at the empty buildings, in my mind I saw scenes from my past playing out again as clearly as if they were happening in front of me.

I approached a bland-looking, grayish building that sat on the bottom of a hill in the city. This was the DEA headquarters where we'd been interrogated. I stopped in front of it on the sidewalk. I remembered being separated from Lisette when the agents walked us in. They took my handcuffs off and led me into another whitewashed room by myself. I remembered looking back at her as I'd gone, and the distant look in her eyes as she stared off at the wall. That was the last time I ever saw Lisette. I'd stood in this same spot on the sidewalk hours later when the agents released the rest of us. We were all free to go, except Lisette. She was the only one who lost her freedom that night, and she hadn't had it back since then.

When I walked to the top of the concrete hill, I faced another memory—the bar that I'd gone to after being arrested, interrogated, and then abruptly turned back to the streets. It was closed now, but I stepped under its awning, out of the rain, to peer in through the windows. With wet hands cupped to the glass, I saw the bar stool where I'd sat next to Chris Cash as he, Frankie, and I swapped lies Lisette had told each of us. We didn't know they were lies until that night. I was sitting in that bar drinking whiskey when I finally realized that she was never really my friend. I remembered watching Frankie pace outside of the bar while he spoke to his wife on the phone. That was the only time I'd ever seen him take a drink.

My phone rang inside my purse. The familiar sound brought me back to real time. I stayed underneath the awning and tried to shake the rain off my hand before I took my phone out to answer. It was my father. "Meili, where are you?" he asked me when I picked up. His voice was distant with the sound of the storm all around me. "When I saw the rain, I went to the courtyard and you weren't there."

"Sorry," I said. "I went on a walk."

"In the rain?" he asked, concerned.

"Well, it wasn't raining when I started . . ."

"Please, come back to the hotel," he said. "Your mother wants to go to sleep, and she's not going to be able to until she knows you're here safe."

"I'll head back now." I put my phone away and took one last look into the bar before I left.

AUGUST 26, 2011

Mike Proctor joined my family outside the federal courthouse on the morning of my sentencing. He had come to dinner with us the night before and tried to prepare my parents for what they might hear in court today. My family was anxious, but instead of coming undone or being stone-faced, our nerves were coming out in smiles and easy laughter. Mike was amazed at how upbeat we all seemed. As we were going through security at the entrance of the building, my mom said, "Now, we want to remember to take a picture for the Christmas card. I thought today would be good since we're all dressed up. Mike, maybe you could take a photo of us after we're done here?" Mike, who was ahead of my mother in the short security line, turned around with a surprised stare.

"You're not serious," he said.

"Well, it's tough to get the four of us all together at once," my mother said casually as she took her shoes off and placed them in a security bucket for screening.

"Uh . . ." Mike gave an awkward laugh. "Let's just see how this goes first and then decide if it's a good day for the Christmas card."

Once all five of us were cleared through security, we took an elevator upstairs to the floor of the courtroom. When the automated doors opened, I saw Ko sitting by himself on a bench at the end of the hallway. His hands were clasped together with his arms resting on his knees, and his foot was nervously tapping on the floor. He would be sentenced today too. "Just a minute," I told my family. My parents stayed back to give me privacy while I approached Ko. "Hey . . ." I said as I walked up to where he was sitting. He rose to his feet when he saw me. He was wearing slacks and a nice button-down shirt.

"Hey," he said. His friendly demeanor hadn't changed since I'd last seen him, but I could tell that he was just as nervous as I was. David had recently been sentenced to ten years in prison, and everyone was getting scared to face the judge. Ko and I exchanged few words. We wished each other "good luck" and went our separate ways. I supposed there wasn't much else to say at this point.

I rejoined my family inside the courtroom as other people around us settled into the pewlike benches. It seemed that no cases had been heard yet today. It was still early in the morning. I sat next to Mike, across the aisle from my parents and Nick. Mike thought it would look better for me to sit separately from them for propriety's sake. I saw Tim Pritchard sitting with Agent Heufelder nearby. They nodded their heads to acknowledge us. I looked at my mother across the aisle. She shot me a giddy grin, displaying her perfectly white teeth. My father smiled and gave a slight wave from behind her. My brother saw them doing this and chimed in with a reassuring smile in my direction. It occurred to me that perhaps I wasn't the only one who was trying to put on a brave face.

Ko's case was one of the first to be called. His hearing didn't last more than a few minutes. Judge Algenon Marbley sentenced Ko to three years and a day behind bars. The extra day was given to make him eligible to do less time if he behaved well in prison. Ko excused himself from the courtroom shortly after he was sentenced. My family appeared to be shaken up after watching one of my codefendants go before me.

My case number was announced next. Mike whispered to me, "We're up." He stood and quickly straightened the jacket of his gray suit. I glanced at my family as I stood. They watched me as I walked into the open court with Mike. We stood side by side in front of Judge Marbley. Tim Pritchard and Agent Heufelder were now standing behind small podiums that faced the judge. The courtroom was silent with anticipation. There were maybe thirty spectators sitting in the pews, including my family and two local reporters, ready to watch everything as it took place.

The formalities began with Judge Marbley asking each of us standing before him to introduce ourselves for the court. Immediately following the introductions, the judge surprised everyone and asked to see Tim Pritchard, Agent Heufelder, Mike, and me for a "sidebar."

When a judge calls for a sidebar, he is asking to see particular parties, usually the attorneys for both the prosecution and the defense, at an area to the side of the judge's bench. The judge will then have a private, off-the-record conversation with the parties that is out of earshot of any jurors or spectators present.

When a sidebar was called, it seemed that we were all caught off guard. Mike had told me that this might happen, but he hadn't expected it to happen before anything else was said. The four of us walked to meet

Judge Marbley as he stepped down from his elevated desk. As we went to him, classical music began to play loudly throughout the speakers in the courtroom so that no one could hear what was being said. The spectators whispered and craned their necks to try to see what was happening. My breath quickened and I felt like crying. It was all happening so fast. I tried to maintain my composure, but it was difficult. I stood directly next to the judge as we created a small circle at the sidebar.

He gave me an authoritative once-over before greeting Mike and the prosecution, then wasted no time in getting down to business. "Agent Heufelder," he said, "would you say that Ms. Cady is the least culpable defendant in this case?" The judge looked at me. I felt a tear coming dangerously close to falling down my face. I tried to be still and hold it all in, but the judge eyed me like he could see right through me. I wiped underneath my eye with my index finger to try to prevent anything from coming out. My nose was starting to run now too. I was a mess, and it was becoming increasingly obvious.

"Your Honor," Agent Heufelder began, "I'd say—" He stopped abruptly when Judge Marbley put up his hand to prevent him from going on. Agent Heufelder seemed stunned.

"Excuse me," the judge said. He turned and walked out of our circle and back to his bench. Mike and I looked at each other, then at the prosecution. Everyone appeared to be just as confused as I was, which made me even more nervous. The judge returned after a moment holding a box of tissues. He walked directly up to me and held them out. It dawned on me that he was offering me a tissue. I gently pulled one out of the box. He continued to hold it out. I took one more. "Thank you," I said meekly.

What a nice man. Or . . . maybe he is just being practical because he's about to sentence me to years behind bars and he knows that I'll have plenty more to cry about. Maybe he doesn't want me to be blubbering all over his courtroom floor.

He turned back to Agent Heufelder. "Go ahead," he said calmly. "Would you say Ms. Cady is the least culpable defendant in this case?"

Agent Heufelder looked the judge in the eye as he answered, "No, Your Honor, I would not say that."

Henry is the least culpable.

The judge tilted his head to look at me. "Hmm," he said. He turned his attention back to the men in our circle and said, "Well, all right. I have a sentence in mind." My heart sank into my stomach. I felt myself losing hold of the hope I'd been clinging to.

Sidebar was over. The classical music stopped and the prosecution, Mike, and I returned to our original positions facing the front of the courtroom.

Once the judge was seated again, he asked me if I had anything I'd like to say before he announced his decision. I apologized to my family, acknowledged the mistakes I'd made, and thanked Mike and the prosecution for their patience with me. To my amazement, I was able to get through the entire statement without my voice shaking too much or cracking from emotion. I guess all those acting classes had finally paid off. I couldn't let my parents see me break down now.

As Judge Marbley spoke leading up to his formal announcement of my sentence, it became obvious that he planned to sentence me to time behind bars. I'd known for a long time that this was probably going to happen, but it became real to me in a way that I wasn't necessarily prepared for when I heard him say things like, "The sentence I impose upon you will be harsh enough, by way of incarceration, that it will limit your ability to commit another crime . . ." I felt my knees tighten, then suddenly release and become increasingly weak.

I'm going to pass out. I am literally going to prison. This is happening. I'm going to pass out right here, in the middle of the courtroom, while the judge is still talking . . .

I wanted to reach to my side and grab hold of Mike's arm to stop myself from falling. I could feel my family's undivided attention as they watched from their seats. The lightness in my knees crept up my legs and began to make its way through my entire body. I'd passed out a few times in my life, and I knew the telltale signs when it was about to happen. I did not want to faint.

What if the judge thinks I'm faking it and he tacks on a few more years to my sentence?

I focused on breathing as I tried to stop the light, tingly feeling from spreading.

Then again, maybe it would be better to be unconscious for this . . .

I braced myself to hear a sentence of more than a year.

Please don't let it be more than a year . . .

One year and one day would mean that I'd be eligible to be locked up for less than a year. My knees began to fold, and I knew I had less than a minute before I was going to pass out. I couldn't hold on much longer. I watched the judge as he talked, but I couldn't process what he was saying because all I could think about was what he was going to say next, and whether it was going to happen before I hit the floor. Then finally, after the longest few minutes of my life, my wait was over.

I held my breath as he began. "Ms. Cady, I sentence you to thirty days in custody, three hundred sixty-five days of home confinement, and three years of probation." Mike's energy beside me completely changed. I sensed his relief, though we didn't look at each other and we kept our faces to the judge. When the judge finished with a few closing remarks, I took in a long, deep breath of air. The tingly sensation in my legs began to fade. As the judge left his bench and walked off, I watched him for a moment with a feeling of deep gratitude. He had given me a second chance. I couldn't have hoped for a better sentence. I was dismissed and free to go. Free. Well, not exactly free yet, but much closer to freedom than I'd expected. I'd been afraid that I'd be sentenced to five years and dragged screaming out of court by armed officers while my family watched on in horror.

The moment we were dismissed, Mike turned to me with a grin. "Now go hug your mom," he said quietly. I rushed to the back of the courtroom, dodging people in my path, to where my family was now standing in the aisle waiting for me. I threw my arms around my mother. We were all overwhelmed with relief. My dad pulled me in for a tight hug. I noticed a glisten in his eyes. "It's over," he said.

We left the courthouse and returned to our hotel to unwind and celebrate. Mike Proctor had become more than just my attorney over the year and a half that I'd known him. He was now a close friend, and someone my family would always hold dear. He joined us in the courtyard of the hotel. My mother brought out a liter of whiskey from the room, an ice bucket, and five tumbler glasses from the hotel bar.

"I bought this yesterday," she said with a smile as she filled each glass with ice and a pour of whiskey. "I figured that whichever direction things went in court, we'd probably want to have it handy."

"Yeah, for very different reasons . . ." Mike laughed. We all nodded and exchanged grave looks with one another. We knew how close I'd come to going to prison for years. Mike raised his drink for a toast. We joined him. After taking a sip, he set his glass down. "Hey, do you still want that Christmas card photo?"

"Oh, yes!" my mom said, getting excited. "Thanks for remembering."

Mike shook his head with a smile. "I thought you were joking when you said that before."

"Oh, no, not at all," my mother said.

We slid the whiskey bottle out of frame and huddled as a family on the outdoor couch. Mike snapped a photo that would be my parents' official Christmas card of 2011, taken by my attorney just hours after I was sentenced to serve time in federal prison. Months later, my mother would take this photo into Costco to have fireworks Photoshopped into the background and add a disproportionately large image of my brother's girlfriend's head, so that it looked like she had been there too. My parents would send this Christmas card to all their friends with absolutely no sense of irony, much to the amusement of my brother and me.

THE DEA ESTIMATED THAT LISETTE'S operation moved seven thousand pounds of marijuana from California to Ohio, garnering $3 million in profits in just eight months. Everyone on Team LL was arrested, and everyone went to federal prison. Those who weren't on the plane on June 14, 2010, were served federal indictments from the government. Each of us pled guilty to at least one felony count of conspiracy and possession of marijuana with intent to distribute. We will all be convicted felons for the rest of our lives, short of presidential pardons. Frankie and Chris Cash were sentenced to one and four years, respectively. Jose, David's weed supplier and connection to a Mexican cartel, got seven years.

After spending more than a year in the grimy confines of a county jail in Ohio, Lisette took her turn to face Judge Marbley in federal court. "I believe, Ms. Lee, that you were naive," he told her. He noted that in her psychological evaluation, she was described as having a substantial "narcissistic dimension," which had influenced her crimes. "You knew it was wrong, but you had a certain fascination . . . It almost appears that you believed you were playing a role." Lisette was sentenced to six years in prison. I read the judge's decision in an article from the *Columbus Dispatch*, a local publication in Ohio that had been following every step of our case.

Hours after reading the article, I was driving in afternoon traffic when I got a call from a restricted number. I answered my phone and heard a familiar voice say, "Meili. Hi, kiddo." It was Daniel, the man who had introduced me to Lisette five years earlier. When I instantly recognized his voice, I felt as though the wind had been knocked out of me.

"Hi . . ." I said.

"How are you doin'?" he asked.

I'd once considered Daniel a close friend, but the trust I'd had in him was long gone. After he introduced me to Lisette, she'd told me he was saying cruel things about me behind my back. I was hurt, and Daniel and I were never friends again. A few months before our arrest I saw him at Lisette's condo. It was awkward at first, but as we tried to make polite conversation we fell into the same friendly rapport we'd always had. I later learned that Lisette had told him I'd been saying equally cruel things about him, though I'd never spoken an ill word. I suspect that Lisette wanted to sever the friendship I'd had with Daniel to ensure that we would never compare stories about her. She poisoned the friendship. I wished that I could still speak to him as a friend and believe that he genuinely cared about me, but I had no reliable reason to believe such things.

"I'm . . ." I said, not wanting to make conversation with him. "Well, I'd say things have been better, but I'm hanging in there."

"I know," he said. "This has been pretty crazy for everyone."

"Yeah," I responded.

"Listen," he said, "I've got Lisette on the other line . . . She wants to talk to you." A jolt of stress and mixed emotions surged through every part of my body. I felt my foot begin to shake as it rested on the gas pedal.

I didn't know how to answer him. My voice wavered slightly as I made a decision. "Why would I want to talk to her?"

Before he spoke, I could almost hear him shaking his head like he couldn't think of a good reason either. He sighed, lost for words. "I don't know," he said.

"I'm sorry, but I can't," I told him.

After a quiet moment, he said, "Okay. Okay, I'll just . . . tell her that it went to voice mail. Hang in there, kiddo."

"Thanks," I said. When I hung up and set my phone in the passenger seat, I considered pulling off the road to get out of my car and try to calm down. I had a feeling that Lisette was hoping she'd find me in a forgiving mood after learning of her sentence. Before our arrest, I would've been shattered by the thought of her spending years behind bars. I cared deeply about Lisette for a long time, and I wanted to think that, on some level, she had cared about me too. I would never know if that was the case, and it really didn't make a difference now. Some damaged part of me missed her. I didn't take any pleasure in imagining her in bad times. Her sentence sounded horrifying to me, but I was numb. By now, she must have known I'd caught on to the fact that she'd lied to me since the day I met her. I suspected that she was waiting with a lie of apology on the other end of that phone call. But I didn't want to hear any more of her lies. I'd already heard enough to last me a lifetime.

It was still difficult for me to believe that Lisette was in jail and she was about to be moved into a federal prison, and that I too would soon spend a month in prison, followed by a year of house arrest. But I'd been through worse. The best friend I'd known was really gone. She would be released one day, just as I would, but she was permanently gone from my world. I could never let her back in. We could never have a reunion. She had to be dead to me, and I would be dead to her. I could never hate her; if I allowed that to happen, I risked the possibility of loving her again.

My phone rang once more. I took my eyes off the road to glance down at it in my passenger seat. It read: RESTRICTED. I ignored it and kept my eyes on the road as I continued down Sunset Boulevard.

ACKNOWLEDGMENTS

I would like to thank two of my best friends—my mother and father—for their unconditional love and support. Through my fault, you were forced to make some extremely tough decisions, and you stayed by my side unwaveringly, though many people wouldn't have done so in the selfless, heroic way that you did. I owe you everything. Anything good that I am, and that I ever will be, comes from you.

Thank you to my big brother for believing in me, for always rooting for me, and for carrying me through times when I wasn't strong enough to carry myself.

Thank you to my agent, Joseph Veltre, at Gersh for taking a chance on me as a new writer and for placing me in the talented hands of my editor, Denise Oswald, at HarperCollins.

Denise Oswald, thank you for giving me one of the greatest opportunities of my life. Thank you for seeing potential in this book and potential in me as a writer. I was so green, but you pushed me to be better at every turn. Your guidance and instincts were always spot-on, and I appreciate your aversion to mincing words. I feel that I learned a great deal from you, and I am so grateful for everything.

Many thanks to everyone at Dey Street and HarperCollins who collaborated on this book.

Thom Hinkle, I'm not sure I would have ever written this book if it hadn't been for you. You took the time to look at the weird blog of the house-arrested waitress who was pouring your Jameson, and then you got her a literary agent. I suppose I should give some credit to the power of Jameson here, too. Cheers, sir. I am forever in your debt.

Thank you to "The Captain" for making me laugh harder than anyone ever could, even during the worst of times in my life. You believed I could be a writer long before I believed it myself, and you supported me when I most needed it. When we were good, we were great, man. I will miss our friendship for many years to come.

Michael Proctor, my wonderful attorney—thank God for you. Your honest approach to my case helped me to overcome my fears of facing the mistakes I'd made. By helping me confront my past decisions, you helped me to better understand them, and to begin to build a positive future.

Michael Schafler—my other, equally wonderful attorney—you are an unsung hero in my case. Your whip-smart legal mind and kind heart helped me immeasurably. You even drove me to and from federal prison in the desert—and you played *Johnny Cash: At Folsom Prison* en route. You went above and beyond, and my family and I will always consider you, Mike Proctor, and Wendy friends of ours. You are truly a unique and great man, and I'm very lucky to have had you on my team.

Wendy Eggleston Carpenter—L.A.'s most beautiful and compassionate legal secretary—thank you for all of the well-timed hugs and tissues you offered me when I most needed them. Your bright sincere smile and great sense of humor always helped me cheer up a bit after tough meetings downtown when I was still searching for a light at the end of the tunnel.

Many thanks to my incredible family members and friends who offered their time and generosity to be my readers: Kimberly Minon, Jason Fuchs, Mike Goldbach, Ashlie, Ben Cox, Kristi, Denise Irwin, and Taylor. Your encouraging comments and positivity helped keep me optimistic when I was feeling overwhelmed. A very special thank you to Uncle Steve, Field, Jorie, Tessa, Nikki and Pom, who read the first draft of the manuscript in its entirety throughout my writing process and gave me notes on every chapter. Each of you never failed to amaze me with your thoughtful critiques and willingness to help.

Minon, thank you for taking me in after my arrest. I don't know what I would have done without you. You gave me solace during one of darkest times of my life. You will forever have my love, friendship, and gratitude.

I'd like to thank the first friend I made in the publishing world, Allie Kingsley, for holding my hand and helping see me through this exciting new adventure. Not only are you a hilarious and talented writer, you're a genuine friend and I adore you.

I'd also like to thank Nikki, an extremely kind and intelligent friend who helped see me through an entirely different adventure—one that began in the G-Unit South wing of Victorville Women's Prison Camp in Adelanto.

Wherever we go in life—whether it's Beverly Hills or federal prison—we are connected to one another through our shared experiences, and we have the power to lift one another up or try to tear one another down. Thank you to the people who have lifted me up.

"Brie," you are proof that it's possible to make authentic, lifelong friendships in Los Angeles. Your faith in the good of people and your willingness to look for it reminds me to keep an open heart.

I'd like to acknowledge the people I wrote about. We are all a part of each other's stories, and we are each the main character in our own—a great equalizer, and my story is no greater than yours for having told it in print.

Thank you to C.A.T.E., the Orb, and my friends who gave me permission to tell stories that involved them. Here's to us making even better stories in the future—and preferably ones that don't end with anyone going to federal prison.

MAKING THE TEAM

When his dreams shattered, Eddie Folger
had to make a new life from the pieces

Eddie Folger

as
told
to

Rhonda Graham

Pacific Press Publishing Association
Boise, Idaho
Oshawa, Ontario, Canada

Edited by Bonnie Widicker
Designed by Dennis Ferree
Cover illustration by Lars Justinen
Typeset in 10/12 Century Schoolbook

Copyright © 1992 by
Pacific Press Publishing Association
Printed in United States of America
All Rights Reserved

Library of Congress Cataloging-in-Publication Data:
Folger, Eddie.
    Making the team / Eddie Folger as told to Rhonda Graham.
       p.   cm.
    "When his dreams shattered, Eddie Folger had to make a
new life from the pieces."
    ISBN 0-8163-1099-8
    1. Folger, Eddie. 2. Pitchers (Baseball)—United States—
Biography. 3. Seventh-day Adventists—United States—Bi-
ography. I. Graham, Rhonda. II. Title.
BX6193.F64A3 1992
286.7'092—dc20   92-6439
[B]   CIP

92 93 94 95 96 • 5 4 3 2 1

Contents

Chapter 1

The Tryout

Crack!

My cousin Bob threw the ball back to me, and I pitched it at him again. He caught it.

Crack!

I watched him take his hand out of his glove and shake it. My arm felt full of adrenaline, and I shifted from one foot to the other, anxious to make the next pitch. I felt as if I could throw the baseball through a wall.

Gene Conley, pitching coach for the AA Pawtucket Red Sox, stood watching me, a grin on his face. In the field behind me, a minor-league player began walking over to where I was pitching the baseball.

Crack!

Gene walked over and took the catcher's mitt from Bob. He crouched down and grinned. "Let's see what you've got, son!"

I threw harder. *CRACK!*

He tossed the ball back to me. Each pitch I threw him seemed to get faster and faster. Gene motioned the player, a catcher, to the bullpen. He walked over and put on a catcher's mask. I was really fired up. Throwing to a professional catcher gave me even more energy. Gene, Bob, and Mike, another cousin, leaned against the bullpen wall and watched me pitch.

"Man, he sure brings it," I heard Gene comment.

I smiled, excitement rippling through me. I knew that if he thought I could throw a fastball, I must be pitching extremely fast.

I pitched the ball faster and faster. I noticed another man walking toward the bullpen. After silently watching me a few seconds, he turned and asked Gene some questions. I waited, barely able to contain my excitement. Could this really be happening? I squinted up at Bob and Mike, who stood watching me. Bob looked at Gene and the other man and shrugged his shoulders.

"I wonder what they're saying," I thought to myself as I continued to pitch.

"Hey, Eddie, why don't you come over here for a minute," Gene called. "There's someone I'd like you to meet."

I jogged over to where they stood by the bullpen door.

"Eddie, this is Don Lock. He is the manager for the Pawtucket Red Sox, and he wants to ask you some questions." Gene clapped me on the shoulder. "Don, this is Eddie. He came here today so I could see him pitch."

Don stood with his arms crossed and rocked back and forth on his heels before he spoke.

"So, how old are you, kid?" he finally asked.

"I'm twenty."

"What team do you play for?"

I took a deep breath. "I don't play for a baseball team, but I do play softball."

Don thought about this a minute. "Where do you go to school?"

"Atlantic Union College, but they don't have a baseball program." I was afraid this might work against me but figured I'd better let him know right away.

His eyebrows shot up in surprise. "So when did you last play baseball?"

"In Little League when I was twelve."

I held my breath as I watched his surprised expression. He chuckled and looked at me with new interest. He stood

6

silently for a moment. Then he asked me my favorite question of the day.

"What are you doing next Wednesday?"

I felt the breath go out of me. "Nothing," I assured him, a grin splitting my face. "Nothing at all!" I could hardly contain my excitement.

"Well, then, I'd like you to come to McCoy Stadium next Wednesday so that a scout for the Boston Red Sox can get a look at you."

"Oh, thank you!" I burst out. "I'll be there! Next Wednesday!"

I ran back to where Mike and Bob stood waiting for me. I knew they'd been trying to figure out what Don Lock had been asking me. My face told them my news even before I had a chance to speak.

"What'd they say?" Bob and Mike asked their question at the same time.

"They want me to come back next Wednesday!" I stopped to catch my breath. "Can you believe it?"

"Man, that's fantastic!" Mike gave me a high-five as he spoke.

"I could tell something great was going on," Bob said as we walked toward the car. "All the players in the field kept asking me who you were while you were pitching to that catcher."

We climbed into the car and started back to Lancaster, Massachusetts. After the initial excitement, we sat silently for a few minutes. My mind raced. I remembered how long I'd wanted to play with the Red Sox, and it hardly seemed real that I'd be trying out for them in a week.

"Remember the sandlot tryouts?" I asked Bob with a laugh. I had tried out for the Red Sox years before in an open tryout. I had never seen a curveball before, and when the pitcher threw me one, I thought it was going to hit me.

Bob laughed with me. "Yeah, you should have seen your face when that ball came toward you. Or the look when you sat down and the guy yelled 'next!' "

"I swore I'd never hear that again." I looked out the window of the car. "And I meant it. I just wish I didn't have to wait until next Wednesday to try out again!"

Bob turned from the front seat and smiled. "Do you remember when you started playing in the men's softball league when you were fourteen? I'll never forget the way you told them to fill up the bases 'cause you'd bring them all home. The guys thought you were all mouth. When you hit that homer, I think they realized how serious you really were."

"Well, I'd been practicing with sticks and rocks in my backyard for so many years, it felt like I'd already hit homers like that a hundred times before." I felt another shiver of excitement go through me. "Do you really think they think I'm good enough to play pro?"

I tried to imagine what it would feel like to step up to the plate with a stadium full of screaming fans. It would be the bottom of the ninth. The bases would be loaded. We'd already have two outs. And I would hit a home run into the stands that would bring everyone in and win the game. I had imagined the scene so many hundreds of times while growing up that I could almost feel the heat of the sun on my face and smell the dust from the field.

"It was sure great of Gene to set this up." I thought again of the tryout and shivered. "Thanks for asking him for me."

Bob turned around in the seat, smiling. "No problem, buddy. I had to see if my big-shot cousin was as good as he thought he was!"

I laughed and playfully punched at him. "Better!" I promised.

Bob and Mike started reminiscing about favorite games. I laughed and added my own comments, but inside my mind raced. It still felt too new, too impossible. I replayed the afternoon over and over in my mind. Each time I got to the part where Don Lock asked me what I was doing next Wednesday, I felt a wave of excitement wash over me.

I remembered attending a Christian high school and college and wishing they had had big athletic programs to excel in. All I ever wanted to do was play ball, and I never thought I'd really get the chance. And now that the chance had arrived, I could hardly believe it was real.

When we arrived home, I jumped out of the car impatiently. My parents met me at the door.

"They've asked me back next Wednesday!" I hugged them both excitedly. "Can you believe it?"

Mike and Bob stood beside me, grinning.

"You should have seen how hard he threw that baseball," Bob added. "It sounded like a cannon shot as it hit the glove."

"Well, son, it looks like you're finally getting the chance you've always wanted," Dad said, his eyes shining with pride. "I'm proud of you."

"Well, I hope next Wednesday goes as well," I answered, half-joking, half-serious. "If it does, I could be going to spring training in Florida!"

Mom squeezed my arm. "I'm sure you'll do a great job."

I looked at Mom and knew she felt happy for me, but noticed some reservation in her eyes. I let it pass, though, as I excitedly shared each part of the day's events.

"Hey, buddy, we'd better run. Congratulations again." Bob gave me a half-hug.

"Yeah, great job today," Mike added. "I'll call you later."

They left, and I turned back to my parents. Dad yawned and looked at the kitchen clock.

"I'd better be getting off to bed. Morning comes too early for farmers." Dad patted me on the shoulder as he walked by. "Try and get some sleep tonight, OK, son?"

I laughed. "Fat chance!"

I looked at the clock on the wall. "I'd better call Dana before it gets too late." I walked to the living-room phone, where I could have some privacy. She picked up the receiver after only one ring.

"Dana, guess what?" I held my breath.

"No, you're kidding, right?" Her voice rose with excitement.

"They've asked me back next Wednesday!"

I held the phone away from my ear as a long squeal came out of the receiver.

"Oh, Eddie, that's wonderful! I'm so excited," she squealed again.

I laughed and cradled the phone closer to me.

"Tell me all about it! I want to know everything that happened!"

I went through the tryout with her, still feeling the excitement I'd felt when it was happening. We hung up twenty minutes later.

"How's Dana?" Mom asked as I walked back into the kitchen.

"Very happy for me," I replied. "I don't think my hearing will ever be the same in my right ear!" I looked at the clock and sighed. "Well, I guess I'd better at least try to get some sleep." I kissed Mom on the cheek and turned to leave. She looked like she wanted to say something, so I stopped.

"What is it, Mom?" I asked.

"Nothing, Eddie." She smiled up at me. "We're very proud of you, and I hope your next tryout goes well." She stopped and chuckled softly. "Your grandfather always said you were the ballplayer of the family."

"Yeah, well, I hope he was right!" I answered, thinking of Wednesday. I yawned and looked at the clock again.

Mom shooed me out of the kitchen. "Time for bed." The questions I'd seen earlier in her eyes no longer seemed to be there.

I prepared for bed quickly and slid between the cool sheets. As I lay in the bedroom where I'd dreamed so many dreams while growing up, I still couldn't believe it might all be coming true in a week.

I replayed the day in my mind again, examining every word and action. As I lay there, I half expected to wake up and find it had all been a dream. It seemed too good to be real.

A car drove by outside, its headlights momentarily lighting the walls to my room. I caught a glimpse of the Red Sox pennant I had hanging over my desk and thought of how long I'd wanted to play for them.

I remembered all the hours I'd spent watching college ball and listening to the announcers talk about athletes who were walk-ons—players who had no scholarship to play but had made the team. Now, as I lay in my darkened bedroom, I wondered if it could possibly happen to me. Could I be good enough to walk on a professional baseball team? Just how good was I?

The questions went around and around until, after several hours, I finally fell asleep.

Chapter 2

Making the Team

Wednesday finally arrived. I hadn't slept much at all the night before. And as we pulled into the parking lot at McCoy Stadium, I could feel the adrenaline beginning to flow through my body again.

"This is it!" I thought as I half-walked, half-jogged to the field.

"Eddie, over here!" Gene Conley waved me over to where he and Don Lock stood waiting for me.

"How are you feeling today?" Gene asked as I joined them. "Ready to throw some more fastballs?"

I grinned. "More than ready. Let me at 'em!"

Gene laughed. "Well, let's get you into some baseball clothes first. I'll show you where the locker room is."

I followed Gene and Don to the locker room, then stepped inside. Pawtucket Red Sox players stopped dressing and stared at me. I smiled, but no one smiled back. Shrugging, I found an empty bench and began changing into my baseball clothes. No one around me spoke, and I knew the players were appraising me as I sat to put on my cleats. It made me nervous to know every one of them had probably been all-American stars in high school and college.

"They're probably thinking, 'Who does this kid think he is?'" I thought as I tied my last shoelace.

I grabbed my mitt and walked back out of the dressing

room. Once outside, I exhaled deeply, suddenly realizing that I had been holding my breath.

"You could have been an all-American if you'd had the chance," I reminded myself as I walked toward the field. "Now's no time to be getting nervous."

I felt my old confidence returning as I walked into the dugout. Out on the field, I saw Gene and Don talking to another man. Gene noticed me and motioned for me to come over. I walked out of the dugout and joined them on the field.

"Eddie, this is 'Lefty' LeFebvre, chief scout for the Boston Red Sox. Lefty, this is Eddie Folger." Gene stood back and let Lefty ask me questions.

"So how old are you?" Lefty asked.

"Twenty," I replied.

"What team do you play for?"

I shifted impatiently. I'd answered all these questions with Don Lock the week before, and now I wanted to get out in the field and do what I did best.

"I've been playing softball in the Boston City League since I was fourteen."

The questions seemed to go on and on. Finally Lefty motioned one of the catchers over, and I started warming up with a few pitches. The players who'd been in the locker room now lined the bullpen wall, waiting to see what I could do.

After a few warm-ups, I began throwing my fastball. And just like the week before, the ball made a loud cracking noise as it hit the catcher's mitt.

Crack!

The catcher tossed the ball back, and I pitched it again.

CRACK!!

Each pitch went faster, and each time the catcher caught the ball, the noise got louder.

"Let's see your curveball," Lefty called out.

I stopped. "I'm afraid I don't know how to throw a curveball," I admitted. I felt a stab of fear. Would this spoil my chance of making the team?

14

"Never mind," he said. "Just keep throwing that fastball."

I threw another pitch, even faster. The one after that felt like my fastest. As I wound up to throw another, Lefty stopped me again.

"Can you hit a baseball?" he asked.

I grinned. "Well, I've hit baseballs only a few times, but I'm a good hitter in softball."

He took this in for a second. "Fine. Go get a bat and take a few swings."

I ran in from the bullpen to the batting cage. As I got there, I saw them again—the all-Americans. I tried to ignore them and began trying out bats.

One of the players walked up to me with a bat. "Here, try this one," he offered.

I took it from him. "Thanks!"

I tried a few practice swings. "Come on, Eddie, you'll do great if you can just get ahold of a couple of pitches," I thought as I stepped into the batter's box. The pitcher faced me, and I could feel the adrenaline starting to flow again. I knew if I could get ahold of the ball, I'd hit it a long way.

The pitcher threw the first ball and I let it pass. It seemed too high. The catcher threw the ball back, and I tapped home plate with my bat as I waited for the next pitch. I caught it right as it came across the plate.

Crack!

The all-Americans craned their necks to watch the ball sail out of the park. I grinned. "Throw me another," I thought. Now my adrenaline was really pumping.

The pitcher threw me another pitch. I hit it out of the park again. The next pitch I hit a low ground ball. The fifth pitch I hit out of the park again.

Lefty stopped me. "Let's go upstairs," he said as he led me off the field. "Go shower and change and meet me upstairs in the front office."

I ran to the locker room and took the quickest shower I ever had. "You did pretty good today, Eddie," I reminded myself as

I struggled into my clothes.

I left the locker room in a rush and ran up the stairs to the front office. As I entered it, I saw Lefty speaking with another man. They stopped talking as I came through the door and turned to me, both smiling.

"Eddie, this is Neil Mahoney, director of player personnel for the Boston Red Sox," Lefty said. "Neil, this is Eddie."

I shook Neil's hand and said hello.

"Lefty says you're quite a ballplayer." Neil appraised me as he spoke.

I grinned and waited for him to go on. My heart felt like it was beating loud enough for both of them to hear. This is it, I thought. This is it!

"Eddie, the Boston Red Sox would like to sign you to a contract for the 1973 season. Are you interested?" His smile told me he knew I'd be interested.

"Where do I sign?" I answered.

He directed me to a contract he had lying on the desk, and I signed it before they could change their minds. After I dated it, I handed it back to him. He looked it over quickly.

"You'll have to take this home for your parents to sign because you're under twenty-one." He looked up at me. "Will that be a problem?"

"No, absolutely not," I assured him. "I'll get it signed tonight."

Lefty walked up and shook my hand. "Congratulations, Eddie. It'll be good to have you aboard the team. Can you stay tonight and watch the game?"

"Yes, of course," I immediately agreed.

Neil handed me the contract and congratulated me again. I folded the contract and put it in my back pocket. I walked out of the office and back down to the field, hardly able to think. The all-Americans were running up and down the field practicing.

"I'm one of you now," I thought, excitement rushing over me. "I've made the team!" I felt like yelling and jumping up and down with joy. Instead, I looked at my watch and decided to try to find something to eat before the game started. I ran to my car and wondered if I'd ever be able to stop smiling.

That evening I met Lefty behind the backstop, and we climbed to our seats together. The warm August night felt so comfortable that I didn't have to wear a jacket. As we sat down, Lefty looked at my muscle shirt and bare arms.

"Where's your jacket?" he asked.

"It's warm out," I assured him. "I don't need a jacket." I looked at the starry sky and then turned to Lefty with a smile.

He gave me a stern look. "From now on you wear a jacket, OK? The Red Sox want you to protect your arm."

Down on the field, the ballgame began, but I had a difficult time paying attention to it. The excitement of being signed to a Red Sox contract overwhelmed me.

"They even care how I dress!" I thought as I watched the action on the field.

The game drew to a close, and Lefty turned to me before we got up to leave.

"I want you to come and practice with the Pawtucket Red Sox for the next three weeks until the season ends." He looked at the field a minute, then back at me. "Think you can make it down here every day?"

"Absolutely!" I promised, smiling eagerly. "I'll be here tomorrow if you want!"

Lefty laughed and slapped me on the back. "That's the attitude we like. I'll see you tomorrow."

He climbed out of the bleachers and walked to the locker room to talk to the team. I stood and stared at the field for a few minutes as the crowd dispersed around me. Once again I saw myself hitting that baseball, winning the game. The excitement overwhelmed me, and I let out a loud whoop of joy.

People stared at me, but I didn't care. I wanted the whole world to know. I wanted to tell them all that the next time they saw a game, I'd be playing with that team! It felt like the magic could last forever.

17

Chapter 3

Local Hero

I got home late that night. The excitement still hadn't worn off, and I rushed into the house to tell my parents. The dark rooms quickly told me they'd already gone to bed, so I undressed and tried to go to sleep. It didn't work. I tossed and turned all night. Every few hours I turned on the light and looked at the contract again. It never failed to send a shiver of excitement through me. Each time I managed to fall asleep, I dreamed of being on the team. Finally, at dawn I got up and started eating breakfast. I was into my second bowl of cereal when my mother wandered into the kitchen.

"Well, it must have gone really well if you're up at this hour," she teased.

"What time will Dad get back from the farm?" I asked, a grin splitting my face. I knew she could tell from the look on my face that I'd made the team, but I wanted to tell both of them at the same time.

"He'll be home for breakfast in a few minutes," she replied.

I sat at the table, watching the clock and straining to hear my father's footsteps on the porch. Finally, after what seemed like hours, he came in.

"I made the team!" I blurted out, unable to contain myself any longer. "They gave me a contract to sign and everything! I'll be making five hundred dollars a month, and I need to report to Winter Haven, Florida, for spring training."

MAKING THE TEAM

Mom gasped and put her hands to her face as Dad came over and gave me a handshake, then a hug for congratulations.

"That's great, son. We're so happy for you! We know how long you've worked for this." Dad clapped me on the shoulder as Mom got over her surprise and gave me a hug.

"I do need you to sign the contract because I'm under twenty-one," I added a little nervously. "But I didn't think that would be any problem."

Dad spoke first. "Let's take a look at it." He sat down, and I handed him the contract. After reading it through, he handed it to my mother to read. She handed it back to him to sign. When no one said anything, I started to get worried.

"Well, are you going to sign or what?" I asked, half-joking, half-serious.

Dad looked at Mom as if to get her to say what they both were thinking. She turned and faced me.

"Eddie, of course we'll sign it. I just have one question, though. What are you going to do about playing on the Lord's Day?"

The question seemed to hang between us as I sat and thought about it. I'd been so excited about making the team that I hadn't thought about God, church, or anything else. I remembered how important Christianity was to my parents and tried to be as gentle as possible in my reply.

"Well," I started slowly. "I've done things your way all my life. Now I'll do them my way."

I waited for their response. Dad picked up the contract and signed it, his face showing no emotion. After he finished, he handed it to Mom, and she signed it too. I sighed with relief. Now nothing could keep me from playing with the Red Sox the next spring.

"Congratulations again," Mom said as she hugged me. I could tell my comment about doing things my way troubled her, but she wasn't going to say anything to me about it.

"Yes, good job, son. We're proud of you." Dad hugged me

again, then handed me the signed contract. "I hope this is what you really want."

"More than anything," I assured him. "More than anything else in the world!"

I got up from the table and headed for the phone. I couldn't wait to get on the road to McCoy Stadium, but I wanted to call my former softball coach first.

"Angie, Eddie here," I said as soon as he picked up the phone.

"Hey, how'd the tryout go?" he asked.

"I made it!" I replied excitedly. "I'm taking the contract back today."

"You're a liar!" Angie Bazydlo laughed. "That sort of thing never happens."

"It did this time." I looked at the clock on the wall. "Why don't you come down with me and watch the final signing?"

"I still don't believe you," he replied, his tone of voice revealing his doubt.

"I'll stop by your place in an hour," I promised and then hung up.

I called Dana and let her know the good news. She screamed twice as loudly as she had the week before. After saying goodbye, I took a quick shower and got ready to leave. Packing my contract carefully in the bottom of my duffel bag, I piled my baseball clothes on top of it, then grabbed my car keys on the way out the front door.

"See you tonight," I called to Mom, who was on her knees, weeding a flower bed in front of the house.

"Eddie, wait." She stood up and walked toward me, brushing dirt off her hands as she walked. "I have a question I feel I really need to ask you."

I stopped and waited patiently for her to continue.

She looked slightly embarrassed. "I've felt the Lord wanted me to ask you this for three months now, and I've always argued with the voice. I told it I couldn't ask you it because it isn't fair." She smiled at me. "But the impression won't leave, so I guess I'd better ask you."

I put my hand on her arm. "It's OK, Mom, really."

She took a deep breath. "Eddie, it looks like every dream you had is going to come true. If something happened so that your dreams didn't come true, would you blame God?"

I thought for a second. "No, Mama, I wouldn't," I answered truthfully.

Mom sighed and looked relieved. "Well, you'd better get down there and get this contract finalized."

I kissed her cheek. "I'll see you tonight."

I got in the car and started the drive to Angie's house. I knew my parents were concerned that I wasn't interested in the church and the values I'd been raised with—but this was my life, and I had to live it my way. I remembered how several church members had criticized me for being so interested in sports and felt angry all over again. I was tired of the petty rules, tired of hearing pleas for money each week from the pulpit, tired of the hypocrisy of certain church members, and tired of being judged. It felt so good to know I'd soon be free from it all—free to live the way I wanted and do what I wanted.

I put all thoughts of the church and my parents out of my mind as I pulled into Angie's driveway. This was my day, my time. I wasn't going to let anything spoil it.

The next few weeks seemed like a dream. The local newspaper ran articles on my signing, and everywhere I went, people congratulated me and wished me luck. I drove down every day to practice with the team and couldn't wait for spring training in Winter Haven, Florida.

As a small thank-you, I brought Lefty fresh vegetables from our garden, but I knew that no gift could thank him for the opportunity to play with the Red Sox.

Three weeks after signing the contract, I went with Mike to a Red Sox game.

"Next year that will be you out there," he promised as we left the stadium together.

"No doubt!" I looked back at Fenway Park as we pulled slowly out of the parking lot. It had been a great game. And the next year I'd be out of the stands and on the field.

We drove with the radio on, laughing and joking with one another.

"Well, I hope you'll remember your true friends when you're rich and famous," Mike joked.

"Only if you treat me with the respect I deserve," I countered, laughing.

Up ahead, a pair of headlights swerved across the median and continued straight toward us. Mike gunned our car, and the other car missed us by inches.

"Whew, that was too close," Mike said soberly, his joking attitude gone.

"Yeah, but we're OK." I brushed off his concern easily. Outside the car, hundreds of stars seemed to blink at me. I had my future mapped out. I felt invincible.

Mike changed the radio station, and our joking resumed. We got home late that night. And as I went to sleep, I knew I'd never been happier in my life.

Chapter 4

The Shattered Dream

The next morning came too quickly. Dad woke me at sunrise to help on the farm, and I dragged myself out of bed reluctantly. After a few grumbles and a hearty breakfast, we headed out to the cornfield. All I could think about in the bright September sunshine was going to Florida for spring training. We climbed out of the truck by the barn, and Dad, shielding his eyes against the light, surveyed the field. Bob Kershner, our friend and fellow worker, joined us.

"I think you and Bob should run the corn blower today," Dad addressed me. "I'll take the tractor and the corn chopper."

I sighed. I hated the corn blower. It was always jamming, and we spent a lot of time unclogging it.

"Sure, Dad," I said out loud, walking over to the tractor with him.

I helped him attach the corn chopper to the tractor, then watched him ride into the ocean of corn. Bob and I looked at the flowing green sea for a few seconds before beginning our work.

"Well," I turned to Bob, "I guess we'd better hook this beast up."

Bob drove his tractor close to the barn, and we hooked the wagon to it. He drove into the field after my father. I checked the corn blower one last time to make sure it was ready, then sat back and waited for Bob to return with a full load of chopped cornstalks that would be used for silage.

The morning sky seemed an impossible shade of blue. I chewed on a piece of grass as I stared across the field. Spring training. The Red Sox. I couldn't keep my mind on anything else. I didn't mind farm work, but it excited me to realize that from now on, my job would be playing baseball. I planned all the perfect pitches, all the home runs I would hit.

The sound of Bob's tractor returning cut into my day-dreaming. I jumped up and helped him back the wagon against the blower. He kicked the tractor into gear, and a lot of corn fell into the blower at the same time. It made us nervous because we were afraid it would clog the machine.

"You don't think the thing will clog up on us today, do you?" I asked, watching the auger move the chopped corn toward the pipe through which it would be blown seventy feet high into the silo.

Bob shrugged in answer. The machine groaned slightly and appeared to be slowing down. I jumped up on the one side to check it. By now the corn looked like it was hardly moving at all.

"Looks like she's stopping up," I commented to Bob as I leaned across the machine to grab a pitchfork.

At that moment, my right foot slipped off the edge and fell into the blower. I screamed and pulled and struggled to get myself out. It seemed to be pulling me deeper and deeper into the machine. Finally, with a great pull, I heaved myself out of the machine and over the side. I hopped away from the blower, then fell to the ground. It was then that I became aware of Bob's screaming.

"Oh my God, oh my God! What should I do?" His face looked ashen.

I looked down at my leg and instantly realized what he was screaming about. My right leg had disappeared from the knee down. I clenched my teeth against the sudden pain.

"Get the truck," I yelled. "Get the truck and drive me to the hospital!" My voice grated out the order with pain.

Bob ran to the truck, then ran back.

"I can't drive the truck! What should I do?" He looked at my leg. "Oh my God, you're bleeding to death!"

"Call an ambulance!" I yelled angrily. "Don't just stand there!" I added a few choice expletives for emphasis.

He ran off in search of a phone, and I sat on the ground holding what was left of my leg.

"Oh, God, I'm going to die," I cried. "I'm only twenty and I'm going to die. No more baseball. No more life." Tears of pain and anger ran down my cheeks as I rocked back and forth holding my leg.

About 150 yards from where I sat, a grain truck pulled up, and the driver began unloading the grain. I could hear him whistling as he stood on the back of his truck, and I tried to call out to him, but the truck motor drowned out my voice.

"Here I am dying, and that guy over there is whistling," I thought wildly. My emotions changed from anger to loneliness. "I'm dying and nobody cares."

I gritted my teeth and willed myself to look at my leg again. It was the same. Gone. Blood stained the ground around me, and I prayed I'd lose consciousness. Bob appeared at my side again.

"What are you doing here?" I screamed at him in panic. "Call an ambulance!"

"I did! I did!" He circled me, trying to figure out what to do.

"Well, call another one!" He looked at me uncertainly. "Go! Go!"

He ran off to call another ambulance, and once again I was left alone. As each minute ticked by, I felt I was getting closer and closer to death. I held onto my leg and sobbed, "I want to live. I really want to live."

Finally, the ambulance pulled up, and the drivers jumped out almost before the vehicle stopped. They ran toward me carrying a stretcher and supplies.

"Grab that plastic bag!" one of them yelled to another. "Let's get it over his leg and get him onto the stretcher ASAP!"

They pried my fingers off my leg, then covered it with a plastic bag to stop the bleeding. After lifting me onto the stretcher, they ran me to the back of the ambulance. Within seconds, we took off, siren wailing. Each bump and turn felt like someone was setting fire to my leg. When I cried out, one of the attendants came over and steadied me. I recognized him as one of the boys I'd played Little League with. I saw tears in his eyes.

"I'm going to die!" I thought, panic-stricken. "I'm going to die!"

The three-mile ride finally ended, and I was rushed into the emergency room of Clinton Hospital. A doctor came toward me with a needle.

"Put me to sleep," I pleaded.

"You're going to be all right," he promised as he gave me a shot.

All around me, nurses rushed to get me stabilized. One cut off my clothes, another checked my pulse, still others examined my leg.

"Doc, I can't feel the shot. Please give me another," I pleaded again.

He gave me another shot, and soon my head began to swim.

"Let's get him into O.R. stat!" I heard the doctor order.

As they wheeled me toward the operating room on a gurney, my thoughts whirled as I drifted toward unconsciousness.

"I'm going to die. I will never play baseball again. No matter what happens in the operating room, my leg is already gone—nothing's going to change that! Now my dream can never come true. I'll never play for the Red Sox. I don't have a leg. I'm going . . ."

Chapter 5

The Hospital

"Eddie . . . Eddie . . ."

The voice called to me out of the swirling, dark fog, and I struggled to open my eyes.

"Eddie . . . Eddie . . ."

I found myself in a pure white room with two attendants dressed in white. Everything seemed bathed in light. Suddenly I knew. I was in heaven! I'd made it!

"Eddie . . . Eddie!"

By now my eyes were focusing better, and I realized that the attendants were nurses. The walls of the room looked a little dingy. In a rush it all came back. A quick glance confirmed it—my leg was gone.

"Lots of people are waiting to see you." The nurse smoothed the covers over me as she spoke. She smiled warmly at me. "Feel up to seeing your family now?"

I nodded, trying to be strong. The awful reality kept me from being able to say anything. I wanted to cry, but I knew my parents would be the first ones allowed into the room, so I forced a weak smile.

Mom and Dad came in together. I could tell both had been crying. Mom sat on the edge of the bed; Dad stood awkwardly, clenching and unclenching his hands.

"How are you feeling?" Mom asked. We all tried so hard to be normal with each other, but no one really knew what to say.

"Fine, Mama. Still pretty numb." I couldn't believe we were having this conversation. I wanted to scream, "It's all gone! I'll never play baseball again!"

Tears ran down Dad's cheeks. "It's all my fault," he mumbled. "I never should have let you work on that machine—" His voice broke and trailed off.

I struggled to prop myself up with my elbow. "Dad, it was an accident. It's nobody's fault. I could have been in a car accident or been hit by a train. It's just an accident." I tried to be as strong as I could.

Mom's shoulders shook as she cried silently. I felt my own tears forming, and I fought to keep them back. They fell anyway. My father broke the silence.

"You know, I've heard of six people who've fallen into corn blowers. You're the only one who made it out alive." He shook his head and wiped at his tears.

"Yeah, I'm glad I came out of it alive. I didn't think I would." As I spoke the words, I felt a bleakness come over me. I was alive, but now what would I do? What was there to live for?

The door opened, and Dana peeked into the room. I smiled weakly and motioned her over. She came to the bed, and Mom made room for her at my side. After setting a huge bouquet of flowers on the night stand, she gave me a hug. Dad cleared his throat.

"Well, son, we'll be back a little later. I think I'll take your mother downstairs and get her something to eat."

Mom got up and kissed my cheek. "We'll be back soon," she promised. They left with a wave.

"They've promised I can spend lots of time with you," Dana said. Her smile was forced as she tried to tease. "I just hope I can stand you that long!" Then her eyes filled with tears. "Oh, Eddie, I'm just so glad you're alive."

I reached out and took her hand. For a minute we just sat silently. The door opened again, and a nurse came in.

"It's time for medication," she told me, a bright smile on her face. "You ready for another shot?"

I grimaced. "If you say so."

Dana got up and blew me a kiss from the door. "I'll be back later," she promised.

The nurse gave me my shot, and soon I could remember nothing but that I'd lost my leg and I'd never play baseball again.

Angie, long-time friend and coach, and Pat O'Toole came to see me toward the end of the day. My eyes filled again as they walked through the door.

Angie sat down beside the bed and silently touched my arm. Pat stood, facing the window. No one spoke. I looked at Angie, tears running down my face, not knowing what to say. This man had trained me, turned raw talent into a professional athlete. He sat, crying, also unable to speak.

After a few minutes, I spoke. "Where the hell do I go from here?" I asked brokenly.

He thought a minute, looking out the window. "You see that sun out there? Thank God you're alive! You still have three healthy limbs, don't you?"

I nodded. Everyone fell silent again. Finally Angie stood. "Hang in there, buddy," he said.

Pat walked over and squeezed my hand. "Yeah, you hang in there." I could see the pain, the questions in his eyes.

They walked out the door, and I looked out the window again. Three healthy limbs. No one played baseball with just three limbs.

The door opened and the nurse came back in. I looked hopefully for a needle on her tray. The last shot had felt wonderful.

"I think I need another shot," I told her.

She frowned slightly. "I'll get one for you. The morphine shouldn't have worn off yet, but . . ."

She walked out and returned with a needle. I obediently took my shot and then floated to sleep.

After two days, the general community was allowed in to see me. They'd supported me so much when I signed my contract; now they felt my loss. Stricken, they came in and out of my room bringing gifts and encouragement. I felt I had to smile and be pleasant for each one of them. And I kept hearing the same thing over and over again—"I know how you feel." I tried to be nice to the people who said that, but I wanted to tell them they had no idea how I felt.

Rounds of doctors visited me and inspected my leg. I knew the doctor who'd performed the surgery had never done one like it before. Everyone wanted to make sure my leg didn't become infected. Each time they told me everything looked fine, I felt a wave of relief. My leg constantly throbbed with pain; medication only dulled it a little. I tried to put on a good show for the doctors, however, because I wanted to get out of the hospital and go home as soon as I could.

The morphine shots became my only way to battle the pain. I tried to get as many as I could. I didn't want to feel anything. Somehow I hoped they could kill more than just the pain in my leg.

Angie brought Kenny Reynolds, a pitcher for the Philadelphia Phillies, to visit me. I knew he'd set the record that year for the most consecutive losses. He walked into my room with a friendly grin on his face.

"Man, it's great to meet you." He held out his hand as he spoke. His energy seemed to fill the room. I smiled and shook his hand.

"How are you feeling?"

"Fine. Just fine." I knew he didn't believe me, but that's what I was supposed to say.

"Hey, I just wanted you to know when I came back to Massachusetts, I was feeling really sorry for myself." He stopped and grew serious. "I think today is the first time I understand how lucky I am." He reached over and squeezed my shoulder.

"Thanks, man." He handed me an autographed picture of himself. I grinned at him, trying to lighten the mood. "You really did have an awful season."

He laughed. "I had a feeling it wouldn't be long before you were up, giving other players a bad time." He looked at his watch. "Well, I'd better run. Get well, OK?"

He shook my hand again, his eyes warm. I smiled back and said goodbye. After he walked out of the room, I looked at the picture again. Sure, he had had a horrible season, but he had a chance to try again. I never would.

After a few days, I became more anxious to get out of the hospital. The doctors kept telling me I had to stay so they could monitor my leg, but all I wanted to do was get out and go home. People kept stopping by, and I felt overwhelmed by the support they offered. Some of my friends even sneaked my dog up to the room so I would feel less lonely. Five days after the accident, a local church elder came up for a visit.

"Hello, Eddie, how are you feeling?" He stood formally by the bed and looked down at me.

I smiled. "Fine." I was surprised he remembered my name. I hadn't made too much effort to attend church for a few years.

He fidgeted, looking uncomfortable. I waited for the usual phrase—I know how you feel—but he said nothing. The silence grew embarrassing.

He finally spoke. "You know, Eddie, this is God's way of punishing you for things you weren't supposed to do."

I felt my anger rising. Ever since my accident, I had felt God had saved my life. I bit back a nasty reply and tried to keep a neutral face. He patted me on the arm and asked if he could pray with me.

"Sure, go ahead," I replied shortly.

He prayed a quick, sanctimonious prayer, then patted me on the shoulder.

"Well, get well soon." He turned and left, leaving me to mull over what he'd said.

"It's no wonder I don't go to church," I muttered to myself as the door shut behind him. "Just lists of don't do this and don't do that!"

33

The days passed slowly. I became more and more discouraged. At night I dreamed that I had my leg and could still play ball. Waking up became my worst time of the day. All I could think about was how I'd been so athletic all my life and now I was disabled. I tried to be cheerful when people visited me, but whenever I found myself alone, I could feel nothing but hopelessness. I kept reliving the accident over and over in my mind. Why did I climb up on that corn blower? What made me slip? I wished I could go back and do it again, and the wishing was so strong it hurt inside.

A week after the accident, my mother brought in a letter for me to read. She handed it to me, then busied herself straightening the flowers around the room.

I smiled as I recognized Herb Douglass's signature. He was a former president of Atlantic Union College, and I'd grown up playing ball with his son. We'd stayed in touch as I'd roomed with his son in college. I read the letter quickly.

". . . Jesus wants Ed's heart and life, and somehow He is going to compensate him for this great turn that Ed will now have to make in his life. Something very useful and beautiful will come out of this if he stays close to Jesus. The hurt will be very, very great. . . . The evil one has done his work, but God will have the last word. . . ."

I put the letter down after reading it and stared at the wall, fighting back tears. I wanted so badly to believe, but everything seemed too impossible. I couldn't see beyond the horrible fear that I'd never walk again, never run or play ball again. What good could come out of that?

"Wasn't that a beautiful letter?" Mom asked as she picked it from the bed where I'd dropped it.

"Sure. I'm glad he wrote it," I replied woodenly. "It's a beautiful letter."

I made it through another few days. People continued to visit. My parents and Dana practically moved into my room with me. The local newspapers ran stories about my accident. Lawyers promised a lawsuit against the company that made the corn blower. I endured it all through a fog of drugs and pain. The doctors told me my leg was healing remarkably well. I didn't care. I just wished they could tell me it had grown back and everything would be like it was before.

The nurses became more and more reluctant to give me morphine shots. One left a brochure for Alcoholics Anonymous by my bed.

"What'd she leave this with me for?" I wondered. "I'm not an alcoholic or anything!" I figured the morphine didn't count.

One day toward the end of my hospital stay, a stranger walked into the room. His military clothing and rigid posture made him appear huge from my vantage point in bed.

"I'm Captain Chuck O'Brien." He reached out and shook my hand.

I motioned him into the chair beside my bed. Since my brother-in-law was serving in the army, I figured he'd been responsible for this visit.

"I know just how you feel," he told me.

I gritted my teeth as I heard the hated phrase for what seemed like the hundredth time.

He reached down, pulled up his trouser leg, and took off an artificial leg and foot. I stared at him, emotions rushing through me. Immediately I knew he understood exactly how I felt.

He put the prosthesis on the bed. "I lost my leg in Vietnam, but it wasn't the end of my life. And I'm here to tell you it isn't the end of yours." He reached into his pocket and pulled out a stack of photographs and handed them to me.

I looked at the pictures in amazement. One showed him skiing; the next showed him playing tennis. I saw pictures of him golfing, walking, looking like a normal, active person.

"What's it like to play sports without a leg?" I asked him as I handed the picture back to him.

"It takes a little getting used to, but it's not impossible." He tucked the pictures back into his pocket and put his prosthesis back on. "It just takes practice. You can't let this beat you."

After he left, the pictures and his words kept going around in my mind. And for the first time since the accident, I began to feel hopeful. If he could ski, I could ski. If he could play tennis, what would stop me?

As I went to sleep that night, I vowed I'd do for others what he'd done for me. And I promised myself I'd be just as good at sports as he was—if not better. It felt good to hope again.

Chapter 6

Chicago

"Well, it looks like we're finally getting rid of you," my nurse teased as she helped me into a wheelchair.

"You'll miss me," I promised as she wheeled me out of the room and down the hall. It felt so good to be going home. The ten days I'd spent in that room seemed like ten years.

"You just make sure you're not back here too soon, OK?" She pushed the wheelchair next to the waiting car and motioned to a couple of orderlies to help me into the front seat.

"I'm not coming back ever!" I promised as they shut the door of the car.

After the orderlies put all my flowers and gifts into the trunk of the car, my sister Nola started the engine, and Dana got into the car. I stared out the window hungrily as we pulled away from the hospital. After ten days of the same walls, the familiar scenery looked new.

When we arrived at Nola's house, she and Dana made a fuss getting me settled on the couch and making sure I was comfortable. Nola fixed all my favorite foods and arranged the television where I could reach it. I tried to enjoy being pampered, but I wanted to get up and move around the house. The pain in my leg limited me to only the most necessary moves. I hated being a burden to my sister, but knew I couldn't be at home by myself with my parents working all day.

For the next few days I watched TV and tried to keep my spirits up. But everything that I watched—from dramas to sports—showed healthy, whole people walking and running around. Every time I looked at my leg, it reminded me that I would never be the same person again. The hope I'd felt after talking to Captain O'Brien now faded as I found myself needing help to get in and out of bed or to the bathroom.

All the emotional support I'd had in the hospital now seemed to have dried up, and I felt terribly alone. Mom tried to help by rubbing my leg whenever it hurt, but I missed the attention people had shown me earlier. Now I knew the support wouldn't last, but the tragedy would.

After a week at home, cousin Bob came to see me. More than any of the other people who had visited me since the accident, I was most worried about seeing him. I knew that he, being an athlete and such a close friend, would be able to identify with me more than most other people.

As Bob walked through the living-room door, I could see him fighting tears and losing. My throat closed as I struggled off the couch and hopped over to him. And even before I reached him, I could feel my tears starting. He held out his arms to me.

"Thank God for what we have left," he cried as we leaned on each other and sobbed together. "I know that's easy for me to say because I have two legs, but God spared your life for a reason."

I nodded and wiped my eyes with the back of one hand. "At least I'm alive." He helped me back to the couch.

We sat down and he looked at me, not knowing what to say. I could tell he not only felt pain for my losing my leg, but he also knew how badly I hurt over losing my dream.

"So, what did the doctors say?" he finally asked.

"I'm doing much better than expected." I tried to sound enthusiastic. "Dad says he's known of other people who've fallen into that machine, you know. I'm the only one who made it out. He thinks it was because of God's protection, of

38

course, and also because I was in good shape. The doctors think I'm healing fast because of my physical conditioning too."

It struck me as ironic that the thing that had saved my life—my athletic abilities—would now be denied me.

Bob stayed for the rest of the evening. We talked about his new job as a teacher in Maryland and my future plans. As he got up to leave, I could see the pain return to his eyes.

"I'll be praying for you," he promised as he left.

"Thanks, buddy." I choked out the words.

From the living-room window I watched his car drive away and felt terribly alone again. Why did this have to happen? I raged inside. Why me?

The depression lingered. I started physical therapy and tried to regain some of my strength. The fight seemed lonely and the rewards few. Everything that had been so easy before now took all my strength. Getting through each day felt harder and harder. And when Dana's parents urged me to come to Chicago to see a specialist there, I jumped at the idea.

"I can quit in Chicago," I thought to myself. "Here in Lancaster, nobody wants to see Eddie be a quitter. In Chicago no one will know."

Before I left, my former softball coach, Angie, made me promise I'd return to Lancaster. I promised halfheartedly. If I quit in Chicago, what could they do about it? I'd be halfway across the country, where they couldn't see me.

Dana's parents made me comfortable in their Chicago home, and we began seeing doctors right after I arrived. Each one examined my leg, went over my medical charts, clucked about the tragedy, and marveled at how well it was healing. I considered myself lucky that I didn't have to go back for more surgery. The rounds grew depressing, however, and I listened to very little of what the doctors said.

I did listen when they refused to fill my prescriptions. It made me angry—I needed those drugs. Desperately I turned to marijuana and alcohol to help mask the effects of withdrawal. The occasional drink I'd taken in Lancaster now turned into a daily habit.

"It eases the pain," I rationalized to myself.

It also numbed me so I didn't need to think about losing my leg and my dream.

After weeks of consultations, I finally got a prescription to go to an artificial limb shop and get a prosthesis. The morning I went, I nervously tried to imagine what the leg would look like. Could they make it look like my real one?

I arrived a few minutes early and sat in the shop's waiting room. I tried to leaf through a magazine but couldn't concentrate. My appointment time arrived, and I hopped up to the front desk.

"I'm Eddie Folger, and I have a ten o'clock appointment with Mr. Dennison.

The receptionist gave me a polished, polite smile. "Please take a seat, Mr. Folger. I'll let him know you're here."

I hopped back to my seat and picked up the magazine again, only to throw it down impatiently. I tried to imagine what it would feel like to walk normally again. As I sat waiting, I pictured the leg being almost like my real one. I'd be able to run and play sports again. I'd fit in on the team again. Instead of getting pitiful stares, I'd be normal and healthy like everyone else.

The door to the back room slammed, and a man came out carrying three blocks of wood.

"Eddie, I'm Denny Dennison. How are you today?"

"Fine, sir," I answered automatically, eyeing the blocks of wood. They couldn't really be my new leg.

He pulled a chair to face me, then sat down. "Eddie, we're going to turn these pieces of wood into a leg for you."

Tears began streaking down my face. I looked at the blocks of wood and wondered how they'd ever make a leg.

He patted my arm and seemed to understand. "I think you'll be pleased when we finish. We can't give you back your original, but this will be the best substitute."

I nodded, unable to stop the tears. I remembered the feeling of leaping for a basket in basketball, jumping to catch a fly ball in baseball. Would I ever experience those feelings again?

"Will I be able to walk?" I asked raggedly.

"Of course," he soothed. "That's the purpose of making the prosthesis. You'll be able to function almost like normal. With long pants and shoes, no one will be able to tell the difference."

I looked into Denny's eyes. Couldn't he understand that "normal" to me meant running, leaping, and pushing my body to the limits?

"Will I ever be able to run again?" I whispered brokenly.

He looked at me compassionately. "No, I'm sorry."

The tears that had been trickling down my cheeks now streamed steadily. I noticed other people in the office staring at me, but I couldn't stop myself.

He seemed to understand and handed me a box of tissues. I stopped crying and tried to concentrate on everything he said. He explained the technical things he'd be doing to fashion the prosthesis and fit it to what was left of my leg. All I could think of was running the bases after I hit a home run, the wind rushing past me, my teammates slapping my hand as I came across home plate. Or the exhilaration of snatching the basketball from an opposing player, racing down the court, leaping, and stuffing the ball into the basket. And now I would never feel any of it again.

That night I had trouble getting to sleep. I kept going over and over the accident in my mind. Each time I tried to replay it a different way. I had refused to go to the farm that day and I still had my leg. Or I had gone to the farm but hadn't gotten on the corn blower and I still had my leg. I thought of the freshly signed, now useless contract, back home in Lancaster and felt sick inside. It represented everything I'd ever wanted. Now what did I have to live for?

I remembered how little I'd cared for school while growing up. All I wanted to do was play sports. I was used to being the best. Now what was left? If I couldn't play sports, what would I do? Who was I?

"Why fight it?" I thought as I turned over and punched my pillow. "Why not give up?"

I got out of bed and lighted a marijuana cigarette. The drug soon calmed me, and I felt myself relaxing. Snubbing the joint out, I crawled back under the covers.

The clock downstairs chimed 2:00 a.m. My pillow felt soaked with tears and sweat. My thoughts turned into nightmares as I fitfully drifted off to sleep.

Chapter 7

Eddie Folger Night

November 11, 1972. While I'd been planning on quitting in Chicago, Angie and other friends in Lancaster were putting together a benefit night for me. I arrived at the Clinton Armory that evening with Dana on one side and Lefty LeFebvre on the other.

As I struggled through the door on crutches, I found the armory overflowed with people. We were led to a small room in the back, and I gasped as I walked in. Kenny Reynolds, pitcher for the Philadelphia Phillies; Dave Gaynor of the Pittsburgh Pirates; Pat Bourque of the Chicago Cubs; Gene Conley, former Celtics, Braves, and Red Sox star; Bunny Lee, state commissioner of softball; and Rico Petrocelli of the Red Sox—all these people I admired so much now turned and greeted me.

"They're all here for you," Dana whispered as the door shut behind us.

I found myself surrounded. "Hey, Eddie, how's it going?"

"Great to see you, man!"

"Hey, won't be long until you're out there throwing a few pitches, eh?"

I smiled and greeted everyone. The tiny room felt alive with people. It didn't seem possible all these people were here for me. I looked again at the sports greats in the room with me. Why had they come here for me? Why did they care? The benefit night was nice, but I knew I was going to quit.

Angie appeared at the door. "We're ready to start," he informed us. "Be listening for your name."

The applause started as the master of ceremonies introduced the first guest.

"Kenny Reynolds, a pitcher for the Philadelphia Phillies!"

The applause grew louder as Kenny left the room, walked down the center aisle, and took his place at the table.

"Dave Gaynor of the Pittsburgh Pirates!"

More applause. I shifted nervously on my crutches.

"Pat Bourque of the Chicago Cubs!"

"Gene Conley, former Celtics and Red Sox star!"

I watched Gene leave the room, remembering how he'd gotten me the tryout. The armory now thundered with applause.

"Bunny Lee, state commissioner of softball!"

I looked around me. Only Rico, Dana, and Lefty remained in the room. The wave of applause and excitement grew larger.

". . . and from the Boston Red Sox, third baseman, Rico Petrocelli!"

Several members of the audience stood and applauded as Rico made his way to the table. I could see him stopping and shaking hands with people as he went. After he reached the table, the crowd went silent.

Gerry Cafarelli, the MC, then gave his final announcement.

"And finally, ladies and gentlemen, accompanied by Dana Demos and Lefty LeFebvre, Mr. Eddie Folger!"

The audience exploded with applause and rose to its feet as I slowly hobbled down the aisle, followed by Dana and Lefty. A chant started from the crowd.

"Eddie! Eddie! Eddie!"

As I reached the table, I noticed all the guests clapping and smiling. Even after I sat down, the applause continued. From my chair, it looked like the entire towns of Clinton and Lancaster stood crying and clapping for me.

As the applause slowly died and the audience took their seats, the MC continued speaking. "And now, some of our guests will say a few words on behalf of Eddie Folger."

Gene and Lefty stood and walked to the mike. It whined a little as they adjusted it to their level. Gene spoke first.

"You know, when I first agreed to take a look at Eddie, I didn't realize what a great athlete he was. But when I saw him throw a fastball, I knew he could really do something in baseball."

I grinned, remembering how Gene's interest in that first tryout had gone from polite to intense. Every time I threw a ball, he seemed to get more and more interested in me. As I listened to him talk, I could almost feel the sun on my shoulders and smell the leather of my mitt.

Lefty nodded in agreement to what Gene said. "I didn't believe you either when you said you had a 'walk-on' for me. I figured if I hadn't seen him and he wasn't an all-American, he couldn't be all that good." He stopped and chuckled. "Well, he's the only boy I ever signed without seeing him play an actual game."

The audience applauded, and Dana smiled proudly at me.

Gene turned and faced me. "Eddie, tonight we want to honor not only your athletic abilities, but also your determination and courage. You are an inspiration to us all."

I smiled politely. It touched me that they cared, but what could they do to make things better for me? Lefty and Gene sat down, and Rico stood up to talk.

"We are not here to dwell on the tragedy," Rico announced in a huge voice. "Tonight is to be a happy night. I hope the people here will enjoy themselves because tonight is about hope for the future and hope for Eddie." I felt so honored as I listened to Rico. I knew he'd just flown in from a funeral in Philadelphia that morning.

Mr. Cafarelli returned to the microphone.

45

MAKING THE TEAM

"Before I introduce our guest of honor, Eddie Folger, I would like to sum up what all of us here tonight feel: The dictionary defines courage as a quality of mind and spirit that enables one to encounter difficulties and adversity with firmness and without fear."

I felt the words wash over me. When had I been courageous? When had I been strong? I had gone to Chicago to quit.

". . . Courage teaches one to be proud and unbending in honest failure, but humble and gentle in success. . . . It instills fortitude when spirits fail, faith when there seems to be little cause for faith, and hope when hope becomes forlorn. It removes one from the commonplace and places him in harmony with himself, with others, with the universe, with God."

The audience fell quiet as everyone strained to catch his words. Beside me, I could see Dana wiping tears from her cheeks, and I struggled to keep my emotions even. I admitted that I knew nothing about courage. I just wanted to make it through that day. And the next day.

"Courage is Lou Gehrig standing silently in Yankee Stadium before thousands of saddened fans and softly saying: 'Today I consider myself the luckiest man on the face of the earth.'

"Courage is Robert Kennedy rekindling the torch passed to him by John Kennedy.

"Courage is John Paul Jones on the brink of defeat, shouting to his enemy from a burning deck, 'I have not yet begun to fight.'

"Courage is Jackie Robinson standing in the Hall of Fame, his thoughts racing back to that spring day in 1948 when he first strolled across Ebbets Field and experienced the insults, the obscenities, and the prejudice of a white-oriented sport."

I felt tears forming behind my eyes, and I fought them back. I gripped Dana's hand tightly.

". . . But perhaps the rarest form of courage of all is the courage to wage a silent, personal, sometimes lonely battle within one's own soul in order to illuminate the very nature

46

and fiber of the soul. It is with great pride and deep admiration that I present at this time such a man."

He turned and faced me.

"Ladies and gentlemen, tonight, here in this hall, Courage is a guy named Eddie Folger."

Immediately the band started playing "The Impossible Dream," and the audience rose to its feet, applauding. I found myself standing, tears streaming uncontrollably down my face. I hobbled to the microphone on my crutches and faced all the friends and strangers who believed in me so much. I couldn't stop the tears. The song grew in intensity, and the applause got louder with it. I looked up to stop the tears and saw a basketball hoop directly above me.

The song ended, and the applause stopped. I cleared my throat before speaking.

"I don't know how to say thank you," I began slowly. "This night means so much to me." I looked up at the basketball hoop again. "I'm going to get my new leg Wednesday and begin physical therapy. In a month I hope to be walking, in two, running, and then hitting again! It won't be long until I'm out on the basketball court shooting baskets!"

The room exploded with applause again. I returned to my seat and sat there while people came by and shook my hand, hugged me, and kissed me. I accepted the hugs with tears in my eyes. Suddenly I knew I couldn't quit on these people. If they thought I belonged in the company of John Paul Jones and Lou Gehrig, I could never quit on them.

The band played in the background, and people walked by with plates of food. The line of people waiting to talk to me seemed to grow longer and longer.

"You're going to make it, Eddie. You're a courageous kid."

"We're proud of you."

"We're praying for you."

The baseball stars made themselves available for autographs. The line of people finally dwindled, and I looked at my mother, who had sat down next to me.

"Mom, can you believe all of this?" I asked her. "I had no idea they were planning anything like this."

She smiled. "Well, Angie was a little worried when you left for Chicago because they had already planned this evening. They made Dana promise she'd get you back here in time."

Angie and Rico interrupted us.

"Excuse me, Mrs. Folger. Eddie, may we speak with you a minute in private?"

I nodded and struggled out of my chair. When we entered a small side room, Rico closed the door behind us.

He faced me, started to speak, then broke down crying. I felt my own tears starting again. After a few minutes, he stopped crying and held out his hand to me.

"I really admire you," he said brokenly. "You had it all, man, and it got taken away. You have so much courage."

I shook his hand slowly. "Thanks." I didn't know what to say. Somehow nothing sounded right. Angie stood to one side, trying to control his emotions.

"The people of Clinton and Lancaster raised ten thousand dollars for you tonight," Angie told me, tears in his eyes.

I felt tears forming. "I . . . I don't know how to thank you."

Angie cleared his throat gruffly and mock-punched my shoulder. "Just get yourself back out on that baseball field, OK?"

"OK," I promised.

Rico grinned, trying to lighten the mood. "Hey, that band sounds pretty good tonight. You think they'd let me play drums with them?"

"Sure, I don't see why not," Angie replied, opening the door.

I struggled back out into the armory. Rico turned to me before joining the band.

"Hey, man, I don't know if I'll get to talk to you again tonight, but keep in touch, OK?" he told me. "I really mean that."

"I'll be at every home game," I promised.

Rico shook my hand again and jogged up to the band. I hopped to the table and sat down. As I watched the crowd, I remembered how I'd wanted so badly to quit in Chicago. Now I knew I could never do it. I could quit on Eddie, but I could never quit on all those people.

Another friendly stranger came by to wish me luck. I thought again of the money they'd so unselfishly donated and felt overwhelmed again. All these people had come to show how much they cared for me. The communities I'd never really noticed while growing up now showered me with what felt like undeserved attention and love.

"You can never quit on them," I whispered to myself. "Never."

Chapter 8

Therapy, Christmas Shopping, and Hockey

November 17. Just a week after the benefit night, and on my twenty-first birthday, I was fitted for my artificial leg. Every day I went to St. Luke's Hospital in Chicago for physical therapy. For the first couple of days, they allowed me to wear my leg only for an hour. I'd walk back and forth between two parallel bars.

"Try a little harder, Eddie," I'd urge myself whenever I felt like quitting. "Just keep trying."

After the first two days, I began wearing the leg a few hours at a time and walking around the hospital on crutches. I kept begging the therapist to let me take the leg home, but she wouldn't let me.

The progress felt slow and the rewards few. I frequently grew frustrated. All my life my body had done exactly what I wanted it to. Now it took all my concentration to do a simple thing like walking.

After a couple very long weeks, I began to get pretty good at moving around with my new leg. Finally the therapist let me take it home, and I began practicing around Chicago. It felt so good to look down and see two feet and a leg—even if it wasn't mine.

I kept my progress secret from my family in Lancaster.

"How's therapy going?" they'd ask every time they called.

"Oh, fine," I'd evade.

51

MAKING THE TEAM

I wanted more than anything to go home walking at Christmas and surprise everyone.

My old enthusiasm came back. I remembered Captain Chuck O'Brien and the pictures of him playing sports. Each time I felt tempted to quit, I thought of those pictures and pushed myself harder.

Walking the crowded and icy Chicago streets with an artificial leg proved harder than I'd anticipated. The revolving doors into stores scared me the most. Each time I tried to go through one of those doors, it caught me either in the forehead or the rear end.

Christmas Eve. After a month of hard work and intensive physical therapy, I flew home and walked off the plane. My parents, who'd been expecting me on crutches, cried when they saw me.

"You should have told us!" Mom wiped her eyes as she laughed and cried at the same time.

"I knew nothing would keep you on crutches for very long," Dad commented, a grin on his face.

They stood back and looked at me a minute. I turned a circle to show off my new mobility.

"Just try and keep me off the basketball court!" I joked.

Christmas. We opened packages, ate well, joked a lot—I felt like a normal member of the family again. Everyone treated me like a real person. Mom pulled me into helping in the kitchen, and my brother gave me just as bad a time as always.

The weekend arrived and the family went to church together. I went because I knew it would make my parents happy. I knew my parents sensed that I had lost interest in spiritual things, but they didn't lecture me.

Early in the new year, a group of friends stopped by the house to visit. I felt like one of them again. After a couple of hours of sitting around joking and laughing together, they started looking at their watches.

THERAPY, CHRISTMAS SHOPPING, AND HOCKEY

"Hey, we're thinking of going down to the rink and playing some hockey. You want to come and watch?" they asked.

"I'll do more than watch," I replied. "How about letting me play on one of your teams?"

They looked doubtfully at one another, and I tried to gain their confidence.

"Relax," I said, tapping my prosthesis. "I'll be a better player with this leg because I won't have to worry about my ankle turning in!"

They still looked doubtful. "Well, OK, if you want," one finally said.

My parents, the boys, Dana, and I piled into cars. When we arrived at the rink, Dana and my parents went to the stands, and I joined the boys in the locker room.

I put on my skates and shin pads quickly.

"Hey, man," one friend teased. "You won't need shin pads on your right leg."

People laughed nervously, then fell silent again. The usual locker-room joking didn't happen. I tried to loosen everyone up a little.

"Hey, did you hear the one about the traveling salesman?" I asked a friend.

He didn't respond. I tried another approach.

"Ron, buddy, I heard about that girl you've been seeing. Quite a looker, huh?"

Ron smiled. "Yeah, she's something," he mumbled.

I gave up trying to joke and started walking around the locker room on my skates.

"This is easier than I thought," I told the guys as I hit a roll of tape against the wall with my hockey stick. "You'd just better watch out when we get out on the ice!"

After seeing me getting around so well on my skates, they loosened up a little.

"Ah, come on!" a friend teased back. "You were never that good at hockey before!"

I shook my fist at him in mock anger and whacked a roll of tape his direction. This seemed to lighten everyone up, and we were laughing and joking as we spilled out of the locker room onto the ice.

I waited until all the other guys were on the ice before I tried getting on. It looked scarier and slipperier than I'd imagined. I tentatively put my left foot on the ice. All OK. Then, holding onto the rail, I put my prosthesis on the ice.

It went right, then left. I held on to the rail, desperately trying to control my foot. I almost fell twice and nearly did the splits before I succeeded in struggling off the ice. The guys watched me, not knowing what to say. I painted a fake smile on my face.

"I guess I'll sit this game out. You guys go ahead."

I turned and walked back into the locker room before they could answer. The tears started before I even sat down. I took the shin pads off, then took my leg off and threw it into the trash can, skate and all. Just then Dad walked through the door.

"I'll never wear it again!" I screamed, tears running down my face. "It's worthless. I felt like I was trying to control a broomstick on a skate out there!"

He sat down beside me, tears running down his own face, and put his arms around me.

"Why, why, why?" I cried. "It's not fair. I was just as good— no, better—than any of those guys out there. Why did this happen? Why?"

Dad didn't reply. He just sat silently with his arm around my shoulders. I looked at my leg in the trash can. It looked ridiculous sticking out with the skate on it. Dad got up, pulled it out of the trash, and handed it to me.

"Put it back on," he told me.

I took the leg from him and stripped the skate from it. I still didn't want to wear it. All I could think of was how well my real leg had worked.

My tears stopped, and I looked at the leg again. Finally,

54

with much determination, I put it back on. Dad slapped me on the back.

"Good for you." He gave me a hand and helped me off the bench. I collected all my stuff from the locker room and headed for the door.

"Basketball and baseball will go better," he promised as we shut the door behind us and headed toward the stands.

"Yeah," I tried to be cheerful. "Hockey never was my sport, anyway."

But as I watched my friends moving so effortlessly across the ice, I fought back another wave of tears. I knew I'd never be like that again. Dad touched my hand and led me up to where Mom and Dana sat waiting for us.

Chapter 9

Opening Pitch

Crowds milled into the stands of Fenway Park for the opening game of the 1973 season between the Red Sox and the Yankees. I stood front row, right beside the Red Sox dugout. Dana stood beside me, and several prisoners of war returned from Vietnam stood behind and on both sides of us.

The organ played traditional ballpark music, and food vendors hawked snacks behind me. I waited nervously for the national anthem and the opening ceremony.

When the Red Sox had called and asked me to throw out the opening pitch at their first game, it hadn't seemed real. Even at the pregame party where we'd mixed with the Red Sox players, it hadn't seemed real. Now, as I took in the crowds, the press people, and the ballpark, I felt excitement rush through me. If I couldn't be out on the field, this was the next best thing.

Everyone stood as "The Star-Spangled Banner" rang out over the stadium. Opening remarks followed. The Yankees and the Red Sox came out onto the field. Then all eyes turned to me as my name was announced over the loudspeaker.

"And throwing out today's opening pitch is a young man named Eddie Folger, a Red Sox hopeful until he lost his leg last fall. Eddie is joined today by Captain Lauren Lengyel, Lt. Timothy Sullivan . . ."

I shifted nervously and smiled what I hoped looked like a

natural smile. Blocking out the rest of the speaker's words, I waited for my cue. It came a few seconds later.

"Play ball!"

I threw the baseball onto the field as cameras flashed around me. Carlton Fisk, the catcher, caught the ball and the game began. I watched each player intently and cheered loudly for the Red Sox. When the Red Sox won, 15-5, the stands erupted with excited fans. After the fans melted away, all the Red Sox team members signed the opening ball for me. I wished that the party could go on forever. But the evening ended, and I had to return to Lancaster and the reality I'd never play ball for the Red Sox.

Wedding plans consumed my time for the next couple of months. Dana and I got married with all the traditional flurry and settled into a cozy apartment together. I knew that if she'd stood by me through my accident and slow recovery, she was the woman I wanted to be married to.

After the wedding, I started working for Continental Insurance, underwriting car and homeowner's insurance. Everything seemed perfect—except I couldn't get rid of my dream of playing ball.

I'd come to terms with the loss of my leg already. Earlier in the year, I'd been at the Walter Reed military hospital when my brother-in-law had open-heart surgery. While there, the doctors asked me to visit with some of the guys on the amputee ward. I saw men with no legs. And men with no arms and legs. By the time I left, I'd stopped feeling sorry for myself and realized that I didn't have a problem.

My local fame continued. The town of Lancaster built a new middle school and named the gymnasium after me. It felt like a double honor when I realized I was the only living person they had named a school building after.

From the outside, everything looked perfect. I had a job, a wife, a little local fame. I got around fairly well on my prosthesis, and most people didn't even realize I was wearing it. But the pain of my lost dream lingered.

I followed the Red Sox avidly. After losing my leg, the team gave me a lifetime pass to their games. I attended every home game and even followed them to New York and Baltimore a few times. While watching them, I could pretend I still played well and I still had a chance of making the team.

Spring season started for the local men's league, and I joined my old softball team again. I thought I could still play ball.

"Some professional players injure themselves and lose several seasons," I bragged to friends. "I lost a leg and I'm not missing even *one* season!"

But not missing a season became my only consolation as I watched most games from the bench. My old teammates never went easier on me just because I'd lost my leg. Because I couldn't hit right-handed anymore, I spent hours practicing my left-handed swing. At the games I did a little pitching and got a few hits. After being a star so long, I suddenly found myself a weak player—and I hated it.

"Will I ever be able to play again?" I wondered as I watched guys I'd easily outplayed the year before hit balls twice as far as I could now.

As the season continued, I gradually got a little better at hitting left-handed. I still couldn't run the bases, so whenever I got a hit, I hopped to first base; then a runner did the rest of the bases for me.

I seesawed between fantasy and reality. After watching Red Sox games, I was sure that I could still play professional baseball. But when I went home and tried to run, I knew I'd never be able to play professionally.

I had little sympathy for complainers. Seated in a restaurant with my sister one day, I couldn't help overhearing a young man complaining about knee surgery.

"I have to keep this cast on for a month," he complained to his companion. "It's not fair. I'll miss basketball season!"

MAKING THE TEAM

As I gritted my teeth, my sister shot me a warning look.

"Don't you dare," she whispered, guessing my intentions.

"I don't know why it had to happen to me," the young man whined, louder this time. "It really hurts too."

I threw down my napkin and stalked over to his table. He looked up at me, surprised.

"Excuse me," I interrupted. "I couldn't help overhearing your conversation." I tapped my prosthesis. It made a hollow wooden sound.

He looked at my leg, then back at me, gulped a couple of times, but said nothing.

"I don't have a knee," I continued. "You really ought to be thankful that you do."

With those words I turned around and left him, stunned into silence. My sister, embarrassed, insisted on leaving the restaurant.

I kept trying harder and harder in softball. My hitting started to improve, and I became more consistent when I got up to bat. But I still couldn't hit the home runs I had been famous for, and I still couldn't run my own bases.

Between my job, my ballgames, and the Red Sox games I attended, I kept myself busy. Dana, a nurse, worked odd hours, and I spent lots of time going to games and parties with my friends.

I could tell my partying bothered my parents. I tried to keep a good façade around them, but they saw through it. "We're praying for you," my mother told me one time. "We believe Jesus has a place for you."

I smiled and said the right things, but inside I didn't care. Things hadn't worked out for me when I had attended church, so now I was going to do things my way.

The last game of the 1973 softball season. I had struggled and practiced all season, but still couldn't play nearly as well as I had before the accident. I watched nervously from the bench as the final inning progressed. Fans sat in the stands behind me.

"Eddie, you're up!" Angie called to me.

I picked a bat and walked to the plate. I'd gotten a hit earlier in the game, but wanted to blow this one over the fence.

The first pitch came toward me, a little high. I let it pass.

"Ball one!" the umpire called out.

The next pitch came toward me. It looked perfect. I swung into it and missed.

"Strike one!"

The crowd seemed to get a little quieter as the next pitch came toward me.

"This is the one," I thought as I swung at it as hard as I could.

The bat and ball connected with the force I'd remembered. Fans of both teams stood up and watched the ball sail over center field and over the fence. The cheering erupted before I dropped the bat and started toward first base. It grew louder as I continued to second and third base. Tears nearly blinded me as I stumbled the last stretch to home plate.

My teammates, the opposing team, and fans from both sides greeted me as I came across the home plate. I found myself surrounded by hugs, backslaps, and photographers snapping pictures.

"Way to go, Eddie!" a player from the opposing team told me.

I wiped the tears from my cheeks and let myself be swept off the field. The game finished with our team winning 24-2 against the other team. That night as we celebrated our win, I felt like a true member of the team again. I had regained their respect as a ballplayer. I wasn't there because I'd once been good, but because I was a good ballplayer once again. It meant everything to me.

Chapter 10

More Dreams Dissolve

"I'm thinking about quitting Continental and going back to college for my P.E. degree. What do you think?" I leaned back in the chair and looked across our small living room at Dana.

She sat on the couch, flipping through a magazine.

"Hmm?" she asked.

"I want to go back for my P.E. degree. What do you think?" My voice took on a note of irritation. Why did I always have to repeat myself with her? Didn't she ever listen?

She arched her eyebrows. "Whatever you want, Eddie." She yawned and closed the magazine. "I know you'll do what you want anyway. It doesn't matter what I say."

I gritted my teeth angrily. "What's that supposed to mean?"

She stood up and dropped the magazine on the couch. "Just what it says. You always think you're right." She walked out of the room before I could answer.

I sat steaming. It always happened this way. The verbal battles that had begun right after we married now marred everything we discussed. As I sat and mentally reviewed our fights, I couldn't believe we'd endured two years together since I'd lost my leg and we'd gotten married.

I followed Dana into the bedroom. She was already in bed, the lights turned off.

"Look, can't we discuss it?" I asked, trying to stay calm.

"Discuss? What a novel idea!" She sat up as she spoke. "Are you starting something new?"

I slammed my fist against the wall. "Forget it!" I yelled. "I'm going out!"

"Fine with me," she spat back.

I grabbed my coat and stomped out of the house. After driving around for half an hour, I stopped in at my favorite bar. I didn't get home until after 2:00 a.m.

The tension increased over the next few months. I quit my job with the insurance company and started college classes again. Dana spent more time at work and with her friends, and I spent more time playing and watching sports.

1975. The Red Sox made the World Series, and I followed every game. It was my life. And when the Red Sox played in the series, I couldn't keep my emotions in check. All I could think of was that it should have been *my* World Series. I should have been on the field, helping my team win.

Weeks dragged by, tensions grew worse, and the fights more frequent. One day I came home and found Dana crying.

"What's going on?" I asked impatiently.

She didn't answer for a minute. "I just called my mom. She's coming out to help me pack. I'm moving back to Chicago." Her voice sounded flat and lifeless.

I felt all the fight go out of me. "When are you coming back?" I finally asked.

Her eyes filled with tears. "I don't know, Eddie. Maybe never."

I sat down on the bed and held my head in my hands. "Why can't we try to work this out?"

She looked at me, anger flashing in her eyes. "Work this out? All you care about is yourself and how you don't get to play baseball anymore. Look, I'm sorry, but I want a real relationship."

I grew angry. "Fine, if that's the way you feel about it, it's probably best you're leaving."

"That's what I thought too," she retorted.

I stood up and grabbed my coat. "I'm going out."

"That's your answer to everything, isn't it?" she screamed. "And you have to *ask* why I'm leaving?"

I stomped out of the house and joined a few of my buddies for drinks. When I returned after midnight that night, I found a note telling me to sleep on the couch.

Dana's mother arrived a few days later. I tried to stay away from the apartment and pretended I didn't care, but I felt like a failure. And when I came home the night after she'd left, I knew she'd never be back.

"Where did I go wrong?" I asked myself. "Why did this happen?"

I combated my loneliness by hanging around with my friends and playing sports. But the loneliness and the ache remained. I tried to pretend it didn't matter, but I knew deep inside that it mattered more than I cared to admit.

I moved back in with my parents and numbly moved through each day. I thought of trying to mend things with Dana—of trying to change my ways. After a few days, I signed up for Bible studies. But the lessons made me feel guilty about the life I was living, and I quit after a few sessions.

The weeks passed slowly, and I became more and more depressed. The sense of failure remained. One night, my parents convinced me to go to an evangelistic meeting with them. I really didn't want to attend, but I knew it would make them happy. As soon as the meeting ended, I got into my car and began driving around town. As I drove past a friend's house, I noticed enough cars parked out front to constitute a used-car lot.

"Must be a party!" I thought as I parked my car.

A car pulled up behind me, and a gorgeous brunette I'd noticed a few weeks earlier stepped out with several friends. I got out of my car quickly and fell in step beside her.

"Hi, I'm Eddie," I told her.

She looked as if she were going to brush me off, but changed her mind when a guy came out of the house and

65

started walking toward her.

"I'm Jacki." She smiled a perfect smile at me, and I felt my heart beat faster.

The guy came up to her. "Jacki, I'd like to talk to you."

"Not now," she replied, taking my arm. "Come on, Eddie."

I smiled smugly at the guy, knowing he was her ex-boyfriend, and walked into the party with Jacki. After I got both of us drinks, we found a place not too close to the stereo to talk.

She looked nervous. "I really shouldn't be talking to you; you're a married man."

"Dana and I separated," I told her. She looked only a little less nervous.

The noise of the stereo made me uncomfortable.

"You want to go for a drive?" I asked hopefully.

She wavered a moment, looking at her ex-boyfriend, who stood watching us. "Yeah, I guess so."

As we walked to my car, I admired her again. Glossy brown hair, blue eyes—I knew everyone envied me for being with her.

We went out for drinks, returned, then drove around some more.

"I want to see you again," I told her.

"Well, I don't know."

I smiled my most winning smile. She smiled back, then sobered.

"I'm still worried about your being married. I don't date married men," she told me.

"I assure you, it's over. Trust me."

She raised one eyebrow. "Trust you?"

I laughed. "I'll call you, OK?"

She thought a minute. "OK," she finally agreed.

I called her the next day. And the next. And the next. I kept calling her until she was convinced I wasn't going to get back together with Dana, and she started dating me. We went everywhere together.

My mother was furious. "How can you run around with another woman when you're still married to Dana?" she asked.

"Mom, it's over with Dana."

She just glared and clamped her mouth shut. I could feel her disapproval every time I left the house to see Jacki.

Jacki fared no better with her father. When one of his friends told him I was married, he became extremely upset. Jacki and I continued to see each other, but hated the pressure.

The pressure only intensified as Jacki and I fell deeper in love with each other. I looked for a way to leave Lancaster. Rescue came in the form of an uncle I hadn't seen or heard from in years.

Fall in Lancaster. I stood on the football field watching the teams play in the crisp afternoon air. My referee's whistle remained in my mouth as I watched for any illegal plays by both teams. At half time I noticed a man walking toward me.

"Hi, Eddie, I'm your Uncle Henry. Do you remember me?"

I thought quickly, then smiled. "Boy, it's been a while. What are you doing here?"

He scratched his head. "Liquidating my antique business and moving to Arizona, for starters."

"Arizona? What for?" I looked at my watch. I still had a few minutes before the game resumed.

"Always wanted to go there. Besides, I bought a ranch. Anyway, I wanted to know if you wanted to help me move." He saw my surprised expression.

"Let me think about it, OK?"

"Sure, take your time, Ed."

I blew the whistle, and the game started again. I threw myself into refereeing. After the game, Uncle Henry waited for me as I collected my stuff and headed for the car.

"I'll be back down in a few weeks. Think about it until then." He shook my hand, then left.

During the next week I barely gave Uncle Henry's offer a thought. School started soon, and Arizona seemed a long way away. Uncle Henry returned, still determined to enlist my help.

"I have bills to pay, and school is starting in a week," I told him.

"Don't worry about your bills, I'll work it out," he promised.

Suddenly the offer seemed more interesting. "How long will it take?" I asked, giving a little.

"Just a couple of weeks," he promised.

I thought about it a few minutes. A couple of weeks didn't seem like long to get my debts paid and earn some extra money besides. Also, as I ran into more and more criticism for dating Jacki, Arizona began to look appealing.

"OK, I'll do it," I agreed.

"Great! I'll have you drive the truck with your Aunt Jean. I'll fly out and join you as soon as I tie everything up here."

We settled all the details about when we would leave. I promised to meet Aunt Jean in a couple of days and start the trip. It felt good to have something to plan for. I still felt like I was drifting without purpose. At least this trip gave me a goal for a few weeks. And as I became excited about the trip, I decided Jacki should come with me.

"Come on, Jacki," I begged. "It'll be fun. A quick, cheap vacation."

"I'll think about it," she answered.

"Call me tonight," I urged.

Jacki agreed to go. However, she let me know that my pleading hadn't persuaded her; her mother had talked her into going.

The evening before we left, I sat outside and watched the sunset. It felt strange to be leaving—even for just a few weeks. I'd never been as far west as Arizona. The only thing I knew about the West centered around cowboys and Indians.

My parents saw me off that morning.

"Drive carefully," Dad called as my brother-in-law and I climbed into his car to drive to my uncle's place in New York State.

"We're praying for you," Mom added.

I thought about Mom's comment as we pulled out of the driveway. I knew she always had prayed for me. Would she ever stop? Despite my frustration with the church and its members, deep inside I hoped she wouldn't.

We stopped at Jacki's before leaving Lancaster.

"All set to go?" I asked her.

"I guess so," she replied, tears starting.

She hugged and kissed her mom. Both were crying. Jacki's mom turned to me as Jacki climbed into the car.

"You take care of my daughter, Eddie Folger," she told me. I could tell that she meant it.

Jacki cried a little more as we pulled out of Lancaster.

"It's only two weeks," I assured her. "It'll be fun."

She smiled. "Yeah. It'll be great."

Chapter 11

Lights, Glamour, and Money

The two weeks turned into months. While Jacki and I waited for Uncle Henry to arrive in Arizona, Aunt Jean put us to work on the ranch for little food and no pay. My debts at home went unpaid. And when I confronted Uncle Henry months later, he refused to pay anything.

"Where are we going to go?" Jacki asked after I had confronted Uncle Henry.

"Well, we could go back to Lancaster . . ." my voice trailed off. I knew we'd return to the same pressure we'd tried to escape.

"We could visit my Uncle Ducky in Las Vegas. I'm sure he wouldn't mind if we stayed with him awhile," Jacki suggested.

I thought about it a moment. Uncle Ducky had been so much fun when we'd visited a few weekends earlier. "Well, it is still warm out here . . ."

"Let's do it," Jacki said.

"OK," I agreed.

We arrived in Las Vegas with a beat-up car, a black lab named Rocky, no money, and no jobs. Uncle Ducky took us in, but I started looking for work and a place to live as soon as I could. We quickly discovered we couldn't afford much.

"Well . . . I suppose it will have to do." Jacki's voice held more optimism than her facial expression.

I looked around the trailer house again—shabby curtains, torn cushions, and rusted appliances. I tried the heater. It rattled briefly before quitting.

"At least the weather's warmer than in Lancaster," I offered hopefully as I looked at the dead heater.

Jacki rolled her eyes at me, walked over to the sink, and turned the tap.

"Well, at least we have water," she joked as she turned off the cold tap and tried the hot. "No hot water, though."

She sat down heavily. I sighed, wishing we could afford more.

"It's only for a little while," I promised. "Only till I get out of poker school and get a decent job."

Jacki looked resigned. "At least Rocky likes it."

I looked at our black lab sprawled on the floor and grinned. "Yeah, he thinks he's in the Hilton."

Jacki sighed. "Well, I guess I'd better start moving our clothes in. You want to get everything settled with the landlord?"

I shrugged, looking at the shabby trailer. "I guess." I walked to the door and opened it. "I'll see you later."

"Later," she called as I closed the door behind me.

I walked to the manager's office, comparing the other trailers to ours. They all looked run-down but in better shape than ours. I decided, as I signed the rental agreement, that we'd found the worst trailer in the worst trailer park in Las Vegas. And I vowed to get out as soon as possible.

We struggled through the next few months while I attended poker school. Every time we wanted to wash up, we had to heat water in an electric skillet. Meals became an adventure as we cooked boxes of spaghetti and old produce we'd been able to buy cheaply before it was thrown out.

When the Nevada Rehabilitation Commission first sent me to poker school, I went because I needed a job. But as I got closer and closer to the end of my training, I realized I was good at dealing cards. I watched all the money being made in the casinos and began to get excited. Maybe I'd make *my* fortune here. Jacki and I could travel back to Lancaster with a motor home and a pocketful of money.

The pocketful of money arrived sooner than I had expected. Right after I finished school and took a job at the Flamingo Hilton, I received $25,000 in a workmen's compensation claim for the loss of my leg. We immediately put the money down on a house. The word of our good fortune spread quickly.

"Hey, buddy, I heard you and Jacki bought a house," my friend from Lancaster congratulated me over the phone. "You think me and my girl can come and visit for a few weeks?"

"Sure, no problem. We'd love to see you," I agreed.

They arrived two weeks after Jacki and I moved in. After they left, more friends came to visit. Jacki began joking that we were running a motel for our friends. I didn't care. Friends always brought lots of drugs and alcohol with them when they arrived.

Drugs and alcohol—the magic combination that allowed me to escape the present and live in the past. Weekends and the parties became my life. Each time my friends and I got high, we talked about what a great ballplayer I'd been. Someone would pull out the old scrapbook, and we'd reread all the clippings, remember all the old days.

I didn't bother to look for a church in Las Vegas. Church meant nothing to me. I knew my parents didn't approve of my living with Jacki or my job in a casino, but I tried not to care.

"This is me," I'd rage to Jacki whenever my conscience began to bother me. "If they can't take it, too bad."

My parents kept in touch with me even though I knew they didn't approve of my lifestyle.

"We're praying for you. . . . God has a plan for your life."

I passed over these sections of the letters or phone conversations quickly. I didn't want to think about God. I didn't want to think about church. All I wanted to do was party and have fun. And they would never know because I knew they would never come out to Las Vegas.

MAKING THE TEAM

October 1978. My divorce to Dana had been finalized the previous spring, and in the fall, Jacki and I drove back to Lancaster to get married. The parties began as soon as we arrived.

"Hey, buddy, we've got a little something for the bride and groom," a friend joked, pressing a package into my hand. "Enjoy!"

I looked at the package. Cocaine. I showed it to Jacki, and she laughed and shrugged.

"How much more do you think we'll get?" she whispered as we looked over our ever-growing stash of drugs and smaller pile of money.

"Enough to get us through the weekend, I hope."

Another friend grabbed my shoulder. "Hey, Eddie, I got a little something for you. . . ."

Drugs and alcohol flowed freely the rest of the night. We reminisced about old times, ranted angrily about the Red Sox losing to the Yankees in the playoffs, and eventually got smashed to the point of almost passing out.

October 14 dawned clear and crisp—a perfect New England fall day. Jacki and I woke after two days of partying and tried to pull ourselves together enough to get married.

"Oh, I'm going to need more than aspirin to get through this," Jacki moaned, holding her head.

"Check the gift pile," I joked, opening a beer for myself.

Jacki rummaged through our drug supply for some pot. We staggered around, trying to get ready. Finally we roused the rest of the wedding party and got everyone into cars.

"We'll meet you at the justice of the peace's house," we called as we pulled into the street.

Behind us we could see people heading in the opposite direction.

"We'll never get everyone together now," Jacki moaned.

We arrived at the house where the justice of the peace waited to marry us. Jacki's parents still hadn't arrived.

"Where are Jacki's parents?" I whispered to my best man.

He turned, his eyes glassy. "How should I know?" he giggled.

I knew he was too high to be of any help. Jacki looked worried.

Fifteen minutes later her parents arrived, and Jacki and I took our places in front of the justice of the peace.

"Do you, Eddie, take this woman . . ."

I looked at Jacki, love breaking through my drug-fogged thoughts. My eyes filled as I saw her looking so lovingly, so trustingly, back up at me. "This is the woman for me," I thought. "No matter what, I can't mess this one up."

"I do." My voice rang with conviction.

"Do you, Jacki, take this man . . ."

I saw my own determination reflected in Jacki's eyes. She squeezed my hand as she replied.

"I do."

"Inasmuch as Eddie and Jacki have pledged their lives to one another, and by the power invested in me by the state of Massachusetts, I now pronounce you husband and wife."

Cheers and applause rang out as I bent to kiss Jacki. Afterward, people came up and congratulated us.

"Welcome to the family," my mother told Jacki as she hugged her.

I felt relief as I watched my parents welcome Jacki without reservations. I'd been afraid that their disapproval of my living with Jacki before my divorce from Dana would affect their acceptance of Jacki. I realized, suddenly, I should have known better.

Jacki's parents came up and congratulated us. Her mother gave me a reserved kiss on the cheek, and her father shook my hand.

"You take good care of Jacki, OK?" I could see him struggling with his emotions as he spoke.

"I will," I promised.

We climbed into cars and went to Jacki's parents' house for the reception. The music blared. My parents chose seats as far from the action as possible. Even from where I stood, I could see their strained smiles as they watched alcohol flow freely.

"I'm sorry." I wanted to say to them. "I'm not sorry I'm doing it, but I'm sorry you have to see it."

Someone pressed a glass of champagne into my hand, and I sipped it. I turned and saw my mother watching me, a sad look in her eyes. I felt a wave of guilt, then I crushed it with anger.

"This is me," I silently told her. "Can you live with it? Can you accept it?"

I looked at the other people at the party. I knew my parents didn't judge Jacki or her parents for what went on at the reception. But me, the son they'd raised to never drink? I swallowed another wave of guilt with a mouthful of champagne.

Mom came up to me, still wearing a strained smile. "Eddie, we're going to leave now. Stop by the house before you drive back to Las Vegas, OK?"

"OK, Mom." I gave her a hug.

I felt a wave of relief as I watched my parents leave. Now I could party without worrying about what they were thinking.

The party grew wilder as we drank and danced. Every time I remembered the pain in my mother's eyes, I had another drink. I didn't want to feel guilt anymore. What right did she have to make me feel guilty?

"Where are you two going on your honeymoon?" someone asked.

"Las Vegas." Jacki laughed. "Isn't that romantic?"

The party continued until midnight. Then Jacki and I got into the car, and I drove to our hotel. She snuggled against me as we walked to our room.

"Eddie?" she asked.

"Hmm?"

"Are you glad we did it?"

I kissed her gently. "Of course I'm glad."

"Good. So am I."

We fell silent for a few moments. When we reached our room, I unlocked the door and turned on the lights. Setting the bags on the floor, I immediately pulled out the drugs. We did cocaine until the sun started coming up. Then we called friends in Las Vegas and told them what a great party we were having. When the drugs finally started to wear off, I started to feel sleepy; Jacki looked like she felt the same way.

"Eddie." Jackie put her head on my shoulder. "I love you."

"I love you too." I hugged her tightly.

She sighed and yawned, then stretched out on the bed. "It was a good party, huh?"

"The best," I agreed, running my fingers through her hair.

The memory of my parents surfaced sharply and in focus. I fought it back down. Jacki had fallen asleep across the bed. I thought about the party and doing more drugs, but decided I'd better lie down.

"Yup, it was the best," I whispered.

Chapter 12

The Never-ending Party

"Eddie was the greatest. Man, you were the best. Remember how many home runs you used to hit?"

I let the words wash over me as my friends looked at the newspaper clippings from when I signed my contract with the Red Sox. In the darkened living room, it was hard to tell the people from the furniture.

"It's just too bad. Talk about bum luck."

I put another line of cocaine on the mirror that lay on the table and snorted it. Perhaps the magic white powder would solve everything. The room began to take on a surrealistic look.

"You could have been another Ted Williams or Tom Seaver."

The cocaine let me leave the living room and my friends and travel back in time to before the accident. I relived the signing, the games, each home run I hit. And I felt free—free of pain, free of responsibility, free to still make the team.

Then, like a bubble bursting, the dream ended and I crashed. Only another line of cocaine or another drink could bring it back. And when the drugs ran out, the dream died. Suddenly, I was back in the living room with my friends. No leg, no dream, and hundred of dollars' worth of drugs and alcohol gone.

I looked around me at the other people. Two or three lay passed out on the floor. One couple staggered out of the room toward the bedrooms. Jacki brushed her hair out of her eyes.

Feeling a wave of guilt wash over me, I went to our bedroom, pulled my Bible out of the night stand, and held it, crying. Jacki came into the room to see if I was all right.

"I'm going to hell!" I yelled, waving the Bible at her.

She leaned against the wall and sighed heavily. "Oh, Eddie, not again."

"It's true. I'm going to hell, and you don't care," I accused.

"I do care," Jacki flashed angrily. "I just don't see how this time is any different from any other. You do this every time you get high."

I gave her a wounded look. She softened.

"Look, I'm a little high myself. Why don't you try to sleep it off?" She walked over to the bed and turned down the covers. "See? Why don't you go to sleep?"

I obediently set down the Bible and crawled into bed, not bothering to get undressed. Jacki collapsed beside me.

The next morning I barely made it out of bed and into the bathroom before vomiting violently. Just when I thought everything was OK, I started again. Finally, after throwing up three times, I shakily left the bathroom.

I stumbled to the kitchen, my head splitting. Grabbing a bottle of aspirin, I washed several down with a can of beer. Another wave of nausea hit, and I fought it with gritted teeth.

"Hey, how's it going?" A friend staggered into the kitchen and greeted me.

"Fine," I managed, wishing he wouldn't talk so loud. Each word seemed to pound into my skull.

"Some party last night, huh?" he went on. "We going to do another one next weekend?"

"Sure, sure, whatever." I would have agreed to anything at that moment.

After a few hours I began to feel better, and I forgot about how ill I'd been. I just wanted to get higher and higher. We sat around comparing party stories, each person trying to top the previous person's tale.

"Well, that's nothing," a friend laughed. "I remember the time we partied and I had to drive home. Remember when the cop stopped me? He asked me if I was drunk, and I said, 'No, I'm Canadian. We all slur our words in Canada.' I can't believe he let me go!"

We all laughed, and I chimed in with another story.

"Remember the time we went to Hollywood to see Santa Fe audition for Motown? What a weekend! We walked up and down looking at the stars on the sidewalk, looking at the street musicians, the hookers drumming up business. Lenny was hot that night. It reminded me of my tryout with the Red Sox."

I laughed at the memory. How long ago had that been? Two years ago? Three? The years merged together with only the weekend parties marking the time.

"Well, I still think last weekend's was the best," I added. "Remember when we were having that contest, seeing who could do the biggest lines of cocaine? Oh, that's right, you guys weren't there."

Jacki threw me a warning look.

"Well, Jacki doesn't think it was funny," I began sarcastically, "but it was."

Jacki got up and left the room. I continued anyway.

"We were doing those lines, and all of a sudden David's girlfriend falls on the floor and starts having convulsions." I jerked around to demonstrate. "We were dying, I mean, she looked like a fish out of water!"

Everyone laughed, and one guy looked at his watch.

"Hey, man, I heard there's a great party going on over at the hotel with Santa Fe. You want to go?"

I jumped up, ready to party again. "Sounds great. Let me get Jacki."

I walked into the kitchen, where Jacki sat staring angrily at the wall.

"Hey, we're going over to the hotel. The band's in town, and they're having a party. Let's go."

81

She ignored me.

"Come on, it will be fun."

She turned and faced me. "You know I don't like it when you talk about what happened to David's girlfriend. She could have died, you know."

"Yeah, but she didn't. Can we go?"

She sighed and stood up. "Sure. Let's go."

Everyone piled into cars and drove to the hotel. The band, Santa Fe, greeted us with hugs.

"Hey, how have you guys been?" the lead singer asked.

We'd been friends with the band since we had first moved to Las Vegas.

"Better than ever." I flashed a smile and pulled a bag of cocaine out of my pocket.

"Whoa, what's this?" He motioned the other band members over. "Looks great!"

"It's the best." I handed the package to him. "Here. Try it."

He took the bag from me and passed it to the other guys. More people crowded into the room, and large amounts of cocaine and alcohol began making the rounds.

"Just one sniff away from paradise," I murmured as I put out my line.

The party continued until sunrise. I drank, did lines of cocaine, and danced with other women when I thought Jacki wasn't looking. As the lights of Las Vegas went off and the sun began spilling across the desert, we left the party and headed for home. I drove wildly, so high I barely knew where we were going.

"Did you have to dance with her? Did you?" Jacki yelled at me.

"It's none of your business," I yelled back, pressing harder on the accelerator.

"I don't know how I put up with you," she screamed back, her drug-dilated eyes shooting anger. "You're just a drugging, drinking, cheating liar."

"Shut up!" I screamed back. "If you don't like it, you can

leave. I didn't ask for this!" I accelerated again. The speedometer said seventy miles per hour, and I had no intention of slowing down.

"Leave? Is that what you want me to do? Fine. I'm out of here!" She opened the door and had one leg partway out before I grabbed her arm. The ground rushed by in a blur.

Shaking, I pulled over to the side of the road and stopped. Jacki crumpled against the seat, crying.

"Oh, Eddie, what was I just about to do? Oh my God . . ."

I sat and held her as she cried. My own heart raced as I imagined her flying out the door and being killed. Finally, our trembling stopped, and I drove home very slowly.

The next weekend we did another round of parties. And the next weekend. And the weekend after that. Each time I felt the pain over losing my dream, I took drugs or took a drink.

My mother kept sending me letters. "We're praying for you. . . . God has a plan for you."

I angrily crumpled them up and threw them away. God has a plan for me? Then why did He take away baseball—the only thing I ever wanted? How could anything good ever come out of that?

The tension between Jacki and me grew thicker. The steady stream of friends living in our house never let up. We fought with the friends and about the friends. We fought about drugs—how much was too much, how much was too little, who was the real addict in the relationship.

I didn't care. I didn't care about the future—at least not any farther into the future than the next weekend and the next party. Each weekend I angrily tried to get higher and higher. Jacki tried to get me to slow down, but I shook her off. I just wanted to forget.

"What do I have to look forward to?" I wondered. "Next year will be the same, and the next too. I have nothing left to live for."

One day, after a night of partying and a morning of being sick, I heard someone knock at the door.

"I'll get it," I called to Jacki.

Opening the door a crack, I blinked against the strong sunlight. It made my already-throbbing head ache even more. A man in a suit stood on the porch.

"Hi. I'm here to see Eddie Folger." He smiled at me, and I managed a smile in return.

"I'm Eddie. What can I do for you?" I still peered through the crack at him.

"I'm the pastor of the local Adventist church. Herb Douglass contacted me and asked if I would come visit you."

I felt a shock go through me. Herb Douglass? How did he find me in Las Vegas? Must have been Mom and Dad, I reasoned. I looked behind me at the living room littered with beer cans and drug paraphernalia and decided I'd better talk on the porch instead. I stepped onto the porch and closed the front door behind me.

"Herb asked me to visit because we're holding a series of meetings at the church, and he hopes you'll attend."

I smiled, thinking, "Attend a meeting in a church? Never!" Hoping I'd appear gracious, I steered the pastor toward his car.

"Look, Pastor," I began.

"Call me John," he offered.

"OK, John. I really appreciate you coming by, but I'm just not ready."

He let the words sink in, then nodded. "Do you mind if I come back someday to visit?"

I shrugged. "No, I don't mind." I stopped and thought a second. "In fact, I'd appreciate it."

The pastor shook my hand and climbed into his car. I stood and watched him back out of the driveway. Jacki came to the front door.

"Who was that?" she asked.

"A minister." I replied absently as I turned and walked back to the house. "No big deal."

But it nagged at me. Why had Herb remembered me? Why

84

had the pastor stopped by now? Why had I told him I wanted him to stop by again sometime?

I pushed the thoughts away. I'd made my choice to go it without the church, and I didn't need it now. I wondered if I ever would.

Chapter 13

I Need Help

"I don't need you! I don't need nobody!"

Clothes flew across the yard as I threw all of Jacki's belongings out the front door. Shoes, clothes, makeup scattered across our lawn and half of the neighbor's, but I barely noticed.

"I can't live like this anymore!" I screamed at the walls of the house.

The phone started ringing, and I glared at it. "Go away," I growled, taking another drink. I threw the empty bottle into the pile on the floor of the kitchen. It gave me a grim sense of satisfaction to know I'd drunk all the liquor in those bottles in a twenty-four-hour period.

The phone started ringing again. "Go away!" I screamed.

I knew it would be my boss, wondering why I hadn't shown up for work.

The phone kept ringing. With a muttered curse I ripped the phone out of the wall, wires and all, then threw it across the room.

I looked down at my prosthesis, took it off, and threw it against the wall too. "Worthless piece of junk," I muttered, picking up the last full bottle of whiskey.

I opened it and took a long swallow, "Cheers!"

Hearing the front door slam, I stiffened.

"Eddie, where are you?" Jacki's angry voice called. "What's going on around here?"

She walked into the kitchen, and her lips curled with disgust as she took in the mess, the destroyed phone, and my completely drunk state.

"I got a call from your boss while I was at work." Jacki tapped her foot angrily. "He wanted to know where you were. And what did I tell him? What could I tell him?"

"Tell him what you want," I snarled, taking another drink. "Do you think I care?"

"Oh, I know you don't care," Jacki screamed, losing control. "That's why you steal from our friends to buy your drugs and alcohol! That's why you're destroying our house!"

"If you don't like it, leave," I yelled back. "Things aren't working in this marriage anyway."

Jacki's eyes narrowed dangerously. "How dare you do this to me," she hissed. "You lying, cheating—"

I whirled around and wrenched the kitchen sink out of the wall. Jacki screamed and cowered against the table. I didn't care. I just needed to get out of there.

I hopped through the house and slammed the front door behind me. As I headed to the car, I knew I didn't care if I ever saw Jacki or the house again. Fifteen feet from the house I stopped. Without knowing why, I turned and slowly made my way back into the house.

In the bedroom I could hear Jacki crying and muttering angrily. Afraid to face her, I went into the bathroom and sat on the edge of the tub, my head in my hands.

"Well, I guess this is it." Jacki's voice broke into my thoughts.

I looked up and saw Jacki standing in the doorway, tears streaming down her face.

"It's over, isn't it?" she half-asked, half-stated.

It felt like all the breath went out of me. "I guess you're right."

Jacki turned and wiped her tears away. "I'll get my stuff and get out of here." She started to walk away.

"Jacki, wait," I called weakly.

She stopped and turned toward me again.

"You can go, but before you go you'd better do me one favor."

She nodded. "What's that?"

"You'd better get me some help." I stopped, my voice choking. "If you don't, I'm going to die." The last few words came out in a whisper.

The color drained from her face. "I'll call someone. Wait here."

She left and I sat, my head in my hands again, trying to stop the room from spinning. I could feel the nausea resulting from the amount of alcohol I'd consumed.

"Just keep it together, Eddie," I gritted to myself.

The room went black for a few seconds then normal. I leaned against the shower wall for support. The nausea seemed worse.

"Eddie, I called a hospital, and they said they'll take you in now."

Jacki's face swam before me, and I took great gulps of air, trying to remain conscious.

"You'd better go. I'm not feeling too well," I mumbled as my stomach lurched again.

Jacki shook her head. "You have to go in." She tried to help me up. "Come on. You can do it."

"I think I'm going to be sick," I moaned as Jacki half-carried, half-dragged me to the car.

She ignored me and buckled the seat belt for me. She backed out of the driveway in a great cloud of dust. The motion of the car and the scenery speeding by made me dizzier. I closed my eyes and leaned against the door.

"Just hang on, Eddie," Jacki commanded. "The hospital's only thirty minutes away. Just hang on."

Her voice seemed to be coming through rolling fog. I strained to concentrate on her words, but missed most of them. Finally, she faded altogether.

"Eddie! Eddie!"

I could hear Jacki's frantic voice, but couldn't open my eyes.

"Eddie! Eddie!"

This time I could feel her shaking me. I tried to answer, but my lips wouldn't move. The seat belt disappeared from around me, and I felt myself being hauled out of the car.

"Eddie, if you don't get up and walk in there on your own, they won't take you." Jacki's voice held a note of panic that I tried to respond to.

I forced my eyes open. A huge building swayed in front of me, and I collapsed against the seat again. Jacki shook me.

"Eddie, come on!"

I opened my eyes and tried to get up. Jacki caught me before I fell back into the car.

"Now, we're going to walk into that hospital," she instructed, her voice strained as she tried to support most of my weight. "Ready now? Walk!"

I took a step, and immediately everything started to go black. I struggled against it. Another step. I could feel myself being dragged through a set of automatic doors.

"You're almost there," Jacki grunted.

A desk loomed ahead. People in white seemed to be rushing all around me. I could feel myself falling, falling.

"You'd better do the paperwork," I mumbled to Jacki before everything went black.

The pain started as the swirling fog receded. Each time I woke up crying in pain, I felt a needle being stuck into my arm, and the fog took over again.

"Eddie. Eddie."

I opened my eyes slowly. A nurse stood holding a glass of water and some pills. I tried to sit up, but my head felt like it would explode. I closed my eyes again, pain shooting through my entire body.

"Here, let me help you."

Her words sounded so loud, so piercing. I flinched at each syllable. She put the pills into my mouth, then held the glass so I could swallow. I gulped down the medicine obediently.

"There. It's only a little Valium to help you feel better," she assured me. "Get some rest."

I nodded, then wished I hadn't. Each movement brought piercing pain. Gradually the drugs started to take effect, and I felt myself relaxing, relaxing, and slipping off to sleep.

When I woke up again, my headache had almost left. My stump throbbed, however, and the bed looked like it had been attacked with an eggbeater. I looked around me. White walls. A window. On the bedside table, my Bible. My Bible? How had it gotten here? A nurse came in.

"Good morning! Feeling better today?"

"Yeah," I answered automatically. I looked again at the Bible. "Did my wife bring this by?" I asked, pointing at it.

"Yes. She brought it in right after we'd admitted you. She said she thought you'd want it."

"Can I see her?"

"No. Not until you get farther along in the program."

"How long have I been here?" I asked.

"Three days." She changed the sheets on my bed while she talked. "You've been pretty sick."

She finished changing the bed and turned to leave.

"Is there anything else I can get you?" she asked.

My leg still throbbed, and I remembered the wonderful floating effects of the Valium. "Yeah. My leg really hurts. Maybe I should take some more Valium."

She frowned. "I'll have to ask the doctor about that."

"Great."

She turned and left the room. I rolled over on my side.

"What the heck am I doing here?" I wondered. "I just had a bad weekend. I don't need to be in the hospital!"

I tried to remember how I got to the treatment center but could recall very little. That's OK, I argued. Lots of people have blackouts. It doesn't mean anything.

"I've got to get out of here," I muttered to myself, wondering where they'd put my clothes.

MAKING THE TEAM

A nurse walked past the door, and I called to get her attention.

"Excuse me!"

She stopped. "Yes?"

"I'm feeling a lot better, and I think I'm ready to go home now. Who do I need to talk to?" I sat up to prove how healthy I was.

"Wait a minute, I'll get the doctor."

The doctor walked in a few minutes later.

"So I hear you're feeling well enough to go home." He looked soberly at me. Pulling a chair close to the bed, he sat down. "Of course you're free to leave, but I think you'd better be aware of the consequences."

I sighed. I didn't need to be here. They had the wrong guy. Places like this were for people who really had problems. I partied only on the weekends.

The doctor continued, "Your insurance company will not pay for the three days you've been here unless you complete the program."

I groaned. I knew I couldn't begin to pay the bill myself. "How long does the program last?" I asked.

"Twenty-eight days." He paused a second. "What do you think?"

"I'll stay, I guess," I reluctantly agreed.

The doctor looked at my chart. "Now, your nurse told me you requested Valium for your leg."

"Yeah. It's really been hurting." I held the stump for emphasis.

He looked straight at me. "I'll tell you, Ed. If you want the Valium, you stay in this room. If you don't want the Valium, you can come out here and have a different room. We want you to do that so you can start meeting people and going to some programs. But if you're going to eat Valium, you're going to stay here."

I thought about it. No contest. "I'll take the Valium."

He handed me two pills. I gulped them down with water

from the glass on the night stand. He stood up to go.

"Let me know if you change your mind."

"OK." I lay back against the pillows and closed my eyes, waiting for the pills to take effect.

Within fifteen minutes, I felt my muscles relax.

"What am I going to do for twenty-five more days?" I wondered drowsily to myself.

Outside the door to my room, I could hear people walking around and talking. Bored, I strained to catch their words, but they eluded me. I looked at the Bible on the night stand. No, definitely not. I counted ceiling tiles. I watched the slant of sunlight change as the day progressed. Outside in the hall, everyone talked and sounded busy. I itched to join their conversations.

"I'm not going to be able to take almost a month of this."

The sound of my own voice in the room sounded hollow and lonely. I massaged my stump. Maybe I didn't really need the Valium.

The doctor returned a few hours later. I was sitting up waiting for him.

"So, are you ready to join everyone else, or do you want more Valium?" he asked.

"I think my leg's feeling better. I don't need any more Valium."

"Great!" He grinned. "We'll move you in with a roommate tomorrow."

I relaxed. I didn't have to spend the next twenty-five days by myself. The doctor checked my blood pressure, then left. I lay on my side, wondering what Jacki was doing. Would she leave me before I got out? I wished I could see her. I looked at the Bible and hoped it meant she still cared and would still be there when I finished the program.

I considered demanding to leave and finding some way to pay for the time I'd been in, but something stopped me. Somehow I knew the drugs and alcohol had to stop. I'd always promised I'd quit getting high when I turned thirty. Now, with my thirtieth birthday only a month away, I knew I needed to stay.

I watched the sun disappear and the window darken. I wondered what the other people in the program would be like. Would they all be strung-out druggies? Again I felt a sense of not belonging in the program.

"It's only twenty-five more days," I told myself. "You can stand anything for twenty-five days."

Chapter 14

A New Kind of God

The counselor came to visit right after I'd been moved into my new room.

"Good morning!" she said briskly, pulling a chair closer to the bed. "I'm Doctor Sylvia Gorton. I'll be your personal counselor for your stay."

"Hi. Eddie Folger."

She shook my hand, then uncapped her pen.

"First thing I want to do is get an idea of what substances you abused and how often."

"Oh, I don't have a problem with that. I just got a little too much this last weekend," I assured her.

She looked straight at me. "I don't believe you."

I gulped. "Well, maybe I did do more drinking than I should have . . ."

"And what else?" she asked bluntly.

I felt myself beginning to sweat. She wasn't going to let go. "Nothing much," I lied.

"You're lying," she told me.

I felt myself starting to get angry. Who did she think she was?

"Look, Eddie, I'm here to help you. I can't help you until you're honest with me. Are you willing to try?"

I looked at her. Her mouth was tough, but her eyes looked kind. I relented.

"OK. I drink every day."

"How much do you drink?"

"A couple six-packs of beer and a couple shots of whiskey," I admitted.

"Any other drugs?" she asked.

"Oh, nothing much." I didn't think the cocaine counted. After all, I could give that up any time I wanted.

"You're lying, Eddie."

What, again? Could she read my mind?

"OK, I did cocaine sometimes."

"How much?"

The questions kept coming at me. I tried to minimize the answers, but she dragged the truth out of me anyway. Finally she seemed to run out of questions. After promising to return the next day, she left the room.

The next morning, a nurse came through my room and woke my roommate and me early.

"Get up! Time for breakfast!"

I groaned. It felt too early to even think about getting out of bed.

"Come on. Up!" She shook the bottom of my bed. "And make the bed after you get up."

Make the bed? I hadn't made my bed in years. The nurse left the room, and I looked at my roommate, who sat yawning on the edge of the bed.

"It's like camp," I joked. "Next thing we know we'll be forced to jog three miles and clean the latrine!"

He grinned and yawned again. "You want the shower first?"

"No, go ahead," I offered.

After showering, we went to a big dining room where all the twenty-eight-day patients ate breakfast together. After I found a seat at one of the tables, an attendant placed a tray of food in front of me. I looked at the unappetizing bowl of oatmeal and pushed the tray back.

"Maybe I'll just have coffee," I told the attendant.

He pushed the tray back in front of me. "Part of the program is that you eat every meal."

"You're going to force me to eat?" I asked, incredulous.

He smiled sympathetically. " 'Fraid so. That's part of the program."

I sighed and picked up my spoon. A distinguished-looking man sitting next to me gave me a small smile.

"Your first day, huh?"

"Yeah. It's like boot camp."

"Worse," he promised.

I studied the cereal, looked at everyone else eating obediently, then slowly started eating.

"You can stand anything for twenty-eight days," I told myself again.

After breakfast we had group meetings. I found myself in a group of very professional men. No bums here, I thought as I listened to them talk about their addictions.

After group counseling, I had personal counseling with my counselor. She started where we'd left off the day before and refused, once again, to let me lie to her. I also found, after years of being able to use my leg as an excuse for my drinking, that she didn't care. The fact that I had only one leg wasn't the issue—my substance abuse was.

After personal counseling and lunch, we had a little free time; then I filled out forms and questionnaires. More group counseling, dinner, then an Alcoholics Anonymous meeting.

I'd never been to an AA meeting before. I sat in the back, where I could listen without being noticed. One of the more distinguished members of our group got up to speak.

"Hi, I'm John, and I'm an alcoholic."

I started slightly. Did everyone really have to say that? I couldn't see myself admitting that. John went on talking, telling about his experience with alcohol and how he decided he needed help.

"I have to take everything one day at a time now," he continued.

97

One day at a time. Up on the wall I saw a chart with twelve steps outlined for recovering alcoholics. Admitting that I was powerless topped the list. Another person stood up as John sat down.

"Hi. I'm Steve, and I'm an alcoholic."

Great, I thought. Are they going around the room? Could I actually admit in front of a room full of people that I had a problem?

"What got me through was a belief in a higher power. A belief in a God."

Several heads nodded in agreement to Steve's last words.

"You have to believe in a higher power," another man agreed.

A higher power. All my life I'd been raised to believe in God. I knew who they were talking about.

"A higher power who is concerned about you, personally. A higher power who offers love and understanding."

Ah-ha, I thought. I'd always hoped God could be like that, but I had been taught only the dos and don'ts while growing up. The people talking described something much better than the picture I'd been raised with. Could God be that accepting and forgiving?

That night in my room, I picked up the Bible and looked at it. Opening it slowly, I turned to one of the texts I remembered from childhood. I read it slowly, then closed the Bible again. Unsure of how to pray, I closed my eyes and just started mentally talking to God.

"God, I don't know what to say or even who You are anymore. Help me to understand and get through this program." I stopped, unsure of what else to say. "Amen."

As I tried to sleep, I tried to remember when I'd last read the Bible and prayed. Ten years ago? Twelve? It seemed like forever.

The next morning, the nurse let me call my father and wish him happy birthday. I didn't know what to tell him. I hadn't called for years, and now I had to call him from a drug-rehabilitation center.

"Hi, Dad, happy birthday!" I said as soon as he got on the phone.

"Eddie! So good to hear your voice! Thanks for calling." He sounded so glad to hear from me that I wondered if Jacki had told them where I was.

"Dad, have you talked to Jacki lately?" I asked, my heart beating faster.

A pause. "Yes, Eddie. She called as soon as you went into the program." Another pause. "And I want to tell you how proud your mother and I are that you are facing your problem and getting help."

I let out a breath I'd been holding. Tears pushed against my eyelids as I heard the love in my father's voice.

"Thanks, Dad," I whispered hoarsely.

"I don't know if Jacki told you, but your mother and I are going to come out to visit when you get out of the program."

"Dad! That's wonderful!" I couldn't imagine my parents in Las Vegas with all the gambling and partying.

"How's everyone at home?" I asked.

"Great," he replied.

We talked for a few more minutes, then rang off. As I replaced the receiver, I thought of my parents coming out for a visit and shook my head. I had never thought they'd come to Las Vegas. And I never realized how much they truly loved and accepted me.

The daily sessions with my counselor became more and more painful. She asked deeper and deeper questions until finally, sobbing, I told her about the real pain behind losing my leg and my dream of playing baseball.

"I have nothing else," I cried. "It's everything I ever wanted . . ."

"And you've been using drugs and alcohol to mask this pain, haven't you, Eddie?" she asked kindly.

I nodded, unable to speak. She let me cry for a minute.

"It's not fair!" I cried brokenly. "It's not fair," I repeated more quietly.

She took my hand compassionately and looked straight at me. "It's done, Eddie. It happened. Now, how are you going to deal with it?"

I sat silently, angry with her for not letting me wallow in my pain, angry with myself for being so emotional. She got up to leave.

"I'm going to let you think about that for a while," she told me.

For the next few days I thought about it constantly. I watched the professional men around me. They lived full lives without baseball. I thought of Jacki. I loved her too much to let her live with my disappointment forever. And slowly, the ache I'd been carrying with me since the accident began to subside.

The AA meetings began to mean more to me. Jacki started attending them with me, and just having her there gave me the strength to stand up and admit my own addiction.

"Hi. I'm Eddie, and I'm an alcoholic."

I looked around the room each time I said that, waiting to see judgment or disgust on people's faces. Instead, everyone applauded me for being strong enough to admit my problems.

The first two weeks went by quickly, and I felt ready to leave the program. Once again I tried to get out early but was told I had to stay the full twenty-eight days or insurance wouldn't pay. It made me restless and edgy to be cooped up in a hospital, when I felt strong and sure I wouldn't go back to alcohol.

The tentative first prayer grew into a daily habit. I found myself having regular morning devotionals out of the "One Day at a Time" booklet. Each time I read a new picture of God or heard one presented in AA meetings, I rushed back to the Bible to study it for myself. The God of my childhood clashed with the God I was now meeting through my study and through other people's testimonies. The two opposing pictures greatly confused me.

"God," I prayed. "I know how I've been raised to see You, but I like the new picture I'm getting of You so much better."

The more I studied and listened, the more convinced I became that God wasn't the tyrant I'd always thought He was. Instead, He offered compassion, forgiveness, and love. The new picture overwhelmed me.

On my last day in the program, I stood up to speak at the AA meeting. I'd been sharing for a few weeks, but this time felt different.

"Hi. I'm Eddie, and I'm an alcoholic," I began. "This program and AA has not only helped me deal with my addiction to alcohol and drugs, but has also taught me about a new kind of God."

In the back, I saw Jacki stiffen slightly. I continued anyway.

"I always believed God sat up in heaven, judging everyone harshly. Through AA I've met a new God, one who loves and accepts me as I am—faults and all."

I could feel my eyes getting moist, but I didn't stop.

"When I lost my leg and my dream, I thought I'd never have anything to live for again. Now, with a God I can love and my wonderful wife Jacki, I have something to keep me going."

Everyone applauded as I sat down. I wiped the tears from my face, then grabbed Jacki's hand tightly.

"Just give me a second chance," I pleaded. "I know I've messed up pretty bad, but I love you, and I think I'm finally getting my life together again."

She leaned over, hugged me, and kissed me gently. "Eddie, I'm here for you, no matter what," she promised. "I believe in you and I'll stand by you." She stopped a minute, her eyes confused. "But this God stuff, Eddie—I don't know . . ."

I grinned. "Not the Eddie you know, huh?"

"It makes me nervous," she admitted. "All the people I know who go around spouting stuff about God are Jesus freaks or fanatics. I don't think I can take that."

"Don't worry. I won't be handing out literature in the casinos," I promised.

She relaxed a little, but still eyed me warily. The meeting ended, and I had to say good night.

"I'll be here early tomorrow to pick you up," she promised.

"The earlier the better. I can't wait to see the outside of this hospital!"

She kissed me good night, and I walked back up to my room. As I prepared for bed, I tried to imagine what it would be like on the outside. I thought of all the drinking and drugs that went along with my casino job, and I began to feel nervous. Sure, I could be sober for twenty-eight days in a controlled program, but could I actually do it around my buddies? Could I really never take another drink?

"God, give me the strength to stay off drugs and alcohol," I prayed. "And help me to keep my friendship with You alive."

Chapter 15

The Visit

My parents arrived a couple of days after I got out of the program. As Jacki and I drove to the airport to pick them up, I tried to imagine what they'd think of Las Vegas.

"They'll see the place as Sodom and Gomorrah," I thought as we arrived at the airport.

I strained to see my parents as the passengers filed off the plane. I never realized how much I missed them until I heard they were coming out to visit. Finally, I saw them coming off the runway.

"Mom! Dad!"

I walked toward them and hugged them both. Jacki followed.

"How was your flight?"

"How is everyone at home?"

"Are you hungry?"

The questions flew fast as everyone tried to ask and answer them at the same time. We collected luggage, piled everyone in the car, and drove back to the house. The questions didn't stop. I kept looking at my parents as we drove, unable to believe they were actually in Las Vegas. The glittery façades on the casinos somehow didn't mix with the stable, steady image my parents possessed.

That night my parents went to my AA meeting with me. As we walked into the room, I knew this would be one of the hardest meetings ever. I didn't just have to admit to being an alcoholic in front of a group of strangers. Now I had to admit it in front of the two people who raised me not to drink and who I'd hurt with my drinking.

The meeting began, and I could feel myself getting nervous. As it got closer to my turn, I smiled at Mom. She and Dad sat quietly watching everything, their facial expressions not giving away their thoughts.

My turn came and I stood up. Clearing my throat, I looked straight at my parents as I spoke.

"Hi. I'm Eddie, and I'm an alcoholic." As I said the words, I could feel my tears starting and could see tears in my parents' eyes.

"Tonight, my parents are here to support me," I said brokenly, "and it means everything to me. I never thought they'd come to Las Vegas. And I never realized how much they cared."

The rest of the group applauded. I continued talking as the applause died.

"You know, my parents raised me in a Christian home. And even though I strayed from their teaching, I never forgot it. And it's their prayers that got me to where I am tonight. In AA I've learned about God again, and I know I need Him to help me beat this addiction. I want to thank my parents for raising me to believe in God and never giving up praying for me, even when it seemed like I didn't care."

I sat back down, tears flowing freely. Mom reached over and squeezed my hand. I felt humbled when I thought of how much my parents cared for me and supported me. I didn't deserve the love they offered so freely.

For the next few days, Jacki and I took my parents sightseeing as well as attending all the AA meetings I needed to. Having them in Las Vegas kept me steady in my decision not to drink anymore. Knowing they were in my house kept me from going to the clubs I used to hang out in and drinking with my buddies. Each time I looked at them, I wanted to tell them how much their visit meant, but I didn't have the words. I tried to show them by keeping my language clean and staying away from the nightclubs.

The weekend arrived, and my parents wanted to go to church. They offered to go by themselves, but I really wanted to go with them.

"Are you sure?" they asked, not wanting to pressure me.

"Yes," I told them.

After getting to know a God I liked through AA, I looked forward to going to church again. I wanted to find a group of people who wanted to learn more about this God as much as I did.

"Are you going to go?" I asked Jacki.

She sighed. "I suppose it can't kill me." She sat silent a minute. "You know, if I wanted to go to church, I'd go to mass. It's at least what I was raised with."

I grinned. "I don't think you'll get my good Protestant parents to mass!"

She laughed. "No more than I'd get my good Catholic parents inside a Protestant church, I suppose."

As we drove to church the next morning, I felt nervous. What would it be like to be back in church? I hoped the pastor would talk about the same type of God I'd learned to love through AA.

The service started shortly after we arrived. I followed it easily. All the years of church while growing up made me familiar with the order of service and the hymns. Finally, after announcements and congregational singing, the pastor stood up to speak.

"We have a burden in our church," he began. "The Lord's word needs to be furthered, and we need the financial support of each of you to do it."

I felt my heart drop. Another sermon on money. Didn't pastors ever talk about the love of God anymore? Why did they always get up and plead money out of their congregations?

"Bring ye all the tithes into the storehouse. . . ."

105

MAKING THE TEAM

The pastor's voice grew grave with concern. All around me I watched his words have the desired guilt-inducing effect on the congregation.

"What ever made me think church would be any different from what I remembered?" I thought inwardly as the pastor droned on.

I got angrier and angrier as the sermon progressed. By the time he finished and we walked out to the car, I had decided never to go back into a church.

Everyone was silent for the first few minutes of the trip home. Finally, Jacki and my mom began talking about what to fix for lunch. I sat and silently seethed. When we got home, Jacki and Mom went into the kitchen, and Dad sat down beside me in the living room.

"Want to talk about it?" he asked.

I gave a bitter laugh. "What's to talk about? Things sure haven't changed, have they? I stay away from church for ten years, and I still hear the same sermon when I come back. Money, money, money. That's all the church leaders are worried about."

Dad sat and listened to me talk. I knew he didn't agree with me, but he let me speak without interrupting. Finally, I ran out of anger and words.

"Eddie, I think the devil's using your feeling on this to keep you away from the church," he finally said. "When God's ready to lead you back to church, He'll lead you; and the devil won't be able to block it."

I thought again about the sermon and shrugged. "If they stop asking me for money, maybe I'll consider it!"

Dad looked as if he wanted to say something, then changed his mind. Sniffing the air, he smiled broadly. "Something smells wonderful. I wonder what's for lunch?"

"Whatever it is, it will be a whole lot better than the hospital food I've been forced to eat for the last month!"

Jacki poked her head around the corner. "Dinner's almost ready. Eddie, will you set the table, please?"

106

THE VISIT

I got up and put the dishes on the table. Five minutes later, Mom announced that dinner was ready, and we sat down together. We all grabbed hands, traditionally, for prayer. I smiled, thinking how warm, how right it felt to be sitting with my family, thanking God for the food.

Dad began praying, and I remembered all the years I'd sat in the family circle praying. I knew this was what I wanted for my family. I could still have God without a church, couldn't I? I didn't have to be in a church to pray.

Dad finished the prayer, and we all let go of hands. The conversation soon turned to Lancaster and all the people we knew there.

"Boy, I sure miss it," Jacki commented as she passed a bowl of potatoes to me. "Remember what it's like at Christmastime with all the snow?"

I pictured it instantly. Lots of white snow, soft lights, Christmas carols. It seemed so real compared to the artificial world of Las Vegas.

"Well, you're welcome back there anytime you want to return," Mom hinted. "I'm sure your parents would love to see you more often," she said to Jacki.

I thought about going back to work at the casino, pitching cards. It didn't hold the appeal it had before. Somehow I couldn't see myself enjoying it without drinking.

We finished the meal, then went for a drive in the desert. That night, as Jacki and I lay in bed, I brought up the subject of Lancaster again.

"Do you really want to go back?" I asked.

"I'd love to. I miss my family so much." She rolled over and looked at me, her blue eyes serious. "And if we ever want a family, I don't want to raise children in Las Vegas."

I thought about that a minute. "You're right. There's nothing for us here and everything in Lancaster. Let's put the house on the market as soon as Mom and Dad leave."

The last few days of Mom and Dad's visit, I dreaded having them leave. I felt afraid to go back to the clubs and casinos that had been my life until now. What if I slid back? What if I started drinking and couldn't control it this time?

We drove Mom and Dad to the airport in silence. It seemed like it would be forever until we saw them again. After checking the luggage, we walked them to the gate. Mom hugged me as their flight was announced.

"We're praying for you," she told me.

She turned and hugged Jacki. "We're praying for you too."

Dad shook my hand. "Keep that relationship with God."

"I will," I promised. I knew I wouldn't stay sober without it.

They disappeared into the plane, and I turned to Jacki, suddenly feeling very alone. She had tears in her eyes.

"I want to go home," she whispered.

"Soon," I promised. "Soon."

Chapter 16

Going Home?

As soon as I was sober, I hated Las Vegas. We put the house up for sale immediately and began planning our move back East. I still regularly attended AA meetings. Everything I saw at work and on billboards seemed to tell me to drink. I couldn't avoid the advertising.

After ninety meetings in ninety days, I got the courage to go back to the club. Santa Fe, the band Jacki and I had been friends with, were playing, and I wanted to see them. I arrived, took a seat, and didn't order a drink. People kept stopping by to talk.

"Hey, Eddie, haven't seen you for a while. Been hiding out?"

"Yeah, I guess so," I joked back.

"Here, let me buy you a drink," a friend offered.

"No thanks, man. I'm clean and sober now. No more partying for this guy." It felt so good to finally say that.

"Really? No kidding! That's cool. You want a soda?"

"That'd be great," I agreed.

The band finished their set and joined the table of friends. When I told them I had gone through rehab, they seemed surprised. I felt a twinge of guilt—Jacki and I had introduced them to cocaine. Would they be able to stop using it as we had?

The rest of the evening passed quickly as we sat around joking and laughing. As I drove home that night, I laughed as I realized they liked me fine without the partying. If only I'd realized that before, I thought as I pulled up to the house.

The weeks dragged by. Real estate agents showed our house, but no one wanted to buy it. Mountains of bills from our partying days were due, and we struggled to pay them back. I still pitched cards, but no longer enjoyed it. Every billboard, hotel façade, and advertisement seemed to scream the artificialness of Las Vegas. We missed our families; we missed the solid New England values we'd been raised with.

I still attended AA meetings. Some of my friends from the group Santa Fe saw the changes in my life and began attending the meetings with me. It eased some, but not all, of my guilt for having introduced them to cocaine.

Nearly a year passed. We painfully paid off our bills and decided to start a family. Jacki became pregnant immediately after going off the pill. I felt scared but excited about becoming a father.

Five months went by. The Christmas season arrived, and Jacki and I decorated a small tree in our living room. We wanted to be home in Lancaster for the holidays, but with the house not selling, we had to stay in Las Vegas.

Two days before Christmas, Jacki called me at work.

"Eddie, I think you'd better get home and take me to the doctor." I could hear the fear in her voice. "Something's not right with the baby. I've called the doctor, and he said I'd be fine, but . . ."

"I'll be right there," I promised, then hung up the phone and rushed home.

I bundled Jacki into the car and drove to the doctor's office as fast as I dared. Questions jumbled around each other in my brain. Would she lose the baby? Was it because we had used drugs for so long?

I brought Jacki into the office and made sure she was comfortable in a chair.

"I need to see the doctor right away," I told the receptionist.

She smiled calmly at me. "I'm sorry, but he's next door at the hospital doing a delivery. Please take a seat."

We waited. Jacki grew paler, and I grew more nervous. The hands on the clock seemed frozen. Jacki moaned slightly.

"I'm going to see how much longer," she said, getting out of the chair.

I looked at the chair she'd been sitting in and saw blood. Grabbing Jacki, I rushed her up to the nurse.

"My wife is going to lie down. Now!"

She took one look at my face and led us to an examination table. Jacki stretched out, her eyes terrified. I paced, watching the clock and praying.

"I know it's because of the drugs," Jacki whispered, echoing my fears. "God's punishing us because of the drugs."

"It'll be fine," I tried to reassure her. I knew she didn't believe the words any more than I did.

"Oh, God, please don't let anything be wrong with Jacki. Please let the baby live."

After what seemed like hours, the doctor arrived. He checked Jacki quickly, shook his head, and turned to us.

"I'm sorry. It looks like you've had a spontaneous miscarriage."

I heard the words, but they didn't register. Jackie had been all right just this morning. How could it happen? The doctor's voice broke into my thoughts.

". . . I don't think we should move you. And I'd like you to stay in the hospital for a few days to recuperate."

I looked at Jacki, lying there crying, and felt helpless. The doctor left us alone for a few minutes.

"Oh, Eddie, I'm sorry. I'm sorry," she cried.

I ran to the bed and tried to hold her. "It's not your fault," I soothed, trying to be strong.

She continued to sob. I just held her, a huge knot in my throat. I remembered all the years I'd abused alcohol and drugs. Could this be the way God was repaying us for those times?

Jacki's voice broke into my thoughts. "Eddie, I can't stay here over Christmas. You have to talk to the doctor. I'm too depressed to be here by myself over the holidays."

"I'll talk to him," I promised, kissing her gently. "I'll try my best. Just relax, OK?"

She nodded, too tired to argue. I went looking for the doctor. The nurse found him for me.

"Is there any way Jacki can come home for Christmas?" I asked. "She's too depressed to spend Christmas in a hospital."

"Only if you promise to keep her lying down. No running around, OK?"

I drew a deep breath before asking the next question. "Doc, will she be able to have any more?"

He gave me a compassionate look. "Yes. After she recovers, she shouldn't have any trouble carrying another baby."

I felt a rush of relief. "That will mean a lot to her."

I brought Jacki home from the hospital. I'd tried to make the house extra cheerful with more Christmas decorations and home-cooked food, but Jacki barely noticed. Depressed, she curled up on the couch and just stared at the tree, not speaking and barely eating.

I tried my best to get her to talk.

"Maybe it's for the best. Maybe there was something wrong with that baby," I said, watching the Christmas lights reflect off the walls.

She didn't answer for a few minutes. "You know, I was starting to believe in this God you've been talking about. I think maybe He doesn't want me to have children because of all the drugs we did."

I struggled to keep back tears. "I don't know, hon. I just don't know."

I wanted to believe in a God who wouldn't punish for past sins, but I feared maybe He let Jacki lose the baby to pay us back for the drugs. I wanted to cry, scream, talk about it, but felt I needed to be strong for Jacki.

Christmas passed and then New Year's. I watched Jacki become more and more depressed, and I didn't know how to help. Sometimes I would come into a room and see her sitting there, crying. And when I tried to comfort her, she refused to be comforted.

At the end of January, two friends of ours, Nick and Toots Marovich, came to visit. An older couple, they were our parents away from home. Nick and I went golfing, leaving Jacki and Toots at the house.

After a round of golf, we came home to take Toots and Jacki to dinner. I noticed Jacki seemed a little happier but didn't have a chance to ask her what she and Toots had talked about. Dinner was the happiest we'd had in a long time. Afterward, back at the house, Toots and Nick left to return to their apartment, and Jacki and I prepared for bed.

"What did you and Toots do today?" I asked as I got in bed and turned off the light.

"Did you know that Toots lost eight babies before she had her first child?" Jacki asked quietly.

"No. You're kidding." I couldn't imagine going through what we'd gone through eight times.

"When I told her I thought God didn't want me to have children, she got mad at me. She looked at me and said, 'I don't want to hear another word about it. Your children will be wonderful.'" Jacki rolled over and looked at me. "Do you think she's right? She made me feel selfish and self-pitying!"

I felt tears in my eyes. God bless you, Toots, I thought. "I think we should try again," I replied.

She sighed. "I just hope it's the right thing."

I felt a stab of fear. "I do too."

Three months later, Jacki became pregnant again. We watched every stage of her pregnancy with apprehension. Would she lose this baby? Was there anything wrong with it?

By this time I hated dealing cards. We kept dropping the price of the house, but it still wouldn't sell. Ever since we'd come to Las Vegas, I'd dreamed of going home with a motor home and a pocketful of money. Now, as we dropped the price of the house lower and lower, I wondered if it would be possible.

113

I still prayed and read the Bible. And I really believed God didn't want us in Las Vegas.

"Please let the house sell," I prayed. "I know You don't want us here. Please let it sell and let us go back home."

Still nothing. The weeks dragged on as Jacki got closer and closer to her due date. Would we have to raise a child in this city? I wondered.

January 23, 1983. We watched the football playoffs on TV while Jackie paced around the house. After the second game, I noticed she looked a little worried.

"I think you'd better call the doctor and get me to the hospital," she told me. "I'm in labor."

I rushed around getting Jacki into the car, calling the doctor, and driving to the hospital. Jacki started timing her contractions, and I started getting nervous. When we arrived at the emergency entrance, the nurses wheeled Jacki straight to labor and delivery.

The delivery room had bright lights and medical people rushing around everywhere. Jacki looked terrified.

"You're going to be fine," I assured her.

"Easy for you to say," she snapped back. "O-H-H-H!"

I grabbed her hand through another contraction. The doctor pushed around and set up the delivery equipment.

"What if this baby's not OK?" Jacki said urgently. "What if there's something wrong with it?"

"There's nothing wrong with it," I assured her, smoothing her hair away from her forehead. "It's fine."

The doctor timed her contractions. "It'll be a little while."

"Did you see the game between Miami and New York?" I asked.

"Yeah, wasn't that a great play that David Woodley made at the end of the second quarter?"

Jacki glared at me.

"I can't believe they scored a touchdown!" I added enthusiastically.

"O-H-H-H-H-H!"

I gripped Jacki's hand through the contraction. When it passed, she glared at both the doctor and me.

"I'm the one having the baby. Could you please stop talking sports and pay attention to me!"

I hid a grin.

"I saw that," she snapped. "And don't think I'll forget you're the one who got me into this mess!"

The doctor grinned and turned away. I guessed he'd heard this exchange between hundreds of couples before us.

The contractions came closer together. I held Jacki's hand and felt helpless as each one ripped through her.

"I can see the head," the doctor announced.

I felt a thrill of excitement. This was really it. I was going to be a father.

More contractions. Jacki pushing. Finally, a small cry.

"It's a boy!" the doctor announced, holding up the tiny human bundle.

He placed our son directly in Jacki's arms. We both cried as we looked at the perfect little boy we'd created. Every toe was there. Every finger was complete.

"Jeffrey," Jacki said, crying. "I want to name him Jeffrey after my brother."

As I watched the tiny bundle eating his first meal, I felt overwhelmed with love and gratitude. I loved this little person with more emotion than I had thought possible. And I felt so much gratitude to God that He'd given us another chance.

After a few days, Jacki and Jeffrey came home from the hospital. With a baby to care for, we became desperate to leave Las Vegas. We dropped the price of the house again. And again. We offered creative financing. Still nothing.

The weeks went by. Then months. We prayed constantly. Every billboard seemed to feature half-naked women, booze, gambling—a world we didn't want Jeffrey growing up in. We wanted him to grow up with his grandparents in a small town with stable, family ideals.

MAKING THE TEAM

September 1983. A prospective buyer came to look at the house. And when he made an offer on the house, I accepted immediately. So what if there was no money down and we had to carry a second mortgage. At least we could get out of Las Vegas. I could see Lancaster in my mind as I signed the final papers. At last, we were going home. Planning to drive back as soon as I could quit my job, I packed Jacki and Jeffrey onto a plane and sent them back to Lancaster.

Chapter 17

One Step Backward

My last night in Vegas. With Jacki so far away, I was lonely. I tried to imagine what going back home would mean. I'd always wanted to go home rich. Now I had to drive home in an old car and join Jacki at her parents' house.

I drove slowly down the garishly lighted streets of Las Vegas. It seemed strange to know I'd be leaving it all and not coming back.

"Eddie, you can't leave without saying goodbye to some of your friends," I said as I drove past our favorite clubs.

I found a place to park, then walked into one of the best clubs on the strip. With the hope of leaving the next day, I felt almost jaunty.

Inside, the slot machines, card tables, and roulette wheels made a dizzying sight. The sounds of money being made and lost overwhelmed me. I felt my pocket. I'd just cashed my paycheck. Maybe I could make a little extra before I went back home.

I sat down at a card table and started gambling. At first I won a little; then I began to lose.

I tried harder. If I couldn't have that motor home, I could at least get the pocketful of cash. After dealing poker for so long, I'd seen people win thousands of dollars. I blocked out the memory of how many more had lost thousands.

"You're going back a failure," I thought as I watched

another set of cards being dealt and saw more of my money disappear.

A waitress came by, and I signaled to her.

"What can I get ya?" she asked, thick makeup covering a tired, drawn face.

"I'll take a beer," I told her. I didn't even think about AA and not going back to alcohol. All that mattered was getting rid of that awful feeling of failure.

The drink came. I swallowed it quickly, enjoying the feeling as the alcohol went down. I finished it and ordered another.

I looked at the cards in my hand. "Hit me," I commanded the dealer. He pushed two more cards toward me. Still no winning combination.

"I fold." I put the cards down and watched my chips disappear in the dealer's bank.

Across the table a man sweated profusely, putting more and more chips on the table. His wife sat beside him, pleading for him to stop gambling, but he ignored her, a frantic expression in his eyes.

"Poor fool," I thought, taking another drink.

Poor fool? Who is the fool here? I caught sight of myself in the mirrored wall and realized I looked just as bad as that man did.

I looked around me. Desperate, lonely people bartered away their money and self-worth for the hopes of getting rich. Slot machines whirled as old ladies hypnotically put one coin after another into the slots. Drinks poured. Prostitutes solicited. I looked at the drink in my hand and fought the urge to throw the glass against the wall.

"What are you doing?" I screamed inwardly, feeling sick.

I got up abruptly from the table, hurried to the cashier to cash in my chips, and almost ran out of the club. As I drove back to the empty house, I felt tears streaming down my face.

"How could you be so stupid?" I screamed at myself. "Don't you care for your wife and that beautiful son God gave you?"

I went home, packed everything I could into the car, crammed the dog in the back, and left town.

When I stopped for gas, I pulled a picture of Jeffrey out of my pocket and taped it to the dashboard. Dressed in a tiny Red Sox uniform, he smiled trustingly at the camera. My guilt knew no boundaries. "If this little boy doesn't mean enough to you to provide for him what was provided for you, you've got a problem!" I yelled at myself.

I kept remembering the drink in my hand, the way it felt so easy going down, the way I hadn't even thought about it before ordering. I pounded on the steering wheel and screamed at myself. "You fool! How can you be so stupid!"

When fatigue finally overwhelmed me, I stopped to get some sleep. But first I phoned Jacki back in Lancaster.

"Hi, Jacki. I'm on my way home."

"That's fast. You packed in a hurry!" Her voice sounded so cheery and loving.

Tears pricked my eyes. I didn't deserve this woman. "Jacki, I slid back last night." The tears and words came out in a rush. "I went to the club to say goodbye, and before I knew it I was drinking. I gambled away most of my last paycheck. I just hope I have the cash to get back home. . . ." Crying, I was unable to continue.

For a minute she didn't speak. "It's OK, Eddie," she finally said. "What's important is that you stopped yourself before it went farther."

"But I took that drink," I yelled into the phone. "How could I do that to you? To Jeffrey?

"Eddie, it's OK. You'll be fine. Remember, one day at a time."

I took a deep breath. "I don't know how I'll forgive myself."

Jacki's voice grew gentle. "Well, you'd better 'cause we need you back here."

"Jacki, I love you," I whispered hoarsely.

"I love you too, Eddie. Hurry home."

I hung up the phone, feeling only a little better than I had before I called. After a few hours of sleep, I started driving again. Jeffrey's picture mocked me from the dashboard, and my guilt overwhelmed me. I called Jacki from my next stop. And the next.

"What kind of father are you?" I yelled at myself. "You get a perfect little son like Jeffrey, and this is how you act!"

I remembered the stable, wholesome home my father had provided for me. I always knew that's what I wanted to give my kids. How would my son respect me when he learned I fell so easily?

"You can't ever do this again," I told myself firmly.

The AA mottos and teaching slowly came back to me. I had to put this behind me and concentrate on today. I had to forgive myself and go on.

"How can I forgive myself?" I asked out loud.

I wondered if God would forgive me. I knew, intellectually, He would, but wondered how He could. I had made so many promises to Jeffrey, to Jacki, to myself, and to God. Now, with them all broken, I wondered how anyone could love and forgive me.

After four long days of driving and berating myself, I drove into Lancaster. As I drove through the familiar streets to Jacki's parents' house, I felt overwhelmed with shame. All my plans were gone. All my dreams dead. Instead of my motor home and unlimited cash, I had nothing, not even self-respect.

"Oh, God, please don't let me do that again," I prayed out loud as I stopped for a light. "Help me give Jeffrey a stable Christian home he can be proud of."

As I got closer to Jacki's parents' house, I wondered what Jacki would say when I got there. She had been supportive on the phone. Would she be furious once I stood in front of her? Seconds after I parked in front of the house, Jacki rushed out to me.

"Oh, I'm so glad to see you," I sighed as I hugged her.

"I missed you so much." She pulled me excitedly toward the house. "You should see my mom with Jeffrey. They get along great."

"Are you angry at me?" I asked, afraid of the answer.

She stopped and looked at me soberly. "No, Eddie, I'm not. And you've punished yourself far too much."

"I'm so sorry," I told her again.

"Eddie, I forgive you. You have to forgive yourself. If you don't, you'll drive yourself—and me—crazy." Her eyes lost their seriousness. "Now can we get out of the driveway and go into the house?"

I grinned, relief flooding me, "Sure. I want to see that son of ours!"

I let the dog out of the back, wrapped my arm around Jacki's waist, and walked into the house.

Chapter 18

Infection, Welfare, and Food Stamps

"What do you mean, I can't get a new leg until I get a job!" I screamed into the phone. "Don't you realize I can't get a job until I get a new leg?"

The patiently polite voice on the other end of the phone infuriated me even further. "I'm sorry, Mr. Folger. That's the policy of the rehabilitation center. If you would like to speak with a supervisor—"

"Never mind," I cut the voice off. "I'll call back later."

"Very well, Mr. Folger."

I slammed down the phone and hopped over to the window. I felt trapped in the little spare bedroom that had become our home in my in-laws' house. Jacki came in, a worried look on her face.

"How'd it go?" she asked casually.

"The usual runaround," I spat back. "Bureaucracies! I hate them! All I want to do is get a job. Can't they realize I can't do that without a leg?"

"How's your stump feeling today?" Jacki asked.

"Better, but I still can't wear the prosthesis." I glared at the useless leg propped against the wall.

"Jacki!" a voice called from another part of the house.

Jacki sighed. "That's Mom. I'd better go see what's going on."

I sat angrily on the bed. Since returning to Lancaster, I'd tried to help my dad on the farm while I looked for a full-time job. But now, with my stump infected and my prosthesis not fitting correctly, I found myself cooped up in Jacki's parents' house. The phone rang, and I picked it up automatically.

"Hello?"

"Hey, is this Eddie? This is Ron. How're you doing?"

"Great, just great," I lied.

"Man, you still looking for a job?"

"Still looking," I admitted reluctantly. "Enjoying the time off, though," I lied again.

"Yeah, well, we're going out tonight, and we wondered if you and Jacki wanted to go with us."

Remembering how little money Jacki and I had to spend made me angry. "No, I'm sorry. Her parents are keeping us under lock and key since we got back." Another lie.

"Well, OK, call me sometime." I could hear the disappointment in Ron's voice.

I hung up the phone, angry all over again. Ever since we'd returned to Massachusetts, we'd hidden in the house, ashamed to admit how broke we were. Other than going to church with my parents, we did nothing.

"God, I thought You wanted us back in Lancaster," I inwardly raged. "This isn't fair. It isn't right. I can't get a job 'cause I don't have a leg. I can't get a leg 'cause I don't have a job. We're putting Jacki's parents out and making life difficult for them. I can't support my family. Please, let something come through."

Nothing. Weeks dragged by. The tensions grew thicker in the house. Jacki's parents didn't like our taking Jeffrey to my parents' church. Jacki, who'd formerly been opposed to any religion, now couldn't seem to study the Bible enough. I grew more and more morose.

"I've got to have a drink," I thought daily, fighting it with everything I'd learned in AA.

I kept repeating the One Day at a Time motto to myself every time I felt tempted to go out with the guys and get drunk. The shame of my last night in Las Vegas stayed with me, and I knew I couldn't do the same thing to Jacki and Jeffrey again.

I called the rehabilitation center two or three times a week, trying to work things out. Every time I called, I got the same answer. I hoped they'd pay for me to finish my P.E. degree. They refused, saying I should get into computers. I hated the thought of computers. Another wall. Still no leg. The tension began to wear on both Jacki and me.

"Eddie, I can't take this anymore," Jacki cried to me. "I need a place of my own!"

I felt anger and guilt in equal proportions. "Well, don't you think I'm trying?"

She glared at me. "I wasn't accusing you. I was just saying that I've got to get out of this house!"

She paced around the room like a caged animal. "I can't take this anymore! I can't live like this anymore! Now Christmas is coming, and I want a place of our own."

"Jacki, I'm trying. Will you let it drop?" I heard the edge in my voice and didn't try to disguise it.

She paced faster. "I want a place of our own . . . I want a place of our own . . ."

I watched her with growing alarm. Then, in a flash, it all made sense.

"I'm taking you to the doctor for a pregnancy test," I blurted out.

She stopped pacing. "A *what*? You're crazy!"

I shrugged. "Well, the only other time you were so intense was when you were pregnant with Jeffrey."

She stopped pacing. "Maybe you're right. Oh, I hope you're not right."

We got an appointment as soon as we could. Jacki and I drove to the clinic together, and I waited while she had the test. Nervously we sat together, awaiting the results. The nurse came into the waiting room fifteen minutes later.

"Good news!" she announced. "You're expecting."

Jacki immediately burst into tears while I jumped up and down, delighted.

"How can we afford another baby?" Jacki cried, her head in her hands.

I hugged her. "God will work things out." I tried to make myself believe it too.

She looked at me like I was crazy, then, slowly, started to smile. I wiped the tears off her face and kissed her.

"It'll work out," I promised.

We decided that with another baby coming, we had to find a place to live. After looking for several weeks, we found a one-bedroom apartment we could afford to live in if we went on welfare. I fought tears as I signed the forms for welfare and food stamps. How could I have come so far from my dream of arriving home rich? I thought of my wealthy friends with important, well-paying jobs and felt bitterly envious.

Jacki tried to make the apartment feel like home, but with only a mattress on the floor for furniture, it was difficult. I felt terrible every time I watched her go out for groceries carrying food stamps to pay for them. I'd always paid my way, always worked for what I wanted. I redoubled my efforts to find a job.

I struggled to keep my relationship with God alive. "God, I don't understand why You're not helping us," I cried. "I'm trying and trying, but nothing's happening. I have to support my family. I have to have a job."

Still nothing. I began to feel desperate. Proud no longer, I called my friends for job leads. They responded immediately, offering leads and support when the leads didn't work out.

At first Jacki and I attended church regularly with my parents. I still wasn't enthusiastic about the church but figured it was a good family day. After a while, though, I began staying home and letting Jacki take Jeffrey to church.

"I'm embarrassed because I don't have a leg," I told Jacki.

Actually I just didn't want to go. It made me angry to sit in church, seething with old resentments.

I attended AA meetings regularly. Somehow my urge to

drink was harder to battle now than it had been when I first quit drinking. More than anything, I craved the escape alcohol offered.

My friends, who'd been faithfully supplying me with job leads, finally secured an interview for me with MCI-Lancaster, a minimum-security prison. By now, with Jacki seven months pregnant, I didn't care what sort of work I did, just so I had something. So what if I didn't know anything about prisons or working with prisoners? It was a job.

On the day of the interview, I hobbled into the superintendent's office on my crutches. I felt terrified.

The superintendent looked at the application I'd mailed in earlier, then at me.

"So you're Eddie Folger," he finally said.

I nodded. "Thank you for agreeing to see me."

He grinned. "Well, your friends gave me little choice. I've been getting calls all week from people all over town, telling me to hire you."

I shifted uncomfortably on my crutches. I needed this job. I needed to convince this man to hire me. "If I get this job, I won't be working it on one leg," I promised. "The rehabilitation center has promised a new prosthesis as soon as I get a job."

He looked at my application again. "Why do you want to work in a minimum-security prison?" he asked.

"I know I have no prison experience, but I'd really like to work here because I think I'd do a good job dealing with the prisoners." I paused. "I really need the job."

He looked again at me, then at the application. "When you get your leg, we'll give you the job."

I almost laughed with relief. "Thank you, sir. Thank you so much. I'll call you as soon as I get my leg!"

He smiled. "I'll look forward to it."

I hurried out of the office and drove straight to the rehabilitation center. On the way over I planned my speech.

"May I help you?" the receptionist asked.

"Yes, I'm Eddie Folger. I need to see the supervisor about getting a leg."

She looked at my crutches and my stump. "Just a minute, please."

I waited impatiently as she phoned him. Finally he came into the reception area.

"Eddie Folger?" he asked.

"Yes." I followed him back to his desk.

"You promised me a new leg as soon as I got a job. Well, I've got a job with MCI-Lancaster, and I need a leg."

He looked through my file. "Let's see here. According to policy, we need written proof that you have a job."

After months of waiting, I could no longer handle my frustration. "Look, here's the phone. Why don't you call over there and have someone bring a letter over?"

He pursed his lips. "Well, that's really not procedure . . ."

"I don't care if it is or isn't," I told him, my voice angry and low. "I'm not leaving this chair until you do."

He looked at me for a second, then picked up the phone. "Number?" he asked.

After a few seconds of conversation, he put down the phone. "They're bringing a letter right over. It looks like we can get you a new leg, Mr. Folger. We'll have you fitted next week." He looked at his watch. "Is there anything else?"

"No. Thank you."

As I drove out of the parking lot, I realized that for the first time in nearly a year, I felt a little hope.

Chapter 19

Uncle Bob's Bible

June 1984. After I started my new job, everything else seemed to fall into place. I had a place to work. I had a new prosthesis. I could now provide for Jacki, Jeffrey, and the new baby due in August.

Even though our financial crisis was over, Jacki continued to attend church. And when she started teaching the cradle roll class, I teased her about it. "If those good Protestant saints knew they had a Catholic teaching their kids Bible stories, it'd kill 'em!" I told her.

"Eddie, the stories of Jesus and His love are the same," she replied. "That's what counts."

I thought about that for a second. When had she started learning the stories? When did she start caring about church so much?

Her voice broke into my thoughts. "And if you're so concerned about the young people in our church, why don't *you* get involved?" she asked.

"I don't know. My work schedule's too unpredictable," I replied.

But I kept thinking about what Jackie had said. I remembered how I'd been sure God had a plan for me when we lived in Las Vegas. Should I get involved? But as I remembered how the church members had discouraged me from playing competitive sports, the old resentments returned. I knew I

129

couldn't get involved.

I watched Jacki become more and more interested in Christianity while I struggled with my doubts and resentments. Sure, I believed in God, but why did church have to come along with it? To her, everything seemed new. I looked at it through the years of hurts and resentments I harbored.

In July, Jackie, Jeffrey, my parents, and I went to visit my Uncle Bob and Aunt Winnie in Connecticut. Of all my relatives, Uncle Bob had been one of the most special. He'd given me my first ball and bat as a kid, and, of all my family, he was probably the happiest for me when I signed my contract and the saddest when I lost my leg.

Uncle Bob and Aunt Winnie opened their home and their arms to us as soon as we arrived. They immediately made Jacki feel comfortable, and she fit right into their family. That evening, we all sat in the living room, late into the night, talking about God and Christianity. Jacki kept asking questions, and Uncle Bob kept finding answers in the Bible.

"Do we have to talk about this all night?" I wondered inwardly as they searched for more answers. I tried to block out the conversation. After all, things were going fine now. God had helped me through the rough times, but now I was doing OK.

"What do you think, Eddie?" Uncle Bob asked, trying to draw me into the conversation. He'd been trying all evening, and I avoided all but the easiest answers.

I yawned. "I think I'm too tired. Maybe I'll go to bed now." I could see that my response disappointed him, but he tried not to show it.

For the rest of the weekend, I avoided all religious topics. Jacki's questions irritated me a little. Why did she have to be so interested?

The two days passed too quickly. As we got ready to leave, Uncle Bob handed me a Bible.

"Here, this is for you. Your aunt and I wanted you to have it."

"Thanks, Uncle Bob," I told him. I looked at the Bible, thinking of how many I already had at home.

He put his hand on my arm. "We'll be praying that all your questions will be answered." He looked at the Bible. "Eddie, don't take anyone else's word for your answers. Go to the Bible and find it for yourself."

I smiled. "I will, Uncle Bob, I promise."

He looked at the packed car. "Well, I guess you'd better get moving."

I gave him a hug, then Aunt Winnie. "We'll see you in August," I promised.

I climbed into the car and started driving home. As I drove and Jacki cuddled Jeffrey, I couldn't help but think about how Jacki's interest in Christianity was increasing while I continued to struggle with old resentments.

"I believe in God," I rationalized to myself. "Isn't that enough?"

I looked at Jacki in the seat beside me. Everything seemed so new to her—so full of promise. I felt a little envious. What if I didn't have the years of resentments to deal with? Would I be as excited about the church?

Jacki and Jeffrey were both sound asleep when we arrived home. I woke Jacki and carried Jeffrey into the house, then unpacked the car while she put him to bed. Finally, unpacked and dressed for bed, I sat down and looked at the Bible Uncle Bob had given me.

Uncle Bob's words came back to me: "Don't take anyone else's word for your answers. Go to the Bible and find it for yourself." I picked up the Bible and opened the cover. Uncle Bob's bold handwriting greeted me.

To Ed,

You're on the only true winning team. With the *only* true captain—Jesus. We love you as Jesus does.

Aunt Winnie and Uncle Bob

MAKING THE TEAM

I put the Bible down and thought about it. The only true winning team. For so long that's all I ever dreamed of—making the team. Somehow I'd never thought of Jesus as a team leader.

August 27, 1984. Jacki called me at work.

"Eddie! This is it. You'd better come get me."

I rushed home and took her to the hospital. Within a few hours, Jacki gave birth to Justin. As I looked at this perfect little boy, I felt overwhelmed with blessings. Only two short months before, I'd been unemployed, without my prosthesis, and on welfare. Now I had a job, a leg, and a second little boy.

The blessings increased. My mom and dad, Jacki's mom and dad, Jeffrey, and our friends all came to the hospital to help us celebrate. In a flash, I remembered the loneliness of Las Vegas and felt so close to my family and friends.

The weekend after we brought Justin home, Uncle Bob and Aunt Winnie came for a visit. I looked for a way to thank him for the Bible. Finally, I caught him alone the morning they left.

"Thanks for the Bible," I told him, leaning against the refrigerator as I spoke.

He looked up from his bowl of cereal. "I'll be praying for you as you study it," he replied seriously.

I squirmed slightly. "Thanks."

Aunt Winnie and Jacki appeared, and the conversation drifted on to other topics. Soon after breakfast they left for their home in Connecticut.

A week later, we got the phone call.

"Your Uncle Bob just died of a heart attack!"

We drove silently to Connecticut for the funeral. A thousand questions tumbled through my mind. Why had this happened? He'd seemed healthy just a week before.

Family members packed the mortuary chapel. As I listened to Uncle Bob's son talk about his father, tears streamed down my face.

"We have a blessed hope," cousin Bob said, his voice breaking. "Dad always loved and believed in Jesus. And someday, we will see him again."

Jacki began to sniffle, and I reached for her hand.

Bob continued: "You all know Dad loved sports. He always said Jesus was his captain." His voice grew ragged. "And I believe Dad made Jesus' team!"

Several amens followed as Bob sat down. I looked at my family. Sure, we mourned, but we believed we'd see him again. I thought again of Uncle Bob's Bible and knew he'd made the team. And, I wondered, could I?

Chapter 20

Making God's Team

"But I don't understand why I should pay tithe," I told my dad. We were having our fifth conversation on the topic.

He patiently listened.

"Why should the church spend my money?" I continued angrily.

"You know, Eddie," he said. "God requests us to return our tithe to Him. When I obey, I don't need to worry about where it goes after I pay it or what the church does with it. That's God's job. I choose to obey God, and that's it."

"But I don't think it is fair the way the church makes it law," I muttered. "Remember when tithe was taken directly out of my paycheck 'cause I worked for a church-owned school? It used to really make me mad!"

Dad refused to argue. "Eddie, all I can suggest is that you test God. See if His promises are true. There were times when your mother and I lived on little more than fifty cents, but God always came through, and He'll do the same for you and your family."

I couldn't imagine how. We'd just moved to a larger apartment and had more expenses. As I looked at the family budget for the next few months, I couldn't see any extra money for tithe. How could I automatically deduct 10 percent from an already-strained budget?

Then my AA mottos came back to me: One day at a time.

I sat in church with the tithe check in my hands. "If all I have to worry about is today," I thought as I filled out that first tithe envelope, "I have enough for today. I can't change the past, and I can't predict the future." I dropped the envelope into the offering plate with a mixture of relief and doubt.

I also resumed attending church regularly. Remembering how much I had despised hypocrites while growing up, I didn't want my own sons seeing one in their father. How would they learn to love church if I just dropped them off and picked them up again after the service ended?

Each time I sat in church, I remembered Uncle Bob's inscription in my Bible. I wanted my sons to grow up with the opportunities in sports that I'd been denied. But as I listened to the pastor speak each week about a loving, forgiving, and compassionate God, I knew I needed to make certain my sons knew about the only true winning team and the only true captain—Jesus.

Gradually my obsession with wealth faded. As I looked at the friends I'd envied so much before, I saw broken marriages and empty lives. In contrast, when I looked at my parents, who had few material things, I saw contentment. And I realized that all the things that I loved most—my family, Jacki, Jeffrey, and Justin—couldn't be purchased. They gave their love freely.

My resentment toward the other church members began to fade as I thought of my motto: Keep it simple. How could I judge them for not being perfect? I learned I needed to take care of Eddie and Eddie's problems—no one else's. I also remembered Jacki's suggestion that I get involved and started working as youth leader in the church.

I struggled with my questions for two years. Long conversations with Dad, my personal Bible reading, my AA mottos, and my new view of God combined to bring answers and changes. Slowly, little by little, resentments disappeared.

1986. When Jacki started studying for baptism, I watched

the process with mixed feelings. Then, on a Friday evening in April, Jacki was scheduled to be baptized.

Waiting for the service to begin, I thought about my baptism years before. I'd been baptized when it was the popular thing to do at my school. It hadn't meant to me what it did to Jacki.

Pastor Ted Modell came to the microphone and greeted the congregation.

"Tonight is a very special occasion. Before we begin, let's have a word of prayer."

As I started to bow my head, a flash of color caught my eye. I turned to see Jacki's parents slipping into the church. A warm feeling flooded me. I knew how much it saddened them to have Jacki leave the church they had reared her in and join my church, but they cared enough about her to attend her baptism anyway.

The prayer ended and the pastor continued, "Jackie Folger has accepted Jesus as her personal Saviour, and we are here to celebrate that with her tonight." He paused and smiled. "Would anyone like to speak a few words first?"

I felt myself getting out of the pew and walking to the front. Standing behind the microphone, I looked out at my parents, Jacki's parents, friends from the church—everyone who loved us enough to make us feel at home in our church. Thoughts raced through my mind. I kept remembering my own baptism, kept wondering about my own commitment.

"Jacki made a great decision when she decided to marry me," I began.

The audience chuckled. I smiled, then continued

"But tonight she's made the most important choice anyone can make. She's decided to make Jesus Christ her personal Saviour "

Amens followed my words. As I sat down, it suddenly struck me. Jacki had made her decision to give her heart to Jesus, but I never had. I had been reared in a Christian home, had attended Christian schools, but had never given my heart to Jesus.

With a lump in my throat, I watched Jacki descend into the baptistry. As tears of joy streamed down her face, I felt a hot wave of jealousy. She got to make her choice free of resentments. She got to meet Jesus as a personal Saviour.

"Jacki, because you have chosen to follow Jesus and have given your heart to Him as your personal Saviour, I now baptize you in the name of the Father, the Son, and the Holy Ghost."

I watched as she disappeared beneath the water, then came up again, her face shining. I fought tears as I saw the pure joy on her face. As Jacki left the baptismal tank, Pastor Modell prayed again.

"Lord, we want to thank You for the decision Jacki made to follow You. . . ."

My thoughts raced. More than anything else, I wanted to trade places with Jacki. I wanted to know what it felt like to be brand new.

Soon Jacki came out of the back room, her hair wet, her eyes shining. I reached for her hand as she sat down beside me.

"What does it feel like to be brand new?" I asked.

Her eyes filled. "I've never been happier."

Another wave of jealousy. I looked at her and wondered if I would ever get to feel what she felt.

Her words stayed with me for days as I worked at the prison. "Will I ever know that kind of happiness?" I wondered again and again

Weeks later, a prisoner—a hardened man—sat in front of me. I looked at his bulky frame and his calloused hands. He looked easily capable of committing the murder he was in MCI-Lancaster for.

"I know I've done some terrible things in my life," he confessed. "But I've changed."

I looked at him suspiciously. Most of the prisoners said that.

"I've found Jesus as a personal Saviour," he continued. "And He's made me brand new."

Brand new. Long after the session ended and the prisoner went back to his cell, his words stayed with me. Brand new. I kept thinking about the prisoner's long criminal record. Brand new. If God could take a murderer and make him new again, couldn't He do the same for me?

I began studying the Bible earnestly. As I read, I remembered Jacki's shining face and the murderer's humble belief in Jesus. Could God really forgive me too? I remembered the drug use, the broken marriage, the defiant attitude.

One late afternoon I sat reading my Bible. And as I read Revelation 21:3-5, it all suddenly became clear.

> I heard a loud voice speaking from the throne: "Now God's home is with mankind! He will live with them, and they shall be his people. God himself will be with them, and he will be their God. He will wipe away all tears from their eyes. There will be no more death, no more grief or crying or pain. The old things have disappeared." Then the one who sits on the throne said, "And now I make all things new!" (TEV).

The old things gone—God will make all things new. I looked at my prosthesis, tears in my eyes. I suddenly had something to hope for, to dream about. I knew that someday God would make all of me new and whole again. And that now, He wanted to make my heart new and whole again.

I finally realized that it all made sense. Uncle Bob's analogy of Jesus as the captain of the winning team now felt personal. He was now the captain of *my* winning team.

As I sat with the afternoon sunlight streaming across the floor, I accepted God's assurance that Ho could make me brand new—not just in heaven, not just today, but every day of my life.

As I remembered all the years of trying to do everything

my own way, a sentence from Herb Douglass's letter came back to me. "The evil one has done his work, but God will have the last word."

Finally, tears on my face, I closed the Bible and sat savoring the peace and joy. I didn't notice Jeffrey standing beside me until he spoke.

"What's wrong, Dad?" he asked, looking frightened.

I put my arm around him and pulled him close. "Nothing, Jeff," I assured him.

I looked at him with pride. My active son, already showing athletic ability. I remembered being his age and worshiping the sports heroes of the day.

"Jeff," I asked, "what's special about Larry Bird?"

He looked at me, puzzled. "Nothing."

I thought a second. "Well, how about Michael Jordan, Roger Clemens, Nolan Ryan, and Wade Boggs?"

"Nothing," he replied. He squirmed out of my grasp and sat on the floor in front of the chair, looking bored.

Now I felt confused. He'd always loved watching sports on TV. I tried another question.

"How about Pastor Thomas? Is there anything special about him?"

Jeffrey looked up at me, his eyes shining. "Oh, yes, Daddy!"

"What makes Pastor Thomas so special?"

Jeffrey's sincere seven-year-old face beamed. "He tells people about God!"

As if struck by lightning, I suddenly realized what Herb Douglass had meant. "Something very useful and beautiful will come out of this."

I had always wondered how anything useful could come out of the loss of my leg and my dream. Now it made sense. God had a plan. It was useful and beautiful, but not because I had signed with the Red Sox, lost my leg, overcome drugs and alcohol, coached sports, or counseled prisoners. It was beautiful and useful because God used these things, through me, to share my favorite promise in the Bible and tell people about the only true winning team, God's team, and its captain, Jesus.

After watching Jeffrey scamper out of the living room, I looked at the Bible in my hands. Yes, it was true. The evil one had done his work, but God had the last word!

"Thank You, God," I whispered. "Thank You."

Epilogue

Eddie continues his involvement in sports through coaching baseball at the Lancaster Middle School and basketball at Browning Elementary. In August of 1991, he held the first annual Eddie Folger baseball camp for boys and girls ages six through twelve. One hundred and twenty-five local youngsters attended the week-long camp. Approximately 150 youngsters are expected to attend the 1992 camp.

Eddie has also become a member of the National Amputee Golf Association and has played in several of their tournaments. He is also helping N.A.G.A. to develop a training program for rehabilitation professionals on teaching physically challenged individuals how to play golf.

Eddie remains employed as a counselor at MCI-Lancaster minimum-security prison. He continues speaking to area high schools, substance-abuse support groups, business groups, and church groups. And each time he speaks, he looks for opportunities to share his favorite Bible promise.

He continues to be active in his church. Presently, he and Jacki serve as the youth department leaders. In the spring of 1991, Eddie was the spring week-of-prayer speaker for grades four through six at Browning Memorial School. His congregation has also asked Eddie to represent them on the board of South Lancaster Academy.

Eddie enjoys watching Jeffrey and Justin play sports. Both

show great promise as ballplayers. But what makes Eddie the happiest is listening to them talk and sing about Jesus.